THE COMPUTER
AND MUSIC

THE COMPUTER AND MUSIC

edited by HARRY B. LINCOLN

State University of New York at Binghamton

CORNELL UNIVERSITY PRESS

ITHACA AND LONDON

Contents

Part Four: Ethnomusicology

Part Five: Music History and Style Analysis

Part Six: Music Information Retrieval

||||||||||||||||||||||||||

Illustrations

Preface

Whether or not computers have now attained their infancy, as is often heard today in this computerized world, their use in the field of music is still at an embryonic stage. This book documents the efforts of a number of composers and music researchers who use the computer in their work, and it illustrates the wide range of possibilities offered by the computer in music composition and research. A third area, computer-assisted instruction in music theory, has emerged too recently to assess its effectiveness or possibilities.

Although the present stage of the computer's contribution to music is embryonic, it would be a mistake to assume that we know what lies ahead, nor can it be said that the uses of the computer in music have evolved systematically. One is struck, throughout these essays, by the multiplicity of ideas and procedures and by the diversity of techniques, terminology, and goals. Those who work with the computer in music today know both the joys and disappointments of being pioneers, the excitement of discovery, and the frustration of failure. Only someone who has prepared programs and data for computer processing can fully realize how misleading in its suggestion of ease is the phrase ". . . and then he fed it to the computer."

The emphasis in several of these essays is on methodology rather than on results. There is still much to be learned, and for most of his work the researcher is dependent upon hardware (equipment) and software (programs) designed for business and the sciences.[1] Developments in both equipment and programs have come at a dizzying pace during the past decade, and it is a challenge to the person in this new area to maintain the flexibility necessary to move with rapid changes and not become tied to outmoded systems.

The range of opportunities and possibilities enjoyed by the composer is, in some respects, wider than that enjoyed by the researcher.

[1] Programming languages designed exclusively for music purposes include MIR, developed by Michael Kassler and described in Chapter XX, and MUSICOMP, by Lejaren Hiller, described briefly in Chapter IV.

The composer may use the computer to write music which will ultimately be played on standard orchestral instruments by performers reading from conventional notation. The style of his compositions may range from a simple counterpoint, based on the so-called rules of an eighteenth-century theorist, to the most recent serial or aleatory techniques. Efforts to imitate older styles have had limited success, and there is little interest in this area today.

The composer may choose instead to develop a vast range of sounds and totally new compositional devices. Some of the sounds may be generated by the computer itself, or the composer may link his efforts on the computer with the remarkable devices in the electronic-music studios found on many campuses. Mr. Brün forcefully argues that "traditional musical procedures have entered the stage where all further possible permutations will no longer possess any new meaning." [2] The widespread use of electronically produced sounds as background to films and television entertainment as well as in popular music adds strength to Mr. Brün's arguments. Whatever procedures are chosen, the many possibilities available pose a challenge to the imagination as well as to the technical skill of the composer. A number of these composers know mathematics, and their literature, as shown by Mr. Hiller's survey, is heavily sprinkled with such expressions as "second order transition probabilities," "random number generators," "sets," "permutation scheme," and "binary choice," to name but a few. In some of this work the new composer imitates, or has the machine imitate, the thought processes of the traditional composer. But it becomes apparent that more and more of the decisions can be left to the computer, and we find ourselves confronted with basic esthetic questions—questions that are succinctly summarized by Mr. Strang. [3]

The researcher, whether in music or some other area, has tended to use the computer to carry out more effectively, or on much larger quantities of data, research methods already developed. In music these include harmonic analysis, various types of indices, and elaborate statistical studies. Among his aims are analysis of harmonic devices, systematic descriptions of the styles of particular composers, comparisons of different styles, and the development of data banks of themes to cite borrowings among composers or to collate widely scattered sources.

The music researcher is immediately confronted with a basic need

---

[2] See Chapter II.   [3] See Chapter III.

when he looks to the computer as a tool. He must convert either the sound of music or the printed musical score to machine-readable data. The first possibility poses complex engineering problems. While it is theoretically possible to digitalize music, that is, to describe every tone by a mathematical measurement of the fundamental pitch and harmonics which comprise the tone, thus far only a limited amount has been accomplished in this field. Attempts to convert the printed score itself have been more successful. One can use letters and numbers to represent the symbols on the page of printed music, and store this representation in the computer memory ready for the various manipulations requested in the researcher's programs.

As yet there is no agreement among scholars on a single music representation. Some researchers have dealt only with the elements of notation of particular relevance to their projects. Others have chosen to represent all the elements of notation. A choice must be made between utilizing a limited system which permits rapid encoding of materials needed for a specific project only or using a broader system permitting greater flexibility and greater possibility of sharing with other researchers for their particular needs. It is unlikely that there will be widespread agreement on a particular representation, and the need for such a *lingua franca* is being reduced with the development of translation programs.

No matter whether one uses a specific or general representation, the encoding of music is tedious and time consuming. It is also expensive, since everything that is encoded must be keypunched. Two hardware developments, long hoped for, would greatly speed this part of the musicologist's work. One is an optical scanner that could read music and convert its reading to the representation. Such a machine is probably farther in the future than was thought a few years ago. A second development, the automated printing of music from a representation, appears to be much nearer. The computer plotter and the photocomposition machine are two devices now undergoing the necessary programming or engineering to permit them to print music.[4]

---

[4] The computer plotter has been programmed to draw a staff and music notation (news article on A. James Gabura's application in *Digital Plotting Newsletter*, May/June 1967, and Jeffry Raskin, "A Hardware-Independent Computer Graphics System," Master's thesis in Computing Science, Pennsylvania State University, 1967). The Ford-Columbia representation, already in use by a number of researchers, was developed by Stefan Bauer-Mengelberg as a graphics-oriented representation for use in a photocomposition machine known as the Photon. The editor, in his work in thematic indexing by computer, is currently testing the use

No one knows what the future holds for computing and music. Those of us who have worked with the computer have found it both a willing and a demanding tool—willing to do prodigious amounts of work in little time but demanding precise and well-thought-out instructions. It is hoped that this book will summarize, for researchers, composers, and other interested readers, the present use of the computer in music and will stimulate efforts to make the computer work more effectively in music composition and research.

HARRY B. LINCOLN

State University of New York at Binghamton

---

of special music characters developed for his project by the IBM Glendale Laboratory at Endicott, N.Y., for use on the high-speed computer printer.

||||||||||||||||||||||||||||

Contributors

EDMUND A. BOWLES, Program Administrator, Humanities, Libraries, Museums, International Business Machine Corporation, Washington D.C.

HERBERT BRÜN, Assistant Professor of Music, University of Illinois

JACK P. CITRON, Los Angeles Scientific Center, International Business Machines Corporation, Los Angeles, California

FREDERICK CRANE, Associate Professor of Music, University of Iowa; formerly at Louisiana State University

JUDITH FIEHLER, Computer Center, Louisiana State University

MARY E. FIORE, Professor of Music, State University College, Buffalo, New York

RAMON FULLER, Assistant Professor of Music, State University of New York at Buffalo

A. JAMES GABURA, Department of Computer Science, University of Toronto

LEJAREN HILLER, Professor of Music, State University of New York at Buffalo; formerly at University of Illinois

BARTON HUDSON, Assistant Professor of Music, West Virginia University

W. EARLE HULTBERG, Associate Professor of Music, State University College, Potsdam, New York

ROLAND JACKSON, Professor of Music, Roosevelt University

THEODORE KARP, Associate Professor of Music, University of California at Davis

MICHAEL KASSLER, Washington, D.C.; Ph.D., Princeton University, 1967; engaged in research in music theory

GERALD LEFKOFF, Assistant Professor of Music, West Virginia University

FREDRIC LIEBERMAN, Assistant Professor of Music, Brown University; formerly at University of California at Los Angeles

HARRY B. LINCOLN, Professor of Music, State University of New York at Binghamton

JOHN LOFSTEDT, 2nd Lt., U.S. Air Force, Norman, Oklahoma; formerly at Macalester College

ALFRED G. LYNN, Systems Analyst, Computer Center, State University of New York at Binghamton

IAN MORTON, Director of Research, Sovik, Mathve, and Madson, Architects, Northfield, Minnesota; formerly at Macalester College

ROBERT E. ROBERSON, Director, Computer Center, State University of New York at Binghamton

WILLIAM STONEY, Professor of Music, Hampton Institute, Virginia

GERALD STRANG, Professor of Music, California State College at Long Beach

BENJAMIN SUCHOFF, Director, The New York Bartók Archives, Cedarhurst, New York

JOHN W. TANNO, Assistant Librarian and Music Bibliographer, Claremont College; formerly Curator of Music Scores and Records at State University of New York at Binghamton

JOSEPH YOUNGBLOOD, Associate Professor of Music, University of Miami, Florida

‖‖‖‖‖‖‖‖‖‖‖ **Part One**

HISTORICAL BACKGROUND

CHAPTER I

Musicke's Handmaiden:
Or Technology in the
Service of the Arts

by EDMUND A. BOWLES

The computer is but the latest in a category of scientific hardware that has been used as a tool by musicians and musicologists alike.[1] In any short overview of their history, one may regard such devices as continuing extensions of man's creative efforts. Indeed, many of them embodied principles that were to reappear later in the computer itself.

The first monumental attempts to develop a large mechanical computer were made by Charles Babbage (1792–1871), a man who hated music, particularly the noise of barrel organs, which he said interrupted his train of thought. Very much a child of the Industrial Revolution, Babbage was obsessed by the idea of harnessing steam power to mechanical computation and of typesetting the lengthy mathematical tables used, for example, in navigation and astronomy. It is remarkable that Babbage was able to accomplish anything at all in an age limited to gearwheels. Under a government reluctant to subsidize such unprofitable research, he was eventually left with two incomplete machines on his hands, embittered, and without funds.

Babbage's first device, the "Difference Engine," was able in theory to compute by successive differences and set type automatically, so that the output would be in the form of printed tables. The "Analytical Engine," embodying a principle we now know as programming,

---

[1] The computer is perhaps better described as a Logic Engine. "They are called computers simply because computation is the only significant job that has so far been given to them. . . . The name has somewhat obscured the fact that they are capable of much greater generality. . . . To describe its potentialities the computer needs a new name—perhaps as good as any is information machine." L. N. Ridenour, "The Role of the Computer," *Scientific American*, 196 (1952), 117.

depended for its operation upon two sets of punched cards, containing nine positions and up to a dozen columns, to tell the machine what manipulations to perform at any stage in the successive calculations. These instructions were maintained in the "store," an embryonic memory. The set of operation cards programmed the engine to go through a set of additions, subtractions, multiplications, and divisions in a prearranged sequence, while so-called variable cards stored the actual numbers to be acted upon by these operations. The real computation was done in what was known as the "mill," a sort of primitive mechanical accumulator. The results were both printed on paper tape and punched on blank cards.[2] Thus, in a very real sense Babbage's Analytical Engine was what we now call a symbol manipulator which, a century before the electronic computer, possessed both a stored program and a means for encoding information.

Neither one of these concepts was new, however, and both had been, and would continue to be, applied to mechanical devices related to music. Around 1840, a fellow mathematician, Ada Lovelace, speculating on the musical possibilities of her colleague's machine, wrote with prophetic insight.

[The Engine's] operating mechanism might act upon other things besides number, were objects found whose mutual fundamental relations could be expressed by those of the abstract science of operations, and which should be also susceptible of adaptations to the action of the operating notation and mechanism of the engine. Supposing, for instance, that the fundamental relations of pitched sound in the signs of harmony and of musical composition were susceptible of such expression and adaptations, the engine might compose elaborate and scientific pieces of music of any degree of complexity or extent.[3]

On the one hand, Babbage's machines were followed in principle by those introduced by Herman Hollerith to the United States, then applied to the Census Bureau, quantitative political research, and from there (deviously) they entered the field of musicology; on the other hand the inherent potentialities hinted at by Lady Lovelace led eventually to computer music.[4]

---

[2] See P. and M. Morrison, *Charles Babbage and His Calculating Engines*, New York, Dover, 1961, esp. Chap. VIII; and L. F. Menabrea, *Sketch of the Analytical Engine* (tr. Ada Lovelace), London, R. and J. E. Taylor, 1843.

[3] R. Taylor, *Scientific Memoirs*, III, London, 1843, p. 694.

[4] It is interesting to note that the same generation produced both Frederick Jackson Turner, pioneer of the quantitative approach to historical research, and

The use of punched holes in cards for the digital storage of information had its origins some fifty years before Babbage in the mechanized weaving of patterns in cloth. Strings of these prepunched cards were used to control the proper lifting in various combinations of the hundreds and hundreds of silk warp threads of the draw-loom. In 1801, J. M. Jacquard, capitalizing on the principles applied by Bouchon, Falcon, and Vaucanson, developed the first fully successful automatic loom. It utilized a series of punched cards, held together like the links of a chain, which programmed the warp and thus the overall pattern of the tapestry being woven.[5]

However, the notion of a stored program can be extended even further backwards in time to mechanical musical instruments. The basis of these devices was either a barrel or cylinder programmed by means of a series of appropriately placed pegs or pins, or a punched paper tape, both of which performed certain mechanical actions when the barrel revolved by means of levers or jackwork. The earliest device of this sort was the carillon, apparently Chinese in origin, and brought to Europe during the Middle Ages. Truly mechanized chimes, depending for their operation upon a large revolving drum provided with pegs which activated the striking mechanism directly, date from the fourteenth century—principally the Netherlands—when they were installed in the belfrys of large cathedrals.[6] For example, the carillon in the Abbey-Church of St. Catherine, near Rouen, was programmed to play the hymn *Conditor alme siderum.*[7]

Mechanically driven organs made their appearance around 1500, when an instrument with 150 pipes was referred to as one of the appurtenances in the Schloss Hohensalzburg. The sumptuous parks of Renaissance princes, lay and ecclesiastic alike, encouraged the installation of hydraulically operated organs, along with all sorts of me-

Herman Hollerith, inventor of the first data processing machinery. In 1890 Hollerith's punched cards, tabulator, and sorter were employed by the U.S. Census Bureau. Seven years later Turner wrote his study of Midwestern political culture. See F. J. Rex, Jr., "Herman Hollerith, the First 'Statistical Engineer,'" *Computers and Automation,* 10 (1961), 10–13; and F. J. Turner, *The Frontier in American History,* New York, H. Holt Co., 1920, pp. 222–242.

[5] On the history of punched cards, see for example A. P. Usher, "The Textile Industry, 1850–1830," in *Technology in Western Civilization* (ed. M. Kranzberg and C. W. Pursell, Jr.), I, New York, Oxford, 1967, pp. 243 f.; and Morrison, *op. cit.,* pp. xxxiii ff.

[6] A. Wins, *L'horloge à travers les âges,* Paris, E. Champion, 1924, pp. 154 f.

[7] A. Ungerer, *L'horloge astronomique de la cathédrale de Strasbourg,* Paris, Société Astronomique de France, 1922, p. 9.

chanical automata and water tricks. All these devices were activated
by means of revolving drums programmed with appropriately placed
cams.[8]

A French engineer, Salomon de Caus, was one of the first to deal
with the theory of cylinders and their programming, or "pinning." His
treatise, *Nouvelle invention de lever l'eau* (1644), includes a hydraulic
engine producing musical sounds in which a water wheel was connected directly to a large revolving drum with pegs which activated a
series of keys. These, in turn, opened valves which allowed air to flow
from a windchest through pneumatic tubes connected to corresponding organ pipes. Caus also invented a hydraulic organ, similarly
constructed, with pins placed in a "musical wheel" which depressed
keys, causing air to be transmitted directly to the pipes.[9] In his
treatise, Caus illustrates, as an example of the pinning, the first six
bars of Alessandro Striggio's madrigal *Che fera fed' al cielo* for
performance by these hydraulically operated instruments.

Following Caus, a succession of inventors took up the problem of
programming cylinders for mechanical musical instruments, including
Robert Fludd, Athanius Kircher, and Johann Ungerer. The revolving-
barrel concept itself led to a parade of devices in the eighteenth
century, such as musical clocks, barrel organs, and music boxes, all
programmed by means of pegs inserted in revolving cylinders of one
type or another. Indeed, Engramelle's treatise, *La Tonotechnie*
(1775), actually speaks of *noter les cylindres,* and the author himself
invented a combination mechanical organ, dulcimer, carillon, and
flute based upon this principle. J. N. Maelzel produced the "Panhar-
monikon," an animated machine orchestra of no less than 42 robot
musicians. The most famous and lasting device, however, was the
music box (*musique à peigne*), constructed by Louis Faure. This
combined for the first time a spring-driven revolving cylinder, the pins
of which in logical or prescribed sequence activated a set of thin,
comblike steel strips. A table or mantle often served as an auxiliary
sounding board.[10]

Until the middle of the nineteenth century the barrel organ and

[8] See A. Protz, *Mechanische Musikinstrumente*, Kassel, Bärenreiter, 1940, esp.
p. 35.
[9] For an English translation, see his *New and Rare Inventions of Water Works*
(tr. J. Leak; 2nd ed.), London, Joseph Moxon, 1701, esp. pp. 28 and 30 and
Plates XVI and XIX.
[10] A. Chapuis, *Histoire de la boîte à musique et la musique mécanique*, Lau-
sanne, Scriptair, 1955, pp. 21 ff.

music box were the only significant mechanical instruments. In 1852 the Frenchman Corteuil devised a perforated strip of cardboard to activate a miniature keyboard, and nine years later J. A. Teste constructed a pneumatic reed-type instrument, the musical notes of which were produced by a system of valves and bellows activated by punched cards.[11] In 1880 the first pneumatic self-playing piano appeared, taking advantage of a perforated sheet of paper which passed over a reed chamber and permitted air to pass through the holes "programmed" into it, thus activating the keys.[12] Numerous fragmentary and isolated efforts such as these were finally brought to mechanical perfection in the "Pianola" invented by E. S. Votey in 1897. In this instrument, a prepunched, perforated paper roll moved over a capillary bridge. Whenever the holes in the roll coincided with the 88 openings in the board, air was transmitted into the mechanism, activating sets of bellows with their corresponding striking linkages. The Pianola was rolled up to a piano so that its fingers, or strikers, hovered directly over the keyboard, note for note.[13]

The phonograph is yet another musical device embodying both the stored program concept and its retrieval. In 1877 Thomas A. Edison worked on a telegraph repeater which embossed the Morse code dots and dashes into a paper tape and later replayed the message any number of times, thus providing an electromechanical instrument for transmitting messages automatically from one station to another. When the punched tape raced through the device at high speed, the

[11] A. Buchner, *Mechanical Musical Instruments* (tr. I. Urwin), London, Batchworth Press, 1959, pp. 25 and 36.

[12] The pneumatically operated keyboard attachment seems to have been first invented by the French engineer Fourneaux in 1863. His "Pianista" was operated by a hand crank which produced the vacuum to activate a set of mechanical fingers which in turn played the keyboard of an ordinary piano. An American device based on similar principles, an automatic organ, was built by John McTammany and exhibited at the Philadelphia Centennial in 1876.

[13] See H. N. Roehl, *Player-Piano Treasury*, Vestal (N.Y.), Vestal Press, 1961, pp. 3–6. This device is not to be confused with the more complicated and sophisticated reproducing piano, or "Vorsetzer," invented by Edwin Welte, and incorporated into a regular piano in this country by the Ampico and Duo Art companies. The recording device cut a roll with the actual key strokes of the artist as he played, as well as his rhythmic patterns, subtle variations in speed, his rubato and accelerando, his dynamics and pedaling. Welte's instrument and its successors would seem to have capitalized on the music-writing machine constructed by Holfeld in 1770. A continuously moving roll of paper was activated by clockwork, and when a clavichord key was depressed, a corresponding lever with a pencil at its extremity drew a line on the paper reproducing the duration of the note being played. See Chapuis, *op. cit.*, pp. 109 ff.

indented combinations of dots and dashes actuating the end of a steel spring gave off what Edison described as a "light musical, rhythmic sound resembling human talk heard indistinctly." Having just devised a revolutionary contribution to the telephone art in the form of a carbon button transmitter applicable to Bell's year-old telephone, the young inventor reasoned that if he could record a telegraph message, he might also be able to record a telephone conversation. His first experimentation led to the utilization of the energy of speech vibrations to indent a moving strip of paraffin-coated paper tape by means of a diaphragm with an attached needle. This in turn led to a continuously grooved, revolving metal cylinder wrapped in tin foil. A recording stylus following the spiral groove indented the sound vibrations into the soft foil. The information thus recorded—speech or music—was retrieved by a reversal of this process. The rest, of course, is history.[14]

Turning now to the principles of encoding and decoding, actually the earliest experiments in electrical communication foreshadowed in primitive form the basis of modern information theory. It was Samuel F. B. Morse who in 1832 developed the first widely successful device to transmit intelligence electrically. The telegraph drew long and short lines on a strip of paper, the sequences of which represented not the letters of a word but their numerical equivalent assigned in a dictionary, or code book, Morse wrote. Six years later this somewhat clumsy system was replaced by the Morse code, which represented the alphabet by various combinations of dots, dashes, and spaces. By this means the dots and dashes indicated electric current, and the intervening spaces between the absence thereof. Thus, in a primitive sense, this "single-current telegraphy" already embodied a two-element code: current and no current, yes and no, or 1 and 0.[15]

Although the nearly limitless possibilities of communication by electricity were only vaguely appreciated at this time, the significance

[14] This ingenious device would seem to have been conceivable only in the mind of a practical inventor or tinkerer such as Edison. Despite the epoch-making contribution of Fourier that a complex wave, or periodic function, could be portrayed by a harmonic series, there was nevertheless nothing to suggest that sound waves, for example, just because they could be represented in this manner, could therefore be recorded and thus, in reproduction, synthesize both speech and musical notes. The bibliography on Edison and the phonograph is too extensive and accessible to be mentioned here. A good popular account is to be found in R. Gelatt, *The Fabulous Phonograph*, Philadelphia, Lippincott, 1954, pp. 17–32.

[15] See for example G. G. Blake, *History of Radio Telegraphy and Telephony*, London, Chapman and Hall, Ltd., 1928, pp. 7–11.

of the transformation of information into electrical form now made for virtually instantaneous transmission of data from point to point, and —more importantly—the possibility of coupling "engines" of one form or another for operating on this information without the mechanical and psychological drawbacks of human intervention.

Some 80 years after Morse, following improvements in telegraphic equipment, it became obvious that a more advantageous system would be one in which all electrical character signals were of equal length. With this in mind, J. M. E. Baudot developed a five-unit, or channel, code with two-condition signaling (that is, each channel either punched or not punched), providing thirty-two character possibilities (2^5) which encompassed the entire alphabet.

The next step was a printing telegraph, and this device, too, can be thought of as digitalizing the information being transmitted and recorded. In 1859 David E. Hughes, a former professor of music, invented a typewriting telegraph, utilizing a pianolike keyboard to activate the mechanism. A paper tape, propelled by a weight-driven motor, recorded in punched form the coded signals sent over the telegraph line to a receiving station.[16]

This keyboard mechanism formed the basis of operation for the early office calculating machines as well, providing a more than casual connection between these devices and the world of music. In the calculator, a rather complicated series of mechanical linkages furnished the means of easy and efficient operation with human aid, as well as a convenient input device for both writing and calculating. D. D. Parmelee patented the first key-driven adding machine in 1850. However, the numerous technical difficulties encountered by the inventors who soon followed led to a technological stalemate, and it was in fact the typewriter which first reached practical fulfillment. Between the introduction of the "literary piano" in 1867 (with an actual keyboard) and widespread use a decade later, the office typewriter evolved into virtually its present form. But now the situation reversed itself, and the commercial success of the typewriter contributed to the development of a practical accounting machine.

By 1877 a young inventor named Dorr E. Felt had perfected a calculator with key-driven ratchet wheels which could be moved automatically by one or more teeth at a time, similar in design to the roller ratchet of a typewriter. Shortly thereafter these two devices,

16 *Ibid.*, pp. 38 and 45.

typewriter and calculator, were combined into a machine that printed the results of computations; and later this fortuitous marriage led to the tabulating machine and the tabulator-typewriter.[17]

Another important development to consider is the principle of sampling. This has been long familiar in the motion picture, which takes advantage of the persistence of vision in presenting a series of still pictures, or samples, which the eye interprets as a continuously moving image. Similarly, based upon the physiological phenomena involved in the process of hearing, it is possible to sample a speech or sound wave, and by transmitting these fragments recapture articulate reproduction by putting the pieces together at the receiving end.[18]

One method of sampling used extensively in telephone communication is pulse code modulation. This is based upon the fact that a continuous electrical or acoustical wave, such as is found in speech or music, can be represented by, and reconstructed from, a sequence of samples of its amplitudes, made at uniformly spaced points along the wave-form. By quantizing these successive samples of amplitude, a representation can be achieved comparable to digitalized text, as in telegraphy, for example. The ear hears the complete sound without detecting the missing segments. Pulse code modulation is thus an economical means of increasing the information-handling capacity of a communications system by sandwiching or interspersing samples from many sources together, transmitting them and then filtering out and reassembling the separate voices at the far end.[19] The ultimate result, of course, is to minimize the amount of information needed to convey the original message.

From Pythagoras to Descartes, theorists and pedagogues devoted considerable attention to the study of music. However, the investigations of Isaac Newton in the late seventeenth century gave such an impetus to the study of mechanics that the scientific aspect of music was virtually neglected for some two-hundred years. However, the development of electricity and telephone stimulated its resumption.

[17] I am indebted to Prof. Derek DeSolla Price, Chairman of the Department of History of Science and Medicine at Yale University, for this information.

[18] It was first demonstrated by Bell System engineers that if, in the transmission of a complex, continuous musical sound—an organ note, for example—the fundamental component is supressed, the ear will supply the missing element and recognize the original pitch of the note. This experiment is described in H. Fletcher, *Speech and Hearing*, New York, Macmillan, 1929, p. 246.

[19] See J. R. Pierce, *Symbols, Signals and Noise*, New York, Harper, 1961, pp. 132 and 250.

Two short-lived inventions typify these attempts to reproduce music electrically. Alexander Graham Bell, with his early dedication to work in speech and hearing, had long been interested in the study of sound reproduction. He not only followed Edison's invention of the phonograph but also in 1880 financed his own laboratory in Washington to promote research relating to sound and acoustics. Together with Charles S. Tainter, Bell devised and patented several means for transmitting and recording sound. At the Philadelphia Centennial in 1876, Elisha Gray (another inventor of a telephone along with Bell) demonstrated his "Electromusical Piano," transmitting musical tones over wires to a fascinated audience. In 1906 an engineer named Thaddeus Cahill introduced the "Telharmonium," an instrument consisting of a series of alternating-current generators which produced pure tones of various frequencies and intensity. Switches permitted the synthesis of tones into any specific spectrum, and a volume control supplied dynamic variation. The device was intended to produce music capable of transmission over telephone lines to household subscribers, but unfortunately Cahill's system never passed beyond the demonstration stage.[20]

However, in spite of an increase in the study of sound, both detailed scientific analysis and the invention of more versatile instrumentalities were required before sound recording, reproduction, analysis, and synthesis were to take place. For example, Prof. Dayton C. Miller pioneered in the development of techniques for studying tone quality in his acoustical laboratory at the Case Institute of Applied Science.[21] A massive attack on understanding the nature of sound, its measurement, and analysis followed the introduction of the audion by Lee DeForest. Once the potentialities of this device as an amplifier and modulator became apparent, the entire communications art underwent a revolutionary development. In October 1912 the vacuum tube was brought directly to the attention of the research laboratories of the Bell System, and its demonstration was to become a landmark in

[20] "The Generation and Distributing of Music by Means of Alternators," *Electrical World*, 67 (1906), 519 ff. This and other later devices are discussed in E. G. Richardson, "The Production and Analysis of Tone by Electrical Means," *Proceedings of the Royal Musical Association*, 66 (1940), 53–65.

[21] One tangible result of this research was Miller's *Anecdotal History of the Science of Sound*, New York, Macmillan, 1935. See especially Chap. V ("Sound in the 19th Century—The Science of Sound") and Chap. VI ("Sound at the End of the 19th Century—The Theory of Sound").

communications history. Shortly thereafter these laboratories began a vast program of research involving a comprehensive analysis of the electrical qualities of speech and hearing in order to obtain better articulation over telephone lines.

This large-scale research program began with an examination of the characteristics of speech. It was followed by a study of the organs of speech and hearing themselves, and was extended ultimately to music and thus to sound in general. The realization that better and more precise instruments had to be developed led in part to the construction of devices to convert sound waves into electrical form and reconstitute them again into sound with a minimum of distortion. The most noteworthy result of these early efforts (specifically, the study of electroacoustic networks) from the musical point of view was the development of electrical, or "Orthophonic," recording in 1925 by J. P. Maxfield and H. C. Harrison.[22]

Electronic musical instruments were an important by-product of these experiments. Their design was based upon the principle of vacuum tube (audion) oscillators, planned and controlled by the experimenter or performer, and combined with amplification and loudspeaker output. Some devices utilized electrical frequency generators, while others employed mechanical (rotary or vibrating) generators to produce the tones.[23]

In 1924 the Russian Léon Theremin invented and demonstrated the "Aetherophone" (later simply called "Theremin") which employed two vacuum-tube oscillators to produce beat notes. Resembling an early radio set, it functioned as a capacitor, deriving musical sounds by the technique of "heterodyning" from oscillations which varied in pitch as the circuit (a wire-loop aerial and metal rod held in the operator's hand) was altered by changing the distance between these two elements. Four years later, Maurice Martenot brought out his "Ondes Musicales" (again, later called the "Ondes Martenot"), a similar, but more advanced electronic instrument. Again, two radio-frequency oscillators were heterodyned or beaten to produce complex wave-forms. Here, instead of a hand-held rod, a moveable electrode was used to produce the capacitance variations. Dutilleux, Honegger,

[22] See Fletcher, op. cit., pp. v–viii; and J. B. Crandall, Theory of Vibrating Systems and Sound, New York, D. Van Nostrand, 1926, Appendix B.

[23] S. K. Lewer, Electronic Musical Instruments, London, Electronic Engineering, 1948, esp. pp. 21–24; and F. K. Prieberg, Musica ex Machina, Berlin, Ullstein, 1960, pp. 198–233.

Messiaen, Milhaud, and Varèse all wrote music for the instrument at one time or another.[24]

Probably the most familiar electronic instrument in these categories is the "Electronic Organ" invented by Laurens Hammond. It employed a system of 91 rotary electromagnetic disc generators, driven by a synchronous motor with associated gears and tone wheels. These tone wheels were shaped so as to generate sinusoidal currents in their associated coils. The wave-forms thus produced could be synthesized into complex tones. Control and programming were achieved through two 5-octave manuals and pedal board. In order to produce all the required fundamental tones and their harmonics, all 91 tone generators were used in various permutations and combinations.

A significant step forward in sound synthesis was achieved in 1955 when Harry Olson of the Radio Corporation of America invented an "Electronic Music Synthesizer." In this device, saw-tooth waves, containing all possible harmonics, are filtered to remove the unwanted ones. The instructions, or program, is put into the machine by means of a typewriterlike keyboard, which punches the commands into a 40-channel paper tape fifteen inches wide, representing binary code numbers describing the desired musical sounds. The roll of paper in turn drives a series of tone generators to produce the actual sounds—the human voice, instruments, or entirely new varieties of sound altogether.[25]

The relationship between experimental music and electronic technology grew not only in commercial scientific laboratories but in forward-looking broadcasting stations and newly established university music studios as well. Profiting by the fortuitous presence of the computer on many campuses, musicians and technologists used this new tool which was able to create any desired wave-form "on command" by means of a sequence of digitalized numerical samples representing the amplitude of that wave of successive points. Together with its ability to accomplish statistical routines, this led to a number of pioneering experiments in computer music. In one type, the machine "composes" music, selecting notes according to mathematical rule or numerical sequence (probability). In a second variety, the computer "plays" music, the wave-form of the notes themselves being

[24] R. Raven-Hart, "The Martenot Instrument," *Wireless World*, 27 (1930), 58.
[25] H. Olson and H. Belar, "Electronic Music Synthesizer," *The Journal of the Acoustical Society of America*, 26 (1955), 595–612. A later version with many improvements was installed in the Columbia-Princeton Electronic Music Studio.

expressed mathematically as a sequence of numbers—including frequency, duration, and intensity—and is converted by an analog device into oscillations which drive a loudspeaker.

Music by chance has captivated composers since the time of Bach. Many dice compositions were produced as parlor games in the eighteenth century, as were puzzle canons in which the solver had to "realize" the second voice. As early as 1949 John R. Pierce and M. E. Shannon of the Bell Telephone Laboratories composed elementary statistical or "chance" music, based upon a repertory of allowable root chords in the key of C. By throwing three specially made dice, and by using a table of random numbers, several compositions were produced. Among their characteristics were eight measures of four quarter notes each, certain specified repetitions, and common tones in the same voice of any two succeeding chords.[26] Seven years later Richard C. Pinkerton wrote simple (or, as he himself put it, "banal") melodies based upon a statistical analysis of 39 nursery tunes. He first constructed probability tables showing how frequently any note followed any other. He then made chance selections from a deck of cards prepared according to these tables.[27] Frederick P. Brooks (now at the University of North Carolina) and his Harvard associates Hopkins, Neumann, and Wright produced computer music, the basis for which was an extensive examination of hymn tunes.[28]

Starting in 1955, Lejaren A. Hiller, Jr., and Leonard M. Isaacson at the University of Illinois began a series of experiments to evaluate a broad spectrum of compositional techniques in terms of their suitability to computer programming. They demonstrated that the machine could either generate musical scores by conventional means or produce an output governed by probability distributions. One major result was the now-famous *Illiac Suite for String Quartet*. For the production of this four-part experiment the computer stored in its memory a numerically coded chromatic scale of about two and a half octaves. It selected notes randomly and rejected them if they violated the established rules of musical composition, producing sequences of

[26] See Pierce, *op. cit.*, pp. 250–261. Mozart himself made up sets of alternative measures of music, and, by means of throwing dice to determine the sequence of measures, a person with no musical abilities could make a variety of "do-it-yourself" compositions.

[27] R. C. Pinkerton, "Information Theory and Melody," *Scientific American*, 194 (1956), 77–86.

[28] F. P. Brooks, Jr., *et al.*, "An Experiment in Musical Composition," *Transactions of the Institute of Radio Engineers* (1957), 175.

letters and numbers which were stored in the computer until a short melody was derived. This was then transcribed by hand into conventional musical notation suitable for human performance.[29]

Max Mathews and his associates at the Bell Laboratories began generating music by computer in 1958. These experiments answered two major difficulties facing composers of conventional electronic music, namely, the generation of complex wave-forms and the precise assembly of noise-free, multiple sounds. The computer produced any variety of these by sampling given wave-forms at regular and frequent intervals (in one program, at the rate of 20,000 times per second), producing thereby series of numbers which approximated the sounds. In the reverse process, digital-to-acoustic conversion, these numerical approximations of the original sound waves were put on magnetic tape, converted into pulses, the amplitudes of which were proportional to the numbers, smoothed out by filtering, and fed to a loudspeaker.[30] Work on computer sound production, originated at Bell Laboratories, has been continued and extended at Princeton University, where the entire original program has been rewritten by Godfrey Winham and Hubert Howe.[31]

The first use of machine methods for the handling and analysis of large masses of quantitative musical data was Bertrand H. Bronson's comparative study of British-American folk songs, which appeared in 1949. By means of punched cards, he coded selected elements of these tunes, including range, meter, modal distinction, phrasal scheme, refrain pattern, melodic outline, upbeat, cadence, and final. In addition, Bronson was able to compile a significant corpus of folk song material with sufficient fullness and accuracy to make comparisons both easy and reliable.[32]

[29] See L. A. Hiller, Jr., "Computer Music," *Scientific American*, 201 (1959), 109–120; and L. A. Hiller, Jr., and J. Beauchamp, "Research in Music with Electronics," *Science*, 150 (1965), 161–169.

[30] See M. V. Mathews and N. Gutman, "Generation of Music by a Digital Computer," in *Proceedings of the Third International Congress on Acoustics*, Amsterdam, 1959, pp. 253 ff.; M. V. Mathews, "An Acoustic Compiler for Music and Psychological Stimuli," *Bell System Technical Journal*, 40 (1961), 677–694; and M. V. Mathews, "The Digital Computer as a Musical Instrument," *Science*, 142 (1963), 553–557.

[31] This has been described by J. K. Randall, "A Report from Princeton," *Perspectives of New Music*, 3 (1965), 74–83.

[32] See B. H. Bronson, Mechanical Help in the Study of Folksong," *Journal of American Folklore*, 62 (1949), 81–86. In a letter to the author (June 13, 1967) Bronson writes, "You ask how I became aware of the possibility of using IBM in

A good many current computer projects in musicology fall into the category of information retrieval—a term perhaps best characterized as "the selective recall of stored factual knowledge." In the subject at hand, the information being recovered or regained from a data bank in machine-readable form is the music itself in one or more of its several dimensions. A conspicuous example is Harry Lincoln's own large-scale project of developing a thematic index of sixteenth-century Italian music. Here, essentially, the computer searches for pattern matches between the encoded themes, or *incipits*, stored on discs and those being investigated. The "hits" are then retrieved and printed out for purposes of identifying anonymous works, duplications, and borrowings.[33]

Owing to the unique problems of musical input—a special vocabulary must be constructed to represent within the computer the multidimensional aspects of each note, including terms of pitch, register, duration, and timbre—musical research was not readily adaptable to machine-record equipment, and had to wait for the arrival of the computer. This necessity of providing data to the machine in its own characteristic digital speech stimulated the development of several musical input representations. Messrs. Stefan Bauer-Mengelberg and Melvin Ferentz, as part of a larger project concerned with automated music printing, have created what has come to be known as the Ford-Columbia system. This is essentially a digital alternate representation of complete musical scores in their every dimension for computer input. Barry Brook of Queens College produced, with Murray Gould, an alphanumeric input called the *Plaine and Easie Code System for Musicke*. Utilizing ordinary typewriter characters, it is a shorthand for musical notation especially useful for incipits and short

comparative tune analysis. My head was full of the practical difficulties of comparing melodies in an objective way, and of my attempts to solve the puzzle. When I discovered that the figures on an IBM card could stand for whatever you chose, letters or numbers, I thought, Why not notes? and I was off! One thing I'm very certain of: I'd never heard of anyone else applying IBM to music, and was terribly pleased with myself for thinking of it!"

[33] In 1924 Béla Bartók remarked that only a systematically scientific examination of the morphological aspects of folk music material would enable one to determine clearly the types, and to draw various conclusions from the transformation and migration of these melodies and their connection with foreign materials. Bartók's own method in fact lends itself to computerization, namely, the skeletonization of melodies yielding *incipits* which can then be encoded on a single punched card. In this way, the pitch contour can be compared as to melodic and rhythmic variants.

excerpts. At Princeton University Hubert Howe, Alexander Jones, and Michael Kassler developed an Intermediary Musical Language (IML) as a practical solution to the problem of feeding musical information into a computer. This particular input utilizes only the 48 characters found in the older standard keypunch machine.[34]

A second major area of computer application in music research is stylistic analysis. Here the machine operates in quantitative fashion on the music itself, identifying, locating, counting, and otherwise codifying the significant components or symbols. For example, program operations can be applied to melodic and harmonic analysis or to the derivation of statistics of frequency distribution. In developing such a taxonomy, and unitizing the musical components for computer processing, the musicologist provides himself with a powerful, multidimensional view of the music itself.

The Princeton project, under the direction of Arthur Mendel and Lewis Lockwood, is a prime case in point of the large-scale application of computer techniques to musical analysis. By means of IML the relevant musical information is translated into machine-readable form, or input, which, by means of a symbolic code, preserves the desired data of every element. A language for Musical Information Retrieval (MIR) then makes it possible to write programs concerning any aspects of the music thus represented, and to obtain the desired results, or output, in intelligible form.

Programs have been written for the analysis of some of the inherently quantitative problems of style in the music of Josquin Desprez (c. 1450–1521). Among those aspects under study are the linear and harmonic components of the style of Josquin's masses, the relationship of music and text and the problems of applying and interpreting the specified and unspecified accidentals (*musica ficta*) that give rise to alternative readings of the pitch-structure of the music. The computer is also being used to process information about certain elements within individual works, such as the location of every type of tritone and diminished fifth as linear and harmonic intervals, together with their occurrence in varying patterns and contexts.[35]

[34] See T. Robison, "IML–MIR: A Data Processing System for the Analysis of Music," in *Elektronische Datenverarbeitung in der Musikwissenschaft* (ed. H. Heckmann), Regensburg, G. Bosse, 1967, pp. 103–135.

[35] See L. Lockwood, "Computer Assistance in the Investigation of Accidentals in Renaissance Music," in *Proceedings of the Tenth Congress of the International Musicological Society*, Ljubljana, 1967.

In the application of computer techniques to the analysis of musical style an important example is the work of Jan LaRue of New York University to evolve computer techniques to describe stylistic characteristics of eighteenth century symphonies. Closely paralleling certain efforts of the literary scholar, he has developed a set of guidelines for musical analysis, quantifying or breaking down the various musical elements into sound, form, harmony, rhythm, and melody.[36]

LaRue has concerned himself mainly with the music of Josef Haydn, and found that the range of the composer's style results from complex interactions between these elements. The first being investigated is Haydn's phrasing and articulation. Taking so-called time-line analyses of exposition sections from the first movements in 30 early symphonies, the thematic functions were keypunched according to their locations on the time-line of the movement. Computer programs were written for the input, compilation, and statistical analysis of this data in order to calculate and display percentile relationships and paired correlations.

Using these computerized techniques of stylistic analysis, LaRue found that Haydn's music is extremely low in redundancy, in other words, has few consistent and repeated conventional patterns. Secondly, the computer brought to his attention for the first time the fact that the composer uses more themes in the second part of the exposition section of his first movements, after modulation to the dominant key, than he does in the beginning of his symphonies in the tonic area.[37]

The computer can also be used as a tool for traditional harmonic analysis. At Roosevelt University, Roland H. Jackson and his associate Philip Bernzott have devised a program for the input and analysis by machine of conventional elements of a musical composition, such as key changes, basic chords, and the measures in which they appear.[38] A discussion of this program can be found in Chapter VIII below.

Allen Forte, of Yale University, has long been working with the computer to help solve some of the basic problems of musical theory.

[36] This general approach follows the principles outlined previously by J. LaRue, "On Style Analysis," *Journal of Music Theory*, 6 (1962), 91–107.

[37] See J. LaRue, "Two Problems in Musical Analysis: The Computer Lends a Hand," in *Computers in Humanistic Research: Readings and Perspectives* (ed. E. A. Bowles), Englewood Cliffs, Prentice-Hall, 1967, pp. 194–203.

[38] This description has been drawn from R. H. Jackson, "Harmonic Analysis with Computer: A Progress Report," *Institute for Computer Research in the Humanities Newsletter*, I (1966), 3–4.

An early effort on his part was aimed at providing insights regarding the coherence and structure of atonal music. According to Milton Babbitt of Princeton the basis of this "has only been partially hypothesized, even less completely tested, and only slightly understood." Having found the traditional forms of musical analysis lacking, Forte designed his approach around linguistic and mathematical models for musical structure, developed a computer program to explore his ideas, then subjected the results to analysis.[39]

One obvious result of such work is a more systematic and objective approach to the analysis of musical style, or content. The computer forces more rigor on the workways of the scholar, at the same time providing the means for a larger and thus more reliable data sampling. One has the feeling that computerized content analysis will lead slowly to a more satisfactory answer as to what *style* really is, at least in its quantitative sense.

Thus, it is readily seen that the computer has already introduced a new set of workways into the field of music, affecting both composition and research. The result has been that composers and scholars alike are coming to terms with techniques unheard of a short generation ago. There has been a corresponding change in the pattern of computer-oriented research, in the number and training of individuals involved in these projects, and in the time interval between their original concept and their ultimate fulfillment.

An important and direct result of this technological innovation in music has been a change in the *dimension* of academic research. The individual scholar, working virtually alone for years with small samples of data gathered slowly and painstakingly (and often jealously husbanding his material from real or imagined predators) is being replaced by teams of people: the researcher and his staff (often his main link with the new world of computers), a programmer or two, and the computer center personnel. These people represent in sum several specialties, and each one plays an important role in the chain of events leading from the initial concept and raw data through the machine to the finished output.

Secondly, there has been a change of pace in intellectual activity. The computer allows the scholar to accomplish in a short time what would have otherwise taken him up to a whole lifetime of drudgery to accomplish. It is well known that the computer can calculate, sort,

[39] An example of Forte's work can be found in his article, "The Domain and Relations of Set-Complex Theory," *Journal of Music Theory*, 9 (1965), 173 ff.

and compare approximately one-hundred million times faster than human beings are able to do. What this means to the musicologist, with his large files of data, is a dramatic shortening of the time interval between his original idea or research plan and its ultimate completion.

Another manifestation of this change of pace has been greater precision of thinking. The necessity of providing a programmar with an extremely precise and lucid explanation of *what* he hopes to accomplish, and *how*, compels the scholar to face these issues explicitly. Furthermore, the ensuing dialogue between musicologist and computer specialist in working out an algorithm for his project forces on the former a higher degree of precision and logic.

An extremely important factor for musicological research is that the computer permits one to broaden his data base, for the first time making possible the comprehensive inclusion of *all* relevant material. No longer does the scholar have to reduce his sampling or his categories of data to the practical limits of hand manipulation. In addition, the machine is far better able to handle in statistical fashion the vast number of variables in every dimension of the musical score, bringing all the complex relationships and patterns to the scholar's attention, thus permitting more reliable generalizations concerning the problem at hand.

Although it is fashionable to consider the computer as being utterly unique, it nevertheless forms a consistent element within the historical context of man's developing technology. Many of its basic operating principles, such as the concept of a stored program, a system for encoding information, and electronic circuitry have been employed before. All these machines, whatever their physiognomy, demonstrate graphically the adaptation of contemporary technology to the practical demands of a specific idea or the aspirations of a particular intellectual discipline. However, whereas these previous devices have been, so to speak, extensions of the hand, the computer, with its logic capabilities endowed with lightning speed, remains uniquely an extension of the mind.

||||||||||||||||||||||||||||||||||| Part Two

MUSIC COMPOSITION

CHAPTER II

From Musical Ideas
to Computers and Back

by HERBERT BRÜN

The link between the computer system and the composer of music is *the program.* The composer may think of himself and his mind and his ideas in any way he pleases, until he decides to use the computer as an assistant. From that moment on the composer must envisage himself, his mind, and his ideas as systems, since only systems can be translated into that language, the program, which can generate their analog appearances in the computer. Under control of a program, the computer system will simulate all the processes in and of the particular system which the program represents. The main problem thus appears at the beginning and again at the end of the entire proposition: Can the composer program musical ideas for a computer, and will the output of the computer contain musical ideas?

Another problem, especially for the more philosophically inclined composer, tends to become more acute as his work progresses. If it should be proven that everything is possible, that every sound, every constellation, every logical or random process is available—in short, if everything thinkable *can* be done—why then go ahead and still do it?

In the following pages an attempt is made to deal with some less obvious aspects of such problems and to propose some methods for analyzing them or even solving them.

Musical ideas are defined by composers of music. Not by philosophers, mathematicians, critics, music lovers, and record collectors. Analysts, commentators, and consumers may occasionally, occasionally even frequently, catch on to what the musical idea of a piece of music is or was. But their recognition of a musical idea, their way of calling it names, their behavior and attitude toward their own interpretation of the composer's work do not define the composer's musical idea. The reaction to a musical creation is a consequence, a product of all the factors which are brought to bear on the moment when the musical idea hits the listener, regardless of this listener's awareness as to what it was that hit him. For most of these factors the listener may be assumed to be responsible. He believes he knows what music is and what music is to be. He is drilled and trained to conceive of certain concepts, to associate certain associations of ideas, to extract from the audible event only what he thinks is worth listening to, and to ignore or even condemn the rest. In theory one might claim that the composer, on the other hand, should be held responsible for the musical idea only. But, as more and more potential listeners have turned composer, such comfortable distinctions will no longer serve, and the best one can do is to state that the composer is responsible for everything *and* the musical idea, while the listener is responsible for everything *but* the musical idea. A composer of music has to be aware of, and to have a penetrating insight into, all the factors which converge to an ideology in the cultural make-up of his contemporaries. He has to come up with an idea, a musical idea, which just passes the accumulated past by not exactly belonging to it, by not conforming to its approved laws, by labeling its claim to eternal validity succinctly as a mere ideology.

Whenever a man finally recognizes and understands the notions and laws that rule his behavior and standards, he will, usually, honor himself for his remarkable insight by claiming eternal validity for these notions and laws, though they be ever so spurious, ever so limited to but temporary relevance. Ideologies flourish on retroactively made-up beliefs which are complacently proclaiming to have found the truth, while skeptics are already busy looking for it again. Under ideological guidance, the desirability of changes of state or law is measured by approved criteria. An idea, on the other hand, usually challenges the adequacy of using approved criteria as standards of measurement, and expressly demonstrates the irrelevance of the *approved* in questions of desirability concerning changes of state or law. It is for this that ideas come under attack; not for being either good or bad, but rather for uncovering the impotence of persisting ideologies. To cover this shame, the ideologically possessed apostle finds himself frequently provoked to advocate indifference, complacency, corruption, or even murder. Often enough, unfortunately, such a defender of an expiring ideology, by proclaiming it to be nature's own law, succeeds in contaminating the more gullible of his opponents, who, unaware of their defeat, then begin to retaliate in kind. The most contagious disease in our human society is the agony of dying ideologies.

Every man's actions, the reasons for these actions, and the aims he proposes to reach with them, all reflect, among numerous other factors, this man's attitude or attitudes toward the ever-present choice offered: either to cooperate with and affirm ideologies, or to search for and try out ideas; either to make already approved criteria his law or to change the criteria according to the law he makes for himself. The composer's attitude will appear in the music he offers; the listeners' choice will influence their concept of, demand for, and participation in contemporary musical creation.

The criteria by which one thinks and the laws by which one acts function in interdependence. Progressing from temporary relevance to eternal obsolescence, by fits and starts, suspended in state at times, at others moved through a process of change, criteria and laws critically reflect each other. As progress in the two areas lacks synchronization, one is always ahead of, or moving faster than, the other. Their relative positions with respect to an assumed maximum of contemporary relevance vary constantly and may, occasionally, differ so widely that all mutual reflection begins to fade. It is in extreme situations like this that radical changes appear to become necessary. Much depends on how aware a man wants to be of such situations and of possible antidotes. The ideologist usually denies, under pressure at most regrets, the existence of both, whereas ideas begin to thrive on just the most drastic analysis of such problems. Musical ideas could be, more than anything else, seismographic analogies to such fluctuations in function between thought and action, criteria and laws, states and changes, elements and the whole.

In order to test the validity of this statement and its assumed premises, as well as to observe the emergence of unpredicted laws inherent in and consequent to such a test situation, I began work on a project which, written down in 1963, has served, and still is serving, as a general program of procedures, goals, and questions for my research activities at the University of Illinois. The Experimental Music Studio of the School of Music and the Department of Computer Science there offer the opportunity and the equipment, in a combination almost unique in the world, to follow up this kind of theoretical and practical investigation. I proposed to do research on the conditions under which a system of digital and analog computers would assist a composer in creating music of contemporary relevance and significance. Two parts of the project reflect, in a rather concise fashion, my concepts of why and how work with computers might help toward a temporary immunity against the ideological infections of intentions and languages. There is, to begin with, a list describing some of the experimental steps to be taken, accompanied by brief comments, and then an essay on the speculative tendency of the project and the terminology used.

Plan for Work on the Project

1. Analysis and definition of recent and earlier systems of acoustical elements and events, which were used as musical material.

> Mainly an investigation of the statistical properties of exploited systems for the purpose of comparative studies.

2. Exploration, theoretical and practical, of the acoustical elements and events which today could be produced, controlled, and organized according to defined intentions of the human mind.

> Experiments in synthetic sound production, with a view to using the results as a foundation for planning the construction of a universal sound synthesizer.

3. Development of a code which, based on the scientific analysis of the physical structure of sound, would allow the programming of computers and sound synthesizers.

> In many a sense the core of the project. This code, in order to be useful, has to be capable of expressing in *computer language* not only the structural conditions of sounds that are demanded, but also the conditions for an organization of elements or events in time. Considering the fact that what is generally called sound structure is, to a large extent, actually also a function of time, first attempts at the solution of the code problem will have to be made in the direction of a time code. If found, the application of such a code to fields other than music should offer possibilities of considerable value. It will take some time, however, to coordinate the theoretical concepts, which will create such a code, with the technological systems, which will have to understand and to answer it. On the other hand, it seems fully advisable to start working on this idea while using such information and such equipment as is already available at computer research centers.

4. The speculative definition of an assumed new limited and conditioned system of acoustical elements and events in disorder.

The communication potential of such an artificial system in disorder depends on the condition that its information content does not at the time of speculative definition surpass presumable future human insight. In this project the new factor which has to be considered is that the quantitative content of the system as well as the presumable power of future human insight are to be augmented by the capacities of high-speed digital and analog computers.

5. The gradual organization of a limited and conditioned system of acoustical elements and events in disorder by way of musical composition.

A large program of experiments designed to investigate the following sequence: the composer's musical idea, the computer system's proposals for organization and realization, and the composer's final selection and choice. The recorded progress and the results of the experiments will be submitted to several different methods of analytical and comparative study.

6. Research on whether and how concepts based on the theory of information and communication could be applied to an analysis of the ways in which communicative creations are perceived, understood, described, interpreted, and finally evaluated by individuals or groups of the respective contemporary society.

It is assumed that in the course of such investigations, some clarification may be reached as to the source, the nature, and the quantity of standards necessary for the evaluation of communications which contain a meaning not previously established. With more knowledge on this subject, it should become possible to work out the foundations for a theory of the function of communicative creation in society, which would at least contribute new aspects of hitherto unsolved problems to existing concepts of history and sociology, and especially of the arts. At the most, this new theory would solve the problems and replace or absorb the existing concepts. All predictions, however, as to the results of these investigations must needs be kept rather vague until research is well under way.

7. The composition, realization, and performance of a musical work
of contemporary relevance and significance with the assistance of a
digital and analog computer system.

No one can possibly say whether any result of this attempt
will correspond to what has, until now, been called a
work of art, or whether it will define what, from then on,
will be called a *work of art*, or whether it will miss altogether
that function in society which makes some creative communication a *work of art*. The contemporary relevance and
significance of the composition should be achieved, not by
appealing to existing means of understanding music, but
rather by creating new means for musical understanding. It
will not only show noticeable changes in the concept of the
acoustical system, not only propose new schemes of organization, but also provoke the creation of new circuits in the
listener's mind. This provocation is the aim and purpose of all
creative and scientific projects. It is in this sense, that the cooperation of composer and computer is considered for here
and now to be a natural idea. Whether it will lead to *music*
or to *electronic brains* or to a new aspect of both, is a question
fascinating enough to render fascinating all attempts at a
satisfactory answer.

The Speculative Tendency of the Project

Man uses the term *chaos* whenever he wishes to ascribe to a
quantity of elements or events what he believes to be the quality of
disorder. In order to get information out of chaos, the elements and
events have to be submitted to a process of organization, whereby
order increases and chaos decreases. As soon as the chaos has disappeared, complete order is installed and no further information can be
expected. The potential of information inherent in a situation of chaos
depends on at least two factors: on the quantity of elements or events
which are assumed to belong to the field of disorder, and on the
number of possible ways in which they can be organized. If the
quantity of elements or events in disorder is a very small one, or if
there exists only a small number of ways to organize them, then the
potential of information, in this particular situation of chaos, will be
small too, and soon exhausted. Usually, though not always, the two
factors seem to function in interdependence.

Wherever man observes chaos, he feels tempted, sooner or later, to apply his powers of organization in order to get information out of this chaos. This temptation is not only an expression of man's untiring curiosity, but also nature's hint at an inevitable necessity. As long as the power of communication of thought is one of the most important pillars of human society, it will be necessary from time to time to renew the sources out of which the means for such communication can be gained. The means for the communication of thought consist of a selection of significant information out of a defined field of original disorder. As soon as this field is fully organized, it cannot yield any more information and thus becomes useless for the generation of communicative means. Established means can be used for the re- peated communication of established thought, but, for the communi- cation of a new thought, it is necessary to generate new means. A new thought is naturally, therefore, always in search of a chaos containing an information potential which would render a particular choice of order significant for this particular new thought.

If a system in a situation of total disorder is said to possess a high information content, this usually means that a great number of differ- ent possibilities for partial or total organization of the elements or events, in this system, are offered for choice. By making a choice, man extracts information from the system. In order that his choice may be significant and the information carry a meaning, however, the relation- ship between the chosen and the eliminated possibilities must be perceived.

When a *chaos* is first attacked by an attempt at organization, it is obvious, therefore, that the information gained will carry very little meaning because too little is known about the other possibilities inherent in the chaos. The significance of first choices can thus not be appreciated. This period of first attack may be called the *experimen- tal* stage in the process of reducing chaos to order. Though seemingly uncommunicative, it cannot be avoided if one wishes to attain to higher degrees of order.

The next period could be called the *speculative* stage. By this time, the quantity of information gained allows for a number of statistical hypotheses as to the direction in which further information and the decrease of disorder in the system might be expected to move. In order to attach significance and meaning to the chosen possibilities at this stage, one has to accept as communicative the relationship be- tween information which has actually been gained, and the eliminated possibilities which are only hypothetically assumed.

In due course the system will find itself in a state of order in which the quantity of information gained allows for a correct definition of the whole system, even though not all the possibilities of organization have been applied. Speculation gradually is replaced by variation. This period could be called the *reflective* stage. Communication becomes easier while the store of information runs low. Further attempts at yet untried possibilities of organization tend to result in repeated significance and meaning, demonstrating, thus, the decline in usefulness of the system as a source for the means of communication of new thought.

The transition to the final, the *administrative* stage, during which a system is totally organized, is an almost unnoticeable process. This is due to the fact that the now wholly communicative system at the same time becomes wholly uninformative. Therefore, the information that a system is dead, can only come from another system which is in a higher state of disorder.

Most systems, as they are found in nature, possess an information content which is so enormous that it usually takes thousands of years of human endeavor to show a noticeable decrease of disorder. Thus an enormous quantity of information must be extracted before the experimental stage is passed and the speculative stage, the first communicative period, may be reached. Out of its need for means of thought communication, the human mind has invented a very effective short cut: using its own assumed limits and conditions as a standard, the human mind conceives of artificially limited and conditioned systems. An artificially limited system reduces, by a priori definitions, the quantity of the elements and events that are offered for choice. A conditioned system reduces, by artificial conditions, the quantity of possible ways of organizing the elements and events in a system. The information potential of artificial systems is expected to be lower than that of *natural, physical,* or *universal* systems. The limits and conditions by which the human mind, at a given moment, defines the artificial system through which communication of thought should become possible, reflect on the limits and conditions by which the human mind defines itself at any given moment of its progress from chaos to order.

The success of every human attempt at the presentation and the communication of a new thought depends on whether a system is found in which the nature of the elements or events in disorder has some bearing on, or affinity with, the nature of the new thought. Not every system will serve all endeavors. It is, furthermore, of utmost importance that the information content of the chosen system does not surpass the limits of presumable future human insight. As a matter of fact, one can say that an essential part of a new thought is the specification of the possible systems in which it proposes to become communicable. Equally, one can deduce from a chosen system some specifications of the thoughts which might be proposed.

A large-scale investigation of the nature of dependence between artificial systems and the human mind would throw light on both.

At least two considerations suggest that such investigation should be conducted with the assistance of computers: (1) limits and conditions are categories which can be expressed in computer programming —the time-saving capacity of the computers could thus be exploited to the full; (2) whereas the human mind, conscious of its conceived purpose, approaches even an artificial system with a selective attitude and so becomes aware of only the preconceived implications of the system, the computers would show the total of the available content. Revealing far more than only the tendencies of the human mind, this nonselective picture of the mind-created system should prove to be of significant importance. It should also be of interest to those engaged in research dealing with the duplication, through electronic devices, of the functions of the human mind.

The research project, meant as a contribution to the pursuance of this aim, would consist of numerous experiments, and should allow for comparative studies of three different but, under the set conditions, interdependent systems: (a) acoustical elements and events; (b) the composer's mind; and (c) the organization potential of digital and analog computers.

If the organization of a system in disorder is attempted with the aim to know all about the system and to render this information communicable, then it may be considered a *scientific project*. Here the system offers not only the means, but also the contents of communication. It speaks for and about itself.

If, on the other hand, this attempt is made in order to mobilize means for the communication of thoughts which transcend the definition of the system, then it may be considered a *creative project*. Here the system offers the means but not the contents of communication. It speaks for, but not about, itself.

All the sciences and all the arts progress in time by way of attacking various systems in various states of disorder with a strategy of interdependence between scientific and creative projects.

Both science and philosophy have suggested that the experience of *time* as an irreversible dimension of movement might be the sensual awareness of a continuous and irreversible replacement of chaos by order, and that, as the beginning of time was total chaos, total order would then be the end of time.

If one uses the terms previously established in this outline, the meaning of the word *music* could be defined as follows:

Music is the result of a continuous attempt to reduce to order the assumed chaos in the system of acoustical elements and events, with the purpose of mobilizing means for the communication of thoughts which transcend the definition of the system [a creative project].

These thoughts, consequently called *musical thoughts*, are the result of a continuous attempt to organize a system, called *composer's mind*, with the aim to know all about the system, and to render the extracted information communicable [a scientific project].

In order to conquer, eventually, the vastness of their respective objects, both attempts have to employ the strategy of probing stepwise into the disordered unknown, with the help of artificial systems. For *music*, the artificial system always consists of a more or less deliberately defined excerpt out of the total mass of possible acoustical elements and events. For *musical thought*, the artificial system consists of a more or less deliberately defined excerpt from the total mass of possible ideas and idea combinations in the composer's mind.

The history of music and of musical thought is the story of such artificial systems, their inception, bloom, and decline, their absorption or replacement by other artificial systems. At the same time, it is a report on the apparent or real progress in reducing to order the chaos in the natural universal system of acoustical elements and events as well as that of the composer's mind.

The idea of composing music, of organizing acoustical events in time with the intent of giving to this time a meaningful variety of movements, is only one of the innumerable attempts of the human mind to repeat, in ever-new ways, the old enjoyable feat of creating order out of chaos. Recent developments in the field of musical composition have shown that the limited and conditioned system of acoustical elements and events, considered *musical material* for several hundred years, has now entered the administrative stage, where all further possible permutations will no longer possess any new meaning. The degree to which contemporary composers are consciously aware of this fact may vary widely. But equally widely varied are the signs giving evident proof for the growth of at least an intuitive suspicion that the system of well-tempered pitches, harmonic spectrums, and harmonic time periodization has had its day, and has now become so thoroughly organized that nothing unheard and unthought of could possibly find, therein, its communicative equivalent. Research in synthetic sound production by electronic means, as well as the sudden emancipation of percussive instruments in contemporary music, the experiments with random and statistical score and interpretation, as well as the rapid *modernization* of popular music— all these are phenomena accompanying the decline of an exhausted system, and indicating the tentative inception of a new one. A further symptom of this state of affairs may be seen in the fact that the term *new*, which was a word of praise in the musical society of the eighteenth century, now has completely lost its flavor of aesthetical approval, and has adopted instead a connotation of reserved tolerance, implying that the experiment is with the listener, and not with the music. This metamorphosis (within such a word's meaning and social function) shows that comfort is found where everything except a new idea communicates easily, and that fear is felt where a new thought might destroy that comfort.

It is more than probable that observations of this kind, though made in the field of music, should also bear witness to certain more general attitudinal trends in our present-day society. In some way which ought to be investigated and interpreted with infinite care, such observations undoubtedly reflect many aspects of the situation in which the human mind finds itself just now. Once the significance of observations made in a specific field is understood, information on the more general system, which made the observations, will have been gained.

The human mind, out of its desire to know itself, creates artificial systems in order to render this knowledge communicable. If the artificial system in which music was understood is now to be replaced by another or larger artificial system, then it should be of great interest to observe how the human mind meets the demands which it poses. To this end, it is necessary to keep track not only of the results —that is, the music—but also to analyze, to register, and to store for further reference each moment of the working composer's mind. If the composer would have to program each of his ideas for a computer system, he would have to define as accurately as possible what he is looking for. It is to be expected that the computer system will respond with far greater a quantity of propositions answering the definition than the composer's mind alone is either conscious of, or able to imagine. At the same time, it would provide for an exact, step-by-step record of all the proceedings between initial definition and final choice. The composer's choice from the computer's propositions would still remain a highly personal decision, but would be taken in a field which is not limited by the prejudicial boundaries of the choosing person's imagination.

My contention is that the understanding of the human mind, which goes into the creation of music, will sooner or later communicate to the listener of music. The more valid the initial understanding proves to be, the more the function of music in society will become of importance and of consequence. All music that today is called beautiful, moving, or entertaining, once was the acute representation of a then contemporary vision of truth in the human mind. In order that the music of our day may add beauty, emotion, and entertainment to future times, we should compose it to represent and to be congruent to our contemporary vision of truth in the human mind. So that the search for this vision be a conscientious one, all that the human mind has created up to this day ought to be mobilized. None of its achievements, be they rational or irrational, be they knowledge or speculation, theory or practice, fantastic intuition or technological construction, should be excluded or even neglected, as long as the search goes on.

Since this project was written down, it has been clearly shown, here as well as elsewhere, that a system of analog and digital computers will indeed assist a composer in his attempt at creating music of contemporary relevance and significance, and also in his research on the meaning of these words. The more the composer works with computers, the more he avoids using the equipment as a glorified typewriter, and the more he has it assist him in mental rather than menial work. This development is reflected in some of the concepts through which the composer sees the computer, and by which he is influenced in his choice of procedures, and in the procedures themselves. As soon as the composer recognizes the computer as a very large and semantically uncommitted system which can adopt any one of the states that its elements and their number allow, he also recognizes how this is an invitation to use this large controllable system as a pseudouniverse in which smaller, artificially limited and conditioned subsystems can be simulated, so that their behavior and structural properties may be registered, recorded, and studied. There are, basically, two ways in which one can accept the invitation. The composer's program may instruct the computer system to simulate a specified subsystem, to operate on it according to specified rules, and to print out (in a convenient, specified code) the resulting states of the subsystem. It largely depends on the specified rules whether the result is predictable or not, whether it represents, unmistakably, the stipulated subsystem and not any other one, whether, as a documentary of the total or implied exploitation of the stipulated subsystem, it shows all the characteristics significant for the composer's intentions, or some, or more, or none. The other way would be that the composer's program defines an initial and a final state of the computer system, and a set of rules, and then instructs the computer system to find and simulate that subsystem, in which these rules will generate an uninterrupted chain of states between the initial and the final state stipulated. Here it will depend on the specified rules whether more than just one subsystem can be found, whether the resultant chain will present a mere record of counting, an exercise in scales, an inventory, or that highly complex progression, facing which the experience of disorder happily meets the knowledge of order.

For some time now it has become possible to use a combination of analog and digital computers and converters for the analysis and synthesis of sound. As such a system will store or transmit information at the rate of 40,000 samples per second, even the most complex waveforms in the audio-frequency range can be scanned and registered or be recorded on audio tape. This not only renders possible the most accurate observation of the nature of sound, but it also allows, at last, the composition *of* timbre, instead of *with* timbre. In a sense, one may call it the continuation of much which has been done in the electronic-music studio, only on a different scale. The composer has the possibility of extending his compositional control down to elements of sound lasting 1/20,000 of a second.

Thus one can say that, potentially, the computer system is a very close approximation to a universal sound synthesizer. If every sound is equally available on order, no particular one carries any significance

by itself. The composer is faced with the problem of how to restrain
the availability of sounds noticeably enough and how to make perceptible the range out of which, with various probabilities, a limited
number of constellations may be selected for actual appearance, so
that each choice attaches that significance to the chosen object which
the composer intends it to carry. The composer, having all at his
disposal, has to create and to define the subsystem in which he wants
his musical idea to expand into a musical event. He has to learn how
to think in systems, how to translate ideas and thoughts into network
systems of interlocking and mutually conditioning instructions, statements, stipulations and equations. At the same time he will have to
open his eyes and ears to the system ruling his social environment, in
order to become conscious of the role which his artificially created
systems play in that environment. Whether they happen to simulate
by affirmative analogy, and by artistic innocence, those ruling systems
he actually means to oppose and to criticize, or whether they simulate,
still by analogy, and maybe ahead of time, that which he hopes for.

CHAPTER III

Ethics and Esthetics of
Computer Composition

by GERALD STRANG

Fifty years ago, the advent of the computer in musical composition would have raised a variety of ethical and esthetic problems. Like any nontraditional instrument, it would have been considered somehow illegitimate, and its employment vaguely immoral. The saxophone, electronic organ, and vibraphone in turn carried the stigmata of illegitimacy.

Similarly, the innovations of Schoenberg, Stravinsky, and Bartók raised questions of esthetic legitimacy. A significant break with tradition was considered both immoral and antiesthetic. The explorers were excommunicated with the verdict: "But you can't call that music!"

By midcentury, ethical and esthetic judgments on such matters had almost disappeared among those who kept in touch with the newer developments. Amplified instruments and synthesizers are being accepted with little concern, except in the strongholds of conservatism such as the symphony orchestras.

We have now witnessed what is very nearly a reversal. Traditionalism is looked on as not quite respectable, and employment of the most recent technological innovations implies, in itself, a degree of merit regardless of the musical vehicle.

The computer as a sound synthesizer, as pioneered by John R. Pierce and Max V. Mathews, offers no unique problems in the permissive atmosphere of the sixties. An enormously complex and versatile instrument, it can be accepted as readily as other new instruments. The mathematical basis of its operation, including the use of numbers instead of notes to communicate the composer's intentions, makes many composers uncomfortable. Performers are disturbed (as they have been by the entire development of tape music) because they see the art of interpretation and performance threatened. The composer (with the aid of engineers and programmers) can now produce a definitive performance without employing a single union musician. The union can be forgiven if the elimination of performers appears immoral to its leaders.

A valid esthetic problem is raised, however, by the "definitive tape" which is the end product of electronic and computer music. Each rendition must by definition be an exact duplicate of every other (except for distortions introduced by the equipment and the acoustical environment). The revitalization of the composition through manifold slight changes in successive "interpretations" is no longer available unless live performance is combined with tape reproduction.

We have been partly conditioned to accept this state of affairs by the ossification of interpretation in recorded music. The Bruno Walter and the Toscanini versions may differ, but the recorded version of each is just as unchangeable as the electronic composition. Perhaps the electronic composer should issue a number of differing versions of his masterpiece to provide grist for the record critics.

Both ethics and esthetics are normative disciplines. They involve judgments of a comparative nature, and they imply standards on which judgments can be based. Absolute standards and criteria are out of fashion these days, but even relativism requires some form of rating or evaluation such that one phenomenon is judged "better" or "more significant" or otherwise superior to another.

Translated into active terms, if the composer accepts any esthetic or ethical responsibility at all, there should be some "oughts." Such terms as *good, bad, better, worse, acceptable, unacceptable* should have meaning and should influence behavior.

Computer composition, when it goes beyond the instrumental— when the computer is allowed to assume some of the compositional functions and processes—raises some issues calling for the examination of the "oughts."

Traditionally, the composer is responsible for every note, nuance, and detail of his composition. It has been considered somehow not quite proper to allow any other hand to participate. Of course, in the modern mixed media (radio, television, movies), orchestrators have been allowed to fill in detail and arrangers have elaborated other composers' music. Such delegation of detail work, under the direction of the principal artist, goes back into the misty past in painting and sculpture. But the *decisions* (at least the main ones) are the responsibility of the artist. And the delegations were always to other men, not to machines.

The computer differs from other instrumentalities in that it can, when properly programmed, make choices and decisions at any level and to any degree desired. The ethical question, in its simplest form, is: What choices and decisions *ought* the composer to delegate to the computer?

The corresponding esthetic question is: What elements of decision making must the composer reserve to make sure that *human* psychological and esthetic values prevail? If computers made music for other computers, who knows what esthetic values might apply?

The computer may take over microprocesses without stirring any misgivings. It may calculate the shapes of wave-forms and endlessly repeat them at the desired frequencies for the necessary period of time. It may add the successive instantaneous values of a number of interacting lines or sonorities to produce composites. It may impose sudden or systematic changes (at the composer's direction) to create dynamic changes, accents, and tempo changes. It may repeat patterns at any level with parameter changes which produce variations. It may carry out the combinations and permutations of a number of interacting patterns.

In short, the mechanical and repetitive aspects of composition may be delegated to the computer. No problems arise as long as the composer makes the determining choices, defines the processes, and issues the instructions.

But inevitably, the composer, with so powerful a tool at his disposal, is tempted to transfer major choices and decisions to the computer. It is cumbersome and complicated to specify all the necessary parameters for each musical event. Composers are accustomed to leaving far more than they realize to the discretion of the performer. A hint, a suggestion, or an example is enough to suggest to a talented performer how he should execute a whole series of related events. A carry-over factor can be built into a computer program, but it lacks the taste and discretion that can be expected from the human performer. Either a complex system of conditional tests and decisions must be provided, or the computer must be programmed to make an arbitrary, that is, random, choice. But the completely random choices are contrary to a fundamental esthetic principal—that art is a planned and organized presentation of related stimuli. The concepts of form, structure, and unity as esthetic criteria leave very little room for random elements.[1]

A truly random occurrence is, of course, scarcely thinkable in relation to a computer. It will select from a so-called random number table, or will carry out a simple mathematical process which is unlikely to produce a repetition in a very long series of numbers, but to the degree that repetition is suppressed, a nonrandom condition is imposed.

The composer finds himself in a dilemma with both ethical and esthetic overtones. Has he the right to leave any musical decision to chance? May he leave minor matters to chance if he controls the important ones? If so, what constitutes a minor matter?

Composing includes a good deal of trial and error. Acceptance or rejection of the result requires an esthetic judgment on the part of the composer. Sometimes the composer arrives at the solution of a compositional problem "accidentally," by "inspiration." Nobody knows how much subconscious logic enters into these cases. That they are chance occurrences is, however, very doubtful. They are probably inevitable results of the thought processes of the composer who is immersed in his material and his hypotheses for using and organizing it.

This semirational, disorderly "stewing over" the material appears to be an essentially human characteristic. The *evaluation* of the products of random processes seems to be a responsibility which the composer cannot avoid.

But the computer can be programmed to eliminate random events which the composer knows in advance he will reject. Thus the composer may permit random choices within a set (for example, the tempered scale or a twelve-tone series). He may further impose rejection criteria based on previous choices, or introduce controls based on probabilities (for example, Hiller's stochastic methods).

He may impose limits between which random choices may be made (for example, pitch choices within a predetermined bandwidth). He may permit limited random variation within a range about a central value (for example, irregular variation of a vibrato rate or a tempo).

In all such cases, limits are set and processes determined by the composer. The computer's "free choice" is narrowly circumscribed.

[1] I am well aware that these criteria have been and are being challenged and that the aleatory is being absorbed into art at an increasing rate. I am not interested in arguing for esthetic verities but only in identifying esthetic problems. The possible abandonment of such criteria is itself a serious problem. In our individualistic art world, each composer must seek his own (hopefully consistent) esthetic system.

The main esthetic judgments are made by the composer, either in setting the conditions, or in evaluating the result. He formulates the criteria, and he retains the power of rejection.

As the computer becomes a more familiar and more widely used tool, there will have to be a great deal of experimentation to find out "what would happen if. . . . ?" Acceptance or rejection must remain the responsibility of the composer.

More sophisticated programming may make it possible to set up hierarchies of conditions such that the computer may simulate more closely the esthetic choices of a particular composer. The composer then recedes a step in the decision-making process. Instead of making each decision at every level, he specifies the conditions and criteria which determine the decisions.

No matter how far-reaching the computer's participation in the compositional process, it remains the agent. The computer does not compose; it carries out instructions. Though its part in the process may increase significantly, the *computer as composer* must be considered a mirage. Nevertheless, it may, before the end of the century, revolutionize music as no previous technological advance has done, without modifying very much the human responsibility for ethical and esthetic judgments.

Music Composed with Computers—
A Historical Survey

by LEJAREN HILLER

This article will review progress in the use of electronic digital computers for composing music, including the preparation not only of substantial scores, but also of compositional tests and experiments carried out in conjunction with analytical studies. Detailed explanations, however, or criticism of the various research or compositional projects described here will not be included, since the primary purpose of this article is documentation.

Computers are basically data-processing devices, even though they can perform certain rather sophisticated operations upon data. In essence, computers accept instructions and data by means of input mechanisms; they then do something with these data; and, finally, they return results to the user of the computer. It is convenient, therefore, to divide musical applications of computers into four principal subdivisions as follows: (1) systems for input-output, storage, and sorting of musical data, (2) musicological and analytical studies, (3) composition with computers, and (4) sound analysis and synthesis. The subject here, then, is the third of these, but where overlapping with other kinds of applications occurs, an effort has been made to be inclusive rather than exclusive.

Some sort of comprehensive survey and bibliography concerned with the use of computers in the field of music is now urgently needed. At present, the most ambitious of such projects is being carried out at Queens College by Barry Brook in collaboration with Gary Berlind.[1] Brook and Berlind have programmed a computer to compile a bibliography of publications on all types of computer

[1] B. Brook and G. Berlind, "Writings on the Uses of Computers in Music," *College Music*, 1 (1967), 143.

applications to music. It is their purpose to keep this bibliography updated by constantly augmenting and systematically revising it as new works are reported.

Other efforts to provide bibliographies or reviews of musical applications of digital computers have been few in number. For example, during 1962, Michael Kassler, then a graduate student at Princeton University, started to compile such a bibliography, but this collection of material remains yet to be organized.[2] William Gale of Stamford, Connecticut, at one time apparently had the same idea, but it is not known what he has done with the materials he collected.[3] Ann Basart's bibliography of serial music contains some literature references on computer music.[4] And two books on experimental music that appeared some years ago provide substantial surveys of such topics as electronic music, electronic music instruments, and many related subjects including, to some extent, computer music. The first book, by Abraham Moles, is primarily technically oriented and incorporates some material on musical uses of electronic computers, either actual or potential.[5] The second book, by F. K. Prieberg,[6] is a carefully documented historical survey of experimental music up through about 1960, including a few pages on computer music. It is an extension of an earlier volume by Prieberg concerned with the impact on music of twentieth-century technology.[7] In 1962 I wrote a technical report describing progress in experimental music in Europe.[8] One of its chapters was concerned with music applications of digital computers and was a first effort to bring up to date portions of a book called *Experimental Music* published by Leonard Isaacson and myself in 1959.[9] Although this book was primarily an account of our own experiments to produce

[2] Letter from M. Kassler, July 20, 1962.

[3] Letters from W. Gale, July 23, 1961, Aug. 29, 1962, Dec. 14, 1962, Sept. 4, 1963.

[4] A. P. Basart, *Serial Music: A Classified Bibliography of Writings on Twelve-Tone and Electronic Music*, Berkeley, University of California Press, 1961.

[5] For computer music, see A. A. Moles, *Musiques expérimentales*, Paris, Éditions du Cercle d'Art Contemporain, 1960, pp. 78–89.

[6] For computer music, see F. K. Prieberg, *Musica ex Machina*, Frankfurt and Berlin, Ullstein, 1960, pp. 103–106.

[7] F. K. Prieberg, *Musik des Technischen Zeitalters*, Zurich, Atlantic, 1956.

[8] L. A. Hiller, Jr., "Report on Contemporary Experimental Music, 1961," *Technical Report No. 4*, Experimental Music Studio, University of Illinois, June, 1962. Part V of this report is on computers and music.

[9] L. A. Hiller, Jr., and L. M. Isaacson, *Experimental Music*, New York, McGraw-Hill Book Co., 1959.

our *Illiac Suite for String Quartet,* it also included some description of other studies in computer applications in music then known to us.[10] Before presenting the material developed since 1959, these earlier experiments need to be reviewed, together with any significant extensions derived from them.

Older Experiments

The four experiments in computer music composition described in 1959 involved the following propositions: (1) a suggestion by R. C. Pinkerton that computers might be used to write simple melodies utilizing probability tables;[11] (2) the generation with a Datatron computer of a tune called *Push-Button Bertha* by M. Klein and D. Bolitho;[12] (3) the generation of simple hymn tunes by Brooks, Hopkins, Neumann, and Wright;[13] and (4) a report that Mozart's Dice Game composition had been programmed for a computer by D. A. Caplin.

Pinkerton analyzed a sample of 39 nursery tunes for first-order and second-order transition probabilities, taking measure position into account. He then set up a simple "banal tunemaker" for the generation of new nursery tunes by means of binary choices—in effect, by flipping coins. He did this by reducing the large set of all possible outcomes for each successive choice to a binary choice between the two most probable outcomes, with all other possible outcomes being assigned probabilities equal to zero. Pinkerton found that his "banal tunemaker" was about 63 per cent redundant because of this binary choice restriction. This compared rather poorly with the value of 9 per cent for the first-order redundancy of the analyzed tunes. Pinkerton showed a typical tune generated by this banal tunemaker in an illustration in his article. He further suggested that an electronic computer could be used for tune synthesis more effectively than his imaginary banal tunemaker. No published evidence has been found that Pinkerton followed up his initial experiments. However, accord-

[10] *Ibid.,* pp. 55–57.

[11] R. C. Pinkerton, "Information Theory and Melody," *Sci. American,* 194 (Feb., 1956), 77.

[12] "Syncopation by Automation," *Data from ElectroData,* ElectroData Division of Burroughs Corp., Pasedena, Calif. (Aug., 1956), pp. 2–3.

[13] F. P. Brooks, Jr., A. L. Hopkins, Jr., P. G. Neumann, and W. V. Wright, "An Experiment in Musical Composition," *IRE Trans. on Electronic Computers,* EC-6 (1957), 175; F. P. Brooks, Jr. "Correction," *ibid,* EC-7 (1958), 60.

ing to Joel Cohen,[14] J. Sowa[15] constructed "A Machine to Compose Music" based on Pinkerton's ideas. He used a somewhat more complex net than Pinkerton's and based it on his own analysis of simple piano music. Although working it out on his machine was a slower process than carrying out the same computations on paper, it did incorporate at least some notion of computer processing.

Pinkerton's article in *Scientific American* describing his project provoked several letters to the editor. For example, J. R. Pierce,[16] noted that "J. J. Coupling has discovered stochastic composition of music in an article 'Science for Art's Sake' in *Astounding Science Fiction,* for November, 1950." (Actually, J. J. Coupling is a pen name used by Pierce when he writes science fiction.) Pierce, who is at Bell Telephone Laboratories, has himself been interested in compositional processes involving chance and stochastic sequences (see below).

A much more sophisticated device than the Pinkerton-Sowa type of "composing machine" was described by Olson and Belar in an article published in 1961.[17] Actually, Olson and Belar built their machine about ten years previous to this, so it antedates just about all the work described in this article. Their machine was not a computer except in the most limited sense. It might be said to produce a kind of "precomputer" machine-composed music. Since it also incorporated a sound-generating system, it was in part a simple prototype of the two later RCA Electronic Music Synthesizers which are described by Olson and his collaborators in other articles.[18]

The Olson-Belar "composing machine," as described, consists first of two random-number generators that employ both free-running and bistable multivibrators (square-wave generators) as their sources of random digits. Since these are operated at quite different orders of magnitude with respect to frequency, it is essentially a matter of

[14] J. E. Cohen, "Information Theory and Music," *Behavioral Science,* 7 (1962), 137.

[15] J. Sowa, "A Machine to Compose Music," manufactured by Oliver Garfield Co., Inc., New York, 1956. I believe that this is the same item that was advertised as a "special" system realizable with the "Geniac, the Electronic Brain Construction Kit." This is a science kit offered for sale to home science enthusiasts.

[16] J. R. Pierce, Letter to the Editor, *Sci. American,* 194 (Apr., 1956), 18.

[17] H. F. Olson and H. Belar, "Aid to Music Composition Employing a Random Probability System," *J. Acoust. Soc. Am.,* 33 (1961), 1163.

[18] H. F. Olson and H. Belar, "Electronic Music Synthesizer," *J. Acoust. Soc. Am.,* 27 (1955), 595; H. F. Olson, H. Belar, and J. Timmens, "Electronic Music Synthesis," *ibid.,* 32 (1960), 311.

chance when the free-running multivibrator shifts its polarity with respect to wave form in relation to the bistable multivibrator. These units are then coupled to a master control and read-out system that permits (a) coded information to be entered into the device, (b) weighted probabilities to be assigned to the control of pitch and rhythm components of the "composition" being generated, and (c) sound output to be produced. The master control system is an electro-mechanical device, essentially a rotary stepping switch and a set of relay trees. The stepping switch is controlled by the rhythm generator and the relay trees by the random-number generators. The relay tree in turn determines what pitch is chosen. All this is directed to a simple sound-synthesizing system that produces sawtooth-wave output sounds.

As input information, Olson and Belar obtained first-, second-, and third-order frequency counts of pitches found in eleven Stephen Foster tunes. All these eleven tunes were transposed to D major, so that the scale which results covers the diatonic range from B_3 to E_3, plus $G\sharp_3$ which occurs several times as an accidental. Relative frequencies of pitch occurrence were thus based on a set of twelve pitches. Second- and third-order transition probabilities, however, were reduced to a base-16 system, because the relay trees in the machine were limited to four bits. In their article Olson and Belar reproduced one of the synthesized Stephen Foster tunes produced with this device.

Klein and Bolitho apparently have not initiated any further attempts to compose computer music, so theirs was also no more than a single effort. *Push-Button Bertha* is printed in the company publication referred to above. Other than in newspaper accounts,[19] this work is mentioned only in an article by Klein himself,[20] which is based on a speech Klein gave at an A.C.M. Convention in Los Angeles in 1956.

The work of Brooks, Hopkins, Neumann, and Wright is somewhat more substantial than the above efforts because it was a serious, if limited, effort to assess the applicability of stochastic models in both the analysis and synthesis of simple music. These authors carried out a statistical analysis of 37 hymn tunes up to an eighth-order approximation. The various transition frequencies so obtained were then used to obtain tables of transition probabilities for synthesizing new tunes.

[19] For example, *The New York Times,* June 5, 1956; Anon., "The First Ballad to be Composed by a Computer," *International Musician,* 55 (Aug., 1956), 21.
[20] M. L. Klein, "Uncommon Uses for Common Digital Computers," *Instruments and Automation,* 30 (1957), 251.

Certain constraints were also imposed such as requiring that all tunes be in C major and in common meter, that the rhythmic patterns conform to the patterns of the original tunes, that the note durations be eighth notes or larger in conformity with the original sample, and that all tunes end on a dotted half note. These authors used basically the same generating process that was employed for the *Illiac Suite;* namely, they first generated random integers, then screened these for acceptance or rejection according to the probabilities in force, and finally provided a "try-again routine" for permitting the computer to rewrite unacceptable passages.

These authors predicted three types of results, all of which were confirmed:

(a) If the order of synthesis is too low, it results in note sequences not contained in and not typical of the sample analyzed.

(b) If the order of synthesis is too high, it results in excessive duplication, in whole or in part, of the original sample.

(c) Between these two extremes, synthesis results in tunes which are recognizably members of the class from which the sample was drawn.

The best level of synthesis seemed to be around sixth order, which is in general agreement with results of work carried out several years ago at the University of Illinois by R. A. Baker.[21] Baker's analysis of selected passages of music by Haydn, Mozart, and Beethoven indicates that a somewhat lower (fourth- to fifth-order) order of analysis and synthesis may be sufficient if a simple enough stochastic model is employed.

Since the original publication of this experiment, another article discussing the same work has been published by Neumann and Schappert.[22] This article is based on a lecture given in Essen in 1958 by Schappert who is presently located at the Institut für Pratische Mathematik at the Technische Hochschule in Darmstadt, Germany.

Finally, with regard to the programming of Mozart's *Musikalische Würfelspiel,* K.Anh.294d, D. A. Caplin described his experiments in some detail in a letter to the author in 1960. This work dates back to 1955, so it ranks among the earliest attempts at computer composition.

[21] R. A. Baker, "A Statistical Analysis of the Harmonic Practice of the 18th and 19th Centuries," D.M.A. Dissertation, University of Illinois, 1963.

[22] P. G. Neumann and H. Schappert, "Komponieren mit Elektronischen Rechenautomaten," *Nachrichte Technische Z.,* 8 (1959), 403.

From his description, it appears that his experiments were aimed at something more than a solution to the Mozart Dice Game alone:

The Mozart Dice Game was originally programmed for the Ferranti Mark computer which had a "hoot" instruction on it. This meant that we could write loops corresponding to each note of the chromatic scale and then play tunes which were "composed." We were then able to make a tape recording of the computer composing and then playing a tune. . . . We have just rewritten this routine for the Ferranti Mercury which is about 20 times faster and this has just been debugged. The tunes now sound quite reasonable. Our first set of experiments bore some resemblance to the work you have carried out, although our efforts were very much more primitive. We took a fixed chord sequence as a harmonic base and using more or less the same kind of rules you quote on page 84 (of *Experimental Music*) we generated tunes so that notes falling on the strong (that is, odd number) beats of the bar were selected from the notes of the appropriate chord. Even-number crotchet and quaver pairs were selected from tables using transitional probabilities.

We generated rhythms according to some fairly simple rules and produced (when we were lucky) rather dull tunes of the sort which one used to hear in Victorian hotel lounges. The day after the programme first worked, Dr. D. G. Prinz, of Ferranti, who was actually doing the detailed coding for this routine, took some of the output to a computer conference at Darmstadt with him and one of the tunes was hotted up by the dance band in the hotel where he was staying and was given a warm reception at its first performance.

This programme was never fully debugged; in particular, your melodic rule No. 5, relating to stepwise motion after a melodic skip was not always obeyed; this led to interesting, if not quite acceptable results.[23]

In this connection, it should be noted that there is now available a new edition of the score of Mozart's Dice Game composition which contains also a brief discussion of the work by K. H. Taubert, who edited the new publication.[24] The old edition,[25] however, is still useful because of the way it provides cardboard squares for each measure which can be arranged by the dice-throwing into a sequence that is inserted into slots provided in the performance parts. Mention might also be made here of an earlier article on this composition written by

[23] Letter from D. A. Caplin, Sept. 21, 1960.
[24] W. A. Mozart, *Musikalishes Würfelspiel*, K.Anh.294d, Mainz, B. Schott's Söhne, Edition 4474.
[25] A corrected and complete reference for this older publication should read: Guild Publications of Art and Music, 141 Broadway, New York; Agent: E. E. Gottlieb, P.O. Box 3274, Olympic Station, Beverly Hills, Calif.

Hermann Scherchen.[26] Recently John Cage and the author have also programmed Mozart's *Dice Game Composition*, as noted below.

Computer Music Composition at the University of Illinois

After completing the experiments that yielded the *Illiac Suite*, Leonard Isaacson left the University of Illinois. In 1958, I was asked by the university to set up an "Experimental Music Studio" that would provide a program of research, composition, and teaching in the areas of computer music, electronic tape music processes, and acoustics. Over the years, this has led to the production of a substantial number of compositions prepared with computers, as well as research in computer sound analysis and score preparation.

A complete list of compositions composed with electronic computers at the University of Illinois up through 1967 is given in Table IV-1. The published literature concerning each of these pieces is reviewed below, or a brief description of them is given so that the reader can have some idea of what they are like.

COMPLETED COMPOSITIONS

(1) *Illiac Suite for String Quartet* (Hiller and Isaacson). The score of this piece was published in 1957.[27] After several brief preliminary reports concerning the experimentation that went into producing it,[28] a full account of its preparation appeared in the book, *Experimental Music*, referred to earlier and reviewed extensively.[29] An article de-

---

[26] H. Scherchen, "Manipulation und Konzeption, I. Mozarts 'Anleitung zum Komponieren von Walzen vermittels zweir Würfel,'" *Gravesaner Blätter*, 4 (1956), 3.

[27] L. A. Hiller, Jr., and L. M. Isaacson, *Illiac Suite for String Quartet*, New Music Edition, Vol. 30, No. 3, Bryn Mawr, Pa., Theodore Presser Co., 1957.

[28] L. A. Hiller, Jr., "Some Structural Principles of Computer Music," *J. Am. Musicological Soc.*, 9 (1956), 247; Hiller, "Musique Electronique," *L'Ère Atomique, Encyclopédie des Sciences Modernes*, Vol. 8, Geneva, Switzerland, Editions René Kister, pp. 110–112; Hiller and L. M. Issacson, "Musical Composition with a High-Speed Digital Computer," *J. Audio Eng. Soc.*, 6 (1958), 154.

[29] The following reviews of this book seem to be representative: G. F. McKay, *J. Research Music Ed.*, 7 (1959), 232; M. V. Mathews, *Proc. IRE*, 47 (1959), 1792; E. G. Richardson, *Nature*, 184 (1959), 1754; P. Westergaard, *J. Music Theory*, 3 (1959), 302; N. Gastinel, *Chiffres-France* (Jan., 1960), 125; R. W. Hamming, *Computing Reviews*, 1 (1960), 16; D. W. Martin, *J. Acoust. Soc. Am.*, 32 (1960), 617; W. Meyer-Eppler, *Archiv der Elektrischen Übertragung*, 14 (1960), 237; T. H. O'Beirne, *The Computer J.*, 3 (1960), 205; I. Anhalt, *The Canadian Music J.*, 5 (1961), 61; W. P. Livant, *Behavioral Science*, 6 (1961), 159; B. Hansen, *Neue Z. für Musik*, 143 (1962), 147; M. Filip, *Slovenska Hudha*,

Table IV-1. Computer music from the University of Illinois

Composer	Title
Completed compositions	
(1) Lejaren Hiller and Leonard Isaacson	*Illiac Suite for String Quartet* (1957)
(2) Lejaren Hiller	"The Flying Lesson" from *Music for "The Birds"* (by Aristophanes) (1958)
(3) Robert Baker	*CSX-1 Study,* for tape alone (1963)
(4) Lejaren Hiller and Robert Baker	*Computer Cantata,* for soprano, eighteen instruments and tape (1963)
(5) Herbert Brün	*Sonoriferous Loops,* for five instruments and tape (1965)
(6) John Myhill	*Scherzo a Tre Voce,* for tape alone (1965)
(7) Herbert Brün	*Non-Sequitur VI,* for six instruments and tape (1966)
(8) Herbert Brün	*Three Pieces for Percussionists* (1967)
Compositions in progress (as of December 1967)	
(1) Lejaren Hiller	*Algorithms I,* for nine instruments and tape
(2) Lejaren Hiller	*An Avalanche for Pitchman, Prima Donna, Player Piano, Percussionist and Prerecorded Tape*
(3) John Cage and Lejaren Hiller	*HPSCHD,* for one to seven harpsichords and one to fifty-one tapes
(4) Salvatore Martirano	*Lo Dissa Dante,* for orchestra *
(5) Herbert Brün	*Infraudibles,* for tape alone
Student compositions	
(1) Frank Moore and Michael Ranta	*Piece for Jazz Set* (1966)
(2) Michael Ranta	*Algol Rhythms* (1967)
(3) James Cuomo	*Zetos 1* through *Zetos 5,* five compositions for various groups of instruments (1967)
(4) Neely Bruce	*Fantasy for Ten Winds, Percussion and Tape* (1967) *

* Only in part a computer-generated score.

rived from the book was published in *Scientific American.*[30] More recently, Sayre and Crosson published a condensation of portions of the same book as a chapter in a book on computers and intelligence.[31]

8 (1964), 128 (also pp. 104 and 112 for photograph and extract from score); P. A. Evans, *Music and Letters,* 42 (1961), 369; R. L. Jacobs, *The Music Review,* 22 (1961), 326.

[30] L. A. Hiller, Jr., "Computer Music," *Sci. American,* 201 (Dec., 1959), 109.

[31] L. A. Hiller, Jr., and L. M. Isaacson, "Experimental Music," in K. M. Sayre and F. J. Crosson, eds., *The Modeling of Mind, Computers and Intelligence,* Notre Dame, Ind., University of Notre Dame Press, 1963, pp. 43–72.

The first three movements of the *Illiac Suite* were played in Urbana in 1956. It has since been played a number of times [32] and twice recorded. The WQXR String Quintet first recorded it in a recording session sponsored by Max Mathews of Bell Telephone Laboratories. One excerpt from this recording appears in a record album issued by Bell some years ago.[33] Recently, a recording of a complete perform- ance by the University of Illinois Composition String Quartet was released by M.G.M. Records.[34]

The existence of the *Illiac Suite,* plus the growth of interest in musical applications of electronic computers in general, has stimu- lated the writing of numerous articles on the subject of computer music in many types of media.[35] Several somewhat more extended articles have appeared in various periodicals, including articles prima- rily intended for students,[36] for nontechnical readers [37] or for readers

[32] In its Jan. 4, 1960, issue, *Newsweek* said of the *Illiac Suite:* "Premiered in Chicago, the stilted, lifeless performance aroused much curiosity but not much envy from flesh-and-blood composers." This was, of course, not the first perform- ance. Unfortunately, just before the concert in question, the quartet engaged to play the *Illiac Suite* refused to do so, declaring it unplayable. So a tape recorder was placed on the stage to play a tape of the 1956 performance for the assembled audience.

[33] "Music from Mathematics," 10" LP, *Bell Telephone Laboratories Record* 122227, 1960.

[34] "Computer Music from the University of Illinois," 12" LP, *Heliodor H/HS-25053, 1967.*

[35] A large number of these, such as most newspaper articles, are of little intrinsic interest; a few of the more substantial are. Anon., "By the Numbers," *Musical America,* 76 (Sept., 1956), 13; E. Cony, "Canny Computers—Machines Write Music, Play Checkers, Tackle New Tasks in Industry," *Wall Street J.,* Sept. 19, 1956, 14B, 1, 12; W. E. Hansen, "This is Music," *Chicago Tribune,* Apr. 12, 1959, Magazine Section; L. A. Hiller, Jr., "Electronic and Computer Music," *St. Louis Post-Dispatch,* May 17, 1959, Music Section; Anon., "Will a Machine Compose a New Symphony?" *The School Musician,* 31 (Jan., 1960), 59 (a synopsis of my article in *Scientific American*); B. Brown, "Why 'Thinking Machines' Cannot Think," *New York Times,* Feb. 19, 1961, Magazine Section. Among other things, Mr. Brown says, "This rather ludicrous extension of the machine-brain equation to artistic creativity perhaps best illustrates its limitations. No machine is ever really likely to contain the artist within its electrophysics. . . ." and so on. See also P. Stadlen, "When Computer Turns Composer," *Daily Telegraph* (London), Aug. 10, 1963.

[36] Anon., "Electronic Brain Composes at University of Illinois," *Illinois Music Educator,* 16 (Sept.–Oct., 1956), 16; L. J. Forys, "Music: Mood or Math," *Notre Dame Tech. Rev.,* 14 (Jan., 1963), 26; B. Lueck, "Synthesizing a Symphony," *Illinois Technograph,* 79 (May, 1964), 6.

[37] Anon., "I. B. Mozart's 42nd Symphony," *Review of Research and Reflection,* 1 (1960), 45 (a review of several articles including mine in the *Scientific Ameri- can* and Leonard Meyer's article in *J. Aesthetics and Art Criticism* on information theory and music); B. J. Novak and G. R. Barnett, "Are Music and Science Com-

principally interested in computer applications.[38] In addition, there exist in European journals two rather thorough commentaries on the work that produced the *Illiac Suite*.[39] Finally, as a consequence of publicity about the *Illiac Suite*, in 1959, I received from its author a copy of a short story, "Das Zwölftonwunder" originally published in Switzerland in 1952.[40] The plot of the story revolved around the idea that a professor at an American university programmed a computer to turn out a piece of music—actually a piece of twelve-tone music—and won a prize with it.

(2) "The Flying Lesson" from *Music for "The Birds"* (Hiller). This is a short piece of theater music in which phrases of a conventional minuet in G major are played on a piano and are answered by equivalent phrases with the same rhythm played on eight other instruments. The instrumental group, however, plays random pitches generated with ILLIAC I, thus providing disorderly answers to highly organized musical ideas, a musical parallel to the stage action.

(3) *CSX-1 Study* (Baker). In 1958, Robert Baker, a graduate student at the University of Illinois majoring in music composition and minoring in mathematics, and I decided to collaborate on writing a new composition to succeed the *Illiac Suite*. We first planned to continue along the same general lines and run a series of experiments solving specific problems in either traditional or more experimental composition methods. For example, we worked out a considerable amount of flow charting and even some programming details for writing fugues. The idea at that time was to produce a second *Illiac Suite*. After some thought, however, this approach was abandoned in

---

patible?" *Music Educators J.*, 46 (June–July, 1960), 44; A. A. Moles, "Muzyka, Maszyny, Kompozytor," *Ruch Muzycyzny*, 6 (1962), 1; N. Slonimsky, "Chamber Music in America," in W. W. Cobbett (ed.), *Cobbett's Encyclopedic Survey of Chamber Music*, 2nd ed., Vol. 3, London, Oxford, 1963, p. 182; Slonimsky, "Modern Music: Its Styles, Its Techniques," in D. Ewen, *The New Book of Modern Composers*, New York, Alfred A. Knopf, 1961, p. 31.

[38] E. C. Berkeley, *The Computer Revolution*, Garden City, N.Y., Doubleday, 1962, pp. 170–171; D. C. Halacy, *Computers-The Machines We Think With*, New York, Harper and Row, 1962, pp. 196–198; R. S. Ledley, *Programming and Utilizing Digital Computers*, New York, McGraw-Hill Book Co., 1962, pp. 371–375.

[39] A. Rakowski, "O Zastosowaniu Cyfrowich Maszyn Matematycznych do Muziki," *Muzyka Kwartalnik*, 7 (1962), 83; J. Hijman, "Elektronishch Componeren?" *Mens en Melodie*, 16 (1961), 141. The first of these articles, by Rakowski, discusses computer composition in light of concepts of information theory and is thus somewhat technically oriented.

[40] F. Ascher, "Das Zwolftonwunder," *Inspiré* (1952), 24.

favor of a more generalized attack on solving problems in computer-music composition. Progress in this direction was reported in several successive publications,[41] some of which deal exclusively with compositional problems while others take up such problems as part of a general discussion of computer applications in music. With the objective of separating procedural logic from specific decisions governing style and structural details, a computer-compiler program was written in SCATRE for the IBM 7090 computer at the University of Illinois. This compiling program, called MUSICOMP, which is an acronym derived from MUsic Simulator Interpreter for COMpositional Procedures, accepts subroutines for various compositional problems and thus serves as a foundation for extended investigations into computer music compositional processes. Baker wrote a brief instruction manual on how to use MUSICOMP [42] that has been expanded and revised in loose-leaf form.[43] Thus far, published descriptions of MUSICOMP have been rather limited and presented in connection with discussion of specific compositions to be described directly below.

The *CSX-1 Study,* written by Robert Baker, is a brief composition for two-channel tape recorder that was intended to be a test not only of MUSICOMP but also of a conversion subroutine within MUSICOMP that permits sounds to be generated by the CSX-1 digital computer. This latter process, devised by J. L. Divilbiss of the Coordinated Sciences Laboratory at the University of Illinois, has been described in an article published by its inventor [44] and in a users' manual issued as a technical report.[45] The *CSX-1 Study* is a short

[41] L. A. Hiller, Jr., "The Electrons Go Round and Round and Come Out Music," *IRE Student Quarterly,* 8 (Sept., 1961), 36; Hiller and R. A. Baker, "Computer Music," in H. Borko, ed., *Computer Applications in the Behavioral Sciences,* Englewood Cliffs, N.J., Prentice-Hall Book Co., 1962, pp. 424–451; Hiller, "Muzyczne Zastosowanie Elektronowych Maszyn Cyfrowych," *Ruch Muzycyzny,* 6 (April 1–15, 1962), 11; Hiller, "Musical Application of Electronic Digital Computers," *Gravesaner Blätter,* 27/28 (1962), 62.

[42] R. A. Baker, "MUSICOMP, *MU*sic-*SI*mulator-for-*COM*positional-Procedures for the IBM 7090 Electronic Digital Computer," *Technical Report No. 9,* University of Illinois Experimental Music Studio, Urbana, 1963.

[43] L. A. Hiller, Jr., and A. Leal, "Revised MUSICOMP Manual," *Technical Report No. 13,* University of Illinois Experimental Music Studio, Urbana, 1966. (Supplements will be issued to this report as circumstances permit.)

[44] J. L. Divilbiss, "Real-Time Generation of Music with a Digital Computer," *J. Music Theory,* 8 (1964), 99.

[45] L. A. Hiller, J. L. Divilbiss, D. Barron, H. Brün, E. Lin, "Operator's Manual for the 'CSX-1 Music Machine,'" *Technical Report No. 12,* University of Illinois Experimental Music Studio, Urbana, 1966.

atonal work for two-channel tape based on systematic permutations of twelve-tone material. It has been performed publicly during the course of lectures by Baker in St. Louis, by me in Darmstadt, and in concerts given in Buffalo and Cleveland in 1964 by the University of Illinois Contemporary Chamber Players. The only known published reference to it appeared in an article in the St. Louis Post-Dispatch.[46]

(4) *Computer Cantata* (Hiller and Baker). A much more ambitious composition is the *Computer Cantata,* completed in June 1963. This composition consists of a series of studies designed to exploit a few features of MUSICOMP and to check it out as far as basic operation was concerned. As described in detail elsewhere,[47] the principal sections of this cantata consist of five "Strophes" that employ in sequence five successive stochastic approximations to spoken English. These five samples of "text," which range from zeroth- to fourth-order approximations, were realized in the ILLIAC I computer and were prepared by Hultzén, Allen, and Miron.[48] Analogous stochastic approximations to these texts were composed, employing a sample of music taken from Charles Ives' *Three Places in New England* as the reference material.

In addition, the *Computer Cantata* contains "Prologs" and "Epilogs" to the various "Strophes" that deal with (a) problems of rhythmic organization for nonpitched percussion, (b) the generation of total serial music employing the model of Boulez's *Structures for Two Pianos—Book I,* and (c) the generation of music with both linear and vertical structure in tempered scales ranging from nine to fifteen notes per octave. For this last study, computer sound realization with the CSX-1 computer was again employed. The *Computer Cantata* was first performed in December 1963 at the University of Illinois by an ensemble conducted by Jack McKenzie, with Helen Hamm as soprano

[46] W. F. Woo, "Learning to Appreciate Electronic Music," *St. Louis Post-Dispatch,* Dec. 4, 1963, Music Section.

[47] L. A. Hiller, Jr., "Informationstheorie und Computermusik," *Darmstädter Beiträge zur Neuen Musik,* Vol. 8, Mainz, B. Schott's Söhne, 1964, 66 pp. A brief review of this book is contained in F. Winckel, "Computermusik," *Musica,* 19 (1965), 45. See also Hiller and R. A. Baker, "Computer Cantata: An Investigation of Compositional Procedure," *Perspectives of New Music,* 3 (1964), 62. This article is derived from an earlier progress report: Hiller and Baker, "Computer Cantata: A Study in Composition Using the University of Illinois IBM 7090 and CSX-1 Electronic Digital Computers," *Technical Report No. 8,* University of Illinois Experimental Music Studio, Urbana, 1963.

[48] L. A. Hultzén, J. Allen, Jr., and M. S. Miron, *Tables of Transitional Frequencies of English Phonemes,* Urbana, Ill., University of Illinois Press, 1964.

soloist, followed by additional performances soon thereafter in Ann Arbor, Chicago, and St. Louis. Udo Kasemets briefly reviewed the Ann Arbor performance,[49] and Donal J. Henahan, the former music critic from the *Chicago Daily News*, has written several fairly extensive articles based on the Chicago performance.[50] More recently, Peter Yates has written descriptions of computer music that concentrate on the *Computer Cantata* as an example for criticism.[51] The score of this piece was published in early 1968.[52] A recording of a performance of the work also appears on the disk containing the *Illiac Suite* referred to earlier.[53]

The principal critical reaction so far seems to center around the question of whether the extension of the stochastic process from zeroth- to fourth-order in the five strophes is really apparent and whether it is sufficient to sustain musical interest. Baker and I intended to be quite objective in applying the stochastic processes, to parallel the text closely, and to restrict controls to linear sequences only. No cross relationships among voices were programmed for the "Strophes," nor was any attempt made to build up "hierarchical structures" of the type discussed in an earlier publication.[54] We wished to examine the musical effect of straightforward increases in order of stochastic control. It is quite easy to hear this increase in organization from "Strophe" to "Strophe," and this is an important point, since there is substantial interest at present in determining just how effective stochastic processes will be in contributing to new types of musical communication. It should be emphasized, however, that we had no illusions that simple stochastic processes would be sufficient in themselves for generating a large body of new compositions.

(5) *Sonoriferous Loops* (Brün). Since Herbert Brün joined the faculty of the University of Illinois in September 1963, one of his principal interests has been to write compositions with the aid of

[49] U. Kasemets, "Report from Ann Arbor," *Musical Quarterly*, 50 (1964), 518.

[50] D. J. Henahan, "A Punchboard Cantata," *Chicago Daily News*, Mar. 4, 1964; "Future Mozart—Will He be A.C. or D.C.?" *Chicago Daily News*, Mar. 8, 1964; "Comments on Classics," *Downbeat*, 31 (Apr. 23, 1964), 33.

[51] P. Yates, "Travels by Ford, II, The Musical Computers at Urbana," *Arts and Architecture*, 82 (June, 1965), 8; P. Yates, *Twentieth Century Music*, New York, Pantheon Books, 1967, pp. 318–321.

[52] L. A. Hiller, Jr., and R. A. Baker, *Computer Cantata* (for soprano, four wind instruments, three stringed instruments, theremin, two-channel tape recorder and ten percussion), Bryn Mawr, Pa., Theodore Presser Co., 1968.

[53] "Computer Music," Helidor H/HS-25053.

[54] "Computer Music," in Borko, ed., *Computer Applications*.

MUSICOMP. The first work he completed is called *Sonoriferous Loops*, written for five instruments and two-channel tape.[55] After several partial performances in 1964 that omitted its tape-recorder interludes, this new computer composition was performed in its entirety at the Festival of Contemporary Arts (University of Illinois) in March 1965. It has since been performed a number of times both in this country and in Europe.

Sonoriferous Loops lasts about 16 minutes and is organized into alternating sections for instrumental ensemble and tape. In the instrumental sections, there are parts for flute, trumpet, double bass, percussion I (mallet instruments), and percussion II (unpitched instruments). Brün defined four parameters for each part, namely, pitch, register, rhythmic unit, and rhythmic mode, and wrote macro orders to govern the choices of each parameter, making use at the same time of some of the internal library subroutines already available in MUSICOMP. The composition is serial in terms of pitch choices in the sense that it uses ML.ROW, a subroutine for extracting single elements from rows and their standard permutations. Brün used this subroutine to obtain twelve different successive pitches and then used subroutine SHUFFL to shuffle the row randomly before repeating this whole process. Brün also defined probability distributions for binary choices of rest or play and for octave registers. These are different for each instrument and for different parts of the composition. Rhythmic modes, that is, basic metrical patterns, and rhythmic units within these patterns were chosen also in accord with assigned probability distributions.

There are five successively shorter instrumental sections or "loops" in *Sonoriferous Loops*. The "loops" differ from one another principally in terms of changes in the rest/play probabilities assigned to each part. Thus, for example, the rest/play proportions for the opening section are flute, 74 per cent; trumpet, 68 per cent; double bass, 50 per cent; percussion I, 32 per cent; and percussion II, 26 per cent, thus giving the flute the most prominent part. In the second instrumental section, the trumpet predominates, and so forth. The computer generated a printout which Brün converted to an ordinary musical score to which he then added tempi, dynamics, and playing instructions (*pizz., sordino, staccato*, and so on).

[55] These descriptions of Brün's pieces are based on notes recently given to me by the composer and on program notes for the 1965 Festival of Contemporary Arts at the University of Illinois and for the 1965 Internationale Ferienkuese für Neue Musik at Darmstadt.

Between each of the above loops, there is inserted an interlude for tape alone employing the method of sound synthesis involving the CSX-1 computer already mentioned above. Three voices were generated for each interlude with defined parameters for pitch, register, intensity, rhythmic mode, and rhythmic unit choices. Each interlude in turn was made up of three "phases" or combinations thereof. Finally, Brün altered the timbres of the sound output on the tapes produced by CSX-1 with the electronic music equipment in the Experimental Music Studio at Illinois.

(6) *Scherzo a Tre Voce* (Myhill). John Myhill, a member of the University of Illinois faculty from 1964 to 1966, is a well-known mathematician who recently became interested in developing ideas in musical composition and sound synthesis. His first piece of computer music was a short composition completed in the summer of 1965. The score was written with the IBM-7094 computer utilizing FORTRAN programming (which was carried out with the assistance of Antonio Leal, a graduate student in mathematics). The output of the IBM-7094 was then transferred via magnetic tape to the CSX-1 computer, so that the final result was generated as three square waves. The only parameter of composition that was deterministically controlled was intensity. The rest were stochastically generated according to the following plan.

(a) *Theme:* Four of eight defined "themes" were designated as "wide," four as "narrow." A certain function $\phi_1(t)$ determined the probability that a wide rather than a narrow theme might be chosen t seconds after the beginning of the piece. Narrow themes were favored at the beginning and end, and wide ones in the middle of the composition. The eight "themes" consisted of eight functions of a real variable. For example, one of the "themes" had the form, $a \sin \beta t$. This meant that t seconds after this "theme" had begun, the voice which had this "theme" had a pitch $a \sin \beta t$ semitones above an "axis" chosen for this particular occurrence of the "theme." Likewise, $\phi_2(t)$ was read to be "fast" or "slow" just as $\phi_1(t)$ was read to be "wide" or "narrow." Finally, $\phi_3(t)$ was read to be "complicated" or "simple."

(b) *Silence:* The function $\phi_4(t)$ gave the probability (for the case that t was an exact multiple of the measure length of 1.2 seconds) that a rest would be chosen in any given voice in the time interval from t to $t + 1.2$ seconds. If such a rest occurred, the theme being generated in the preceding measure of that voice was resumed after the rest.

(c) *Method of Approximation:* The function $\phi_5(t)$ determined the probability that the curve associated with the theme in any particular measure and voice would be followed strictly rather than approximated by the nearest of six randomly chosen equal-tempered pitches. Thus, $\phi_5(t)$ was the probability of a *glissando* and was so set as to be greatest at the beginning and at the end of the piece.

(d) *Rhythm:* $\phi_6(t)$ was the probability (given that a *glissando* had *not* been chosen) that one of 15 periodic rhythms would be used. Again, it was greatest near the middle of the piece. If one of these 15 was not used, a random procedure was used to choose note lengths.

(e) *Tonality:* The random pitch selection method was modified so that certain pitches would predominate in certain randomly determined sections. These favored pitches proceeded in their order of appearance according to the cycle of fifths.[56]

(7) *Non-Sequitur VI* (Brün). This composition, which lasts about 15 minutes, was commissioned by Radio Bremen and was first performed in that city in May 1966. It is scored for flute, cello, harp, piano, two percussion, and two-channel tape. It is also the first computer composition produced at Illinois that exploits our provisional digital-to-analog sound synthesis system.[57] In *Non-Sequitur VI,* just as in *Sonoriferous Loops,* choices of musical parameters depend primarily upon various probability distributions entered as data into the computer. A principal difference, however, is that this time, compared to what was done in programming *Sonoriferous Loops,* the choices actually made in each short section of the composition were constantly inspected in order to refine the starting distribution. When each new section was reached, this process was repeated starting from new initial distributions. In effect, this routine consisted of the successive refinements of the probability distributions according to the actual environment being generated.

Structurally, *Non-Sequitur VI* differs from *Sonoriferous Loops* in that the tape sections overlap with the instrumental sections rather than alternate with them. According to information provided by Brün, "the programming of this work mainly reflects the continuous search for answers to two questions: (1) What is the minimal number and power of restrictive rules that will select from randomly generated sequences of elements that particular variety of element-concatenations satisfying the conditions for either recognizable or stipulated

[56] This description is based on notes given me by John Myhill.

[57] G. R. Grossman and J. W. Beauchamp, "A Provisional Sound Generating Program for the ILLIAC II Computer and D/A Converter," *Technical Report No. 14,* University of Illinois Experimental Music Studio, Urbana, 1966; A. B. Otis, Jr., "An Analog Input/Output System for the ILLIAC II," *Technical Report No. 18,* University of Illinois Experimental Music Studio, Urbana, 1967.

'musical' forms and events? (2) Could a combination of stochastic choice rules with heuristic, multivalent, decision-taking procedures contribute an apparent 'musical' coherence to a chain of changes of state in a structural system?"

Non-Sequitur VI was performed in April 1967 in Chicago by the University of Illinois Contemporary Chamber Players with the composer conducting.

(8) *Three Pieces for Solo Percussionist* (Brün). In 1967, Brün produced three pieces for three percussionists as follows: (a) *Plot,* written for Michael Ranta who has since performed it at Urbana, Interlochen, Warsaw, and Paris; (b) *Touch and Go,* written for Allen O'Conner, and (c) *Stalks and Trees and Drops and Clouds,* written for William Youhass. These last two pieces were scheduled for performance in early 1968.

For each of the three pieces, Brün wrote a FORTRAN program which produced an output tape for the CALCOMP plotter to draw a score on transparent paper. The "notation" of these scores makes use of a selected set of symbols already available in the CALCOMP library (triangles, circles, lines, and so on). The "language" of the scores is given by the distribution, size, and position of symbols on each page of the score; in effect, each page is a plot of dynamic level versus time. Once the performer is provided with a short introductory explanation of the notation, he is able to perform directly from the score. The result is a novel and interesting way of using an existing computer output system for the direct production of a score which can be used without modification for performance. Brün is now engaged in developing a system of musical symbols that will be incorporated into the symbol library of the CALCOMP plotter.

COMPOSITIONS IN PROGRESS

(1) *Algorithms I for Nine Instruments and Tape* (Hiller). Three new related compositions are being completed, called *Algorithms I, II and III.* These are scored for flute, clarinet, bassoon, trumpet, harp, two-channel tape, percussion, violin, cello, and double bass. Work on these pieces was started about two years ago, and three articles have been written during this time that serve in part as progress reports.[58]

[58] L. A. Hiller and J. W. Beauchamp, "Research in Music with Electronics," *Science,* 150 (1965), 161; Hiller, "Programming a Computer for Musical Composition," in G. Lefkoff, ed., *Papers from the West Virginia University Conference on Computer Applications in Music,* Morgantown, West Virginia University Li-

The first of these refers to computer music composition only briefly in the context of reviewing electronic methods for research in music; the last two articles are based specifically on computer applications in music, that is, composing music with computers.

As explained in both these latter articles, *Algorithms I* will incorporate more complex structural relationships than the *Computer Cantata* possessed. The plan was well set as of December 1967. The composition consists of three movements as follows: I. The Decay of Information (2 minutes duration); II. Icosahedron (3 minutes); III. The Incorporation of Constraints (4 minutes). It should be noted that this is a revision of a six-movement plan described in the articles referred to above. Each movement of the work will exist in four "versions," any one of which can be chosen for a given performance. Each "version" will reflect small but systematic and important changes of parameters inserted into the various compositional subroutines written for this work. Consequently, *Algorithms I* not only will serve to demonstrate that such changes can drastically alter the overall effect of a given general musical structure, but also will permit the controlled and identified isolation of the specific effect of a particular musical parameter on the impression of the whole. The process is thus a novel application of a standard type of experimental design.

Sound synthesis for the two-channel tape for *Algorithms I* is being achieved by a two-step process that involves two subroutines, DIGAN and INTRFC. DIGAN is inserted into compositional routines and accepts choices of pitch, rhythmic duration, dynamics level, timbre choice, and attack and decay time. DIGAN then calls INTRFC which stores these data on a digital tape in a special digital format. This is done in the IBM-7094 where all our compositional work is done at present. This tape is then transferred to the ILLIAC II where it provides the input data for the provisional sound-generating program described above. *Algorithms I* will thus be the first piece in which both the compositional process and direct digital-to-analog sound synthesis are achieved in one integrated routine. These programs not only eliminate punching data cards for sound synthesis, but also serve as prototypes for programs we shall be writing for an integrated system employing IBM-360/50 and IBM-360/75 central processing

brary, 1967, pp. 63–88; Hiller, "Some Compositional Techniques Involving the Use of Computers," in H. Von Foerster and J. W. Beauchamp, eds., *Music by Computers*, New York, John Wiley & Sons, in press.

units, and an IBM-1800 satellite computer to which we shall attach A/D and D/A converters.

Performances of a "version zero" of the three movements of *Algorithms I* were given in Chicago and in Urbana during 1967. This "version zero" was set up to test the main routines of the three movements and employed dummy subroutines for some of the compositional subroutines that were not yet operational.

(2) *An Avalanche for Pitchman, Prima Donna, Player Piano, Percussionist and Prerecorded Tape* (Hiller). This is a short satirical composition based on a script written by Frank Parmon, a playwright. The script is a critique of propaganda extolling our current "cultural explosion." A setting for it is provided in which a lecturer on this subject competes for the audience's attention with a soprano singing miscellaneous arias, a performer on a trap set, and a player piano. The computer is used to generate a piano-player roll by a process devised by J. L. Divilbiss. Divilbiss has written a routine which will cause a CALCOMP plotter to inscribe all the markings of a player-piano roll on its output. Given these guide markings, it is relatively easy to cut the roll for actual use. The player-piano part will be based upon a shuffled assortment of ninety themes taken from the conventional nineteenth-century symphonic literature. Since this program is operational, it is expected that *Avalanche* will have been completed by early 1968.

(3) *HPSCHD* (Cage and Hiller). John Cage is currently at the University of Illinois as a member of the Center for Advanced Study. This project is a new composition of indeterminate length entitled *HPSCHD*, for one to seven harpsichords, and harpsichordlike sounds recorded on any number of tapes up to fifty-one. The tapes are both composed and synthesized on the IBM-7094-ILLIAC II system. The first job was to write a new subroutine for MUSICOMP called ICHING which generates first and second choices of integers between 1 and 64 according to the rules of changes defined by the I-Ching process. Although ICHING provides a random distribution of these integers considered as monograms, it generates nonrandom distributions of all the sets of digrams that depend in turn upon the storage pattern of integers in the I-Ching reference table.

This subroutine is being used to choose pitch levels in equal-tempered scales from 5 to 56 pitches per octave, intonational deviations from these pitch levels, and, finally, durations for every pitch level so chosen. One scale will be used for each of the fifty tapes mentioned above (the 12-tone scale being omitted from the set). Programming up to this stage has been finished as of end of 1967.

It is proposed next to generate for each of these scales melodic patterns derived from an analysis of melodic structure in Mozart's music. Possibly this analysis may be done at least in part by statistical techniques of the type developed by Robert Baker for analyzing the harmonic practices of Haydn, Mozart, and Beethoven.[59] In the concert performance of HPSCHD, harpsichordists will play passages of music derived by computer programming from Mozart's *Musikalisches Würfelspiel* while being accompanied by the above-mentioned tapes.

(4) *Lo. Dissi Dante* (Martirano). This is a composition for orchestra in four movements that will contain computer-generated materials in its third movement and possibly elsewhere. In preparing the computer materials, Martirano has worked with Joseph Mercer, a graduate student in mathematics. They have written a FORTRAN program that has produced pitch choices, and they are considering extending their work to include control over rhythmic choices.[60]

Martirano chose a particular twelve-note row and broke it up into four trichords. These trichords, a transposition, and two inversions of them were then represented in the computer by a four-by-four matrix. One property of this matrix was that any complete route through the matrix or any quadrant of the matrix yielded a complete row. Rows and columns of the matrix were then used to produce "solo" pitch lines with the remaining three-by-three matrices being used simultaneously to produce "accompaniments" for the "solos." This scheme was used to generate the eighteen sections of score Martirano desired for the third movement of the composition. In addition, other constraints upon pitch choices were programmed, such as, for example, a routine for minimizing pitch redundancies of adjacent "accompaniment" cells. In other words, three-by-three matrices that provide accompanying materials in successive sections of the score were searched and internally shuffled in such a way as to spread apart as much as possible trichord repetitions. This program was completed during 1967, but the complete composition is as yet unfinished.

(5) *Infraudibles* (Brün). This composition, intended for computer-synthesized sounds on tape, is being produced by a FORTRAN program run on the IBM-7094. The computer generates data to be converted into sounds by the ILLIAC II D/A system referred to

[59] See R. A. Baker, "A Statistical Analysis," *op. cit.*
[60] This description is based on notes given me by Salvatore Martirano and Joseph Mercer.

earlier.[61] According to notes provided by Brün, by "substituting the addition of periods for the modulation of frequencies, the composer is able to extend the time and duration control he applies to the macro-events of his composition also to the infrastructure of the event-forming sounds. Thus, 'pitch' becomes a result of composition instead of functioning as an element. The same holds true for the concept of sound timbre. To be studied and evaluated remain the differences between complex wave forms that are the result of instantaneous addition of amplitudes, on the one hand, and the results of the periodic repetition of sets containing sequences of different single periods on the other hand. Both the analysis of available results and corresponding revisions of the composition are in progress at present" (December 1967).

Brün has published lectures and articles which give reasons why he uses computers for musical purposes.[62] Brün defines creative activity, such as composing music, as involving the extraction of order out of chaos. He says that any such processes, in practice, go through four stages—experimental, speculative, reflective, and administrative—as information is removed from a given system (that is, a given musical style). He says that the "history of music and of musical thought is the story of . . . artificial systems, their inception, bloom and decline, their absorption or replacement by other artificial systems. At the same time, it is a report on the apparent or real progress in reducing to order the chaos in the natural universal system of acoustical elements and events as well as that of the composer's mind." Brün feels that traditional music is now in its "administrative" state and that the inception of a new system, an "experimental" one, justifies the use of new devices such as computers. These instruments, in turn, will assist greatly in providing unbiased definitions of the elements of the new system.

STUDENT COMPOSITIONS

Since 1958, courses have been taught at the University of Illinois in acoustics and electronic and computer music. A short article written in 1963 describes our course of instruction at that time.[63] Since then, we

---

[61] See G. R. Grossman and J. W. Beauchamp, "A Provisional Sound Generating Program," op. cit., and A. B. Otis, Jr., "An Analog Input/Output System," op. cit.

[62] H. Brün, "Chaos and Organization," ICA Bulletin, No. 166 (1967), 8; Brün, "On the Conditions under Which Computers Would Assist a Composer in Creating Music of Contemporary Relevance and Significance," Proceedings 1st Ann. Conference, Amer. Soc. University Composers, Apr. 1966, pp. 30–37.

[63] L. A. Hiller, Jr., "Acoustics and Electronic Music in the University Music Curriculum," Amer. Music Teacher, 12 (Mar.–Apr., 1963), 24.

have further expanded the curriculum to include two two-semester courses offered in alternate years, "Composition with Tape" and "Composition with Computers." In the latter, student composers (mostly fairly advanced graduate students) are introduced to SCATRE, FORTRAN, ALGOL, and MUSICOMP to the extent that they begin to write programs on their own and to produce computer music compositions. A number of such pieces have been written to date as shown in Table IV-1.

(1) *Piece for Jazz Set* (Moore and Ranta). This is a short study, written in ALGOL; it contains complex rhythmic combinations and can be performed by two percussionists on unpitched percussion instruments. Frank Moore had extensive programming experience with Herbert Simon previously at Carnegie Institute of Technology. He presently is programming MUSIC V with Max Mathews at Bell Telephone Laboratories.

(2) *Algol Rhythms* (Ranta). Michael Ranta, who is a percussionist himself, used an ALGOL program in writing this extended composition for solo percussionist. He performed the piece in Urbana in the Spring of 1967 and again since then in Europe, where he is currently living. He is presently revising the composition.

(3) *Zetos 1 through Zetos 5* (Cuomo). This is a series of short compositions for various instruments as follows: (a) *Zetos 1, . . . , 4*, for trumpet, violin, cello, and trombone; (b) *Zetos 2, . . . , 2**, for flute, tuba, and two-channel tape; (c) *Zetos 3, . . . , 5**, for five double basses and tape, subtitled, "A Garden of Glissandi Flowers"; (d) *Zetos 4, . . . ,**, for two-channel tape, incidental music for "Waiting for Godot"; and (e) *Zetos 5, . . . , 3*, for a trio of diverse instruments.

Cuomo programmed all of these pieces in SCATRE and MUSICOMP. He has also provided the following descriptions of them: *Zetos 1, . . . , 4* is a simple experiment in probability control of density employing a seven-note scale. *Zetos 2, . . . , 2**, based on the jazz blues form, consists of twelve 12-measure choruses. Probability changes are substituted for harmonic changes. Parameters so controlled include rhythm, octave choices, timbre, density, and instrumentation. The tape part was written to conform with the instrumental parts, and was prepared with our ILLIAC II system. *Zetos 3, . . . , 5** is a short experiment with the use of "beats" in a very low register. It consists of glissandi in the five parts that move from a closely voiced microtonal structure to an open texture. *Zetos 4, . . . ,** is a four-minute tape piece that can be used on an overture for Beckett's play. The tape is entirely computer sound. Finally, *Zetos 5, . . . , 4* is "an experiment in phrase generation" for string quartet that is not completed at this time.

(4) *Fantasy for 10 Winds, Percussion and Tape* (Bruce). This is not a computer composition in its entirety, but rather makes substantial use of computer-composed materials as well as computer-generated sounds. The piece, not entirely finished at this writing, is in three movements. Two sections of the second movement are being produced by means of standard MUSICOMP subroutines. Pitches in these sections are being chosen according to probabilities of occurrence of the twelve tones in the chorales "Old Hundredth" and "Now thank we all our God" played in B♭ and E, respectively. Rhythms are chosen from a set comprised of whole notes, half notes, quarter notes and quarter-note triplets with emphasis on the latter values to give the effect of a march in $\frac{6}{8}$ time. Probabilities of rest and play are also varied.

Also, in the third movement, tape cues are heard, prepared by the ILLIAC II digital-to-analog conversion process. One channel of the tape begins with the pitches of "Old Hundredth" played rapidly and spread over six octaves. The tape gradually becomes more ordered until it ends with the tune in its correct rhythm. The other channel of the tape does the same thing with the other chorale tune.

Other American Experiments

Important experiments in computer music composition have been carried out at Bell Telephone Laboratories, where John Pierce and Max Mathews have directed a program of experimentation with computer applications in speech and music for a period now of about ten years. Mathews has pioneered the use of computers for the direct generation of speech and musical timbres by means of digital-to-analog converters, a research activity that has culminated with the writing of the program MUSIC IV for sound synthesis designed to operate in an IBM-7094 computer, and a new program MUSIC V, now being written for a more modern computer. This work, of course, is not the subject of the present review, although it is obvious that it is a parallel and equally important development. An article published several years ago by James Tenney[64] provides a clear description of MUSIC IV as well as references to earlier publications.

Pierce and Mathews have also been quite interested in computer

[64] J. C. Tenney, "Sound-Generation by Means of a Digital Computer," *J. Music Theory*, 7 (1963), 24.

music composition as well as sound synthesis. Pierce, because of his interest in information theory, has considered its applicability in the arts as well as other fields. This has led him to investigate methods for stochastic composition and, in turn, for composition with computers. For this reason, Pierce and his colleagues at Bell Laboratories devised several simple techniques for the generation of various types of elementary stochastic music. These experiments are described by Pierce in two publications.[65] The second of these, in particular, should be singled out as a substantial discussion of information theory applied to art. Most of the results of these experiments in stochastic composition are recorded on an LP disk referred to earlier.[66] None of these experiments, however, are computer music. Some of the experiments with MUSIC IV and with other processes developed at Bell Laboratories, however, are of such a nature that they can be said to incorporate at least some aspects of computer composition. For example, Mathews and Miller[67] have written a short paper describing a process they call "pitch quantizing." This paper discusses the question of whether it is useful to examine a computationally simple algorithm to see if it has any musical sense, as opposed to programming some set of algorithms corresponding to a successful but traditional musical routine. Mathews and Miller suggest that an approach such as theirs might be the starting point in the development of new musical styles. "Pitch quantizing," specifically, generates not only well-known chords and intervals contained in tonal and 12-tone music, but also structures built upon arbitrary numbers of steps in the octave or on no scale at all. At the same time, Mathews and Miller have also devised a new graphical notation not unlike that used by Stockhausen for his *Studie II* for handling successions of pitches of any frequencies and not just those employing the ordinary chromatic scale. Four plots against time are required for any voice, namely, $262\log_2$ frequency, loudness, duration in beats, and duty factor (that is, staccato and legato).

Mathews and Miller wrote a "quantizing algorithm" in order to obtain some control of intervals between voices. For example, a "Voice 2" might be quantized against a "Voice 1," such that "Voice 2" is caused to shift to the nearest 3rd, 4th, 5th, or 6th away from "Voice 1."

[65] J. R. Pierce, *Electrons, Waves and Messages*, Garden City, N.Y., Hanover House, 1956, pp. 271–274; and Pierce, *Symbols, Signals and Noise*, New York, N.Y., Harper and Bros., 1961, pp. 250–267.

[66] "Music from Mathematics," *Bell 122227.*

[67] M. V. Mathews and J. E. Miller, "Pitch Quantizing for Computer Music," *J. Acoust. Soc. Am.*, 38 (1965), 913A.

Then "Voice 1" shifts to its next pitch and the process repeats. More generally, a voice may be quantized against several other voices using logical "and" or "or" operations to build up tables of allowable frequencies. In general, this program is somewhat like counterpoint in that the algorithm takes two or more separate voices and makes minimal adjustments in their frequencies in order to satisfy prescribed quantizing rules. On the other hand, it is limited in that there are no sequential constraints.

Mathews and Miller used three methods for evaluating this algorithm: (a) generating a polyphonic musical example (this, however, prevented them from separating the effect of polyphony from the effect of the algorithm); (b) generating an orderly sequence of ascending chords; (c) generating a sequence of random chords.

They then "composed" a piece for two voices, the score of which is shown in the article in graphical form. The frequency lines were chosen to fall on no known scale, and the melodic intervals were also forced to be unique. Two arbitrary timbres were chosen to distinguish the intervals. The following versions of this composition were then generated: (1) original composition; (2) "Voice 2" quantized against "Voice 1," allowing only major 3rds, 4ths, 5ths, or 6ths as vertical intervals; (3) "Voice 1" quantized into ordinary 12-tone scale; (4) "Voice 1" quantized into a "Key of C"; (5) both voices quantized into a "Key of C." Their reaction was that the greatest change toward "harmoniousness" seemed to occur between the third and fourth versions.

Mathews and Miller finally generated a series of random three-note chords following a similar logic starting with a uniform distribution over a two-octave range. They found that quantizing logic had less effect here than other changes. Nevertheless, they felt that a quantizing algorithm can exert a strong control over dissonances and can even be used to generate standard triads. The advantage is that "harmonizations" can be achieved even if a melodic line follows no scale at all. For example, with an equal-interval scale of 34-notes in two octaves, this gave a quite interesting result that almost seemed to define a timbre rather than a chord.

More recently, Mathews and Rosler [68] have devised a graphical method of input to the MUSIC IV program employing a light pen on a cathode ray tube attached to a small computer that in turn serves as

[68] M. V. Mathews and L. Rosler, "Graphical Language for the Scores of Computer-Generated Sounds," unpublished manuscript.

a satellite to the IBM-7094. Mathews and Rosler were interested in doing this in order to eliminate the tedious business of having to prepare large numbers of data cards representing a composition to be converted into sound. In addition to providing merely a new form of input, Mathews and Rosler also wrote some algorithms among the new routines "by means of which the computer generates parts of the music." This is accomplished by "an algebra for combining graphical functions, which is especially useful for computer-aided composing." For example, the computer can "average between two melodic or rhythmic lines or gradually convert one rhythm or melodic pattern to another." This was actually done with *The British Grenadiers* and *Johnny Comes Marching Home* to produce a curious result in which one tune slowly converts to the other and back again. Other functions include such things as self-synchronizing functions for altering rhythmic patterns and the pitch quantizing function already described. Mathews and Rosler raise the question as to whether the computer is being used to compose music. They point out that their algorithms are "deterministic, simple and understandable, no 'learning' programs are used; no random processes occur." Nevertheless, the results are unplanned in fine detail by the composer, so it is clearly apparent that the computer is aiding the composer in writing music in much the same way it does when details are left to chance to a greater degree.

James Tenney, Associate Professor of Electrical Engineering at the Polytechnic Institute of Brooklyn, has been very much involved with sound synthesis via digital-to-analog conversion. A number of his compositions involve a greater or lesser degree of decision making and specification of details by the computer. A list of his computer compositions (including some also for instruments) is shown in Table IV-2. All save the last one were composed when he was at Bell Telephone Laboratories, 1961–1963. Tenney has written a full account of his experience at Bell Laboratories. This report provides a systematic record of his compositional ideas as he refined them from composition to composition as listed in Table IV-2.[69]

In brief, Tenney sought more and more to incorporate into his compositions an increasingly greater degree of "variety" that would be realizable in the tape medium. By variety he meant measurable parameters that could be expressed in terms of the concept of entropy as employed in information theory. In practical terms, this meant that

[69] The list of J. C. Tenney's pieces in Table IV-2 is based on notes he sent me and on his unpublished manuscript, "Computer Music Experiences, 1961–1964."

Table IV-2. Computer compositions by James Tenney

Title	Medium	Duration
(1) *Four Stochastic Studies* (1962)	Monophonic tape	11 minutes
(2) *Stochastic String Quartet* (1963)	Instruments or monophonic tape	3 minutes
(3) *Dialogue* (1963)	Monophonic tape	4 minutes
(4) *Radio Piece* (1963)	Monophonic tape	2 minutes
(5) *Ergodos I* (1963)	Two monophonic tapes	10 to 18 minutes
(6) *String Complement* (1963)	Instruments	Indeterminate
(7) *Phases* (1963)	Monophonic tape	12 minutes
(8) *Ergodos II* (1964)	Stereo tape	Up to 18 minutes
(9) *Instrumental Responses* (1964)	Instruments	Indeterminate
(10) *Music for Player Piano* (unfinished)	Player piano roll	3 minutes
(11) *Fabric for Che* (1967)	Stereo tape	10 minutes

Tenney incorporated into his compositions random sequences generated by means of RANDH, one of the generators of MUSIC IV. He allowed, within various specified controls of mean values and ranges, random generation of sequence of note duration, amplitudes, frequencies, and other parameters. The successive refinements of his compositional ideas are embodied in compositional programs entitled PLF2 and PLF3.

The tape compositions listed in Table IV-2 are the result of more and more complex compositional programs. With the earliest, *Four Stochastic Studies*, three parameters (note duration, amplitude, and frequency) were permitted to vary randomly from note to note, but mean values and ranges were changed after every one or two seconds. Various settings for sound duration ("clang" duration in Tenney's terminology), number of voices, and note probabilities made up the four studies. These studies were written with PLF2.

Dialogue, the first piece written with PLF3, incorporated controls of more parameters, specifically amplitude modulation rate, amplitude envelope, and wave-form specification. This in turn gave more control over timbre. With *Ergodos I*, Tenney attempted to explore means for shaping the large form of a piece, in other words, how might a broad field of possibilities be defined such that the character of this "field" might yet be perceptible. In *Ergodos I*, Tenney shaped only the beginning and end of the piece, leaving the center section free. This work consists of two ten-minute monaural tapes that can be played either forward or backward, either alone or together. The tapes are statistically symmetrical front to back and have an average density of sound such that the tapes might be interesting played either alone or together. With *Phases,* on the other hand, Tenney imposed a greater control of parameter choices by imposing a set of slowly oscillating sinusoidal functions upon some of the parameter choices—specifically, amplitude, note duration, and noise parameter. Finally, in the last tape composition, *Ergodos II,* that he completed at Bell Laboratories, Tenney made use of the two-channel stereo output provided by MUSIC IV. This piece contains a minimum of "shaping." It is similar to *Ergodos I* but without the controls imposed at the beginning and end of *Ergodos I.* The tape lasts 18 minutes, but Tenney specifies that it may be played in either direction for any length of time and may be started and stopped at any point.

As shown in Table IV-2, Tenney also completed several computer compositions for instruments. In the first of these, *Stochastic String Quartet,* Tenney wrote a program specifying metrical and rhythmic choices and subdivisions thereof. Tenney later experienced the familiar difficulty of having string quartets performers refuse to play his music.[70]

The next two instrumental pieces are expressed in much more indeterminate notation. For example, *Responses,* performed by the University of Illinois Contemporary Chamber Players in 1966 in conjunction with *Ergodos II,* consists of a sheet of score for each instrument divided into quadrants. The performer is instructed to perform while listening to *Ergodos II* and to select a notation from a quadrant of the score that relates his sound antiphonally to the sound on the tape. The remaining instrumental piece, *Music for Player Piano,* is intended to last about three minutes. It is completely composed, but the player-piano roll is not yet cut. J. L. Divilbiss, at the University of Illinois, currently has this material and intends to record it in four versions, forward, backward, turned over (inverted around the center of the roll) and turned over and backwards to yield four "versions" of the same piece.

[70] It is curious to note how many computer pieces have been written for string quartet—our own *Illiac Suite,* Tenney's *Stochastic String Quartet,* Xenakis' *ST4,* and Champernowne's *Music from Edsac,* particularly since string-quartet performers seem to be among the least receptive to newer compositional ideas such as computer music.

It might be noted also that Tenney emphasizes in his paper the growing influence upon him of many of the concepts of John Cage, particularly the idea that sounds should be permitted to happen and be appreciated for their own sake, rather than be subjected to stringent subjective controls of the traditional type.

Another composition of a much different sort was produced in 1964 by Mother Harriet Padberg of Maryville College of the Sacred Heart outside of St. Louis. The computer work was carried out under the direction of Professor W. A. Vezeau of the Mathematics Department of St. Louis University.[71]

Her compositional method is based on the idea of first subdividing the octave into twenty-four steps. These are not tones in equal temperament, however, but rather the 24th to 47th harmonic partials of a fundamental of 18.333 cps. It follows, therefore, that the 24th partial is 440 cps. The 48th partial is, of course, the octave of this, and the steps within the octave are separated by equal numbers of cycles per second. Consequently, the scale is linear rather than logarithmic with large scalar steps in its low range and with smaller and smaller steps as the pitch increases. Second, Mother Padberg associated a letter of the alphabet with each note of this scale, doubling up V and W and associating Y with either I or Z. Third, she defined a tone row by means of any 12-letter meaningful phrase and further defined ways of developing rhythms from ratios of consonants to vowels. With the addition of further rows for dynamics and voicing or orchestration, she was then ready to write computer programs for generating compositions based on these schemes. Mother Padberg first wrote a computer program in FORTRAN for an IBM-1620 computer to enable her to write a canon for two or four voices. Later, however, she was able to expand and generalize this idea by writing a more generalized program for an IBM-7072 computer. This latter program permitted her to generate canons in two or four voices based on one to three tone rows with the further option of producing a "free fugue." The construction of this "free fugue" was based on the idea that a tone row and its transformation constitute a "group" to which transformations of group theory are applicable. The result is a *Canon and Free Fugue* which has since been converted into sound by Max Mathews.

Mother Padberg concludes that while her "computer-composed"

[71] Mother H. A. Padberg, "Computer-Composed Canon and Free Fugue," unpublished doctoral dissertation, St. Louis University, St. Louis, Mo., 1964; and other letters and papers (personal correspondence).

Canon and Free Fugue may be lacking in aesthetic appeal, it never-theless has qualities traditionally associated with both absolute and program music. It is "a logically conceived, unified composition inte-grally bound to its 'title' in melody and rhythm and not dependent on outside connotations for its explanation or development." It might be noted that, if the project seems willful and arbitrary, it is certainly no more so than many other compositional schemes being used today. It is hardly necessary to point out that mathematical permutations of sets of numbers are considered quite proper when done in the name of serial composition. Moreover, the association of names of notes with words or anagrams has long been used to provide musical themes and mottos. This seems already to be a realization of a way of composing music based on written messages proposed by Cazden in what are apparently meant to be satirical essays.[72]

There remain several items to mention in which syntheses of musi-cal passages were done primarily in order to check analytical results. One of the most interesting and important of these was carried out some years ago by W. R. Reitman, a psychologist, in collaboration with Marta Sanchez, a composer. This study, described in detail in a technical report written by Reitman,[73] is an attempt to extend to musical composition the work on general problem-solving of Newell, Shaw, and Simon.[74] This is an application of heuristic programming, that is, an attempt, as Reitman says, "to incorporate in computer programs processes analogous to those used by humans in dealing intelligently with ill-structured problems." [75] These include the discov-ery of theorems in mathematics and logic as Newell, Shaw, and Simon have done, the formation of scientific hypotheses, the selection of moves in chess, and the composition of music. Reitman says that "one can invent a hierachy of complexity which runs from elementary symbolic logic, to chess, and then to music. The solution of a logic problem is defined by the theorem to be proved. . . . Artistic works,

[72] N. Cazden, "Staff Notation as a Non-Musical Communication Code," *J. Music Theory*, 5 (1961), 113; and "How to Compose Non-Music," *ibid.*, 5 (1961), 287; see also Cazden, "The Thirteen-tone System," *The Music Review*, 22 (1961), 152.

[73] W. R. Reitman, "Information Processing Languages and Heuristic Program-ming," *Bionics Symposium* (WADD Tech. Report 60–600), Wright-Patterson Air Force Base, Ohio, Directorate of Advanced Systems Technology, 1960.

[74] A. Newell, J. C. Shaw, and H. A. Simon, "Report on a General Problem-Solving Program," The Rand Corp., P-1584, Dec., 1958.

[75] W. R. Reitman, *op. cit.*, p. 410.

however, may well have to satisfy networks of tests which themselves change as work progresses."

To test his ideas, Reitman then worked with Sanchez to create a heuristic program simulating the behavior of a composer writing a fugue. He recorded everything the composer said or did as she described her working method over a period of several months. Their analysis of the data made it evident that the computer would first have to be taught the elements of music, so they programmed it to compose simple melody, harmony, and counterpoint. Then, to solve the problem of original composition, they incorporated into their program an already existing "General Problem Solver" written by Newell, Shaw, and Simon in 1958.[76] The successive stages of refinement of the fugue are provided as illustrations in Reitman's technical report. This work seems interesting for two reasons at least. First, it provides a prototype for heuristic programming for composing music, a technique thus far unexplored but very likely a powerful technique for music composition if it is sufficiently developed. Second, it is the one study so far that attempts directly to explore the compositional process itself as people do it. This is, of course, of great interest to psychologists as well as to musicians.

Another paper which should be mentioned has been written by Pikler,[77] who defined "musical transfer functions" as processes that bring about the transfer of musical signals from one locale or environment to another. Although Pikler is primarily concerned with performed music and electronically produced music on tape, he does also include processes of musical composition as areas to which his "transfer functions" apply. For this reason, he makes reference in his article to our work with ILLIAC I to produce *Illiac Suite*.

Finally, a study that involves both analysis and synthesis with computers has been set up by Jacob T. Evanson. Evanson has not yet published any of his results, but several years ago he sent me a number of examples of chorale tunes and a substantial description of his work up to that time.[78] Evanson's study is reminiscent of that of Brooks, *et al*, discussed above in that he was primarily interested in developing a statistical scheme of analysis of relatively simple musical

[76] A. Newell, J. C. Shaw, and H. A. Simon, *op. cit.*

[77] A. G. Pikler, "Musical Transfer Functions and Processed Music," *IRE Trans. on Audio*, AU-10 (1962), 47.

[78] Letter from J. T. Evanson, Sept. 8, 1964.

materials—in this instance, Bach chorales. Evanson wrote a program in IPL-V to generate matrices of transition probabilities to define "states," that is, successive choices of pitches, rhythms, and perhaps most interesting, sequences of notes such as melodic phrases. He felt that his program was efficient for analyzing "anything that can be represented as a 'monophonic sequence of symbols'—e.g., melody, harmonic progressions, hokku, etc." Although Evanson was primarily interested in analysis, he also did some "synthesis" from his matrices and produced a number of zeroth- through third-order approximations of chorale melodies.

French Experiments in Computer Composition

Considerable interest in computer music composition exists in Paris, principally because of experiments carried out by composers Pierre Barbaud and Yannis Xenakis. In addition to the work of these two composers, there exist publications which deal in greater or lesser detail with questions raised by this new process of composition.

Since about 1960, Pierre Barbaud, to a substantial degree in collaboration with Roger Blanchard, has worked on processes for computer music composition. Barbaud is a well-known composer of film music, while Blanchard is best known professionally as a choral conductor. Their experiments have been carried out at the "Centre de Calcul Electronique de la Compagnie des Machines Bull," a large manufacturer of computers and data processing equipment. In 1961 Barbaud provided me with some brief publications describing their work [79] and explained that his objective was the traditional one of creating order among "musical objects" such as the twelve tones of the ordinary chromatic scale. He proposed to use mathematics to eliminate those arrangements "considered to be without interest," employing a computer for the necessary calculations. Barbaud also cited the historical precedent of using musical games for their work.[80]

[79] P. Barbaud, "Avenement de la musique cybérnetique," *Les lettres nouvelles,* 7 (Apr. 22, 1959), 28; Barbaud, "Musique Algorithmique," *Esprit,* 28 (Jan., 1960), 92; Anon., "Sur deux Notes les Mathématiciens de l'avenir composent un symphonie complète," *Courrier Bull,* 49 (Oct., 1961), 16; Anon., "La musique algorithmique," *Bulletin Technique de la Compagnie des Machines Bull,* 2 (1961), 22.

[80] Including an anonymous eighteenth century work in the Bibliotheque nationale: *Ludus melothedicus* (*sic*) *Anonym. s.d.* (1754), B.N. V[8] 1137, Dept. de Musique, which contains calculations "par lesquels toute personne composera differèns menuets avec l'accompagnement de basse en jouant avec deux dez même sans sçavoir la musique."

By the fall of 1961, Barbaud and Blanchard had completed one basic program for music composition. This generated a species of twelve-tone music produced, first, by the random generation of a tone-row and, second, by the synthesis of extended structures from this tone-row by various combinatorial operations. The various available combinatorial operations were also randomly chosen. Thus, the structure of the resulting music was very much governed by chance. They used a standard textbook on combinatorial mathematics as their guide to programming.

As revealed in two technical publications from the Compagnie des Machines Bull,[81] the actual operation applied by Barbaud and Blanchard to obtain pitch choices consists of addition and subtraction (transposition musically), multiplication (interval expansion), sign change around a chosen point (inversion), and other more complex operations such as recurrence and circular permutation. Rhythms and octave displacements were randomly chosen at the same time. The results were printed out in a simple alphanumeric notation and then scored by the composers. The finished music was used for several purposes, principally a film score and a computer piece. This latter composition has been recorded on a 10″ LP disk.[82] A review of this recording has also appeared.[83]

Barbaud and Blanchard subsequently worked on a computer program for tonal music. They completed a logical scheme for programming for this admittedly much more complex problem, but in 1961 the actual programming and generation of the music resulting therefrom had been held up pending completion of a new arrangement with the Compagnie des Machines Bull. In the meanwhile, they tested their scheme by throwing dice to obtain chance sequences to insert into the scheme. Subsequently, they succeeded in programming this or some similar scheme to produce a computer program that generated a popular song. This achievement has been reported in the popular press.[84]

In 1966, Pierre Barbaud published in book form a full account of his

[81] See footnote no. 79 above.

[82] P. Barbaud and R. Blanchard, *Imprévisibles Nouveautés-Algorithme I,* performed by an orchestra directed by R. Blanchard, 10″ LP, Critère Productions R. Douatte, CRD 430A.

[83] A. A. Moles, "La Musique Algorithmique, Première Musique Calculée," *Revue du Son,* 93 (1961), 28.

[84] Anon., "The Machine Closes In," *Time,* 79 (Feb. 16, 1962), 65.

work to that time.[85] This book is divided into three sections concerned with (a) general considerations regarding musical automata, that is, computer programs for composition, (b) a detailed description of two types of compositional programs, and (c) reprints of actual programs completed by Barbaud.

In the section on general considerations, Barbaud is concerned first with presenting a method of encoding musical parameters such as pitch and rhythm and with setting up matrices that permit combinatorial operations to be carried out on the elements of these matrices. He then points out that the formulation of these matrices permitted him to write the three ALGOL computer programs reproduced later in the book, namely ALGOM 3, ALGOM 4, and ALGOM 5. The central part of the book gives a detailed description of these programs. ALGOM 3 and ALGOM 4 are concerned with "chromatic music." Obviously, these represent further development of the two types of investigations started by Barbaud some years earlier. Barbaud's description of his work is detailed, specific, and clear. At the time of writing this article, I have not yet seen or heard examples of music prepared with these programs.

The second set of experiments to be discussed here involves the stochastic music of Yannis Xenakis, a composer whose background includes architecture and mathematics as well as music. Of interest for our present discussion is Xenakis' use of mathematical computations for writing some of his musical scores. Xenakis employs statistical calculations that incorporate, among other things, elements of the theory of probability, the use of Poisson distributions, and elements of the theory of games.

Xenakis has described these processes in a series of articles published in the *Gravesaner Blätter*.[86] He calls his work stochastic music because it is derived from choice processes governed by probability distributions. The earliest and one of the best known of these is *Achorripsis*, the score of which has been published for some time.[87] The mathematical basis for the structure of the composition depends

[85] P. Barbaud, "Initiation à la composition musicale automatique," Paris, Dunod, 1966.

[86] Y. Xenakis, "La Crise de la musique serielle," *Gravesaner Blätter*, 1 (1955), 15; "Manipulation und Konzeption, II," *ibid.*, 6 (1956), 28; "In Search of a Stochastic Music," *ibid.*, 11/12 (1958), 112; "Elements of a Stochastic Music—I to IV," inclusive, *ibid.*, 18 (1960), 84; 19/20 (1960), 140; 21 (1961), 113; 22 (1961), 144; "Stochastic Music," *ibid.*, 23/24 (1962), 156.

[87] Y. Xenakis, *Achorripsis*, Berlin, Bote und Bock, 1959.

on the use of Poisson distribution to scatter the controlled musical elements uniformly over each of the sections of the composition. A more precise description would be the generation of a matrices defined to represent timbre choices versus time that conform to a Poisson distribution of statistically chosen elements.

Recently, Xenakis recast his theoretical writings in the form of a monograph entitled *Musiques Formelles*.[88] The critical reaction to this book, not surprisingly, is quite mixed. For example, Daniel Charles, in a recent essay [89] considers Xenakis' work, including his theoretical writings, to be of central importance to current developments in European music, while Michael Kassler [90] reviews the book in a manner that is highly critical of its content, particularly of terminology.

In 1961 Xenakis worked out an arrangement with IBM in Paris to use an IBM-7090 computer to compose music according to his stochastic schemes. He learned FORTRAN programming for this purpose. By early 1962 he completed this program and then employed it to generate stochastic choices for musical parameters such as pitch, rhythm, playing styles, and so forth.

In Chapter 4 of *Musiques Formelles*, Xenakis describes how he recast the mathematical basis for *Achorripsis* into FORTRAN programming and then allowed the computer to produce a series of compositions in which variations in structure, duration, and orchestration were accomplished by means of data input cards. Xenakis' logical flow charts and portions of his FORTRAN program are also reproduced in *Musiques Formelles*. It should be noted also that German and English translations of this same chapter of *Musiques Formelles* have recently appeared in *Gravesaner Blätter* along with a disk recording of ST/4-1,080262 performed by the Bernede String Quartet.[91]

Because various publications (including Xenakis' own) have not made it clear just which of his compositions have been obtained by computer programming and which have not, Xenakis was asked to clarify this when he visited Urbana in March 1967. Xenakis remarked that the only program he has thus far completed is indeed the pub-

[88] Y. Xenakis, "Musiques Formelles," *La Revue Musicale*, Vols. 253–254, Paris, Editions Richard Masse, 1963.

[89] D. Charles, "Entracte: 'Formal' or 'Informal' Music?" *Musical Quarterly*, 51 (1965), 144.

[90] M. Kassler, "Review of 'Musiques Formelles' by Y. Xenakis," *Perspectives of New Music*, 3 (1964), 115.

[91] Y. Xenakis, "Free Stochastic Music from the Computer," *Gravesaner Blätter*, 26 (1965), 79.

lished one. He would like to continue along this line, but the chance for further extensions of this work have not yet arisen. In any event, Xenakis went through the list of his music given in a booklet prepared by his present music publisher [92] and checked off the pieces composed entirely or in part by means of the computer program (see Table IV-3). As seen, this list is substantial. A few words of explanation are in order.

Table IV-3. Computer compositions by Yannis Xenakis

Title	Instrumentation	Date Completed
ST/48-1,240162	48 instruments	1962
ST/10-1,080262	10 instruments	1962
ST/4-1,080262	String quartet	1962
Amorsima-Morsima	10 instruments	1962
Morsima-Amorsima	Piano, violin, cello, double bass	1962
Atrées	10 instruments	1962
Stratégie, Jeu pour deux orchestres		1962
Eonta *	Piano and five brass instruments	1964

* Only in part a computer-generated score.

First, several of the works, namely ST/10-1,080262, for ten instruments, ST/4-1,030762 for string quartet, and ST/48-1,240162 for forty-eight instruments, have coded titles. The titles are systematic in that ST stands for "stochastic"; 10-, 4-, 48-, and so on, stand for the number of instruments scored; 1, 2, and so on, stand for the first composition, the second composition, and so on, written for the number of instruments previously specified, while a number like 080262, for example, stands for 8 February 1962. Incidentally, *Atrées* is apparently also called ST/10-3,060962.

In any event, the first of all these works to be performed is ST/10-1,080262. This was presented at a special concert in May 1962 at IBM headquarters in Paris by an instrumental group conducted by Konstantin Simonovic. Thus this concert precedes by some seven months a concert in Athens containing the two computer compositions described by Slonimsky in his recent survey of contemporary Greek

[92] M. Bois, *Iannis Xenakis, The Man and His Music*, London, Boosey & Hawkes, 1967.

music.[93] At least one report of the Paris concert has appeared in the American popular press.[94]

Second, a different aspect of Xenakis' interest in the use of mathematics for music composition is exemplified by his two compositions for two orchestras, *Duel*, completed in 1959, and *Stratégie*, completed in 1961. In both these compositions, Xenakis employs the theory of games to set up a competition in performance. He proposes that the two orchestras face one another with their conductors back to back. Each conductor can choose from one or more of the sections of the composition and play it for an indeterminate time (greater than 15 seconds in *Stratégie*). At each successive choice by either conductor, a score is computed and added to a total on a scoreboard visible to the audience. At the end of the performance the conductor with the greatest number of points is declared the winner of the contest. Scores are achieved by consulting matrices constructed by Xenakis which assign weights to six basic "tactics," to silence, and to combinations of tactics. Each conductor chooses, whenever he can, a tactic which he thinks will accrue points to his score. In *Stratégie*, the basic tactics are: I. "Wind instruments," II. "Percussion," III. "String instruments struck by hand," IV. "Pointillistic playing of stringed instruments," V. "String glissandi," and VI. "Sustained string harmonics."

Each of the tactics, therefore, is a section of musical score and in the case of *Stratégie*, each was compiled from materials generated with the IBM-7090 computer.

Duel, the earlier piece, was not composed with a computer but seems otherwise to be rather similar. It has apparently not yet been performed.

Third, *Eonta*, the most recent composition on the list, according to Xenakis, was composed only partially with materials produced by the FORTRAN computer program.

Disk recordings of some of these works are available. Already listed is the recording of *ST/4*. *Eonta* is available on a French disk along with *Metastasis* and *Pithoprakta*.[95] Tape recordings of most of the other pieces also exist.

Interest in computer applications to music has caught the attention of other musicians in Paris as well. In substantial part, I believe, this

[93] N. Slonimsky, "New Music in Greece," *Musical Quarterly*, 51 (1965), 225.
[94] Anon., "Inside Stuff-Music," *Variety*, 227 (July 11, 1962), 65.
[95] Y. Xenakis, "Metastatis, Pithoprakta, Eonta," 12" LP, *Le Chant du Monde* LDX-A8368 (monaural), LDX-A48368 (stereo).

can be attributed to the efforts of Abraham Moles to investigate the ways in which cybernetics and information theory might be used to explain how artistic ideas are communicated. Moles, whose background includes physics and psychology as well as music, has been directly involved with developments in experimental music in Paris for a number of years. His book [96] summarizes much of his theoretical thinking and speculation about acoustics, aesthetics, psychological perception and information as applied primarily to musical communication. As noted in the reference, an English language edition of this same book prepared by Joel Cohen has recently been published. Dr. Moles' book reviewing developments in experimental music was referred to earlier.[97]

Dr. Moles' idea, as presented in his monograph, centered upon defining what he calls "semantic" and "aesthetic" modes of information transmission. More recently he has extended his ideas toward developing definitions that permit him to write flow charts for various types of experiments for generating music for computers. Because of his interest in applying concepts of information theory to music and its perception, Dr. Moles has continued to be concerned with the "cybernetic" aspects of musical composition and has thus developed an interest in computer applications to musical problems. This interest is reflected in some of his more recent publications.[98]

In addition to Moles' publications, some papers have also appeared that are based on conferences sponsored by the Service de la Recherche of RTF (the *musique concrète* group headed by Pierre Schaeffer in Paris). In 1960 the organization published a monograph on many aspects of experimental music as derived from a conference sponsored by the Service de la Recherche in 1960. This volume includes two articles that deal with aspects of computer music, the first of which, by Reynald Giovaninetti [99] is a brief historical survey of

[96] A. A. Moles, *Théorie d'Information et Perception Esthétique*, Paris, Flammarion, 1958; *Information Theory and Aesthetic Perception*, English edition prepared by J. Cohen, Urbana, University of Illinois Press, 1965.

[97] A. A. Moles, *Musiques expérimentales*.

[98] A. A. Moles, "Perspectives de l'Instrumentation Électronique," *Reuve Belge de Musicologie*, 13 (1959), 11; also "The Prospect of Electronic Instrumentation," *Gravesaner Blätter*, 15/16 (1960), 21; A. A. Moles, "The New Relationship between Music and Mathematics," *Gravesaner Blätter*, 23/24 (1962), 98.

[99] R. Giovaninetti, "La Revolution des Musiques Experimentales," *Situation de la Recherche, Cahiers d'Études de Radio-Télévision, Nos. 27–28*, Paris, Flammarion, 1960, pp. 57–62.

the development of experimental music in the twentieth century. Toward the end of this article Giovaninetti refers to computer music and its composition by means of programming. He describes very briefly the work of Barbaud and Blanchard and of Xenakis discussed above.

A more substantial article on computer topics was prepared for the same monograph by Michel Phillipot.[100] This article in turn is a synopsis of a symposium in which François Le Lionnais led the discussion. Le Lionnais' remarks can be summarized as follows.

After asking whether the idea of music composed with a machine is good or bad, he proposed to inspect the results thus far available (in 1960). He said that the transfer of compositional responsibility appears quite limited; however, there are two major areas in which useful results might be achieved: (1) the generation of music, and (2) the preparation of research results that disclose information regarding the compositional process. Three major studies were then reviewed, the work at the University of Illinois involving the *Illiac Suite,* the work of Barbaud and Blanchard, and the stochastic composition of Xenakis. Later on, the work of Klein and Bolitho, Pinkerton, and of Brooks, Hopkins, Neumann, and Wright were also mentioned.

Le Lionnais then discussed various methods by means of which constraints might be imposed upon a random musical structure. He mentioned rules of exclusion such as those used in the *Illiac Suite,* but suggested that more general procedures might also be profitably investigated, namely, procedures based on asking how much information might be removed from a system in order to yield a given perceptible musical structure. He pointed out that many composers used statistical procedures, not merely to produce random music, but also to reduce chance by the introduction of constraints. He then returned to a discussion of banality and noted how this is related to the historical and sociological conditioning of the listener.

The symposium discussion was then turned over to Dr. Moles, who brought up the topic of the composer and the machine and how they interact. He pointed out first that the function of the computer depends on its property of feedback of both information and controls. This provides for "regulation," either external or internal. When properly applied, these functions permit the computer to operate as an "intelligence amplifier" as defined by Ross Ashby.

[100] M. Phillipot, "La Musique et les Machines," *ibid.*, pp. 274–292.

English Experiments in Computer Composition

Three experiments in computer music composition were carried out several years ago in England, one at Cambridge University by D. J. Champernowne, one at London University by Stanley Gill, and a third, a study of change ringing by D. A. Papworth. Since all of these experiments involve the study of the generation of music according to specified "rules of composition" and since each, at least in part, employs some rules of serial composition, or equivalents, it is convenient to discuss them together at this point.

D. G. Champernowne of Trinity College, Cambridge, is a member of the faculty of economics who has used the computer at Cambridge University to solve problems in his field. In 1961 he became interested in programming musical composition and in his spare time developed two programs for musical composition that are quite effective within their prescribed limitations. These were first described in a report written several years ago.[101] Champernowne, apparently, has not yet written an article for publication describing his programming. This is too bad, since it would seem that what he did worked out quite successfully within the specified constraints on the compositional process. The two programs for musical composition are the following:

Synthesis of Victorian Hymn Tunes. After an inspection of typical hymn tunes, Champernowne developed a set of empirical rules for composing such music. He then wrote a computer program that consists of four distinct parts: (a) the generation of random numbers; (b) the generation of the top melodic line; (c) the generation of harmonic support; and (d) printout in alphanumeric notation. He provided for rhythmic variety, passing notes, neighbor notes, and appoggiaturas. Moreover, the program could be used to harmonize given tunes, since part (b) of the program could be by-passed, and independent melodic data could be used instead. With this program, he could generate only one phrase at a time, so awkward transitions sometimes occurred between the end of one phrase and the beginning of the next phrase.

Synthesis of Serial Music. Champernowne also wrote a program for the synthesis of a species of twelve-tone serial music in which a systematic permutation scheme permitted the production of a composition about 200 measures long. He applied some arbitrary rules that

[101] L. A. Hiller, Jr., "Report on Contemporary Experimental Music, 1961," *op. cit.*

eliminate, I believe, certain dissonances. It is interesting to note that this music, superficially at least, bears some resemblance to that of Barbaud and Blanchard.

Champernowne then arranged a three-movement "composition" for string quartet out of these materials consisting of (a) a set of "Victorian humn tunes," (b) the serial piece that serves as a sort of middle-movement scherzo, and (c) a series of harmonization of well-known tunes like "Rule Brittannica." Because Champernowne was unable to induce a string quartet at Cambridge to play his music, we asked him to send us a set of performance parts from which we assembled a score and prepared a tape recording of a performance by a string quartet at the University of Illinois. I find sections of this *Music from Edsac* quite entertaining, particularly the harmonizations in the last movement.

Stanley Gill is a well-known mathematician and computer specialist who works at the Digital Computer Laboratory in the Department of Electrical Engineering of the University of London. His program for computer music composition was prepared to create a sample of background music called *Variations on a Theme of Alban Berg* for a B.B.C. television program on the subject of "Machines Like Men" that was broadcast on August 20, 1962. This is a piece of music written with a simple serial technique and is scored for violin, viola, and bassoon. Gill has published an account of his work [102] that includes an illustration reproducing twelve bars of the score.

Although Gill's composition is simple in concept and is governed by no overall structural plan—deficiencies Gill clearly recognizes in his article—the program does contain one very interesting feature, a feature I believe useful enough to incorporate in a subroutine in our own MUSICOMP. This is his "tree process" that serves as an alternate procedure to a "try-again routine" for generating sequences of music that conform to "rules of composition" and yet permit developing musical sequences to avoid "dead-ends." What he did was essentially the following. At any moment, eight competitive versions of a partial composition, not necessarily of the same length, were stored in the computer. These "competitors" represented various trials of the composing process carried out as far as some choice, i. When this choice i was then made, one of the eight branches was selected at random and the new choice added to it. The result was then evaluated according

[102] S. Gill, "A Technic for the Composition of Music in a Computer," *The Computer J.*, 6 (1963), 129.

to criteria specified by the programmer, and the "weakest" of the nine sequences then present (the "other seven" plus "parent" and "offspring") was discarded, and the best eight were stored. The process was then repeated over and over until a composition of the desired length was obtained. A clever way of insuring that the compositional process went at a reasonable rate was the insertion of a bonus for length *per se* of a sequence being evaluated and a penalty for a sequence that often seemed to lead to blind alleys. Figure 2 in Gill's article referred to above shows an example of a generated tree structure.

Gill used some of the standard primitive twelve-tone operations (transposition, retrogradation, inversion, voice shifting, and so on) to produce this composition, but it is obvious that it is a perfectly general logical process suitable for any style of music. The work was also performed on a program of computer music given in Chicago in April 1967.

Professor Gill was instrumental in promoting a competition for computer music compositions held in conjunction with the Congress of the International Federation for Information Processing in Edinburgh in August 1968.

The third experiment, reported in a paper by D. A. Papworth,[103] involves programming a method of composition called "change ringing," a permutational technique that developed over the centuries in connection with the ringing of church bells, particularly in England. The standard descriptive treatise on change ringing was written by J. W. Snowden,[104] and recent mathematical treatments of the subject have been published by Rankin[105] and Fletcher.[106]

Papworth programmed change ringing for a PEGASUS computer. As he notes, the problem of change ringing can be described mathematically as follows: Given the numbers, 1, 2, . . . , n, representing church bells of different pitches in descending order, find rules for generating in some order all $n!$ permutations or "changes" or subsets thereof. However, the following restrictions must be observed: (1) the

[103] D. A. Papworth, "Computers and Change Ringing," *The Computer J.*, 3 (1960), 47.

[104] J. W. Snowdon, *Standard Methods in the Art of Change Ringing*, Leeds, Whitehead and Miller, 1940.

[105] R. A. Rankin, "A Campanological Problem in Group Theory," *Proc. Cambridge Philosophical Soc.*, 44 (1948), 17.

[106] T. J. Fletcher, "Campanological Groups," *Amer. Math. Monthly*, 43 (1956), 619.

first and last permutations of any sequence or subsequence must be the original row, 1, 2, . . . , n, which is known as a "round"; otherwise, no two rows may be the same; (2) in any row, no number may occupy a position more than one place removed from its position in the preceding row; (3) no number may remain in the same position in more than two consecutive rows.

Papworth solved the particular system of change ringing called "plain bob major." Changes on eight bells are called "major," and "plain bob" is the simplest kind of change, namely that in which consecutive rows differ by as many exchanges as possible. Papworth discusses this method of change ringing in some detail in terms of its subsequences called "treble lead" and groups of these subsequences that make up "courses." Papworth was concerned, first, with proving that "plain bob major" is sufficient to generate all 8! or 40,320 possible permutations of eight numbers, and, second, with generating sample compositions starting with random numbers. Specifically, each successive "lead-end" (the first row of each treble lead) was tested against all previous lead-ends and stored if new. Alternately, it was rejected and a new lead-end generated. Papworth says that his greatest difficulty involved making a composition end with rounds at the correct point. To achieve this, Papworth found it necessary to write "alteration routines" to have the composition come out right.

As noted above, Papworth's work stimulated Bernard Waxman and me at the University of Illinois to write an analysis and generating program for change ringing for our own use. As we saw it, the basic problem involved in change ringing is the generation of permutations of n discrete symbols following some set of given rules. Using this basic idea and some of the conventional rules of change ringing, subroutine RING was written so that it would generate sequences of numbers that symbolize different permutations on a set of tones. In our first experiment the basic rule was followed that each sequence must be different from all others, with the exception of the first and last. There are also additional constraints which may or may not be used depending on how restricted one wishes the permutational set to be.

We have used the usual methods of forming new lead-ends and the sequences between lead-ends as described above, namely, "plain bob," and "singles." The program was written to choose one of the possibilities at random within set constraints. One of the constraints chosen was that any change must keep the order of the last tone and leading tone the same as "plain bob." The program will produce any number of sequences of tones on any set of six or more tones, up to the point where all possible sequences have been generated. For example, with six tones it is possible to generate at most 6! or 720 sequences.

This program can be used to generate such things as sequence of rhythmic variations and changes in dynamics as well as sequences of tones. Waxman and I have prepared a rough draft of a short report and description of this project. This report will be put into final form after the subroutine has been used in the production of *Algorithms II*.

Other European Experiments

Other European experiments in computer composition are for the most part quite recent, and publications concerned with them are few or nonexistent. Several fragmentary or marginal items need also to be mentioned for completeness.

G. M. Koenig, formerly with the W.D.R. electronic music studio in Cologne, several years ago became director of the electronic music studio in Utrecht, Holland. He has both expanded its electronic music facilities and instituted a substantial program of computer usage, principally for compositional purposes.[107] Koenig uses ALGOL for his computer programs. Among other things, he has offered a course in computer composition.

Koenig has written an essay based on a lecture he gave at several American universities (including Illinois) in 1965.[108] Koenig suggests that computers provide the essential means for realizing composition in which the sound patterns and the rules of composition are closely linked. He illustrates with flow charts some simple examples of useful compositional routines such as the generation of a twelve-tone series. He compares deterministic and chance means of producing components of a score, pointing out that chance is "serviceable" if a process requires variants or if minor details are unimportant. Koenig hopes to build up a basic library of compositional routines that describe "the context of certain musical parameters and leave it to the composer to determine initial values or the limits of statistical distribution." He also proposes a direct linkage to a digital-to-analog converter for

[107] See "Equipment and Working Methods of the Studio for Electronic Music at the University of Utrecht," multilithed information sheet obtained from G. M. Koenig.

[108] G. M. Koenig, "The Second Phase of Electronic Music," unpublished manuscript, 1965.

sound synthesis. It is interesting to note the resemblance to our own thinking regarding building up a library of compositional subroutines, the main difference being perhaps the emphasis Koenig gives to serial compositional techniques.

Koenig has sent me a more recent unpublished manuscript that is a quite explicit description of his first major project in computer composition.[109] This is an outline of "Project 1" a series of programs first written in FORTRAN II at the University of Bonn in 1964 and later reworked at Utrecht in ALGOL 60. Basically, "Project 1" permits the production of a number of compositions—versions—that vary from one another within a number of fairly tight constraints that fit Koenig's compositional ideas. "Project 1" consists of a main program, a number of subroutines governing parameter choices and two subroutines ALEA and SERIES. ALEA generates random integers (like our own ML3DST) and SERIES generates rows of lengths specified by the user (like our own REIHE). The main program, which is quite elaborate, provides for the generation of timbre, rhythm, pitch, sequences, octave register, and dynamics. Values for these parameters are generated by subroutines dependent on ALEA and SERIES. Values so produced are then used to provide materials for "form sections" that make up the total composition being generated. Koenig points out that the users of this program must specify a certain number of input data concerned with tempi, "entrance delays," the number of points in time for each form section and a few other items. Beyond this, his influence on the course of the program is rather minimal, so Koenig prefers to call each piece produced by "Project 1" a "variant" or "version" rather than an independent composition.

Knut Wiggen, a Norwegian composer recently appointed director of the new electronic music studio at Swedish Radio in Stockholm, is also very much concerned with computer composition. When he visited Urbana in November 1965, he had the printout of a new computer composition with him. He provided the following information concerning his work.

Wiggen started producing computer compositions in 1963 using a Swedish SAAB computer in Stockholm, writing his programs in a form of ALGOL. He first wrote *Wiggen-1* a technical exercise for piano that he does not consider to be an authentic composition. *Wiggen-2* (not then otherwise titled), however, is a different matter. This is the first

[109] G. M. Koenig, "Project 1," unpublished manuscript, 1967.

of ten projected computer compositions that will constitute an album of pieces that may or may not be played in sequence or in its entirety. *Wiggen-2* is the second piece of the projected set of works. All of these pieces will be composed with a computer, and most will be realized in computer sound alone. In 1965 Wiggen apparently still had a few errors in his program that caused some erratic printout of his results, but he felt confident that these were quite minor. The first work was projected to be around 10 to 15 minutes long, and to be based on an interaction between two more-or-less independent growth-decay patterns. The first of these bears some relationship to biological growth patterns in the sense that it permits of a continual proliferation of "rules of composition" that in turn govern probability distributions for choices of musical parameters. For example, the first rule states that the first pitch choice can be random because no composition yet exists, but the succeeding tones can no longer be chosen at random but only in relation to the now existent first pitch choice. The constant addition of rules as the composing process develops is thus a kind of compositional method by accretion of presumably significant restrictions of the information content of the piece. The second pattern is then superimposed on this first pattern and seems to be somewhat analogous to the occurrence of "events," chance or otherwise, that might interrupt or otherwise alter this steady process of accretion.

Georg Heike, a composer employed at the Institute for Communications Research at the University of Bonn has expressed interest in using computers for composition especially since he has already written other music based on "order-disorder parameters." He has written an article on information theory and music composition [110] in which he outlines some of his ideas along this line. For example, he distinguishes simple Markoff chains that lead to what he calls "microstructures" from "structure types" for larger sections of a score. By this he means parameters relating, for example, to the beginning, middle sections, and ending of a composition. Heike then presents a very simple flow diagram of how a compositional process might be programmed for a computer.

Yehoshua Lakner, an Israeli composer, has developed a generalized theory of tonal organization which he hopes to evaluate with the help of a computer. Lakner's theory, as described to me in 1965, rests on the assumption that one can define a motif for a musical composition

[110] G. Heike, "Informationstheorie und Musikalische Komposition," *Melos*, 28 (1961), 269.

which will contain "conditioned objective factors" which in turn will
lead to the subsequent musical treatment of this motif through application of many permutational operations (reflection, transposition,
sequencing, and so on). In effect, these motifs seem to be simple
generating structures, and, in fact, Lakner claims that all common-
practice music of the eighteenth and nineteenth centuries can be
explained in terms of operations on the motif of the common major
triad and its "reflection," the minor triad. Lakner says this is only one
of many conceivable motifs, and illustrates his ideas by treating the
motif DEF. As I understand it, Lakner claims that his operational
scheme not only is more general than, and inclusive of, the traditional
body of common-practice compositional techniques, but also would
provide a common ground for unifying contemporary compositional
practices. Lakner has published one article [111] that presents in some
detail a graphic method of representing pitch relationships. The
graphic notation apparently is one by-product of the more generalized
set of ideas embodied in Lakner's complete theory.

As far as I know, Lakner's theory of tonal structures remains still
only a proposal rather than a result. Although there seem to be some
useful procedures embodied in the theory, the claims for the theory
that Lakner sets forth are based on the traditional view that presumes
that a composer would automatically wish a tonally coherent composition. Lakner seems also to be concerned only with pitch relationships,
to the neglect of other components of music such as rhythm, dynamics, and timbre.

Algorithms for Generating Folk Tunes

Another type of computation involving musical-score generation
relates to folk-song analysis and synthesis. All the studies of folk music
that conclude with attempts at synthesis originate thus far in Eastern
Europe. This presumably reflects strong governmental support for
folk-music research in that part of the world. The earliest example
originates in Russia. In 1961 R. Kh. Zaripov [112] published a paper
describing the generation with a URAL computer of "folk melodies"
of the structure:

[111] Y. Lakner, "A New Method of Representing Tonal Relations," *J. Music
Theory*, 4 (1960), 194.
[112] R. Kh. Zaripov, "An Algorithmic Description of the Music Composing
Process," *Doklady Akademiia Nauk SSSR*, 132 (1960), 1283. English translation
appears in *Automation Express*, 3 (Nov., 1960), 17.

$$a_1\beta_1a_2\beta_2\gamma_1\gamma_2\gamma_1\gamma_3\delta\beta_3$$

where the symbols, a, β, γ, and δ refer to four-bar melodic phrases of differing rhythmic structure. Thus, all a's had to have the same rhythms, likewise all β's, and so forth. These rhythms were generated at random within constraints governed by folk song style, that is, the rhythms were basically simple and uncomplicated. A random choice of $\frac{3}{4}$ or $\frac{4}{4}$ meter was permitted at the beginning of the generating process. Secondly, the computer was instructed to assign a pitch to each note of each rhythmic pattern, but a_2 was allowed to be different from a_1, and so on. These pitches were first generated at random and then screened by a series of constraints such as: (1) the piece must be in an *ABA* form with *B* contrasting to *A* (I interpret this to mean that *A* is $a_1\beta_1a_1\beta_2$, that *B* is $\gamma_1\gamma_2\gamma_1\gamma_3$ and that *A* returns with $\delta\beta_3$); (2) each phrase must end on I, III, or V; (3) successive large melodic skips in one direction are forbidden; and (4) no more than six small melodic steps are permitted in one direction; and so on.

These are, of course, easily programmable rules of composition that did work to produce recognizable melodic lines. An example of Zaripov's results is printed in his article. This work, incidentally, has been severely criticized by Wright.[113]

At the time of writing, I have not yet been able to obtain a copy of a second article written by Zaripov.[114] I have been told that Zaripov has also written a book on the subject of cybernetics and music. In addition, Brook and Berlind have listed one other Russian article on folk music synthesis.[115]

A second body of work is being carried out at the Computing Center of the Hungarian Academy of Sciences in Budapest. This research activity seems to be quite extensive in scope, embracing folk-song analysis, synthesis of simple musical melodies, the use of an accordion as a direct data input device to a computer, and, finally, the analysis of dance movement and choreographic notation. In 1965 Dr. E. N. Ferentzy, one of the principal investigators in this research

---

[113] H. Wright, *Computing Reviews*, 2 (1960), 105.

[114] R. Kh. Zaripov, "O Programirovanyii Processza Szocsinyenyija Muziki" ("Programming the Process of Music Composition"), *Problemi Kibernetyiki*, 7 (1962), 151.

[115] R. G. Bukharov and M. S. Rytvinsskaya, "Simulating a Probabilistic Process Connected with Composing a Melody," *Kazan Universitet Uchenyia Zapiski*, 122 (1962), 82, referred to in Brook and Berlind, "Writings on Uses of Computers," *op. cit.*

program sent me manuscripts and a large monograph on computational linguistics [116] that contains several articles relating to music studies described below.

The interest at the Budapest institute in dance movement is rather outside the present topic even though it has obvious parallels to studies of music. Ferentzy, as a matter of fact, emphasizes this very point in the last article in the above citation. He says that the results of his study of folk dance steps seem to correspond, at least in terms of mathematical analysis, to some of the operations commonly employed in the serial composition of music. (Incidentally, in this connection a similar but much more limited study of dance movement was carried out several years ago by Joseph Thie, a physicist residing in Chicago, who sent me a manuscript describing computational choreography.) [117] He has also written a short article suggesting applications of computers in all the arts including music, dance, literature, and drama. [118]

The experiments in music seem to originate with the work of Havass on folk-music analysis and synthesis. [119] In this paper, Havass outlined an analysis with a computer of a group of 100 folk tunes contained in the collection *Ötfoku II* assembled by Zoltan Kodaly. Havass felt this to be valid experimentation, yet he remarks that ". . . it cannot be the primary goal of programmers to have the machine compose pieces of music because the whole process of composing cannot be formalized and so the works which a computer can compose are only dilettante works which fail to have the creative power and depth of a piece composed by a composer." Because of this attitude, Havass concluded that computers are useful only in (1) correlation analysis between synthesized and real music, (2) the statistical investigation of folk music, (3) correlations of music to linguistic differences among nations, and (4) the analysis of music theory.

Havass' work, in actuality, bears close resemblance to the work of Zaripov discussed above as well as to the earlier work of Brooks *et al*

[116] F. Kiefer (ed.), *Computational Linguistics*, Vol. III, Computing Centre of the Hungarian Academy of Sciences, Budapest, 1964. Relevent articles in this publication are the following: (a) M. Havass, "A Simulation of Music Composition. Synthetically Composed Folkmusic," pp. 107–128; (b) E. N. Ferentzy and M. Havass, "Human Movement Analysis by Computer: Electronic Choreography and Music Composition," pp. 129–188; (c) P. Braun, "On a Human Movement Analyzer," pp. 189–204.

[117] J. A. Thie, "Computation Choreography," unpublished manuscript.

[118] J. A. Thie, "Computers in the Art," *Computers and Automation*, 10 (1961), 23.

[119] M. Havass, "A Simulation of Music Composition," *op. cit.*

discussed above. He adapted the standard Markov model of a musical composition as his point of departure. He defined "vectors" describing not only the standard musical parameters such as pitch, rhythm, and intensity, but also constraints such as rules of composition or statistical frequencies obtained by analysis.

Havass also had to devise an input language with existing input equipment because the input accordion mentioned above was not operational at the time his work was carried out. The format of his input is described on pp. 117–120 of his article. Finally, he devised routines to obtain (1) pitch choices, (2) rhythmic choices either in relation to previous pitch choices or in terms of choosing "bars" or "bar groups," (3) form, and (4) tonality. Form, of course, is defined here only in terms of simple four-line folk tune structures. According to Havass these synthesized results were played at the I.F.M.C. meeting in Budapest in 1964 and have been recorded on tape. I have not heard these particular examples, but have heard samples of czardas tunes similarly prepared. Dr. Ferentzy has a tape of these interspersed with standard cabaret tunes of this type. The purpose of this experiment was to see whether the synthetic tunes can be distinguished from the others.

In July, 1966, Ferentzy moved to the University of Toronto. He left a progress report of his work at Washington State,[120] work he intended to continue at Toronto. Although Ferentzy's primary interest is music analysis, a brief statement of his ideas seems useful here because his programming could easily be adapted to composition as well.

In this report, Ferentzy said that he has developed a generalized Markov analysis for the stylistic analysis of music that is realized as a FORTRAN IV program. Ferentzy claimed that this program permits alternative schemes of analysis to be employed in contrast to other existing programs all of which are confined to particular schemes of analysis. Moreover, his program might be used to analyze the relationships of not just pitches but of up to 16 different musical parameters, and any combination of these. Thus far, he had made some test runs of his programs using a limited set of tunes (about 100) as input data.

Another feature of Ferentzy's program was its capability of being used to search for "almost identical" musical examples, that is to say, close variants. Internally, the program stored musical data in a matrix

---

[120] E. N. Ferentzy, "Progress Report on the Project, Analysis of Musical Styles by an Electronic Computer, Sponsored by Washington State University," unpublished report, Pullman, Washington State University, 1966.

form with rows of the matrix corresponding to musical parameters. Equivalence relationships were then defined so that the model was used to perform a generalized Markov analysis to any desired depth and compute transition probabilities among the stored parameters.

Ferentzy has also published an article [121] which discloses much of the theoretical background of his present method of style analysis. Moreover, in this article are presented examples of simple nursery tunes generated from data contained in his analytical matrices. He was careful to stress that these are extremely primitive results of scientific rather than aesthetic interest.

A third investigation of the use of computers for folk tune analysis and synthesis originates in Czechoslovakia. This study was carried out by Zdenck Fencl, a programmer at the Computing Center of "Business Machine Enterprise" in Prague. In 1965 Fencl sent me a description of his experiments in manuscript form.[122] Since then he has published a short account of his work.[123]

Fencl has written an algorithm for the synthesis of melodies as a test of the sufficiency of an analysis of simple Czech folk tunes. He selected 87 folk tunes possessing an $A_1A_2BA_2$ structure in 16 bars in $\frac{2}{4}$ or $\frac{3}{4}$ meter and in major keys. He computed matrices giving second-order Markov transition probabilities for harmonic structure, rhythmic duration, and melodic sequences. The matrix for harmonies was simple, since it was limited to tonic, dominant, and subdominant. The matrices for rhythms and melodic tones were considerably more complex, since some seven different rhythmic values and diatonic melodic tones spanning an eleventh occurred in these tunes.

Fencl tested his results by the synthesis of numerous monodies employing a four-part algorithm which consisted of: (1) the determination of the form, (2) the composition of the harmonic line, (3) the selection of meter and the choice of rhythmic values, and (4) the composition of the melody. In this algorithm, the programmer could choose the form and the meter while the computer generated the rest of the material employing a Monte Carlo method of computation that uses probability tables derived from the frequency matrices ob-

[121] E. N. Ferentzy, "On Formal Music Analysis-Synthesis: Its Application in Music Education," *Computational Linguistics*, 4 (1965), 107.

[122] Z. Fencl, "COMA, Description of the Computer Music Algorithm," unpublished manuscript dated June 1965 with "Results of the Computer Music Algorithm Composing a Monody Containing 16 Bars," dated May 1965.

[123] Z. Fencl, "Komponující algoritmus a obsah informace" ("A Composing Algorithm and Information Contents"), *Kybernetica*, 2 (1966), 243.

tained from the analysis discussed above. Except for some adjustments in composing the melodies, second-order Markov values were used throughout.

He also computed information contents and redundancies by means of the standard Shannon equation for each measure of the given structure employing the matrices referred to above. A plot of redundancies versus measure fluctuates as one might expect with maxima of 100 per cent being obtained in measures such as bar 8, where a cadence is required. In general, redundancies were moderate and were higher for digrams than for single-parameter choices.

One additional investigation of folk songs also originates from Czechoslovakia. Sychra [124] has computed the statistics of interval usage in 576 Moravian folk songs subdivided according to type. He has also analyzed rhythmic usages in 378 of these folk songs. The songs are taken from collections of Poláček, Bartoš, Janáček and Vasa. Sychra's main concern was with analysis including the use of information theory to interpret the results; however, he also did a certain amount of synthesis, that is, computer composition, as a check on his analytical work. The programs for synthesis made use of frequency distributions given in tables of data published with Sychra's article. He felt that the computer-composed folk tunes were not too satisfactory and required a certain amount of touching up to be convincing. He attributes this to the incompleteness of the compositional programs in terms of defining all the factors that impart the style representing the original songs.

Miscellaneous

This survey is concluded by listing miscellaneous publications which refer but briefly or incidentally to computer music composition. For example, articles not infrequently appear that are concerned with the long-established tradition of regarding mathematics and music as closely related. Articles that mention computers in this context include publications by Cohen [125] and Coexeter. [126] A similar example is con-

[124] A. Sychra, "Hudba a Kybernetika" ("Music and Cybernetics"), *Nové Cesty Hudby*, 1 (1964), 234.

[125] J. E. Cohen, "Some Relationships between Music and Mathematics," *Music Education J.*, 48 (Jan., 1961), 104.

[126] H. S. M. Coxeter, "Music and Mathematics," *Canadian Music J.*, 6 (1962), 13.

tained in a recent book by Portnoy [127] in which he considers the relationship of music to science. Portnoy discusses "Music Machines," including under this title electronic music and electronic music synthesizers as well as computer music, and gives a brief account of these systems for composition and an evaluation of the way in which they may affect the creation and performance of music in the future.

Sometimes, however, such articles are diatribes against developments in contemporary music. Examples include recent articles by Missal [128] and Lamb. [129] Missal denounces developments such as serialism and electronic music as well as computer music. Writings of this kind have been criticized by Appelton, [130] who at the same time seems also to take a negative attitude toward most of the experimental music he discusses. Among numerous other items, the *Illiac Suite* comes in for criticism, being characterized as having "a monotonous texture" and as being "dull because it satisfies neither aesthetic" of predictability and personal choice or random choice. The composer is accused of "wanting to have his cake and eat it too." More recently, Appelton also took a dim view of an oral report given on computer music. [131] Short nontechnical articles that attempt to justify computer applications in the humanities and music without really going into any details have also appeared. An example is a recent article in *Electronic Age* by J. A. Shaw. [132] Reports on current developments intended for an informed musical public have also appeared. For example, Ivor Darreg, a Los Angeles composer, has prepared rather extensive descriptions and a useful commentary on many developments which he feels affect the present state of music. [133] Computer music is one topic he treats among other items such as electronic and concrete music, the Schillin-

[127] J. Portnoy, *Music in the Life of Man*, New York, Holt, Rinehart and Winston, 1963, pp. 171–181.

[128] J. Missal, "The Fallacy of Mathematical Compositional Techniques," *American Music Teacher*, 12 (Nov.–Dec., 1962), 25.

[129] H. Lamb, "The Avant-Gardist—A Product of Process," *Music J.*, 22 (Jan., 1964), 22.

[130] J. Appelton, "Aesthetic Direction in Electronic Music," *The Western Humanities Review*, 18 (1964), 345.

[131] J. Appelton, "Report from Yale: Festival of Contemporary American Music," *Current Musicology*, 2 (1966), 65.

[132] J. A. Shaw, "Computers and the Humanities," *Electronic Age*, 24 (Spring, 1965), 26.

[133] I. Darreg, "Special Bulletin of 1963 on Electronic Music, with Supplement, March, 1966" and "Should Music be Composed with the Aid of 'Systems'?" mimeographed manuscripts available from the author.

ger system, unusual scales and temperaments, and so forth. Another example is a recent article by Stockhausen,[134] who reports to German readers observations gathered on a prolonged visit to the United States. He stresses the growing importance of automation to electronic music processes, mentioning technical developments in Europe and Japan. Although he is concerned primarily with automated processes for electronic sound synthesis, he does briefly discuss musical automata and composing machines.

In 1960 at the University of North Carolina computer laboratory in Chapel Hill, I was given a proposal for programming sixteenth century counterpoint by F. N. Young, Jr. Sample compositions were to be analyzed for their melodic, harmonic, and rhythmic patterns in order to assemble a set of tables of probabilities from which the computer would select at random, sifting the selections for coincidence with a set of basic rules of counterpoint. Thus, the experiment is reminiscent of *Experiment 1* and *Experiment 2* of the *Illiac Suite* except that weighted choices rather than random choices of parameters would be screened through the rules of composition. I have not heard since whether tangible results have been obtained with this program.

Finally, the survey is completed with references to several articles taken from the bibliography compiled by Brook and Berlind, several of which seem to be no more than brief news items.[135] The first two of these, judging by the title and dates of publication, possibly refer to Klein and Bolitho's work discussed above among the older experiments. The third and fourth of these articles refer to Barbaud and Blanchard's work mentioned in the section above on French experiments. Two further listings [136] are of perhaps greater interest, especially Leitner's publication.

[134] K. Stockhausen, "Elektronische Musik und Automatik," *Melos*, 32 (1965), 337.

[135] See footnote no. 1, and Anon., "Composer: The Brain," *Melody Maker*, 31 (July 21, 1956), 2; Anon., "Gulbransen Piano Used as Electronic Brain Writes 1,000 Popular Songs an Hour," *Piano Revue*, 115 (Sept., 1956), 21; Anon., "Les Principes de Composition de la Musique Algorithmique par des Ensembles a Traiter l'Information," *Electro Calcul*, 4 (Mar.–Apr., 1962), 19; Anon., "La Cybernetique et la Musique," *Disques* (Aug., 1962), 58.

[136] P. Leitner, "Logisch Programme für Automatische Musik," *Staatsprufungsarbeit an der Tech. Hochschule Wein*, 1957; K. L. Hartmann, "Versuch eine Mathematische Musiklehre," unpublished manuscript, Vienna, K. L. Hartmann, 1962.

CHAPTER V

MUSPEC

by JACK P. CITRON

The program to be described here represents an attempt to bring the use of computers as a tool in musical composition closer to the realm of established musical thought. The user of this program is expected to think in terms of rhythms, pitches, and chord structures rather than mathematical functions of time, frequencies, and frequency couplings with no voice-leading control. However, this does not restrict his thinking to existing pitch systems, traditional rhythms, or conventional harmonic forms. As such, the program may be used to produce results which conform to any style the user is capable of defining or to advance musical thought in an evolutionary manner.

The first of two blocks of data used as input to the program contains stylistic control information. In this data block, the user defines any pitch system desired, the subset of pitches which may be used for root tone selection, a scale of intervals from which root tone continuity will be established, interval assemblages which define the allowed harmonic structures, and voice-leading specifications which, besides controlling the linear continuity of the voices that serve as accompaniment, establish the chord structures to be extracted from the total harmonic structures. Interdependent rhythmic and melodic information to be used for melodization of harmony as well as the initial reference root tone, chord structure, and voicing are also specified.

The second data block consists of any set of numbers at all— whether abstractly chosen or purposely contrived. This block of data is used by the program to serve as the selector control function. Each number is used by the various algorithms to establish successively from the raw material in the first data block the new root tone, the harmonic structure built on that root, the voiced chord selected from that harmony, and the rhythmically ordered melody notes which are to be played with this accompaniment.

In June 1967 the output of the program was a printed listing of the notes and time durations in proper sequence (but not in musical notation). If the necessary hardware were available, the computer could be programmed to convert this output into digital information capable of further conversion to analog signals for recording purposes. Until such hardware is available, the results must be transcribed into conventional notation for instrumental performance—providing such instruments exist.

Oddly enough, the original justification for developing these methods grew out of a study on the use of computers in aural pattern recognition.[1] In that study, primitive hardware allowed investigation of complex sounds but not with the complex temporal continuity which characterizes music. The main feature of that study was to have the computer convert information into sound according to various algorithms. The user was then to observe by ear qualitative differences capable of labeling or differentiating between various kinds of information. It is our contention that the less abstract the sound (the more musical), the less training an observer would need to carry out routine observations with such a method. This naturally leads to the question as to what general musical procedures can be used algorithmically to convert abstract data into musically sensible sound, allowing of course for the observer's musical heritage and experience. Experience with nonmusicians who have written songs but need assistance putting them into musical notation shows very clearly that our culture has developed a subconscious harmonic sense which plays a dominant role in controlling conscious estimates of sensibility in a piece of music. This explains the rationale behind our choice of method, that is, the composition of a voiced harmonic continuity and its subsequent melodization.

We have used the program to generate and compare "thematic motives" characteristic of such things as the persistent lines of chemical substances, the travel-time entries of the various phases of seismic disturbances (the same disturbance as recorded at different observatories and different disturbances as recorded at one observatory), and excerpts from lists of data representative of other phenomenological recordings such as electrocardiograms, stellar luminosity plots, densitometer tracings from various types of spectroscopic studies, and so on.

[1] J. Citron and A. Hurwitz, "Use of computers in aural pattern recognition," IBM Los Angeles Scientific Center Report 35.017, 1966.

Although at present, these techniques are being used only for musical purposes, in the near future, when hardware for on-line sound production is readily available, practical technological use could also be made of such methods to perform rapid diagnosis or qualitative analysis of incoming signals. Incidentally, this projected use of the program as a "musical spectroscope" suggested the name, MUSPEC.

In the following sections, instructions for using the program are combined with explanations of what the user might consider state-ments in the MUSPEC language. These statements make up the data for the program. The use made of each statement is described along with the input card format.

Tonal System

The pitch system in which the music is to be composed is given symbolically in the composer's own notation. At present, he may specify up to 24 two-character symbols. We intend to increase this to at least one hundred symbols shortly. In the following three examples, the first illustrates one way of entering the seven-note scale: C, D, E, F♯, G, A, B♭. The second is the twelve-tone scale, and the third might represent an octave of quarter tones.

TONSYS C D E FS G A BF
TONSYS C DF D EF E F GF G AF A BF B
TONSYS C C° DF °D D D° EF° E E E° F F° GF °G G G° AF °A
    A A° BF °B B B° (on a single card)

The only fixed part of this format is the mnemonic "TONSYS" starting in column one of the card.

The tones named on this card will be referenced on other data cards and throughout the program by their numerical positions on the TONSYS card. For example, pitch number four implies the symbol "FS" from the first card, "EF" from the second, and "°D" from the last of the three cards shown above. The program converts all computed notes back into the symbols read in on the TONSYS card for the printed output.

Note that there is no reason other than convention to order the pitches monotonically according to frequency. Thus the pitch system itself could be a specific tone row or even contain certain notes more than once. It is also possible to enter octave specifications here, and this is our main reason for increasing the size of the pitch system which can be read in.

Root Tone Scale

The scale of allowed root tones upon which chords may be constructed is entered on one card. The mnemonic starting in column one for this card is the word "ROOTS." The order of the entries following the mnemonic is of significance whenever root tone cycle continuity is being selected. The entries themselves are numbers corresponding to pitches named on the TONSYS card. Examples of the ROOTS card could be:

ROOTS 1 11 9 7 6 3 2
ROOTS 3 6 2 5 1 4
ROOTS 1 2 3 4 5 6 7 8 9 10 11 12 13 14 . . .

The highest value entered, however, must correspond to an entry on the TONSYS card. The first note of the root tone scale is used as a reference root during the very first calculation of harmonic continuity. Thus, the first chord actually to appear as output is computed as being some interval away from the first root in this scale.

The Scale of Root Tone Progressions or Cycles

The numbers punched in the CYCLES card give the allowed root tone progressions according to the ordered root tone scale. Consider as an example the following set of three cards.

TONSYS C D E F G A B
ROOTS 3 4 1 6 2 5
CYCLES 5 2 3 5 2 5

Suppose the first cycle selected by the program from the CYCLES card is 3. Since the reference root is the first ROOTS entry, 3, the first calculated root tone is 6 (which is 3 steps away in the root tone scale) or the pitch A. If the next cycle selected is 2, the following root will be 5 or the note G. Now a cycle of 5 would specify the root tone number 2 or D. Notice that in this particular example the choices of cycles are effectively weighted 3 : 2 : 1 according to the frequency of occurrence of the entries 5, 2, 3 in the CYCLES card.

Harmonic Structures

Up to twelve cards may be used, each specifying a harmonic structure. Structures are defined by numbers which enumerate the intervals (in the TONSYS scale) separating consecutive notes of the structure. Consider the following two cases.

1) TONSYS C DF D EF E F GF G AF A BF B
   ROOTS 1 4 5 7 9 11
   STRCTR 4 3 3

This structure card specifies a seventh chord of the same type built on any allowed root tone, for example: (C, E, G, B♭), (E♭, G, B♭, D♭), and so on.

2) TONSYS C D E F G A B
   ROOTS 1 2 3 4 5 6
   STRCTR 2 2 2

Here the structure depends entirely upon the root tone chosen, for example: (C, E, G, B), (D, F, A, C), and so on.

The information on these structure cards is used for melodization as well as harmonic composition. Certain members of each structure can be referenced on "voicing" cards to constitute actual chords, while "melody" cards will designate structure entries to fulfill the melodic function. All structure cards for a given run should have the same number of entries. There can be up to eight intervals in any structure. This limit of eight as well as the limit of twelve structures per run can be increased if desired by some simple program alterations. In order to weight the probability of choosing particular structures more heavily, their respective STRCTR cards may appear more than once in the same data set. A structure such as:

STRCTR 4 3 4 3

will control the construction of a harmonic vector with five components. The currently selected root tone is structure component one. Component two is the note which lies an interval of four units away in the pitch system (TONSYS card). The components numbered 3, 4, and 5 follow, separated by intervals of 3, 4, and 3 respectively. Now, for purposes of voicing and melodization, the structure will be referenced according to its five components regardless of the actual notes which the components in turn reference.

Voicing the Harmonic Continuity

Voicing cards, as already pointed out, isolate the structure entries which will actually be used for chords. In addition, they control the voice leading between chords. The position of an entry on the voicing card implies the note of the structure in the present chord, while the entry in that position gives the structure note in the next chord to which that voice must move. Thus the card:

VOICNG 1 3 4 2

controls voice movement as shown below.

Old structure component	New structure component
1	1
2	3
3	4
4	2

The card shown also implies that chords in this run contain just four notes. All such cards in the same run should have the same number of entries with a possible maximum of nine. Up to twelve VOICNG cards may be used in any run. Relative weighting of the various voice leadings can be accomplished as in previous cases by using multiple copies of certain cards.

It is important to realize that no entry can appear twice on the same VOICNG card, and no numbers may be skipped as entries. In order to get chords with doubled functions or skipped functions, one must set up the STRCTR card to provide unique consecutive numbers for each chord component. For example:

STRCTR 4 3 9 - - -

provides a major triad with doubled third as the first four structure notes in the twelve tone system. Similarly

STRCTR 4 6 4 - - -

provides for a ninth chord in four part harmony. Thus, one need never use invalid cards of the following types:

VOICNG 2 1 2 3   (invalid because "2" appears twice)
VOICNG 1 3 4 5   (invalid because "2" is a skipped entry)

Voicing the First Chord

The card used to carry out this function takes on two forms:

1) CHORD1 1 3 4 2
2) CHORDP 1 3 4 2

The first card simply states that the initial reference chord (used to calculate the chord which will actually appear as chord number one in the output) is ordered: root, third structure tone, fourth tone, second tone. The second card shown above gives the same voice ordering, but the P in column 6 of the card also causes structures and root tones to be "Phased" in all calculations. The most obvious way to employ this feature is to use as many structure cards as there are root tones and order them so as to correspond in the desired fashion. For example:

```
TONSYS C DF D EF E F GF G AF A BF B
ROOTS 1 10 8 6 5 3
STRCTR 4 3
STRCTR 4 3
STRCTR 4 3
STRCTR 3 4
STRCTR 3 4
STRCTR 4 3
CHORDP 1 3 2
```

These cards assure that whenever a chord is built on C, A, G, or D, it will be a major triad. Chords built on F and E are similarly guaranteed to be minor triads. Had CHORD1 been used with the same structure cards, major and minor triads would be selected with a 2 : 1 probability in favor of major (regardless of the root tone) because of the ratio of major structure cards to minor structure cards.

Basic Rhythmic Groupings

Rhythms are handled in two levels of control. The "basic rhythmic group" cards outline an overall or "macrorhythmic" control.

```
BSCGRP 2,6/−1,4/1,3,2
```

This card first establishes two units of time (bars or beats or whatever the composer has in mind as a unit) which may contain up to a maximum of six attacks. This is followed by one unit of time beginning with a chord change (signalled by the minus sign) and containing up to four attacks. Another single time unit follows with a maximum of three rhythmic attacks and a minimum of two attacks specified.

In general then, the first numeric entry on a BSCGRP card always commands a chord change. Any negative duration entry does also. Maximum attack numbers must be specified following each duration entry. Minimum attack numbers come next but are assumed to be one if omitted. A slash separates consecutive groups of three items—duration, maximum number of attacks, minimum number of attacks—and the third item may or may not appear explicitly in any group. As a second example,

BSCGRP $4,7,3/-2,5,2/1,2/1,1$

provides for four units of time with from three to seven attacks followed by two units which begin with a change of chord and contain from two to five rhythmic attacks. Next is a single time unit with one or two attacks and finally one more unit duration with a single attack.

Spaces are optional between numeric fields here and may replace the commas shown. A slash may be replaced by a dollar sign ($) if a continuation card is required for the next group of three items. Up to 48 entries—16 groups of duration, maximum number of attacks, and minimum number of attacks—may make up one BSCGRP statement and may run over as many cards as are required.

Relative Durations

"Microrhythmic" attack patterns are specified as relative duration groups. It is easiest, but not necessary, to break these down or expand their time values into integers. That is, either series of notes shown below

can be described by the following card:

RELDUR 3 1 2 2 −1 3 2 2

Note the use of the minus sign to specify a rest of the given duration (−1).

In execution, a basic rhythmic group is selected first. Then a relative duration group is chosen. This choice is checked against the first of three (or two) fields on the BSCGRP card to see if the number of attacks (including rests as attacks) falls within the specified maximum and minimum. If it does not, another relative duration group is selected and checked. If none of the RELDUR entries are found to be satisfactory, a message to this effect is printed, and the job terminates. When a group with the necessary qualifications is found, the relative durations are assigned absolute values to fit within and fill out the fixed time span given by the basic group duration entry. For example, the above RELDUR card would be acceptable for the first field in the card, as

BSCGRP 1 8 / −2 10 4 / −1 6

The durations would become 3/16, 1/16, 1/8, 1/8, −1/16, 3/16, 1/8, 1/8. The next group of fields on this BSCGRP card then goes into effect, and a new RELDUR group is selected. For our convenience, suppose exactly the same group used above were selected again. This time the durations would be set to 3/8, 1/8, 1/4, 1/4, −1/8, 3/8, 1/4, 1/4. Now the next set of BSCGRP entries becomes effective, and, if the same relative duration set were again chosen, it would be rejected, because the maximum number of attacks allowed here is six. Thus another relative duration group would be selected to complete the specifications of the basic rhythmic group. When the BSCGRP is completed, another is chosen, and the entire process is repeated.

One further feature of the RELDUR card allows the composer to force certain microrhythms to apply to particular macrorhythms. To use this feature, one punches any nonblank character other than a number, minus sign, or decimal point as the last entry on the card. This card is then restricted in its use to apply only to the previous BSCGRP card throughout the program. To apply one rhythm to more than one basic rhythmic group but not all, the card containing that rhythm (RELDUR) must be duplicated as many times as required so as to have one in the data block for each of the BSCGRP cards in this category.

Melody

Melodies are entered as strings of integers representing notes selected from interval structures.

STRCTR 4 3 4 4 3 2
STRCTR 4 3 3 3 2 3
MELODY 2 5 4 7 7 3 6

If the first structure shown were in effect and built on the note c in the twelve tone system when the melody shown was selected, the melodic result would be:

E E♭ B A♭ A♭ G F♯

If the first structure shown were in effect and built on the note C in the melody would be:

E D♭ B♭ F♯ F♯ G E♭

Without other specification, a melody once chosen remains in effect until the relative duration group in effect has been satisfied. However, an alphabetic B or C may be punched as the last entry on a MELODY card to signify that this melody, once in effect, is to remain so until the current "Basic" rhythmic group or "Chord" structure is completed. In any case, the melody is cycled over if necessary until a new choice must be made because of the macrorhythmic specifications.

The composer can phase the melodic lines punched on cards with either the macrorhythms or microrhythms (or both) by using the same number of melodies as rhythms of the desired type(s) and ordering the cards of the two (or three) classes in a corresponding manner.

Lines

The second data block is preceded by a card with the word "LINES" starting in column one. Hereafter, we'll refer to this block as "line data." Any comments desired for printing as a heading on the musical output may be punched after LINES starting in column eight.

Up to ten cards may follow with 14 numbers on each fitted into a FORTRAN 14I5 format. We'll refer to these numbers as "lines." The last card of this block must have an integer from 1 to 3 punched in column 72. If a 1 is used, another set of line data must follow immediately, begining with the card containing the word LINES. A 3 is used to indicate a whole new data deck follows—new musical information and new lines. A 2 means that no more data follows.

The numbers comprising the line data are taken one at a time and used to select material from the musical data. The methods used to choose say a particular structure out of the N structures read in as data are similar to those which musicians use in decoding chordal notation into scalar notation. For example, conventionally speaking, we immediately recognize the ninth chordal tone as the second scale step. But the general method used is to compute the scale step as the residue of the chord tone number (9 here) modulo 7 (the number of unique scale tones) with unit index (first scale step is numbered 1 not 0). Thus if 9 chord structures are read in, and the line data entry is 137, structure number 1 is selected since 1 is the residue of 137 modulo 9 (with unit index).

The actual choice of material starts with the selection of a root tone cycle from the cycle scale (which was read in as data on the CYCLES card). This cycle is defined as the residue of the first line entry modulo the number of cycle scale entries. This establishes the next root tone. On this root will be built a structure selected from the structure list—considering this list as a kind of scale—and using the same line in exactly the manner already described. The voicing choice is made next by the same method, and thus the chord is specified in detail. Next, a macroryhthmic selection is made. A microrhythm is then chosen and tested against the macrorhythmic specifications as to maximum and minimum numbers of attacks allowed. If the chosen microrhythm does not satisfy the specifications, the next one in the microrhythmic scale or list is tested, and so on until an acceptable one is found (or all are found unsuitable causing the program to stop with an explanatory error message printed out). Finally, a melody selection is made from the list of those entries, and we now have a complete set of musical entities in force.

Basically, each line is used to establish a chain of chosen items as outlined in the previous paragraph. Situations can arise in the course of the program execution where the members of the chain are not quite as outlined above. For example, if an intermediate duration in the current macrorhythm calls for a new chord, the next line in the line data assumes control, and new root tone cycle, structure, and voicing selections are made. The same macrorhythm is still in effect, and processing continues as before. Microrhythms are chosen when appropriate according to the code (or lack of one) specified when the current one was read into the computer.

The chain of selections triggered by a given line is unique to a degree depending on certain "scale" sizes and whether or not "phasing" is requested on the CHORD1 card. Phasing keeps each line constant throughout the time it is in control. When not phased, the value of each line is purposely modified after certain selections in the chain, in order to prevent such phasings in cases where coincidental scale sizes would cause them. Whereas quite different lines could reduce to the same residues with phasing control, modifying these lines by dividing them by the same number (say the number of entries on the CYCLES card) and then taking residues will usually give different results. Now, dividing these numbers by the number of structures, before taking the next set of residues, makes equal results still more unlikely for the next calculation in the chain.

Summary

A minimum set of statements has been described which forms the nucleus for a musical composition language. The statements are collected for reference purposes in Table V-1. The data cards used to

Table V-1. Statements in the MUSPEC language

Statement type	Entries * (N)	Statements † (N)
Block 1 ‡		
TONSYS C D EF F . . .	24	1
ROOTS 1 3 11 2 5 7 . . .	24	1
STRCTR 1 5 12 10 3	8	12
VOICNG 1 3 2 4	9	12
CYCLES 2 2 3 5	12	1
CHORDx § 1 3 2 5	9	1
BSCGRP 2,6/−1,4,2/1,3,2 ($)‖	48	16
RELDUR 5 2 2 1 1 1 −4 (x) #	16	20
MELODY 1 3 2 5 5 4 (x) **	16	20
Block 2		
LINES (comments for printing)	—	1
1978 3424 7651 82 8 . . . ††	14	10

* Maximum number of entries per statement.

† Maximum number of statements of this type per block.

‡ Order of cards in Block 1 does not matter except where specifically required for phasing purposes.

§ Here x equals 1 or P for unphased or phased.

‖ Dollar sign ($) in place of slash (/) indicates data continues on next card.

If x (any alphabetic) is used, this rhythm applies only to previous BSCGRP card.

** Here x can be B, C, R, or blank.

†† Fill fields from beginning with FORTRAN 14I5 format. Last card has 1, 2, or 3 in column 72.

produce a short example (actually part of a complete composition) are listed in Figure V-1. The length of this example is controlled by the number of "lines" in block 2 (the five numbers on the card following the LINES card). Each set of data produces five melodized

```
TONSYS    C   DF   D   EF   E   F   GF   G    AF   A   BF   B
ROOTS    12  11  10  9   8   7  6   5   4   3   2   1
CYCLES    7  11  7  11  7
STRCTR    4  3  3  4  4  3
STRCTR    3  4  3  4  3  4
STRCTR    3  4  4  3  3  4
STRCTR    4  3  4  3  4  3
STRCTR    4  3  3  3  5  3
CHORDP      4  1  2  3
VOICNG    3  4  1  2
VOICNG    1  2  3  4
VOICNG    3  4  1  2
VOICNG    4  1  2  3
VOICNG    3  4  1  2
BSCGRP    2,3/    -2,4/    -2,3/-2,3/-4,6,6/-4,1
BSCGRP    4,6,6/-4,6,6/-4,6,6/-4,1
BSCGRP    2,3/-2,4/-2,3/-2,4/-2,3/-2,4/-4,1
BSCGRP    4,6,6/-2,3/-2,3/-4,6,6/-4,1
BSCGRP    2,3/-2,4/-2,3/-2,4/-4,6,6/-4,1
RELDUR    1  1  2
RELDUR    1  1  2
RELDUR    1  1  3  1  1  1
RELDUR    1  1  3  1  1  1
RELDUR    1
MELODY    1  4  6  3  7  4
MELODY    6  2  6  3  6  4
MELODY    5  2  4  1  5  2
MELODY    6  3  4  1  5  2
MELODY    7  6  3  2  7  6
LINES     MUSPEC  EXAMPLE                                         3
 2424  3272  7126  1108  2755
TONSYS    C   DF   D   EF   E   F   GF   G    AF   A   BF   B
ROOTS    12  11  10  9   8   7  6   5   4   3   2   1
CYCLES    7  11  7  11  7
STRCTR    4  3  3  4  4  3
STRCTR    3  4  3  4  3  4
STRCTR    3  4  4  3  3  4
STRCTR    4  3  4  3  4  3
STRCTR    4  3  3  3  5  3
CHORDP      4  1  2  3
VOICNG    3  4  1  2
VOICNG    1  2  3  4
VOICNG    3  4  1  2
VOICNG    4  1  2  3
VOICNG    3  4  1  2
BSCGRP    2,1/-2,1/-2,2/-2,1/-4,5/    -4,2
BSCGRP    4,2,2/-4,2/    -4,2,2/-4,1
BSCGRP    2,1/-2,1/-2,3/-2,1/-2,3/-2,1/-4,1
BSCGRP    4,2,2/-2,3/-2,3/-4,2/-4,1
BSCGRP    2,1/-2,1/-2,3/-2,1/-4,4,4/-4,1
RELDUR   -1  1  2
RELDUR    1  1  2
RELDUR    1  1
RELDUR    1  1
MELODY    3  5  2
MELODY    3  7  3
MELODY    3  6  3
MELODY    5  3  4
MELODY    5  1  4
LINES     COUNTERPOINT FOR MUSPEC EXAMPLE                          2
 2424  3272  7126  1108  2755
/*
```

Figure V-1. Data cards used to produce musical example shown in Figure V-4

chords for output. The second data set was constructed from the first by replacing certain rhythmic and melodic information with acceptable contrapuntal values. Thus, the two cases produce individual results which may be played simultaneously. Figures V-2 and V-3 show the two sets of computer output, and Figure V-4 gives the musical transcription of both showing the common harmony and labeling the melodies 1 and 2.

We felt such a language was necessary for two somewhat related reasons: first, to provide the majority of professional composers and arrangers in our culture with a means of communicating in a natural

```
                                                               LINE  =   2424
ROOT = C    CHORD = C  E  G  B
                                              4.0 BEATS     8.0 SUBDIVISIONS
    RHYTHM =     0.50   0.50   1.50   0.50  0.50   0.50
    MELODY =       GF     G      B      C    D      E

                                                               LINE  =   3272
ROOT = DF   CHORD = DF  E  AF  B
                                              2.0 BEATS     4.0 SUBDIVISIONS
    RHYTHM =     0.50   0.50   1.00
    MELODY =       GF     E      GF

                                                               LINE  =   7126
ROOT = GF   CHORD = DF  E  GF  BF
                                              2.0 BEATS     4.0 SUBDIVISIONS
    RHYTHM =     0.50   0.50   1.00
    MELODY =       GF     E      C

                                                               LINE  =   1108
ROOT = B    CHORD = B  D  GF  BF
                                              4.0 BEATS     8.0 SUBDIVISIONS
    RHYTHM =     0.50   0.50   1.50   0.50  0.50   0.50
    MELODY =       DF     D      BF     B    DF     D

                                                               LINE  =   2755
ROOT = E    CHORD = B  D  E  AF
                                              4.0 BEATS     1.0 SUBDIVISIONS
    RHYTHM =     4.00
    MELODY =       DF
```

Figure V-2. Computer output from MUSPEC example

way with computers, and second, to speed the day when the average man can hear a piece of "computer music" and not be forced to agree with those who hold that technological progress implies the defeat of the human spirit. Further, we felt these statements formed a sufficient set for the following reason. Until sound-producing hardware is available at our installation, there is little point in constructing routines to control properties directly associated with the output wave form such as timbre, volume, accents, vibrato, and so on. And since the composer's logical methods for orchestrating the harmonic accompaniment depend very strongly on such matters, we have chosen to leave the harmonic output in its present primitive form. Various schemes concerning these matters and others (such as basic compositional procedures other than melodization of harmony, and operational methods involving group theory and matrix representations) have been

CCUNTERPOINT FOR MUSPEC EXAMPLE

```
ROOT = C    CHORD = C   E   G   B
                                        4.0 BEATS    2.0 SUBDIVISIONS
      RHYTHM =    2.00  2.00
      MELODY =       D      G
```

LINE = 3272

```
ROOT = DF   CHORD = DF  E   AF  B
                                        2.0 BEATS    4.0 SUBDIVISIONS
      RHYTHM =    0.50  0.50  1.00
      MELODY =       AF    BF    AF
```

LINE = 7126

```
RLOT = GF   CHORD = DF  E   GF  BF
                                        2.0 BEATS    4.0 SUBDIVISIONS
      RHYTHM =   -0.50  0.50  1.00
      MELODY =          DF    AF
```

LINE = 1108

```
ROOT - B    CHORD = B   D   GF  BF
                                        4.0 BEATS    2.0 SUBDIVISIONS
      RHYTHM =    2.00  2.00
      MELODY =       GF    E
```

LINE = 2755

```
ROOT = E    CHORD = B   D   E   AF
                                        4.0 BEATS    1.0 SUBDIVISIONS
      RHYTHM =    4.00
      MELODY =       F
```

Figure V-3. Computer output from counterpoint for MUSPEC example

Figure V-4. Musical transcription of computer output for MUSPEC example (Figure V-2) and of counterpoint for MUSPEC example (Figure V-3) showing common harmony and labeling the melodies "1" and "2"

planned to some extent in the hope that we will be prepared if the time should arrive when we can direct more attention to this fascinating field.

|||||||||||||||||||||||||||| Part Three

ANALYSIS OF MUSIC

CHAPTER VI

Webern's Use of Motive
in the *Piano Variations*

by MARY E. FIORE

The recently discovered sketches of the *Piano Variations*, Opus 27, have established that Anton von Webern composed the first twelve measures of the third movement as the theme of the composition. In the first three measures of this theme the motives which constitute the source of the twelve-tone row and the basis of the entire composition are stated.[1] The very first sketch for this composition is of the source motive and the resultant twelve-tone row. It is reproduced with the final version of the same passage and analytic data (see Figures VI-1, VI 2, and VI 3). The first motive—the first four notes of the third movement—is used in the completed score as first stated. The other possibility sketched by Webern, f'♮ as a replacement for the d'♮, forming tritone with the b♮ rather than the minor third, does not reappear in the sketches.[2] The second motive, five notes—notes five through nine of the third movement—was subjected to eleven revisions. The resultant row was revised almost that many times. In each revision, the motive and then the resultant row is sketched. Again the minor third seems to have been a goal, although both the minor third and the tritone are emphasized in the final version of the second

[1] The composer's sketches for the *Piano Variations* were made available for this study through the courtesy of the Moldenhauer Archive and Universal Edition, A. G. Vienna.

[2] The following system of octave designation is used throughout this article.

CC   C   c   c'   c''   c'''   c''''

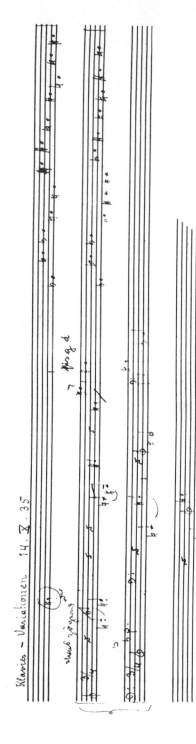

Figure VI-1. Anton Webern's sketch of *Piano Variations*, three staves. From Webern's autograph sketchbook in the Moldenhauer Archive, Spokane, Washington. By permission of the Archive and Universal Edition, Vienna.

Figure VI-2. Piano Variations, printed score of third movement, bars 1 to 5. Musical excerpt is used by permission of the original publisher, Universal Edition A. G., Vienna.

```
                    CLASSIFICATION OF MOTIVES
                    INTERVALS IN SEMI-TONES

CLASS           CHORD TYPE      CHORD
                INTERVALS       MELODIC MOTIVE

TRITONE         6,11,14,29,     (THEME(M2))59L12,53*D,48L12,45*B,30*D,
MINOR 3         5,13,16,        (THEME(M1))68*B,63L11,55*B,52L11,
                6,11,14,29,     (THEME(M2))59L12,53*D,48L12,45*B,30*D,
                19,32,          (THEME(M3))82*A,61L13,50L13,
BOTH            6,11,14,29,     (THEME(M2))59L12,53*D,48L12,45*B,30*D,


              WEBERN, PIANO VARIATIONS, III, 1-5, THEME
```

Figure VI-3. Piano Variations, computer output of theme

motive. The last three notes of the twelve-tone row are not identified as a third motive in the analysis. New intervallic relationships are not stated. These notes, measures four and five of the movement, were not the focus of the revision. The motives are delimited by silences and changes of dynamics.

Analysis of groupings of three or more notes indicate that each of the ten variations—three in the first movement, one in the second movement, and theme with five variations in the third—with the exception of the ninth, is delineated by a distinctive use of the characteristic intervals from one or the other of the two motives. The usage is summarized in Table VI-1. The three-note groupings defined are chords and melodic groupings delineated by slurs. The unique identity of each of the ten sections, nine variations, and theme, is also defined by texture and rhythm [3] and by the composer's labels in the sketches. Relatively few defined three-note groupings with neither tritone nor minor third among the intervals are used in the variations analyzed.

The use of the minor third in juxtaposition to the major seventh in contrast to the tritone is a focus of the composition. The minor third is emphasized and "sealed off" at the final cadence.[4] The change in Webern's late works from an emphasis on the preferred tritone, half-an-octave,[5] to the minor third in juxtaposition to the major seventh is

[3] Armin Klammer, "Webern's *Piano Variations,* Op. 27, 3rd Movement," *die Reihe,* Vol. II, 81–92.

[4] Anton Webern, *The Path to New Music,* Bryn Mawr, Pa., Theodore Presser, 1963, p. 52.

[5] *Ibid.,* p. 55.

Table VI-1. Summary of source motive usage by variation

Source motive	Type of grouping	Characteristic interval (in semitones)	Variation	Movement	Measures
2	Chord	Tritone(6)	1	I	1–18
1	Slur	Minor third(3)	1		
2	Slur	Tritone(6)	2	I	19–36
2	Chord	Tritone(6)	3	I	37–54
1	Slur	Minor third(3)	3		
2	Chord	Tritone(6)	4	II	1–22
1	Melody *	Minor third(3)	theme	III	1–12
2		Tritone(6)			
1	Chord	Minor third(3)	6	III	13–23
2	Slur	Tritone(6)			
2	Chord	Tritone(6)	7	III	24–33
2	Chord	Tritone(6)	8	III	34–44
Not defined in these analyses†			9	III	45–55
1	Chord	Minor third(3)	10	III	56–66
	Slur				
2	Chord	Tritone(6)			

* Silence delimited melodic groupings isolated in the composer's sketches.

† The grouping of notes and the relationships among the groupings used in the ninth variation are based on principles not yet defined in these programs.

demonstrated in this work.[6] The technique of using two closely related motives as the theme for a set of variations is completely developed in the later *Variations for Orchestra,* Opus 30.[7] The use of intervals as structural determinants and the change of focus from the tritone to the minor third are thus interpreted as part of the meaning of Webern's statement to the poetess, Hildegarde Jone, that in the *Piano Variations* he had achieved something that he had had in mind for years.[8]

The advent of high-level, nonnumeric programming languages has made it possible for the musician to use the digital computer to analyze music using his own analytic techniques. It is no longer necessary for the researcher to think of his analysis in terms of the data structures of tangential disciplines. He can now analyze musical

[6] Henri Pousseur, "Da Schoenberg a Webern: Una Mutazione," *Incontri Musicali,* Vol. I, 3–39.

[7] M. E. Fiore, "The Variation Form in Webern's *Oeuvre,*" read at The Fourth Webern International Festival, August 1968.

[8] Frederich Wildigans, *Anton Webern* (tr. Edith Temple Roberts and Humphrey Searle), London, Calder and Boyars, 1966, pp. 147–148.

events—chords, motives, dynamic changes—and their interrelationships in terms of only the basic premises of music analysis he has adopted.

The data structures of mathematics are useful and appropriate for analyses making use of the principles embodied in them. However, to be forced to use a data structure that does not reflect the intrinsic structure of the data or the rationale of the analytic procedure being used is at best inconvenient. In using SNOBOL3 Programming Language [9] the musician is permitted to work with music on its and his own terms; he may use data structures borrowed from mathematics, define his own structures, or program the computer to define structures based on and developed dynamically by the analytic process itself.

An analysis of the entire score of the *Piano Variations* by Webern for harmony as a function of the theme and variations form was done entirely by digital computer using the SNOBOL3 Programming Language.[10] It was possible to program the analysis using only music analysis techniques and structures. The computerized results confirmed the noncomputerized analysis [11] as well as the impression of listener and performer. One would have been alarmed if it had not been thus. That the results of this SNOBOL analysis of the *Piano Variations* reflect the composer's intent is documented by the sketches which have recently been made available.

The analysis consists of three main programs, each of which is comprised of several smaller units of program. The first main program relates the encoded staff notation [12] to another code to be used in the analytic programs, and groups notes according to changes of dynam-

[9] D. J. Farber, R. E. Griswald, and I. P. Polonsky, "The SNOBOL3 Programming Language," *The Bell System Technical Journal,* July–August (1966), 895–944.

[10] The author gratefully acknowledges the assistance of Anthony Ralston, Director, and the staff of The Computing Center of State University of New York at Buffalo. The Center implemented and up-dated SNOBOL3 for this project. It also provided the use of an ATS terminal for the preparation and editing of the manuscript. The Computing Center is partially supported by NIH Grant FR 00126 and NSF Grant GP 5675. The project was also partially supported by a grant-in-aid from The Research Foundation of State University of New York.

[11] M. E. Fiore, "The Formation and Structural Use of Vertical Constructs in Selected Serial Compositions," unpub. dissertation, Indiana University, 1963.

[12] The author is grateful to Stefan Bauer-Mengelberg and Melvin Ferentz for instruction in the use of their Ford-Columbia representation and to Allen Forte for instruction in the use of the SNOBOL programming language in conjunction with the music representation.

ics and tempo. A second code is needed in order to extract pitches from the staff notation with its unequal whole and half steps and clef changes. The originally encoded staff notation is preserved in order to refer to the composer's spelling of chords and disposition of notes on the staves. The codes are not translated but only referenced one to the other. Thus, an exact mapping of the analytic evidence to the original score is always retrievable.

Each event in the referenced code is read: PITCH(POSI-TION(DURATION))ARTICULATION. The referencing of a staff code into a pitch code associates the effective clef with each note, assigns a specific pitch code to each note and deletes the accidentals. Identical pitches governed by different clefs are equalized by adding a constant, 12; identical pitches governed by different staves, upper or lower of the two-stave system, are equalized by subtracting a constant, 50, from the notes written on the lower staff. The octave of the partially processed staff-notation code is determined by dividing the code by the number of codes in one octave, 7, and redetermined in the chromatic scale by multiplying the quotient by the number of notes in the octave, 12. The remainder in this division process is used as an indirect reference to a statement assigning the proper number of half-steps to each interval above the note of reference, g.

A double-digit number is arbitrarily assigned to each note, twelve different notes and twelve different numbers defined in each octave. The code, 60, is assigned as g' on the treble staff, thus, 72 as g'', 84 as g''', and 38 as g. Distinctions between enharmonic equivalents: for example, 68 as e''♭ or d''♯, are retrieved by referencing. Twelve POSITIONS are defined in each measure of the fifth variation, first variation in the third movement. The number of POSITIONS in each measure is variable dependent on the configuration of note values used in the context.[13]

The second main program, which accepts the results of the main program as input, locates chords, simultaneities, of a specified number of notes and duration, and groups and names them according to the constituent intervals. The figuration used is a twelve-note variant of the seven-note figured bass notation of diatonic music, for example, the major triad in twelve-note figuration, 7,4, and the same triad in figured bass notation, 5,3.

The program defines chords resulting from overlapping durations.

[13]Allen Forte, "A Program for the Analytic Reading of Scores," *Journal of Music Theory*, Fall 1966, pp. 330–364.

In addition it deletes notes from chords at the positions at which the duration is no longer effective. It was not programmed to specify the chords that are simultaneously articulated. This program also identifies silences throughout the texture, inserts markers, and deletes the rests.

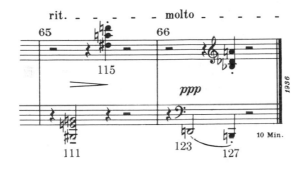

SAMPLES OF EACH OF THE PROGRAMS

STAFF NOTATION IN FORD-COLUMBIA REPRESENTATION
INPUT

```
/65,*ZRIT.*Z,RH,RQ,  *VDIM.*V,73=11,71=H,66+H*B,  RQ,  44=Q*D,11=Q,2
7+Q,RQ,  RH,RH,  /66,RH,RQ,  77*XF,*VPPP*V,68=HL61,  RQ,  23*XG,24=Q,
20-Q,18-Q*D,66=QL61*D,  RH,RH,  //
```

ANALYTIC CODE
INTERMEDIATE OUTPUT

```
/65,R((109)4),R((109)2),60((111)4),57((111)4),49((111)4)*B,R((11
3)2),R((115)2),58((115)2)*D,53((115)2),47((115)2),R((117)4),R((1
17)4),/66,R((121)4),R((121)2),31((123)4)L61,R((125)2),62((127)2)
*D,54((127)2),51((127)2),28((127)2)*DL61,R((129)4),R((129)4),//
```

FINAL OUTPUT
CLASSIFICATION OF CHORDS AND MOTIVES

CLASS	CHORD TYPE INTERVALS	CHORD MELODIC MOTIVE
TRITONE	5,11,	(10(115))58*D,53,47,
MINOR 3	3,11,	(10(111))60,57,49*B,
		(10(113))60,57,49*B,
	3,	(10)123)31L61,28L61*D,
	8,11,34,	(10(127))62*D,54,51,28*DL61,

WEBERN, PIANO VARIATIONS, III, 65-66

Figure VI-4. Piano Variations, measures 65 and 66, with samples of each of the programs. Musical excerpt is used by permission of the original publisher, Universal Edition A. G., Vienna.

Melodic motives, identified by slurs in the score, are also retrieved from the second main program. The Ford-Columbia Code provides for the marking of slurred notes with an L, mnemonic for ligature, and an identifying number. The location of the first and last notes of any slurred group is trivial. The intervening note in three-note slurred melodic motives was defined to be a note with a POSITION larger than that of the first note of the group, smaller than that of the last, or other tagged note of the same group, and not bearing an L number of its own.

In the third main program, the grouped notes, chords, and slurred melodic motives, are classified by intervallic structure, that is, groups with minor third, with tritone, with both minor third and tritone, and with neither minor third nor tritone. The figured basslike notation is used for CHORD TYPE. Thus, the silence-delimited first motive of the theme is analyzed as 5,13,16, CHORD TYPE, five semitones from the highest e''♭, 68, to b'♭, 63, thirteen semitones from the same e''♭ to the d'♮, 55, and sixteen semitones from the same e''♭ to the b, 52. See Figure VI–4 showing measures 65 and 66 with samples of each of the programs.[14]

The groups of notes that include a minor third are identified with the first motive of the theme, and those with either tritone or both tritone and minor third are identified with the second motive. Few groups of notes with neither of the two isolated intervals are used in the *Piano Variations*. In the tenth and last variation, only chords considered to be derived from one of the two motives are used. The minor third of the first motive is used at the final cadence, to "seal off" the first idea.

Computerized, nonnumeric analysis is an invaluable aid to both analytic and historical music research. Any analytic process that can be defined and executed on a music score can be programmed. Analytic evidence of an entire composition, even an entire *oeuvre*, can now be based on explicitly stated criteria, structured and restructured according to various hypotheses, and mapped or directly related to the original score.

[14] The author's programs in SNOBOL3 for the IBM 7044 are available on request.

CHAPTER VII

Toward a Theory of
Webernian Harmony, via Analysis
with a Digital Computer

by RAMON FULLER

Almost all music composed between 1600 and 1900 is described by classical harmonic theory in the following way.

First, it consists of a succession of well-defined sets of tones (called "triads" and often sounded simultaneously as "chords") which succeed each other according to fairly well-defined rules and help to establish a key center. Second, each chord contains or implies a root tone which partly absorbs other tones in the chord into its overtone series (or into the overtone series of one of its lower octaves), and, third, every tone in the music (with almost no exceptions) is related to such a chord, either by being a fully consonant member or, if dissonant, by resolving to a chord member. Specific rules were usually followed in preparing and resolving dissonances.

In the twentieth century, many composers discarded or modified the old chordal patterns and rules in favor of other techniques and more dissonant sonorities. This is especially true of Anton von Webern (1883–1945), whose music has been much discussed of late, representing as it does the purest form of serial, or tone-row composition. A tone row is a carefully ordered arrangement of the twelve tones of the chromatic scale, which, together with its mirror forms, is used as the basis of a piece of music. The twelve-tone technique can be briefly described as the art of arranging tones of the row in the vertical (octave placement) and horizontal (temporal) dimensions in such a way as to achieve musical variety and structure without disrupting the order of the row. The way this is accomplished in Webern is not well understood, except for certain obvious limitations imposed by the method of composition: only tones contiguous within the row may be

sounded simultaneously (with the exception of certain liberties sometimes taken in rearranging subsets within the row); choice of octave
placement for any tone is free, but often crucial to the musicality of a
passage, as any experienced serial composer will say.[1]

It is often assumed that the twelve-tone technique as used by
Webern represents a complete break with the older harmonic thinking described above. This is correct, as far as compositional technique
is concerned, but is it strictly true of the music as perceived? For
instance, in listening carefully to Webern compositions one hears
points of harmonic reference which stand out from the dissonant
texture. In Figure VII-1, for example, the C♯ in bar 2 is heard as a

Figure VII-1. Anton Webern, *Variationen* (*Piano Variations*), Opus 27,
First Movement. This excerpt is used by permission of the original publisher,
Universal Edition A. G., Vienna.

consonance with the F♯, so that one fleetingly hears the F♯ as a root,
in spite of the strong dissonance with G. The C♯ is not sounded
simultaneously with the F♯. Thus *tones in the neighborhood* of a

---

[1] The perceptual importance of the vertical dimension can be demonstrated by
a simple example. Take three tones, say C, D, and E, as elements of a chord. Any
of the three tones can be perceived as the chord root, given the right vertical arrangement and assuming a favorable context. Whether or not one agrees that
roots have meaning in Webern, it is evident that the vertical ordering of a set of
tones is very important perceptually—although it has been studied only superficially, as far as serial music is concerned. Thus the concept of octave equivalence
needs to be qualified, if not drastically modified.

root, as well as those simultaneous with it, may be part of its harmonic complex. Several such triadic complexes are intermingled in bars 1 and 2: F♯, C♯; G, B, F; B, F♯; C♯, F, B; E, B.

This way of looking at the music immediately raises several questions: (1) How can one identify the most important (strongest) roots? Or in other words, what conditions in this music will cause a tone to be perceived as a root? (2) Are such roots important in the musical structure? (3) Are there any significant connections between the strongest roots, or do they occur at random? Are there rules of succession? (4) What other phenomena are related to Webern's use of root complexes?

The answers to questions 2, 3, and 4 naturally depend on the answer to question 1. As we have seen above, the analyst will have to examine each tone in its musical context, and identify and measure the conditions that work for or against its being a root. Since many conditions must be considered for each tone, and since these conditions may interrelate in complicated ways, it is natural to consider the computer as an analytical tool, and computer language as a medium in which to formulate the theory. Further reasons for using the computer are as follows.

In the first place, writing a computer program forces one to put his theory into explicit, logical form; the program and its description then become important theoretical documents.

Secondly, the analytical theory, being embodied in the computer program, may be checked and revised very simply—if the basic programming logic is flexible and general enough. Revising a good program will usually involve only changing the weights of some factors, or adding new subroutines to account for newly recognized factors. The theory may be checked by analyzing special data both with the computer and by other means, and comparing results.

A third reason is that once the program is running and generalized, compositions can be analyzed as fast as they can be transcribed into a computer-compatible representation. This gives the theorist greater opportunity to test his theory on a variety of musical examples.

Having decided to use the computer in this fashion, the theorist must make two further choices before writing the program: how to represent the musical score to the computer, and in which of the several available languages to write the program. Since the original analytical conception required floating point numbers, FORTRAN was chosen rather than SNOBOL,[2] of the two languages then [3] known by the author.

The choice of FORTRAN in turn led to representing the musical score as a set of arrays, one array for each relevant aspect of the music. Among these are pitch (identified to the computer as the array, IP, and represented by the integers from 1 to 88, with the integer 91 reserved for those rests actually representing silence); the measure in which a tone is attacked (MESA); the measure in which it is released (MESR); its duration (DUR); the position of its attack (ATT) and of its release (REL) within the measure. Other information (such as musical intervals, structural time spans, and so on) can be calculated from these arrays by the program, since all the symbols used are numbers.

At this point, it is desirable to define some words that will be used in a special way:

Root: the tone currently being examined as a root whether or not it in fact turns out to be an important root.

Partial: a tone a major third, perfect fifth, or minor seventh (plus any number of intervening octaves) above, or the harmonic (not mirror) inversions of these intervals (plus intervening octaves) below the root. The minor seventh is not considered a partial unless it is supported by another partial nearby.

Root interval: the interval between the root and the tone currently being examined as a partial to the root.

Interfering tone: any tone other than a partial or root that intervenes (in time) between root and partial, or is simultaneous with either or both.

Rest: rest symbols indicating actual silence between tones or sonorities are considered part of the pitch structure; those occurring simultaneously with tones or chords are ignored. Each silence is represented by one number in the pitch array, regardless of how many rest symbols are printed in the score to represent it.

Record: used in the computer jargon sense—for our purposes, a set of data representing a musical score, or section thereof.

Scan: a short section of a record to be examined in the course of the analysis.

---

[2] SNOBOL arithmetic is limited to integers.
[3] Autumn, 1966.

Description of the Computer Program

According to good programming practice, a main program calls subroutines to do the actual steps of the analysis, as follows:

ISCN1. The first step in the root analysis of a given tone is to fix the limits of the scan within which partials might reasonably be heard in reference to the root. It was hypothesized that a tone can have little root influence beyond five tones in front or five tones in back of itself, in Webernian context. This brings the total scan to eleven tones, except for the following conditions: tones simultaneous with the root are counted among the five forward tones, and again among the five rear tones of the scan; the scan is lengthened to include any tones sounded simultaneously with the fifth tone on either side of the root; rests are counted as two tones, since in the Webern *Variationen* (*Piano Variations*) they seem to delimit phrases; the scan is appropriately shortened for a root near the beginning or end of the record. Thus the musical context influences the length of a scan. Once the scan is fixed, the calling program, using other subroutines, tests each tone in the scan to determine whether it is a partial. This is accomplished by calculating the "mod 12" value of the root interval, and comparing the result with appropriate numbers. If the root interval is a minor seventh, its scan is searched for other partials; if none are found, the minor seventh is not considered a partial.

INVERT. This routine is called each time a partial is found. It assigns a temporary "harmonic field strength" to the root interval, taking into account whether it is harmonically inverted, whether it is in "exact partial position" (for example, whether a perfect fifth is actually a perfect twelfth, corresponding with the third partial of the overtone series—if so, the root interval is considered stronger than otherwise), and how many octaves apart the root and partial are. Inversion weakens a root, as do intervening octaves (except when the root is below the partial, and the vertical span is less than or equal to exact partial position). The result is stored in a variable, DINV.

CONTEX. This routine analyzes the context in which the root interval is found, that is, it accounts for the possibility that tones immediately preceding or following the root interval may weaken the harmonic effect of the root. For instance, a tone preceding the root interval may tend to absorb the root if it bears a root relationship to the root; a tone following the root interval may tend to cause the root to be perceived as a nonharmonic tone (as when a perfect fourth resolves to a major third). CONTEX makes the initial definition of a variable, YNTRFR, which is used in the final calculation of the root strength of the root interval.

RTINFR. This routine calculates the interference offered by a tone within the scan of the root interval (including tones simultaneous with the root or partial, and tones sounded temporally between root and partial). This root interval scan has previously been defined by a routine, KDOPRM. RTINFR calls another routine, WHST (for *which set*) that tells it which of four possible sets of tones a given tone belongs to, with respect to the root: (1) partials to the root, (2) roots to the root, (3) pure dissonances to the root,[4] or (4) different[5] roots to one of the partials, or partials to one of the partials.

These sets are weighted according to the amount of interference one of their members will offer a root interval, for example, set 1, no interference; set 2, strong interference; set 3, medium interference; and set 4, weak interference.

A weight corresponding to the set the interfering tone belongs to is added to YNTRFR (except that if it belongs to set 1, the program moves on to test the next tone in the root interval scan); then additional weight is added for each of the following conditions found as, for example, when: (1) interfering tone is below the root; (2) interfering tone is between the root and the partial (in the vertical dimension); (3) interfering tone occurs simultaneously with either the root or partial or both; (4) root and partial do not overlap each other, in time; (5) interfering tone lies (temporally) between the root and partial, the root appears before the partial, and the interfering tone is vertically close to the root. This may cause a shift of the perceptual level from the root to the interfering tone, making it more difficult to relate the partial to the root. If the root and partial are attacked simultaneously, only tones simultaneous with both are considered interfering tones, conditions 4 and 5 are not considered, and condition 2 is changed to read, "interfering tone is below the partial."

---

[4] The augmented fourth and minor second (and inversions and octave extensions) are considered pure dissonances because they are neither roots nor partials to the root or any of its partials (as partials and roots are herein defined). An exception to this (not allowed for in the present version of the program) is that the tone an augmented fourth from the root can be a root to the major third of the original root, if supported by one of its own partials (since the minor seventh requires such added support according to our present theory).

[5] For instance, if the root is C, its partial, E, has another root, A.

When the weights of all interfering tones and their conditions have been added to YNTRFR, DINV is divided by YNTRFR, to obtain the final harmonic strength of the root interval; the result is stored in HFST, and added to the dimensioned variable, HFS, which will contain the total harmonic field strength of the root after all of its root intervals have been analyzed. HFS, HFST, YNTRFR, DINV, the root, and the partials are all printed out, each time they are finally defined.

After each tone has had its harmonic field strength calculated and printed out, a search is made for harmonic patterns. A moving scan of about nine tones is set up (more, if either of the end tones is simultaneous with others), from which the three strongest roots are chosen by a little sort routine, RTSORT. The scan bumps along through the record in six-tone leaps, so that several tones overlap between each adjacent pair of scans. Thus, about one-third of the tones in the score are selected as strong roots, tested for the following conditions, and results printed out.

1. Do the other two strong roots in the scan belong to the harmonic system of the present root? The harmonic system of a given root includes the roots of those major triads which have a tone in common with the major triad of the given root; for example, the harmonic system of C includes, besides itself, G, F, E, A, A♭, and E♭.

2. How many tones within the scan of the root belong to the harmonic system of the root (regardless of their root strengths)?

3. How many of each type of interfering tone occur simultaneously with the root?

4. How many of each type of interfering tone occur within the scan of the root?

Some Analytical Results and Theoretical Discussion

Three structural phenomena having to do with roots are found in the Webern *Variationen*, first movement (see Figure VII-1): direct clashes between roots; perceptual separation of temporally adjacent, related roots; and complete harmonic fusion of a group of simultaneously sounded tones into rooted sonorities.

The identity of a given root is probably less important than the fusion or nonsimultaneous harmonic connection associated with it. Nevertheless, in locating the roots, one also pinpoints harmonic connections and disjunctions which define the structural layers of the music, and hence help delineate the overall perceived form, or *Gestalt*, of the composition.

The computer program selected the roots in the passage analyzed below (see Figure VII-1). This will illustrate the theory as it has developed so far. Note the role of dissonance in separating harmonic layers.

In bars 1 and 2 G♮ is root to B♮ and F♮ (with E♮ as a supportable dissonance which also "resolves" to the C♯); F♯ is root to the C♯ in bar 2 and to the B♭ in bar 3. We thus find a direct clash between the two strongest roots in the neighborhood. The F♯ strongly interferes with the rooted complex, G♮, B♮, F♮, E♮, just at the moment when it would have become a firmly fused harmony. The appearance of the C♯ then transforms the F♯ (retrospectively) from an interfering tone to a root, and brings some feeling of resolution from the tensions both within the G♮ complex and between the F♯ and G♮.

In bar 3, A♮ is root to the C♯ in bar 2 (note that C♯ is a partial of both A♮ and F♯; the author perceives it to be related more strongly to the F♯ than to the A♮, which agrees with the computer analysis). G♯ in bar 4 is root to the C♮'s and E♭'s in bars 3 and 5.

Bars 5, 6, and 7 form the retrograde of bars 1, 2, and 3, in both notation and harmonic analysis, except that the C♯ in bar 6 is strongly perceived in relation to A♮, rather than to F♯. This disagrees with the computer analysis which again makes the F♯ the stronger root of the C♯. In both places, however, A♮ and F♯ were both selected as strong roots, so the error here is a fairly subtle one. The two D♮'s in bars 3 and 5 are heard as neighboring tones to the two C♯'s.

In bars 3, 4, and 5, there are three structural layers, separated by dissonance, harmonic inversion, and vertical distance: on the bottom, the two A♮'s; the B♭, E♭, C♮, G♯ complex in the middle; and the two D♮'s and two C♯'s on top. In bar 6, when the D♮ resolves to C♯ (a partial of A♮), the top and bottom layers are joined harmonically; the middle layer remains separated.

Again in bars 8 and 10, there are the three layers, harmonically separated by dissonance: F♮ and A♮ on top, and E♮ and C♮ on the bottom, separated by the F♯ and E♭ vertically between them. The two outer layers might have fused to form an F♮ chord, or at least registered harmonic motion, were it not for the separating dissonances, the inversions, and the vertical distances involved. Bar 9, in contrast, is harmonically fused: the D♮, G♯, C♯ complex is not only coherent in itself, but is also felt to belong to the following (also coherent) complex, which has B♭ as its root. This is true partly because of the common tones between the two complexes, and partly because the dissonances (C♯ and G♮) can both be supported by the root, B♭.

In conclusion it may be said that the use of the computer has affected my present harmonic theory in two important ways.

For example, the first, simpler version of the analysis program gave unsatisfactory results because it did not account for enough relevant harmonic factors. This was made dramatically clear by the very literal manner in which the computer carried out the analysis; no unconscious factors operated to rescue the analysis from the inadequacies of the theory. The author was thus persuaded to take a much closer look at his assumptions, with profitable results, which were incorporated into the present version of the program.

In the second place, the computer, unlike a human, cannot make an analysis in terms of whole chords which it recognizes, but instead must look at each tone and its context to decide whether (really to what extent) it is a root. This kind of thinking affected the whole theory—assigning weights to various conditions, setting up a scan for each root, evaluating the context of a root interval—all of these being aspects of both the program and the theory that grew out of the manner of thinking required by the computer.

In its present stage of development, the program (CONHAN, for CONtextual Harmonic ANalysis) performs quite satisfactorily in choosing the most important roots of a musical passage in Webernian style. There are a few discrepancies, such as the relationships between the C♯, F♯, and A♮ noted above in the discussion of bars 5 and 6; but these are not disastrous, since a good part of the analysis must still be done without the computer, and so minor corrections are easily made.

Perhaps the least satisfactory part of both the program and the theory is the attempt to find larger "harmonic systems." This idea was an early hypothesis made before the concepts of separation were fully formulated. At this writing, a revision of the program is underway, which should yield a more complete and accurate description of a musical structure in terms of the present harmonic theory, as revised and expanded with experience. It is fully expected that the computer will continue to be important in every stage of the theoretical development.

CHAPTER VIII

Harmony before and after 1910:
A Computer Comparison

by ROLAND JACKSON

The decisive changes that came into music c. 1910 (somewhat earlier among the Viennese composers, somewhat later in Stravinsky) affected all aspects of musical style, but none perhaps as drastically as harmony. Almost overnight the system that had prevailed for centuries, the building up of chords in thirds and the scheme of chord connections that has come to be called "functional," tumbled to the ground. And in its place there ensued a kind of harmonic anarchy, at least in the beginning, a style in which harmony was no longer central, as the main organizer of the musical design, but rather surrendered this position to other elements such as rhythm or texture.

But the nature of the change still needs some clarifying. Are there remnants of tertian structure abiding in post-tertian pieces? Did some new form of harmonic logic develop to replace the old functional connections? These and similar questions are not easily answered, partly because the chords themselves (both in pre- and post-1910 compositions) tend to be so very complicated, partly because the mind feels itself so very taxed in remembering harmonic details of this kind. For these reasons the decision was made to enlist the services of the computer, which for problems like this turns out to be an ideal research tool.[1] For—after having been programmed to do so—it shows itself capable of analyzing each of the chords, from the most simple to the most complex, within a given piece.[2] And, what seems even more

---

[1] This study was initially presented (in more abbreviated form) at the national meeting of the American Musicological Society in New Orleans on December 27, 1966. I should like to express thanks to my student Philip Bernzott, who assisted me in many ways, especially in the working out of the computer programs.

[2] These programs are rather generally described in two abstracts: Roland Jackson and Philip Bernzott, "Harmonic Analysis with Computer—a Progress Report,"

significant, it can keep these chords "in mind" (better than a human could) while it makes comparisons of various kinds, pointing out, for example, some of the differences between one piece and another or one composer and another.

The idea essentially was a simple one: compositions from a little before and from after the style change were encoded for computer analysis[3] and then subjected to various analytical routines carried out by the machine. Although only a very few pieces were included, the results already contain some points of interest—more suggestive, to be sure, than definitive. Here follows a list of the pieces or excerpts that became part of the survey (see Table VIII-1).[4] It will be noticed that

Table VIII-1. Compositions encoded for musical analysis

Composer	Tertian	Post-tertian
Schoenberg	*Verklaerte Nacht*, m.1-100 (1899)	*Serenade* (from *Pierrot Lunaire*) (1911)
Berg	*Piano Sonata* (1908)	*Lyric Suite*, 1st mvt. (1926)
Webern	*String Quartet*, m.1 80 (1905)	*String Quartet*, Op. 28 (1938)
Stravinsky		*String Quartet*, 1st mvt. (1914)
Scriabin	*Quasi Valse*, Op. 47 (1906)	
Varèse		*Intégrales* (1923)

the three Viennese composers are each represented by an earlier and a later work, while Scriabin's earlier work is balanced by later pieces by Stravinsky and Varèse.

The comparisons divide themselves into three principal categories: (1) those involving the chordal or intervallic content of the pieces;

ICRH Newsletter, Vol. I, 9 (1966), 3-4; and Roland Jackson, "The Computer as a 'Student' of Harmony," in *Proceedings of the Tenth Congress of the International Musicological Society*, Ljubljana, 1967.

[3] The encoding method is described in Roland Jackson and Philip Bernzott, "A Musical Input Language and a Sample Program for Musical Analysis," to appear in *American Musicological Society, Greater New York Chapter Symposia Proceedings 1965–1966, Musicology and the Computer* (ed. Barry S. Brook), Flushing, N.Y., 1967. I should like to express gratitude here to two of my students in particular, Mr. David Goodman, who coded all of Varèse's *Intégrales* (minus the percussion instruments) and Mr. Richard Moerschel, who double-checked most of the coded material.

[4] The following abbreviations will be adopted throughout the present article: Schoenberg, *Verklaerte Nacht* = VN; Schoenberg, *Pierrot Lunaire* = PL; Berg, *Piano Sonata* = PS; Berg, *Lyric Suite* = LS; Webern, *Quartet*, 1905 = Q(05); Webern, *Quartet*, 1938 = Q(38); Stravinsky, *Quartet*, 1914 = Q(14); Scriabin, *Quasi Valse* = QV; and Varèse, *Intégrales* = I.

(2) those involving the dissonance content; and finally (3) those involving what shall be called the "recurrent chord" content. Each of these will now be described in greater detail.

Chordal and Intervallic Content

The computer program was designed to find out just which vertical combinations (no matter how brief or fleeting) made up a given musical piece, and for what percentage of its total duration. Each sonority was, therefore, treated as an isolated entity, but in the end each of its appearances was totaled together to arrive at the overall percentage. This program leaned heavily upon a chord table and an interval vector table,[5] against which the successive chord forms occurring in a piece were matched. These two tables are purely numeric (the chords being represented by 12-digit numbers: .100100100010 stands for a diminished-minor seventh chord; while the interval vectors are assigned 6-digit numbers: .001110 stands for a major, or minor, triad) as are also the chords in the composition (in my scheme of coding), which greatly facilitates the comparisons. In this way we are enabled to see at a glance the harmonic "palette" employed in a particular piece, just how many different sonorities were brought into play, which intervals assumed prominence, and many other details concerning chord color.

A comparison between the tertian and post-tertian works points immediately to some striking changes (see Table VIII-2). Consider, for instance, the abrupt cessation or decline in use of a number of traditional sonorities: triads (of all four types), minor-minor and diminished-seventh chords, major-minor seventh chords (that is, V7), and French sixth chords. Only the *Lyric Suite* movement shows, significantly, a residue of these "chords-in-thirds."

Now, looking at the total number of different vertical sonorities to appear in these same compositions, we see, somewhat surprisingly, that Schoenberg and Berg, in their post-tertian works, call upon even more kinds of chords than in their earlier pieces (see Table VIII-3).[6] The movement from *Pierrot Lunaire* seems especially astonishing in

[5] A list of interval vectors is published by Allen Forte as part of his article "A Theory of Set-Complexes for Music," in *Journal of Music Theory*, VIII (1964), 145–148. This list I have numbered and correlated with my own list of chords of 0-12 pitch classes. One correction to Mr. Forte's list might be made here: of the distinct 7-note sets, set no. 8 should read 454422 rather than 454442.

[6] The total number of 0-12-note chords is 352, and does not include transpositions, octave displacements, or Rameau-type inversions.

Table VIII-2. Comparisons of chord content

Per cent of	Tertian			Post-tertian			
	VN	Q(05)	QV	PL	LS	Q(38)	Q(14)
Single notes	5	12	18	24	4	27	0
Intervals	8	6	19	13	2	36	16
Triads	16	27	9	2	8	3	0
Minor-minor and dim.- minor 7th	15	3	1	0	7	0	0
Dim.-7th	9	0	1	0	2	0	0
Major-minor 7th	5	1	2	0	4	0	0
French sixth	1	5	8	0	2	0	0

Other sonorities, making up a total of 100%, are not included in this table.

this regard, since 153 different sonorities appear within the relatively brief time span of 53 measures. Stravinsky and Webern, on the other hand, move in the very opposite direction, adopting a more sparse or ascetic chord vocabulary in their later pieces.

Still another program was designed to take percentages of the number of pitch classes sounding simultaneously at various points during a composition, that is, the proportion of the total duration taken up by chords of 0 pitch classes (rests), of 1 pitch class (single notes), of 2 (intervals), and so on (see Table VIII-4). In this way one arrives at an impression of the "relative density" of a composition. We notice, for example, that the earlier works tended to emphasize four-note chords (mostly in the form of seventh or incomplete ninth chords); although Webern's first quartet, exceptionally, showed a greater abundance of three-note sonorities, due mostly to the importance of augmented triads in the section that was tested. The later pieces reveal two opposing tendencies, toward simpler and at the same time toward more complex chord forms. Webern, as might be

Table VIII-3. Comparisons of total number of chords used

Tertian			Post-tertian			
VN	Q(05)	QV	PL	LS	Q(38)	Q(14)
90	68	36	153	99	33	27

Table VIII-4. Number of pitch classes employed

| No. of PCs | Percentage of total duration of composition | | | | | | |
| | Tertian | | | Post-tertian | | | |
	VN	Q(05)	QV	PL	LS	Q(38)	Q(14)
0	1.03	4.40	2.95	.78	1.51	9.07	
1	5.76	11.61	17.75	32.15	3.83	26.54	
2	7.90	6.55	18.63	10.77	2.06	39.15	15.86
3	22.60	44.37	21.00	4.48	22.68	22.56	58.41
4	48.18	32.40	34.02	9.14	61.23	2.65	25.24
5	13.66	.64	4.73	18.63	7.86		.48
6	.84		.88	23.97	.80		

expected, displayed an unusually high proportion of rests: nine per cent in his later quartet (and already four per cent in the early one). Both Webern and Schoenberg show a significant increase in the use of single notes (while, surprisingly, Stravinsky's quartet movement is entirely lacking in 0 and 1 note chords). On the other hand, Schoenberg's *Serenade* (tested without *Sprechstimme*) [7] revealed an uncommonly large number of six-note chords (almost 24 per cent), and Berg's *Lyric Suite* movement an even more noteworthy proportion of four-note chords (61 per cent), no doubt because of the favor accorded seventh-chord formations in this piece.

Turning now to a more detailed consideration of the kinds of chords employed, we find the following sonorities as most prominent within the total time span of the compositions (see Table VIII-5).

Here one is struck in the Schoenberg excerpt by the rather large percentage of seventh chords—diminished-minor, major-minor, and diminished—making up fully a quarter of the total sound duration, and by the significant proportion of time taken up by the minor triad (8 per cent). Webern, however, even in 1905, seems to have been less inclined to incorporate this voluptuous sounding seventh-chord vocabulary into his work, allowing triads instead—and especially the augmented triad—to assume the central position. Scriabin, aside from emphasizing single notes (18 per cent), allotted about a quarter of his

[7] The movement from *Pierrot Lunaire* was tested both with and without the part for *Sprechstimme* in an effort to determine whether the *Sprechstimme* notes in any way contributed to or detracted from the harmonic design. In this piece at least, the latter seems to be the case, since the voice part occasionally "cancels out" recurrent harmonic patterns that are present in the accompaniment.

Table VIII-5. Sonorities used most prominently in the early pieces

Sonorities	Percentage of total duration of composition		
	VN	Q(05)	QV
Rest		4.40	
Single note	5.76	11.61	17.75
Min. 3rd	3.30		
Maj. 3rd		4.49	9.76
Min. triad	8.09	4.00	
Maj. triad	4.08	9.18	7.10
Aug. triad		12.74	
Aug. 4th + min. 7th		4.08	7.98
Dim.-min. 7 chd.	12.50		
Maj.-min. 7 chd.	4.85		
Dim. 7 chd.	8.87		
Fr. 6 chd.		4.53	7.98
V9 chd.			4.14
Aug. triad + min. 7th			12.72

total sound duration to three quite closely related sonorities: the French sixth chord, the "dominant" ninth chord (without a fifth), and the augmented triad plus minor seventh. A rather special interest involved finding out how much of the total time was taken up by Scriabin's so-called "mystic" chord (that is, C F♯ B♭ E A D, or its transpositions). Interestingly enough, this chord never once appeared in its complete form; and yet of the 36 total chord forms, most would form parts of this basic chord. For example, chord number 22 (.100000100010), which makes up 7.98 per cent of the total, represents its lower three notes (and 85 per cent of the time this chord, like the parent chord, appeared in root position).

A separate routine indicated on which scale degrees the roots of chords [8] most frequently appeared. Here no particular pattern of emphasis emerged except in Scriabin's piece, which gave striking evidence of a strong F-major orientation. For of the French sixth chords two-thirds occurred on D♭, of the ninth chords three-sevenths on C, and of the major triads three-fourths on F.

[8] The assigning of roots to chords is, of course, somewhat arbitrary. My procedure was, whenever possible, to arrange the notes into tertian formations, in which the "bottom" note would be considered the root.

A further program tested the interval vectors in these earlier works. Generally the minor second was slighted (and was almost totally absent in Webern's piece), which points to a less "harsh" sound than in the later pieces. In *Verklaerte Nacht* two (of the 64) vectors made up nearly 30 per cent of the total: .001110 (12.17 per cent) and .012111 (17.35 per cent). And in Scriabin's *Quasi Valse*, looking at its vectors in general, there was an interesting emphasis upon the major second, major third, and augmented fourth. By adding together the percentages for each interval within the interval vectors, we arrive at the following totals (that is, for how much of the total duration chords contained minor seconds, major seconds, and so on):

Intervallic Content of Scriabin's Quasi Valse

Interval	Percentage of total duration
Minor 2	8
Major 2	50
Minor 3	27
Major 3	67
Perfect 4	24
Augmented 4	51

Turning our attention now to the later compositions, one is impressed most strongly by what seems a deliberate avoidance of the tertian chord forms (Berg's *Lyric Suite* movement providing the only exception). Stravinsky's *String Quartet,* for example, is a most unusual movement, in which the entire continuity is made up of four separate ostinato patterns, one for each instrument. The notes of these patterns are as follows:

Cello	*Second violin*	*First violin*	*Viola*
C Db Eb	C♯ D♯ E F♯	G A B C	C♯ D

These ostinato notes coincide variously as the composition proceeds. But what at first might seem to be an arbitrary or accidental congruence of tones is in reality a cleverly calculated organization. For of the 27 chord forms not a one fits the traditional tertian mould (despite the fact that tertian chords could easily have been obtained from the ostinato notes present). The most prominent of the chords used are the following (some of which can only be indicated by their decimal form, in which a "1" stands for the position of a note in the octave):

Most Frequent Chord Forms in Stravinsky's String Quartet

Chord forms	Percentage of total duration
Min. 2nd	12.50
.111000000000	7.69
.100000110000	7.45
Aug. 4th + maj. 7th	7.69
Perf. 5th + maj. 7th	14.18
Min. 3rd + maj. 3rd	8.17
Maj. 2nd + min. 3rd	7.69
.100111000000	6.49

Three chords in particular stand out; and one notices also their stationary position tonally, for the first is always based on the note D, the third on the note B, and the second almost invariably on the note D (see Example VIII-1).

Example VIII-1.

From this, one draws the conclusion that Stravinsky had something like a basic sonority in mind, one consisting of a minor second plus some other note or notes spaced at varying distances. This may be seen more clearly by examining the interval vector content, wherein the following four forms make up over 50 per cent of the piece:

.111000	9.13%
.101100	8.17%
.100110	18.26%
.100011	15.14%

In fact, every one of the interval vectors contains a minor second. And this, along with the persistent ostinato melodic patterns, must contribute to the general feeling of flatness or lack of dynamic direction that prevails in the composition.

Webern, in the opening movement of his Opus 28, shows a characteristic preference for simple sonorities. Of a total of 33 different chord forms, 28 correspond with the first, and most simple, chords in the chord table. These include mostly rests, single notes, and intervals, which appear in the following percentages:

Most Frequent Sonorities in Webern's Opus 28 (First Movement)

Sonorities	Percentage of total duration
Rest	9.07
Single note	26.54
Minor 2	6.41
Major 2	5.08
Minor 3	10.84
Major 3	11.72
Perfect 4	3.09
Augmented 4	1.99

These constitute, then, about 75 per cent of the composition. Triads are not altogether excluded, but are relatively unimportant (minor triad: 1.10 per cent; major triad: .88 per cent; augmented triad: .44 per cent).

In Varèse's *Intégrales* (of which only the first 38 measures came under consideration in this particular test) four chord forms made up most of the continuity. The principal sonority is a seven-note cluster built on the note A (23 per cent). It appears, at least in this excerpt, that Varèse, like Stravinsky, prefers to keep his chords stationary, that is, built on particular scale degrees.

Chord Content in Varèse's Intégrales (*m. 1-38*)

Chord forms	Percentage of total duration
Single note	58.55 (mostly on B♭)
Maj. 3 + min. 7 + maj. 7	7.00 (all on B)
.111110110000	23.33 (all on A)
.111111111110	1.55 (all on C♯)

Once again Berg's *Lyric Suite* movement represents a more conservative posture. One notices a de-emphasis of minor seconds and augmented fourths, and (as in the tertian pieces) a stressing of minor and major thirds, as well as perfect fourths. In all, 69 different interval vectors were employed; but, of these, 12 accounted for more than 50 per cent of the total continuity, a striking indication that a prevailing unity of sound exists in this work.

Dissonance Content

One's method of analyzing dissonances reflects, to be sure, some personal bias. In this project, for example, dissonant intervals were measured from the lowest note in a chord (rather than from its root), and rhythmic stress was not included as part of the definition. Briefly, the machine was instructed to examine each vertical sonority, no matter how transitory, determine which of its notes were dissonant, and then, on the basis of voice leading, assign these dissonances to various categories such as escape tone, retardation, and so on. Most problematical was to tell the machine what to do when it encountered sonorities containing both a sixth and a fifth, or a major and a minor third, both of which were consonant in themselves but created a dissonant clash because of their combination. It was decided to regard as dissonant whichever note or notes moved melodically from the point of dissonance to resolution. In conclusion the computer tabulated the percentage of each type of dissonance, and added a further break-down by interval and by pitch class of dissonance.

In comparing the early and late pieces one notices a marked de-crease in the use of dissonances involving traditional voice leading, and in their place a greater frequency of what I have called free dissonances (that is, a dissonant note both leapt to and from, or one with a rest immediately preceding or following). Since the actual quantity of dissonances does not noticeably change, one suspects that the "highly dissonant" effect of much post-tertian music may be due more to a greater freedom of voice leading than to dissonance *per se*. A dissonance, as Stravinsky says, "is neither required to prepare itself nor be resolved"; it becomes, as we have noticed with the chord content as well, "an entity in itself." [9]

This change becomes evident when we compare the kinds of disso-nances that assumed most prominence in the earlier works with those of the later works (see Table VIII-6).

The distribution of dissonances by pitch classes showed an empha-sis on certain pitches in the earlier works, but no noticeable distinction in the later ones (except in Stravinsky's *Quartet*, due to its peculiar ostinato structure). Thus in the opening of Berg's *Piano Sonata* most of the dissonances fell on A, B♭, D, and G; whereas in the *Lyric Suite* the pitches are about equally represented (each taking between 7 and 11 per cent).

In comparing the actual intervals of dissonance little difference between early and late works could be discerned. Webern's *Quartet*, Opus 28, second movement, however, did seem unusual in that of the 47 dissonances only 4 were minor seconds and 3 were major sevenths. These sharper dissonances were probably intended to provide climac-

---

[9] See his *Poetics of Music*, New York, Vintage, 1956, pp. 36–37.

Table VIII-6. Comparative frequency of dissonances
(only the highest percentages are given)

| | Percentage of types of dissonances | | | | |
| | Tertian | | Post-tertian | | |
Dissonances	Q(05) (M. 1-11)	PS	LS	Q(38) (2nd Mvt.)	Q(14)
Appoggiatura	11				7
Escape tune	15	12	24		
Free	17	16	34	88	35
Lower auxiliary					7
Parallel	13			12	5
Passing tone	16				7
Retardation					13
Suspension	8	26			
Upper auxiliary					19

tic emphasis since they all appear quite close together, about two-thirds of the way through the piece.

Finally, the computer printout permits an easy scansion of what might be termed "dissonance rhythm," that is, the rate of dissonant notes compared with the passage of time. In the *Verklaerte Nacht* excerpt, for instance, we notice a highly uneven rate of change. The opening measures (1–10) fluctuate from few to many (due in part to voice doublings) to fewer dissonances.

Rate of Dissonances in Verklaerte Nacht

This stands in marked contrast with the more static dissonance rate in Webern's *Quartet,* Opus 28, second movement, wherein nearly every measure contains the same number of dissonances.

Recurrent Chord Progressions

An initial step in the programming of more long-range harmonic relationships may be seen in the testing for recurrent chord succes-.sions.[10] For the present, a repeated pattern was defined as any sequence of 2, 3, 4, or more chords, irrespective of their tonal positions (thus a pattern of a minor triad to half-diminished seventh chord to

[10] This program owed much of its initial stimulation to John Selleck's and Roger Bakeman's "Procedures for the Analysis of Form: Two Computer Applications," *Journal of Music Theory,* IX (1965), 281–293. I am grateful to Mr. Selleck for sending me a copy of the FORTRAN program described in the article.

single note, and so on, was considered, no matter if the roots or position of these sonorities changed).

The program was designed to take each two successive chords in a piece, then look for a match throughout the remainder of the piece. The same is done for three-chord successions, then four, and so on, until no match is found, at which point the program is terminated.

On the basis of this analysis the "harmonic form" of a composition becomes clearly visible, and might be reconstructed as a diagram, as I have done here with Scriabin's *Quasi Valse* (see Table VIII-7). This diagram, to be sure, is somewhat disproportionate to the original, since the chord numbers take up more space than do the chords in the actual music. In all, fourteen nonexpansible patterns (some of them very brief) were discovered in the Scriabin piece. It seems significant that only rarely are these patterns repeated more than one time, and that usually a repetition stands in close proximity to the original statement.

Turning to a general comparison between several pieces, Table VIII-8 indicates: (1) the total number of repeated patterns occurring in a piece; (2) how often these patterns appeared independently of a larger pattern (that is, the encircled numbers in Table VIII-7 above), how often they were repeated once, twice, or more than twice; (3) the number of chords making up the patterns; and (4) how often the patterns were repeated within a measure or two of the original presentation. In the earlier works we observe a greater frequency of patterns containing more than two chords (45 in VN as opposed to 4 in PL). Both *Verklaerte Nacht* and the early Webern *Quartet* exhibit fairly lengthy patterns of 16 and 22 chords respectively. It may seem curious that *Pierrot Lunaire* (minus the part for *Sprechstimme*) does contain a 19-chord pattern—due to a repeated accompanimental figure beginning in measure 30—which is, however, canceled out by the *Sprechstimme*. Both the early and late pieces show a considerable number of patterns that are repeated only once, and usually in close proximity to the original statement. Thus in the *Pierrot Lunaire* example of 28 patterns in all, 17 were repeated once, 13 in consecutive measures; and in the *Lyric Suite* 82 (of 94) were repeated once, 31 in consecutive measures.

Some of the patterns uncovered by the computer pose an intriguing question: Is the repetition part of the composer's artistic intention, or has the machine simply come across accidental correspondences? In an example such as the following taken from the first part of Webern's *Quartet*, Opus 28, the relationship indeed seems fortuitous since it involves different chord roots, positions, spacings (see Example VIII-2). And yet the fact that the recurrence takes place immediately may

Table VIII-7. Repeated chord patterns in Scriabin's QUASI VALSE *

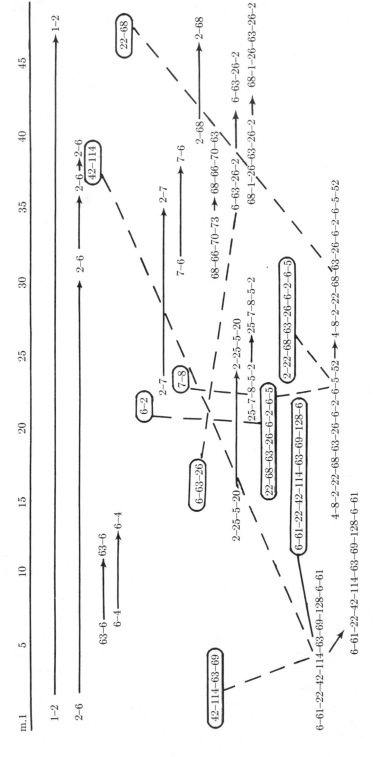

* Numbers indicate position of chord in the chord table; circles and dotted lines indicate that the pattern is only part of a larger pattern.

Table VIII-8. Repetitions of chord patterns

	Tertian		Post-tertian			
Repetitions	VN	Q(05)	PL	PL *	LS	Q(38) (2nd Mvt.)
(1) Total no. of repets.	97	81	28	26	94	10
(2) No. occur. indep.	29	15	2	6	4	1
No. repeated once	62	49	17	14	82	7
No. repeated twice	5	10	5	6	7	2
No. repeated more than twice	2	5	4	0	1	0
(3) 2-chd. repets.	17	60	24	19	85	9
3-chd. repets.	24	12	4	2	5	1
More than 3-chd. repets.	21	9	0	5	4	0
Longest repet.	16-chd.	22-chd.	3	19	6	3
(4) No. of repets. in consec. meas.	40	17	13	9	31	8

* Not including the part for *Sprechstimme.*

Example VIII-2.

m. 5-7

m. 8-9

point to its deliberate use. If this is the case the computer has revealed to us what may be an important form of variation technique (purely intervallic in nature) that we would normally have overlooked.

The same question arises in the following repetitions from Schoenberg's *Pierrot Lunaire*, but in reference to an even more minute pattern, consisting of two intervals, a diminished fifth followed by a major third, which recur each time with different notes, different rhythms, etc. (see Example VIII-3). Again the pattern is stated in close proximity, making its conscious use as such at least plausible.

In summary, we have noticed especially the sudden decline in the later pieces of the use of traditional, or tertian, types of chords, the abandoning of smooth or conventional voice leading in the resolution of dissonances, and the general absence of lengthy repeated patterns of chords. Thus one's initial impression is of a general lack of harmonic order in the later works (with the *Lyric Suite* providing the most notable exception). At the same time, however, a few hints of possible new kinds of organization suggested themselves. In the use of dissonance one piece (by Webern) showed a quite calculated placement of more acute intervals at the climax of the continuity. And, as we have just observed, repetitive intervallic patterns may have been consciously employed by Webern and Schoenberg. But the most interesting and tangible new development, observed especially in

Example VIII-3.

m. 27   m. 29   m. 30

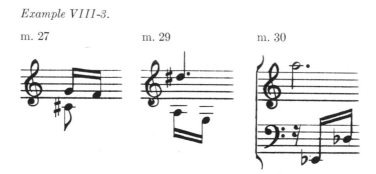

Webern, Stravinsky, and Varèse lay in what seems their deliberate selection of certain harmonic colors within a given composition, thereby limiting themselves to a few predominant sonorities which do not return in any set order but are heard frequently enough to provide a sense of unity within the piece as a whole. And in the discerning of all these (possibly) new forms of harmonic ordering, the computer has shown itself to be a most invaluable, if not indeed indispensable, guide.

Automated Discovery of Similar Segments in the Forty-eight Permutations of a Twelve-Tone Row

by GERALD LEFKOFF

In each group of forty-eight permutations of the twelve pitch classes which are derived from a twelve-tone row by the traditional procedures of inversion, retrogression, retrograde-inversion, and transposition, there are segments of various permutations in the group which are similar to each other in certain ways. This paper is concerned only with permutation segments which are similar in either of two ways, namely (1) identical unordered pitch-class sets (that is, segments which have identical pitch classes) and (2) identical ordered pitch-class sets (that is, segments which have identical pitch classes in the identical order). The second type is a subclass of the first type.

The frequency, size, location, and content of permutation segments with identical pitch classes (ordered or unordered) is unique to each permutation group. While the conditions which determine the recurrence of such segments within a group can be formalized, the actual recurrence within a group depends upon the particular ordering of the pitch classes in the row. Hence these recurrent segments must be searched out independently for each permutation group. Computer programs which discover all recurrent segments of the type mentioned are described in this paper. If the discovery of these recurrent segments is of use, the automated discovery of these patterns by computer is of value in that it is more efficient and often more accurate and thorough than a manual search.

Three uses are suggested for lists of recurrent permutation segments. First, they may be used in association with compositional procedures in determining characteristics of the row which may be emphasized or avoided and in selecting particular permutations used in the composition. Secondly, they may be used in association with analytical operations. These may include the operations of reconstructing the probable permutation structural scheme used by the composer, of searching for motives and chordal entities, and of searching for relations of pitch-class sets which produce a kind of "tonality." Thirdly, they may be used in association with the theoretical exploration of permutation groups to answer such questions as the following: What are the frequency and association limitations on recurrent permutation segments in the forty-eight permutation group? What significant classifications of tone rows according to recurrent permutation segments in the permutation group can be stated?

In the version of the program used to produce the examples, the twelve pitch classes are represented by the integers 0, 1, 2, . . . , 11. Zero can represent any pitch class like a movable "do." (Another version of the programs will use note letter names in which C replaces zero.)

The input is the twelve integers which represent P_0, the prime form of the row with a transposition value of zero. The program prints out the forty-eight permutations as shown in Figure IX-1. The prime (P) and retrograde (R) permutations, and the inversion (I) and retrograde-inversion (RI) permutations are placed side by side respectively. The column headings 1, 2, 3, . . . , 12 following the letters P, R, I, and RI indicate the ordinal position of the pitch classes in the permutations below. The row headings 0, 1, 2, . . . , 11 in the columns below the letters P, R, I, and RI indicate the transposition value of the permutation which follows. Each row of twelve integers, read from left to right, represents one of the permutations in the group.

The individual permutations are designated in the subsequent program in the usual manner with the letters P, R, I, and RI followed by the transposition value of the permutation. A standard arrangement of the permutations in the group is used in which the P and I forms with identical transposition values begin with the same pitch class, and the P and R forms and I and RI forms, respectively, with identical transposition values exchange their first and last pitch classes. In the example, the first pitch class of the P and I forms and the last pitch class in the R and RI forms correspond to the transposition value. This correspondence is not required however by the program.

The location of a permutation segment in the group is designated

Permutations of a Twelve-Tone Row   149

48 FERMUTATICNS DERIVED FROM AN ORDERED 12 PITCH CLASS SET

PRIME

P	1	2	3	4	5	6	7	8	9	10	11	12
0-	0	11	7	8	3	1	2	10	6	5	4	9
1-	1	0	8	9	4	2	3	11	7	6	5	10
2-	2	1	9	10	5	3	4	0	8	7	6	11
3-	3	2	10	11	6	4	5	1	9	8	7	0
4-	4	3	11	0	7	5	6	2	10	9	8	1
5-	5	4	0	1	8	6	7	3	11	10	9	2
6-	6	5	1	2	9	7	8	4	0	11	10	3
7-	7	6	2	3	10	8	9	5	1	0	11	4
8-	8	7	3	4	11	9	10	6	2	1	0	5
9-	9	8	4	5	0	10	11	7	3	2	1	6
10-	10	9	5	6	1	11	0	8	4	3	2	7
11-	11	10	6	7	2	0	1	9	5	4	3	8

RETROGRADE

R	1	2	3	4	5	6	7	8	9	10	11	12
0-	9	4	5	6	10	2	1	3	8	7	11	0
1-	10	5	6	7	11	3	2	4	9	8	0	1
2-	11	6	7	8	0	4	3	5	10	9	1	2
3-	0	7	8	9	1	5	4	6	11	10	2	3
4-	1	8	9	10	2	6	5	7	0	11	3	4
5-	2	9	10	11	3	7	6	8	1	0	4	5
6-	3	10	11	0	4	8	7	9	2	1	5	6
7-	4	11	0	1	5	9	8	10	3	2	6	7
8-	5	0	1	2	6	10	9	11	4	3	7	8
9-	6	1	2	3	7	11	10	0	5	4	8	9
10-	7	2	3	4	8	0	11	1	6	5	9	10
11-	8	3	4	5	9	1	0	2	7	6	10	11

INVERSION

I	1	2	3	4	5	6	7	8	9	10	11	12
0-	0	1	5	4	9	11	10	2	6	7	8	3
1-	1	2	6	5	10	0	11	3	7	8	9	4
2-	2	3	7	6	11	1	0	4	8	9	10	5
3-	3	4	8	7	0	2	1	5	9	10	11	6
4-	4	5	9	8	1	3	2	6	10	11	0	7
5-	5	6	10	9	2	4	3	7	11	0	1	8
6-	6	7	11	10	3	5	4	8	0	1	2	9
7-	7	8	0	11	4	6	5	9	1	2	3	10
8-	8	9	1	0	5	7	6	10	2	3	4	11
9-	9	10	2	1	6	8	7	11	3	4	5	0
10-	10	11	3	2	7	9	8	0	4	5	6	1
11-	11	0	4	3	8	10	9	1	5	6	7	2

RETROGRADE INVERSION

RI	1	2	3	4	5	6	7	8	9	10	11	12
0-	3	8	7	6	2	10	11	9	4	5	1	0
1-	4	9	8	7	3	11	0	10	5	6	2	1
2-	5	10	9	8	4	0	1	11	6	7	3	2
3-	6	11	10	9	5	1	2	0	7	8	4	3
4-	7	0	11	10	6	2	3	1	8	9	5	4
5-	8	1	0	11	7	3	4	2	9	10	6	5
6-	9	2	1	0	8	4	5	3	10	11	7	6
7-	10	3	2	1	9	5	6	4	11	0	8	7
8-	11	4	3	2	10	6	7	5	0	1	9	8
9-	0	5	4	3	11	7	8	6	1	2	10	9
10-	1	6	5	4	0	8	9	7	2	3	11	10
11-	2	7	6	5	1	9	10	8	3	4	0	11

Figure IX-1. Forty-eight permutations derived from an ordered 12-pitch-class set

by reference to the permutation in which it is found, followed by the integers in parenthesis which indicate the ordinal location of the first and last position occupied by the segment. Hence the designation $RI9(3\text{-}7)$, indicates a permutation segment which is found in the RI permutation with a transposition value of nine which begins with the third position and ends with the seventh.

For each permutation segment there are eleven other segments which are found in the same ordinal position in the same permutation form which have the identical intervallic relationship between the pitch classes although the pitch classes themselves differ. In the program only one of these segments is given. The rest can be easily calculated. Hence, if the ordered set $\{0, 5, 1\}$ is found at $P3(7\text{-}9)$ then the set $\{1, 6, 2\}$ is found at $P4(7\text{-}9)$, the set $\{2, 7, 3\}$ is found at $P5(7\text{-}9)$, the set $\{9, 2, 10\}$ is found at $Po(7\text{-}9)$, and so forth. These related segments are found by adding, in Modulo 12, the same transposition value to each of the pitch classes in the segment and to the transposition value of the permutation form. Only the prototype of the group of twelve is listed in the program for the sake of simplicity in the output, since excessive output tends to obscure the elemental relationships.

The choice of prototype of the recurrent segments are as follows. For the ordered sets, that transposition of the permutation is used in which the first pitch class is zero. The choice of prototype for unordered segments is somewhat more involved. Since these sets are unordered, the actual pitch classes may occur in any order in various permutation segments. In the prototype the pitch classes are given in ascending order, and the transposition chosen is such that the first pitch class is zero, and the smallest interval span between the first and last pitch classes is used. If more than one transposition yields the same minimum interval span, the transposition which yields the first lowest number after the zero is selected. This is a standard form which is often used to represent classes of pitch-class sets. However, in this program the prototype of unordered pitch-class sets represent actual pitch classes. Hence, if the unordered pitch-class set $\{0, 3, 4, 8\}$ is found at $RI2(3\text{-}6)$ then the unordered set $\{3, 6, 7, 11\}$ is found at $RI5(3\text{-}6)$, and so forth.

Some ordered pitch-class sets retain their identity under the operation of retrogression or retrograde-inversion at one of the twelve transpositions. When listed in the output, these types are labeled R or RI, respectively. The ordered set $\{0, 1, 7, 6\}$ is an example of the type which retains its identity upon retrogression and is labeled R, and $\{0, 1, 3, 4\}$ is an example of one which retains its identity upon retrograde-inversion and is labeled RI.

Some unordered pitch-class sets retain their identity at several transpositions. An example is the set $\{0, 1, 3, 6, 7, 9\}$. This set retains its identity under two transpositions (0 and 6). This includes a transposition of zero under which all sets retain their identity. Some unordered pitch-class sets retain their identity upon inversion. An example is the set $\{0, 1, 3, 4\}$. Most unordered pitch-class sets which retain their identity upon inversion also retain their identity under several transpositions. The set $\{0, 4, 8\}$ (the augmented triad) is an example of such a set. When listed in the output, the unordered sets are labeled according to the operations under which they retain their identity, as follows. A set which retains its identity only in the prime form is labeled P. One which retains its identity in both prime form and inverted form is labeled PI. The letters P or PI are preceded by the integer which indicates the number of transpositions under which

```
1PI  0  1
       P 1( 1- 2)      R 1(11-12)
       I C( 1- 2)     RI C(11-12)
       P 5( 3- 4)      R 5( 9-10)
       I 8( 3- 4)     RI 8( 9-10)
       P11( 6- 7)     R11( 6- 7)
       I 2( 6- 7)     RI 2( 6- 7)
       P 7( 9-10)      R 7( 3- 4)
       I 8( 9-10)     RI 8( 3- 4)
       P 8(1C-11)      R P( 2- 3)
       I 5(1C-11)     RI 5( 2- 3)

1PI  0  4
       P 5( 2- 3)      R 5(1C-11)
       I11( 2- 3)     RI11(1C-11)
       P 2( 7- 8)      R 2( 5- 6)
       I 2( 7- 8)     RI 2( 5- 6)
       P 6( 8- 9)      R 6( 4- 5)
       I1C( 8- 9)     RI1C( 4- 5)

1PI  0  5
       P 5( 4- 5)      R 5( 8- 9)
       I 8( 4- 5)     RI 8( 8- 9)
       P 8(11-12)      R 8( 1- 2)
       I 5(11-12)     RI 5( 1- 2)

1PI  0  2
       P11( 5- 6)     F11( 7- 8)
       I 3( 5- 6)     RI 3( 7- 8)

1P  0  4  5                             0  1  5
       P 5( 1- 3)      R 5(1C-12)      I 0( 1- 3)      RI 0(10-12)
       P 5( 3- 5)      R 5( 8-10)      I 8( 3- 5)     RI 8( 8-10)
       I1C( 8-10)     R11C( 3- 5)      P 7( 8-10)      R 7( 3- 5)
       I 5(1C-12)     RI 5( 1- 3)      P 8(10-12)      R 8( 1- 3)

1P  0  1  4                             0  3  4
       P 5( 2- 4)      R 5( 9-11)      I11( 2- 4)      RI11( 9-11)
       I 2( 6- 8)     RI 2( 5- 7)      P 2( 6- 8)      R 2( 5- 7)

1PI  0  2  7
       P11( 4- 6)     F11( 7- 9)
       I 3( 4- 6)     RI 3( 7- 9)

1PI  0  1  2
       P11( 5- 7)     F11( 6- 8)
       I 3( 5- 7)     RI 3( 6- 8)
       P 8( 5-11)      R 8( 2- 4)
       I 6( 5-11)     RI 6( 2- 4)

3PI  0  4  8
       P1C( 7- 9)     F1C( 4- 6)
       I1C( 7- 9)     RI1C( 4- 6)
       P 6( 7- 9)      R 6( 4- C)
       I 6( 7- 9)     RI 6( 4- 6)
       P 2( 7- 9)      R 2( 4- 6)
       I 2( 7- 9)     RI 2( 4- 6)

1PI  0  1  4  5
       P 5( 1- 4)      R 5( 9-12)
       I C( 1- 4)     RI C( 9-12)

1P  0  1  4  8                          0  3  4  8
       P 5( 2- 5)      R 5( 8-11)      I11( 2- 5)      RI11( 8-11)
       I 2( 6- 9)     RI 2( 4- 7)      P 2( 6- 9)      R 2( 4- 7)
       I 8( 7-10)     RI 6( 3- 6)      P10( 7-10)      R10( 3- 6)

1PI  0  1  2  7
       P11( 4- 7)     F11( 6- 9)
       I 3( 4- 7)     RI 3( 6- 9)

1P  0  3  4  5                          0  1  2  5
       P 2( 5- 8)      R 2( 5- 8)      I 3( 5- 8)      RI 3( 5- 8)
       I 5( 9-12)     RI 5( 1- 4)      P 8( 9-12)      R 8( 1- 4)

1P  0  1  4  5  8                       0  3  4  7  8
       P 5( 1- 5)      R 5( 8-12)      I 3( 1- 5)      RI 3( 8-12)
       I 6( 6-10)     RI 6( 3- 7)      P 2( 6-10)      R 2( 3- 7)

1PI  0  3  4  5  8
       P 2( 5- 9)      R 2( 4- 8)
       I 8( 5- 9)     RI 8( 4- 8)

1P  0  1  4  5  6  8                    0  2  3  4  7  8
       P 5( 1- 6)      R 5( 7-12)      I 3( 1- 6)      RI 3( 7-12)
       I1C( 7-12)     R110( 1- 6)      P10( 7-12)      R10( 1- 6)

1PI  0  1  2  5  7  9
       P11( 4- 9)     F11( 4- 9)
       I 3( 4- 9)     RI 3( 4- 9)

1PI  0  1  2  4  5  7  8  9
       P 6( 2- 9)      R 6( 4-11)
       I 3( 2- 9)     RI 3( 4-11)

1P  0  1  2  4  5  6  7  8  9           0  1  2  3  4  5  7  8  9
       P 6( 1- 9)      R 6( 4-12)      I 3( 1- 9)      RI 3( 4-12)
       I1C( 4-12)     R11C( 1- 9)      P11( 4-12)      R11( 1- 9)

1PI  0  1  2  3  4  5  7  8  9 10
       P 2( 1-10)      R 2( 3-12)
       I 3( 1-10)     RI 3( 3-12)

1PI  0  1  2  3  4  5  6  7  9 10
       P11( 2-11)     R11( 2-11)
       I 8( 2-11)     RI 8( 2-11)
```

Figure IX-2. Recurrent unordered pitch-class sets

The Computer and Music

it retains its identity. The minimum is one (for transposition of zero), and *P* is always present. The set {0, 3, 4} is labeled 1*P* since it retains its identity only in prime form for transposition zero. The set {0, 6} is labeled 2*PI*, since it retains its identity as prime under two transpositions and its identity under *I* for two transpositions. The set {0, 1, 3, 6, 7, 9} is labeled 2*P*.

The ordered sets which are labeled *R* and *RI* and the unordered sets which are labeled *PI* or which retain their identity under more than one transposition of necessity are found in more than one of the permutations in the group. Hence the special attention which they receive in the program.

Figure IX-2 is the list of recurrent unordered pitch-class sets (size 2 to 10) with their locations, which occur in the permutation group found in Figure IX-1. Figure IX-3 is the list of recurrent ordered pitch-class sets (size 2 to 12) with their locations, which occur in the permutation group found in Figure IX-1. The permutation group in

```
RECURRENT ORDERED SEGMENTS

RI    0 11                    0  1
      P C( 1- 2)              I C( 1- 2)
      P E( 9-10)              I E( 9-10)
      P 7(10-11)              I 5(10-11)
      I 7( 2- 4)              P 5( 3- 4)
      I 1( 6- 7)              P11( 6- 7)
      RIC( 6- 7)              RI 2( 6- 7)
      R 4( 9-10)              RI E( 9-10)
      RI 4( 2- 3)             R 8( 2- 3)
      RI 5( 2- 4)             R 7( 3- 4)
      RI11(11-12)             R 1(11-12)

RI    0  6                    0  4
      P 1( 2- 3)              I11( 2- 3)
      P1C( 7- 6)              I 2( 7- 8)
      P 2( 6- 5)              I1C( 8- 9)
      RI 6( 4- 5)             R E( 4- 5)
      RI1C( 5- 6)             R 2( 5- 6)
      RI 7(1C-11)             R 5(10-11)

RI    0  7                    0  5
      P 4( 4- 5)              I E( 4- 5)
      I 4(11-12)              P 8(11-12)
      P 3( 1- 2)              RI 5( 1- 2)
      RI 3( 6- 5)             R 5( 8- 9)

RI    0 1C                    0  2
      P 5( 5- 6)              I 3( 5- 6)
      RI 1( 7- 6)             R11( 7- 8)

      0 11  7                 0  1  5         0  4  5         0  8  7
      P C( 1- 3)              I C( 1- 3)      R 5(10-12)      RI 7(10-12)
      RI 5( 2- 5)             R 7( 3- 5)      I1C( 8-10)      P 2( 8-10)

      0  6  5                 0  4  3         0 11  3         0  1  9
      P 1( 2- 4)              I11( 2- 4)      R 4( 9-11)      RI 6( 9-11)
      RI1C( 5- 7)             R 2( 5- 7)      I 1( 6- 8)      P11( 6- 8)

      0  1  E                 0 11  4         0  5  4         0  7  8
      P E( 3- 5)              I 7( 3- 5)      R 9( 8-10)      RI 3( 8-10)
      I 5(1C-12)              P 7(10-12)      RI 9( 1- 3)     R 3( 1- 3)

RI    0  6  4                 0  4  8
      P1C( 7- 5)              I 2( 7- 9)
      RI 6( 4- 6)             R 6( 4- 6)

RI    0 11 1C                 0  1  2
      P 6( 5-11)              I 6( 9-11)
      RI 4( 2- 4)             R 8( 2- 4)
```

Figure IX-3. Recurrent ordered pitch-class sets

Figure IX-1 is that used by Schoenberg in his *Fourth String Quartet, Opus 37.*

The format of the output found in Figure IX-2 is as follows. A blank line appears before the appearance of each recurrent segment. At the very beginning of the next line the segment type is labeled (*1P, 2PI, 1PI,* etc.). This is followed on the same line by the pitch classes which occur in the recurrent set. If the set does not retain its identity upon inversion, two sets appear on this line, the second set being the inversion of the first. If the set retains its identity upon inversion, only one set is given. Beneath the appearance of each set is a listing of the locations of its appearance in the permutation group. This list is in two columns with locations in *P* and *R* forms with the same transposition side by side, and in *I* and *RI* forms with the same transposition side by side.

The format of the output found in Figure IX-3 is as follows. A blank line appears before the appearance of each recurrent segment. At the very beginning of the next line the symbols *R* or *RI* appear if the set retains its identity upon retrogression or retrograde-inversion. If the set does not retain its identity upon retrogression or retrograde inversion, four related ordered pitch classes appear on the one line. Taking the first set for reference as a prime form, the second set is its inversion, the third set is its retrograde form, and the last set is its retrograde inversion. If the set retains its identity upon retrogression or retrograde-inversion, only two sets are listed in which the second is the inversion of the first. Beneath the appearance of each set is a listing of the locations of its appearance in the permutation group.

CHAPTER X

FORTRAN Music Programs Involving Numerically Related Tones

by IAN MORTON and JOHN LOFSTEDT

Three FORTRAN programs coupled to numerical definitions of tonal material are described in this article. Two programs for composition and one for the analysis of tonal music are discussed.

Tonal music relies on pitch relationships which can be described numerically by the first four integral primes (1, 3, 5, 7), the first four reciprocal primes (1/1, 1/3, 1/5, 1/7), their multiples (9, 15, 21, 25, 27, etc.) and submultiples (1/9, 1/15, 1/21, 1/25, 1/27, etc).

The interval of the perfect fifth, C to G, for example, may be described as the function 3 since the frequency of G is 3 times that of C. Moreover, since musical tones are related logarithmically to the base 2, the musical octave (the power of 2) has no meaning in this theoretical framework, and G may be said to be related to C by the function 3 irrespective of the octave in which either may appear.

It is also worth noting here that the relationship between G and C may also be described as the function 1/3, since C is obviously 1/3 the frequency of G when G is 3 times the frequency of C. A musical interval does not care whether it is described from below upward or from above downward.

The harmonic major third, C to E, for example, may be similarly described as the function 5 since the frequency of that E is 5 times that of C. As in the case of the perfect fifth, either or both tones may be multiplied or divided by any power of 2 without doing violence to their relationship. It should also be noted again that if E is 5 times C then C is 1/5 E.

As we have seen in the cases of the intervals just described it is not possible to know which tone of an interval, if either, is derived from the other. A tone is said to be "derived" from a "root" when its frequency is the result of multiplication or division of the root frequency by a prime number. A minimum of three tones is required to produce a discreet musical unit which contains an identifiable tone of derivation and tones which are clearly derived from it.

Ambiguity of "roothood" is present, then, with any two isolated tones. It is also present in a structure of three or more tones when no one of the tones can be a root (for example, the diminished triad and the diminished seventh chord), and in any structure in which there are two or more possible roots (for example, the augmented triad).

The simplest possible musical construction in which a tone of derivation is clearly defined is the major or minor triad, which, when major, may be described as three tones at the 1-3-5 relationship (C-G-E, respectively).

A major tonal system (key) can be constructed by disposing three roots at the 3 function from one another ($1/3$-1-3) and erecting major triads upon each. If we take C_1 as the root of the tonic triad, the root of the dominant triad will be G_3, and the root of the subdominant triad will be $F_1/3$. The tonic triad will then be C_1-G_3-E_5; the dominant triad will contain G_3-D_9-B_{15}; the subdominant triad will be composed of $F_1/3$-C_1-$A_5/3$. Since it is more convenient to deal only with integral numbers we clear the fraction by multiplying all of these numbers by 3. The tonal components of our major key now become F_1, C_3, A_5, G_9, E_{15}, D_{27}, and B_{45}.

The minor triad is symmetrical with the major and is an equally primitive unit. It can be described most conveniently and powerfully by the first three reciprocal prime numbers: $1/1$-$1/3$-$1/5$. This view of the minor triad defines it as a manifestation of frequency division in the same manner as the major triad was defined as a manifestation of frequency multiplication. Thus in describing the traditional A-minor triad (A-C-E) we take E to be the tone of derivation as $1/1$, A then becomes $1/3$, and C becomes $1/5$. We will call this triad E minor instead of A minor since E, not A, is its tone of derivation ($1/1$).

A minor tonality (key) may be constructed by taking three roots at the 3 function as we did with the major mode but dividing the frequency of each root by 1, 3, and 5, instead of multiplying. Let us take E_{15} from the major numeric scale as our tonic root ($1/1$). The tonic triad will then consist of E_{15}-A_5-C_3; the dominant triad will contain A_5-$D_5/3$-F_1; the subdominant triad will be composed of B_{45}-E_{15}-G_9. The numerics of the major and minor systems are seen to be the same with the exception of D27 in the major system and D5/3 in the minor. To clear the fraction we again multiply all elements by 3 and obtain for the combined major-minor system: F3, D5, C9, A15, G27, E45, D81, and B135. To compare the two D's we multiply D5 by successive 2's to place them in the same octave: D5, D10, D20, D40, D80. Their relationship is that of the syntonic comma, 81/80.

It is well known that the 7th (F) of the dominant seventh chord in major (GBDF) is not the same frequency as the note F which acts as the root of the subdominant triad (FAC). The two tones remain undifferentiated in our traditional musical notation, however. In order to achieve a precision not afforded by orthodox notation it is necessary, therefore, to add one more numeric to our series—G27 times 7 (F189). To view the nature of the difference between F189 and F3 (the root of the subdominant triad) we multiply F3 by successive 2's to place the two F's in the same octave: F3, F6, F12, F24, F48, F96, F192. By dividing F189 and F192 by the common divisor 3 we find the relation between the two F's to be 64/63.

The 7th of the dominant seventh chord in the minor mode (AFDB) is the 1/7 function of the dominant tone of derivation A15. Since it is obvious that we shall be left with another fraction by such a division let us multiply all scalar elements by 7 before we divide: F21, D35, C63, A105, G189, E315, D567, B945, F1323. The 7th of the minor dominant seventh chord will then be A105/7 or B15. To compare B15 with B945, the root of the minor subdominant chord (B-G-E) we multiply B15 by successive 2's to place the two B's in the same octave: B15, B30, B60, B120, B240, B480, B960. Dividing B960 and B945 by the common divisor 15 we find their relationship to be 64–63.

So that we could be assured of quotients which would remain integral in a complete numeric system it became clear that we required a number for the tonal center that was minimally $1 \times 3 \times 3 \times 5 \times 7$. To provide one additional primitive division we chose C as $1 \times 3 \times 3 \times 3 \times 5 \times 7$, or 945. F then became 315 and G became 2835. Other notes were derived by multiplications and divisions by 3, 5, and 7, resulting in the system shown in Table X-1.

The note name assignments need not be fixed. Any note which acts as a tonic may be assigned to 945. If D is assigned to 945, then G is 315 and A is 2835, and other note names shift accordingly. Thus the numerics stand for common tonal relationships rather than fixed names of notes. The interlace of the simplest to the most complex relationships is contained in the numerics and not in letters with attached musical accidentals—sharps, flats, and naturals. This numeric description of relationships permits both precision and flexibility in musical analysis and composition, and, of course, such symbolism is handled with particular felicity by the computer equipped with the FORTRAN compiler.

Table X-1. Numeric description of tonal relationships

Note name	Function	Note name	Function	Note name	Function
0	0	0	0	0	0
D♭	1	C♭	7	B♭♭	49
A♭	3	G♭	21	F♭	147
F	5	E♭	35	D♭	245
E♭	9	D♭	63	C♭	441
C	15	B♭	105	A♭	735
A	25	G	175	F	1225
B♭	27	A♭	189	G♭	1323
G	45	F	315	E♭	2205
E	75	D	525	C	3675
F	81	E♭	567	D♭	3969
C♯	125	B	875	A	6125
D	135	C	945	B♭	6615
B	225	A	1575	G	11025
C	243	B♭	1701	A♭	11907
G♯	375	F♯	2625	D	18375
A	405	G	2835	F	19845
E♯	625	D♯	4375	C♯	30625
F♯	675	E	4725	D	33075
G	729	F	5103	E♭	35721
D♯	1125	C♯	7875	B	55125
E	1215	D	8505	C	59535
B♯	1875	A♯	13125	G♯	91875
C♯	2025	B	14175	A	99225
A♯	3375	G♯	23625	F♯	165375
B	3645	A	25515	G	178605
F✕	5625	E♯	39375	D♯	275625
G♯	6075	F♯	42525	E	297675

Before proceeding to the description of our programs it must be noted that the musician's dearly held concepts of the "inharmonic" tone and "chromaticized" chord dissolve in the presence of the numerical description of tonal relationships. The "passing tones," "neighboring tones," "suspensions," "retardations," "anticipations," "appoggiaturas," "added tones," and, God save the mark, "free tones" can readily be identified numerically. To illustrate, the "passing" or "neighboring" tone B appearing with the C-E-G triad produces the minor triad B-G-E along with C-E-G to form a compound triadic structure. The B obviously has a specific, identifiable numeric relation with all three tones of the C-E-G triad. "Chromatic," "altered," "colored," "clouded," and even "corrupted" chords can also be identified with reasonable ease and precision. The so-called "Neapolitan Sixth" chord related to C945 is simply composed of D♭63-F315-A♭189. By eliminating the fanciful jargon of traditional music theory and replacing it with a numeric description of tonal relationships FORTRAN becomes an eminently useful tool for tonal composition and analysis.

The more fruitful if not the more interesting of our composition programs was the second, which we called Comp II. The first step in the Comp II program was to read in several tables and two initializing chords. We provided tables for the determination of the line and space position of notes on a staff, the selection of new chord roots, and the choice of rhythm patterns.

Once the tables and initializing data were stored, the computer selected a rhythm pattern for the first measure. The tables provided measures of various rhythmic combinations from which the computer chose one measure at random. Several sets of measure tables were developed to correspond to musical tempi and styles. These included Adagio in $\frac{4}{4}$, Moderato in $\frac{6}{8}$, and the like. A set of measures was selected to be stored for each composition or movement. A complete measure was selected from the stored table with the aid of an IBM random-number generator. This complete measure provided the number of events in the measure and the actual time values. For example, one measure of four events might consist of four quarter notes. The computer stored the number four (4) in an area called EVENT and the values Q,Q,Q,Q in NOTE. A new musical incident (chord or rest) was written for each value in EVENT, and when all the values in EVENT were computed a new measure was chosen. Since the program did not include an examination of earlier measures to determine the nature of the new measure but relied only upon random selection of prescribed patterns, the temporal character of the music was not always logical or convincing.

After the selection of the new measure individual chords were chosen. The computer examined the two initializing chords or those just previously determined and chose the next musical event from tables. The initializing or previously written chords were first examined for mode progression (that is, major to major, major to minor,

minor to major, minor to minor). Four sets of tables were prepared, and the table to which the computer went depended upon the mode progression. The tables were set in a three dimensional array. One dimension of the array contained all possible roots of Chord I; the second dimension contained all possible roots of Chord II (these two dimensions were identical, of course); the third dimension contained the numbers 1 and 2, one of which was randomly selected. Two values for the new event were at each point of the array. These two values included: the chords of the major tonalities of C and G, the chords of the minor tonalities of E and B, and rests. The random selection of 1 or 2 caused the selection of one of the two optional events. Recycling loops which the computer might have generated were defeated by this random feature.

An illustration of the procedure outlined above follows. Say the computer found the mode progression of the two previously written chords to be major to major. The root progression was, say, C945 to G2835. These conditions will lead the computer to a table which provides, say, C945 or B14175 as the optional responses. The random number generator will select one of the two values.

By using tables, tight control was maintained over the output, but a measure of freedom was injected by permitting random selection of one out of a possible two events in the final decision.

The selection of the new root being complete, the computer next determined the position of each voice of the composition—soprano, alto, tenor, bass. We divided the musical staves into 61 increments, and assigned a note name to each increment. These notes included the first four sharps and first four flats. The C below the bass staff was numbered 1, C♯ 2, and so on, until we reached the C above the treble staff which was equal to 61. A rest was given the value 62. We also divided the ranges of the four voices to conform to commonly accepted limits.

The soprano voice was computed first, followed by the bass, and the inner voices, in that order. To determine which note of the new chord should be given to the soprano the computer first examined the function of the soprano note in the previous chord and observed its staff position. It then noted the mode of the previous chord. (If the previous event was a rest the computer examined the chord before the rest.) The new soprano note was determined with a view toward providing interesting harmonic-melodic relationships by changing the melodic function in successive chords (a practice which incidentally all but eliminated parallel fifths and octaves), and producing a "normal" musical line. For example, if the mode progression was major to major, and the previous soprano note was a funtion 3, the tables provided that the function of the new soprano note would be either 1 or 5. The computer then determined which of these values was closer on the staff to the last soprano note and selected it.

The bass was determined next by conditions set by the new soprano note. First the mode of the new chord was examined, then the function of the new soprano note was observed. These two conditions determined the selection of the new bass voice from one or possibly two values. In the example given in connection with the soprano voice, the mode of the new chord was major, and the function of the new soprano note was, say, 5. Under these circumstances the bass was ordered to take the 1 function. Within the range of the bass voice there exist two staff positions which correspond to the function 1. The computer selected the staff position of the new note on the "closest note" basis after considering the staff position of the previous bass note.

Once the outer voices were determined the inner parts were filled in. We prepared our program to insure that all three functions of a chord (1, 3, and 5, or 1/1, 1/3, and 1/5) were included. (In our composition programs no dominant seventh chords were included, though, of course, the 7 and 1/7 functions were required for the analysis program.) If one of the outer voices was at the 1 function and the other at the 5 function, one of the inner parts took the 3 function. If both of the outer voices took the same function, the inner voices took the other two. If after three voices were chosen all functions were present the fourth voice doubled the 1 or 3 function whichever was closer on the staff. Our program provided for alternation of priority between the alto and tenor voices—first the alto had first choice and then the tenor. With this method of inner voice determination neither alto nor tenor often received a function 5 because the outer parts, having first choice at the available functions, left the inside voices with a limited selection.

The computed chord was lastly examined for crossed parts between the soprano and alto, and tenor and bass. (Crossing of tenor and alto voices was considered to be musically acceptable.) If the soprano note was found to lie below that of the alto, it was sent to the staff position one octave higher; if this action resulted in a note above the range established for the soprano, it was returned to its original staff position, and the alto note was dropped an octave. An identical procedure was conducted for the tenor-bass parts.

An interesting outcome of this last routine was an occasional and admirable leap in the musical lines. These sudden changes to new pitch levels overcame some of the computer's tendency toward aimlessness and created a pleasant musical surprise from time to time.

In a previously developed composition program called Comp I we relied more fully upon numeric manipulation and less on prepared tables. The new root value was found from tables, and the mode of the chord emanating from that root was found by consulting a table of mixed major-minor progressions. The function of the last soprano note was found by dividing the soprano numeric by the root numeric if the mode was major, and dividing the root numeric by the soprano numeric if the mode was minor. This calculation set up the conditions for the determination of the new soprano, and selection was made by multiplying or dividing the new root numeric by the calculated function. The other voices were found in a similar manner, provision being made, of course, for inclusion of all functions of the triad and suitable doubling.

One advantage to be gained from calculating voices in this manner is the ease with which a program may be expanded, since the need for making major revisions in the table values is greatly reduced. Simple multiplication or division permits easy expansion to include advanced numerical combinations, while the table method limits a program to a specific range of values.

Both Comp I and Comp II contain many powerful features. At present, to be sure, both programs produce a conventional four-part music not unlike that achieved by music students at the end of their first year of collegiate study. Both programs, however, like good students, are capable of a more advanced form of composition.

Our analysis program examined a work of music, recorded the number of chordal roots and the number of times each fell on a given beat of a measure. The chord roots were identified by the numerics of Table X-1. The computer examined the data given to it and stored the following results: (1) the number of times the root appeared in the piece; (2) the number of times one root followed another; (3) the number of times one root preceded another; and (4) the number of times a root fell on a certain beat of a measure.

Because numerics can be employed for every instant of every measure, the detail in this kind of analysis is considerable. "Passing tones," and other "inharmonic" tones, can be integrated numerically to provide a detailed harmonic evaluation of any tonal work. The program is equally useful in statistically evaluating the melodic content of a piece by "plugging in" melodic numerics instead of roots.

Some integration of root progression with melodic progression, both stated in numeric terms, may yield new insights into the very nature of music. The coupling of FORTRAN to numeric tonal descriptions makes such a study possible.

Theoretical Possibilities

for Equally Tempered

Musical Systems

by WILLIAM STONEY

Of the many proposals that have been put forward for novel systems of tempered tuning over the past four centuries, not one has yet found general acceptance among composers or performers as a practical alternative to the limitations inherent in the conventional 12-semitone system. The purpose of this study is to re-examine the subject of equal temperament, utilizing the computer as a means of investigating all of the possibilities within a given set of limitations.[1] From such a study we may hope to discover one or more temperaments of interest to experimental composers, at the very least we may expect to gain added insight into some of the reasons for the hardy survival of the conventional 12-semitone system.

One of the most ancient and universal notions in the theory of music is that the ear takes pleasure in those tone combinations whose frequency ratios can be expressed in small whole numbers. These ratios can readily be deduced by utilizing instruments of the mono-

[1] This project formed a part of the research undertaken by this writer as a Fellow of the Cooperative Program in the Humanities at Duke University and the University of North Carolina during the 1966–1967 academic year. We wish to acknowledge gratefully the assistance of Mr. Hamilton Hoyler, Director, Duke University Department of Data Processing, in making computer time available and in arranging for the capable assistance of Mr. Dick Pritchard as programmer. Dr. Frederick P. Brooks, Director, University of North Carolina Department of Information Sciences, and Mrs. Bonnie Bain, Secretary for the Cooperative Program in the Humanities, provided helpful suggestions utilized in writing the detailed memorandum submitted to Mr. Pritchard as a guide for writing the program. Special mnemonic terms coined for this study are explained in the body of this paper. The computer used was an IBM 360 Operating System, Model 30, and the language used was FORTRAN IV (E level subset).

chord class and observing the inverse relationship which exists between string length and musical pitch for a stretched musical string of given length, diameter, and tension.

The laws governing string vibration were known to the ancients, and it is thus that we find the small number ratios forming the foundation of musical theory in the Hellenic world [2] and in medieval Arabic culture.[3] It is from these two sources that Western musical theory descended, but with a pronounced tendency toward the simplification of the materials used for scale building.

The intonation system of medieval Europe is presumed to have been Pythagorean,[4] which is a term that has come to mean any system in which all intervals are derived from the ratios of the octave (ratio 1:2) and the perfect fifth (ratio 2:3) and various manipulations of these two ratios. In such a system the major thirds were too wide and dissonant to permit the development of triadic harmony. The gradual increase in the significance of major and minor triads, observable from the middle of the fourteenth century onwards,[5] led to the development by the sixteenth century of the system of meantone tuning for keyboard instruments, thus providing pure thirds in the more common keys at the cost of perceptibly narrowed fifths.[6] During that period we may also infer that the problems of fretting instruments of the lute and viol class were laying the groundwork for the evolution of equal temperament.[7] In this latter system, which has been in general use for about the past century and a half,[8] fifths are imperceptibly narrowed, thirds deviate considerably from their theoretically just intonation, and the pitch distance covered by a semitone is the same throughout the scale. Triads are tolerably well in tune and, indeed, have a brighter sound than in either meantone or just intonation, and all keys sound equally well in tune.[9]

[2] See J. Murray Barbour, *Tuning and Temperament: A Historical Survey*, East Lansing, Mich., Michigan State College Press, 1953, pp. 15–24.

[3] See Al-Farabi, Bk. I, in Rodolphe d'Erlanger (tr.), *La Musique Arabe* (6 vols.), Paris, Libraire Orientalists Paul Guenther, 1930, Vol. I, 92–117.

[4] Gustave Reese, *Music in the Middle Ages*, New York, W. W. Norton, 1940, p. 161.

[5] A. Tillman Merritt and Willi Apel, "Harmony," *Harvard Dictionary of Music* (ed. Willi Apel), Cambridge, Mass., Harvard University Press, 1950, p. 324.

[6] Alexander Wood, *The Physics of Music*, 6th ed. revised by J. M. Bowsher, London, Methuen, 1964, p. 190.

[7] Cf. Barbour, *op. cit.*, p. 57.

[8] Cf. Wood, *op. cit.*, pp. 192–93.

[9] Cf. William Braid White, *Piano Tuning and Allied Arts*, 5th ed. revised, Boston, Tuners Supply, 1946, p. 65.

The computer program with which this paper is concerned was designed to explore the intonation characteristics of all of the theoretically possible equally tempered systems, starting with the conventional 12-semitone system and carrying the investigation up to a limit of 144 degrees to the octave. For present purposes we shall limit our discussion to systems of not more than 72 degrees. The assumption was made throughout this study that the interval of the perfect octave (ratio 1:2) was to retain its just (that is, determined by its theoretical ratio) intonation.

The studies of numerous experimenters in this area have been summarized in Mandelbaum's dissertation *Multiple Division of the Octave and the Tonal Resources of 19-Tone Temperament*,[10] and it must be admitted at the outset that the various proposed systems described by Mandelbaum have remained on the periphery of musical evolvement in Western culture. There are, however, two justifications for reinvestigating the question of experimental temperaments. The first of these is the facility with which the computer enables one to explore all of the possibilities. Second, the use of electronic devices by experimental composers has removed earlier practical barriers to the exploration of new temperaments.

The first problem which presented itself was the question: How do we determine what really is true intonation? The studies of Barbour[11] and Shackford[12] have demonstrated that just intonation has not necessarily been a characteristic of Western musical practice. The discipline of ethnomusicology offers little support for a mathematical theory of intonation because in so many isolated communities of the world intonation varies according to local tradition.[13]

On the other hand, just intonation is considered to be the ideal in theory, though flexible in practice, in the writings of Helmholtz[14] and Lloyd,[15] and the use of pure ratios has been eloquently advocated in

[10] Meyer Joel Mandelbaum, *Multiple Division of the Octave and the Tonal Resources of 19-Tone Temperament*, Ann Arbor, Mich.: University Microfilms, 1961, pp. 134–218.

[11] Barbour, *op. cit.*, pp. 197–99.

[12] Charles Shackford, "Some Aspects of Perception III: Addenda," *Journal of Music Theory*, VI, 295–303.

[13] See, for example: Colin McPhee, *Music in Bali*, New Haven, Yale University Press, 1966, pp. 36–55.

[14] Hermann L. F. Helmholtz, *On the Sensations of Tone as a Physiological Basis for the Theory of Music* (trans. Alexander J. Ellis; ed. Henry Margenau) New York, Dover, 1954, pp. 323–327 *et passim*.

[15] Llewelyn S. Lloyd, *Intervals, Scales, and Temperaments*, ed. Hugh Boyle, London, Macdonald, 1963, pp. 82–91.

both theory and practice by the American experimentalist Harry Partch.[16] Still further support for just intonation may be found in the preoccupation with pure ratios in the musical theory of ancient Greece,[17] and of the medieval Arabic world,[18] and (in the observation of this writer) in the performance practice of the best Hindu and Carnatic musicians, as well as the better Japanese koto players.

Our solution to the dilemma of divergent attitudes about intonation must therefore be to forego any attempt at prescribing what should be the practice of musicians; we shall simply investigate and classify the theoretical possibilities. The procedure for evolving such a classifica-

Ratio	Cents value	Ratio	Cents value
8:9	203.910	10:12	315.641
8:10	386.313	10:13	454.214
8:11	551.318	10:14	582.511
8:12	701.955	10:15	701.954
8:13	840.527	11:12	150.637
8:14	968.825	11:13	289.209
8:15	1088.268	11:14	417.507
9:10	182.404	11:15	536.950
9:11	347.408	12:13	138.573
9:12	498.045	12:14	266.870
9:13	636.617	12:15	386.313
9:14	764.915	13:14	128.298
9:15	884.358	13:15	247.740
10:11	165.004	14:15	119.443

Figure XI-1. Printout of the essential ratios

tion may best be discussed by referring to specific examples of the computer printout.

The first phase of the program was concerned with computing the theoretical values for the ratios found in the fourth octave of the harmonic series, in terms of cyclic cents (see Figure XI-1). Cents are a kind of system of musician's logarithms—anticipated by Woolhouse,[19] and used extensively by Ellis [20]—in which the logarithm of the octave ratio (1:2) is converted to equal 1200 cents and the

[16] Harry Partch, *Genesis of a Music*, Madison, Wis., University of Wisconsin Press, 1949.

[17] Barbour, *op. cit.*, pp. 15–24.

[18] D'Erlanger, *op. cit.*, Vol. I, pp. 91–116 and 172 ff.

[19] Wesley S. B. Woolhouse, *Essay on Musical Intervals, Harmonics, and the Temperament of the Musical Scale*, London, J. Souter, 1835, pp. 12–18.

[20] Helmholtz, *op. cit.*, pp. 446–456.

logarithms of all other ratios are expressed in terms of this value. Any interval in the conventional 12-semitone temperament is an even multiple of 100 cents, thus affording an immediate comparison between the familiar tempered scale of the Western world and the intonation of any other musical system.

It will be observed, in Figure XI-1, that the ratios used are confined to those found in the fourth octave of the harmonic series. All lower ratios may be found by using an appropriate multiple. For example, the perfect fifth (ratio 2:3) may be taken as the ratio 8:12; the just major third (ratio 4:5) is taken as 8:10, and so on. As a practical

DEGSYM 12

ORDNO	Cents value	HARFAC	Deviation
0	0.000	8	0.000
1	100.000		
2	200.000	9	−3.910
3	300.000		
4	400.000	10	13.687
5	500.000		
6	600.000	11	48.682
7	700.000	12	−1.955
8	800.000		
9	900.000	13	59.473
10	1000.000	14	31.175
11	1100.000	15	11.732
12	1200.000	16	0.000

Deviations Summary:
8:12   −1.955
8:10:12   AVER 10.427 MAX 10:12 −15.641 MIN 8:12 −1.955
8:10:12:14   AVER 18.846 MAX 12:14   33.130 MIN 8:12 −1.955
8 THRU 15 AVER 27.111 MAX 9:13   63.383 MIN 8:12 −1.955

Figure XI-2. Printout of the analysis of DEGSYM 12

limitation to the present study it was decided that the ratios should go no higher than those of the harmonic series fourth octave.

Figure XI-2 shows the computer printout for analysis of the conventional 12-semitone temperament; since the analyses of higher systems follow the same procedure and format, this example will serve to illustrate the rest of the program. By way of vocabulary: DEGSYM is mnemonic for degree system, that is, tempered scale system; ORDNO is mnemonic for ordinal number, which is the number for a specific degree in a particular system as reckoned upwards in pitch from the assumed starting point. "Cents value" is the pitch distance in cyclic cents of a specific ordno as reckoned upwards from ordno zero. HARFAC (mnemonic for harmonic series factor) is synonymous with the word harmonic, HARFAC 8 being the eighth harmonic, HARFAC 9 the ninth harmonic, and so on. A minus sign in the deviation column indicates that the tempered version of a harmonic is flat, or lower than its just pitch by the indicated number of cents; absence of a minus sign means that the deviation is sharp, or higher than its just pitch. Two additional columns which were in the printout are not included in the example. One showed frequencies in cycles per second for each ORDNO, with ORDNO 8 taken as 220 cps. The other column was reserved for special comments on extent of deviation, and on relative spacing.

In the data shown under the heading *"Deviations Summary"* (Figure XI-2) all deviations were computed with respect to the just cents values shown in Figure XI-1. In the first line, opposite the ratio 8:12, is given the deviation for the interval of the fifth. In the second line, opposite the ratio 8:10:12, is shown the average extent of deviation for all of the essential intervals formed by the major triad (8:10, 8:12, and 10:12), after which follows a listing of the interval with maximum deviation, and the one with minimum deviation. Line three applies the same procedure to the intervals contained in the third octave of the harmonic series (8:10, 8:12, 8:14, 10:12, 10:14, and 12:14), and line four carries the same procedure into the fourth octave of the harmonic series.

The data given in the printout for any particular degree system permits us to examine that system, by inspection, from five different points of view. First, those systems having the lowest deviation for the perfect fifth would yield Pythagorean intonation. Second, those systems showing lowest deviation average for the major triad would be suitable for approximating just intonation. Third, systems having low deviation averages for the intervals contained in the third and fourth octaves of the harmonic series (and especially the fourth octave) would enable one to utilize these intervals in experimental music. Fourth, systems of degrees numbering 24, 36, or any multiple of 12, would be compatible with the conventional 12-semitone temperament. Finally, systems with a high extent of deviation for the simpler intervals of the fifth and third (systems of 13 or 14 degrees, for example) would produce highly artificial intervals and scales.

One further concept which was written into the program must be discussed briefly; this is the concept of relative spacing. When a

HARFAC represents the mean term in a proportion of three integers, its pitch location in "Cents values" should be nearer to the higher tone than to the lower. Consider, for example, the location of the fifth within the octave as conforming to the proportion 2:3:4. The fifth must obviously be nearer in pitch to the upper octave than to the lower; otherwise the result might be a tritone and not a fifth. Or again, considering the major triad as being the proportion 4:5:6; the third of the triad is the mean term of this proportion and must be nearer in pitch to the fifth than to the root in order to avoid producing a neutral triad. For this spacing, normally used for the fifth within the octave and the triad third within the fifth, we may use the term "proportional spacing."

As we move to higher ratios, the ear becomes satisfied with a lesser degree of accuracy. Using the scale of A-major for reference, the first three tones of the scale—a, b, and $c'\sharp$ [21]—should conform to the proportion 8:9:10; but in this case the ear is satisfied with note b equidistant in pitch between notes a and $c'\sharp$. We may call this latter kind of spacing "neutral spacing."

If, on the other hand, the note b were nearer in pitch to note a than to $c'\sharp$, the result would represent not the ratio 8:9:10 but the reciprocal of this ratio, and we may term this "inverse spacing." Since this program dealt with superparticular ratios rather than scales, the possiblity of inverse spacing was rejected. The computer was programmed to require proportional spacing in locating HARFAC 12 with respect to HARFACS 8 and 16, and HARFAC 10 with respect to HARFACS 8 and 12. Either neutral or proportional spacing (dependent upon the nearest match for "Cents values") was permitted in locating HARFAC 14 with respect to HARFACS 12 and 16, HARFAC 9 with respect to HARFACS 8 and 10, 11 with respect to 10 and 12, 13 with respect to 12 and 14, and 15 with respect to 14 and 16.

The procedure for DEGSYM 12, as shown in Figure XI-2, was applied to all of the tempered systems falling within the limits of this study, and the results for each system were printed out. Essential data for each system was then copied onto a separate index card to permit ordering the systems according to various criteria. Our conclusions derived from this study may be summarized as follows:

---

[21] In designating pitch by letter names, we have used lower case letters to indicate the range extending from low c (an octave below middle c) upwards through b below middle c; if a prime sign (′) follows a letter designation, that note is to be read an octave higher in pitch.

1. The conventional 12-semitone temperament yields greatest purity of intonation in the simpler intervals of the fifth and fourth, moderate deviation for thirds and sixths, and the rather large deviation of 31 Cents for the seventh harmonic. The existence of the eleventh and thirteenth harmonics is doubtful.

2. Any improvement over the 12-semitone temperament, for purposes of just intonation, would require at least 19 degrees to the octave.

3. A 17-degree system yields good fifths (705.9 Cents) but too wide thirds (423.5 Cents). A 19-degree system yields nearly just thirds; its fifths are 7 Cents narrower than just. A 22-degree system yields a reasonable approximation of just intonation through the twelfth harmonic, and good relative spacing but too sharp intonation (by 32 Cents) of the thirteenth harmonic. The fifth is 7 Cents wider than the just value.

4. A 24-quartertone system yields a highly accurate approximation of the eleventh harmonic and a satisfactory approximation of the thirteenth harmonic. Fifths and thirds retain their present intonation, but the nearest approximation of the seventh harmonic is a quarter tone lower than in DEGSYM 12, thus making HARFAC 14 (as 950 Cents) neutrally spaced with respect to HARFACS 12 and 16.

5. Systems of equal temperament may conveniently be classified as positive systems, or systems with wide fifths, and negative systems having narrow fifths. These may further be listed in roster form in ascending order of fifth deviation as follows:

Positive systems (wide fifths)
0 to 1 Cent fifth deviation: systems of 41 and 70 degrees.
1 to 2 Cents deviation: systems of 29 and 58 degrees.
2 to 4 Cents deviation: systems of 46, 63, 17, 34, 51, and 68 degrees.
4 to 8 Cents deviation: systems of 56, 39, 61, 22, 44, 66, and 71 degrees.

Negative systems (narrow fifths)
0 to −1 Cent fifth deviation: systems of 53 and 65 degrees.
−1 to −2 Cents deviation: systems of 12, 24, 36, 48, 60, and 72 degrees.
−2 to −4 Cents deviation: systems of 67 and 55 degrees.
−4 to −8 Cents deviation: systems of 43, 31, 62, 50, 69, 19, 38, and 57 degrees.

6. Systems omitted from the above list have greater than 8 Cents fifth deviation.

7. Temperaments of 19, 24, 29, 34, and 39 degrees have neutral spacing of the seventh harmonic, raising the possibility that these systems may be inferior to some others in relative spacing.

In summary of the above, systems (in ascending order of average deviation for HARFACS 8 through 15) of 72, 58, 53, 70, 65, and 41 degrees yield low fifth deviation of 2 Cents or less, very good relative spacing, and acceptable approximation of harmonics 8 through 15. A temperament of 31 degrees has merit, but the fifth deviation of −5 Cents is relatively large. The most promising low-order systems are those of 24, 22, and 19 degrees. For these last three systems practical experimentation over an adequate period of time and utilizing suitably designed instruments would be required in order to assess their respective deficiencies and merits.

CHAPTER XII

Root Progression and

Composer Identification

by JOSEPH YOUNGBLOOD

This study sought to determine whether a composer's identity is revealed through the distribution of root progressions in his music.[1] Stated differently, it sought to determine whether the way that chords are connected is a minor encoding habit that would remain fairly constant throughout the works of a single composer and would differ significantly from one composer to another.[2] Although the hypothesis that root progression distribution does constitute such a feature was not strongly confirmed, neither was it flatly rejected; thus, the plan is to continue the study with enough additional data to obtain a clearer picture.

Root progression seemed a particularly good feature to study, partly because objective procedures for determining roots have been formulated,[3] and partly because it is unlikely that a composer would consciously manipulate root progression, especially a composer of linear counterpoint or of allegedly atonal music.

Four works were chosen for analysis: three string quartets and one clarinet quintet. Three date from a single five-year period, before the publication of *The Craft;* these are by three different composers, all of stature. The fourth work dates from after *The Craft;* it is by one of the first three composers, who is also the author of *The Craft.*

[1] This study was supported in part by a grant for Summer Research in the Humanities by the University of Miami. Computer time was made available at the University of Miami Computing Center, Professor Carl M. Kromp, Managing Director.

[2] Cf. William J. Paisley, "Identifying the Unknown Communicator in Painting, Literature, and Music: The Significance of Minor Encoding Habits," *Journal of Communication,* IV (1964), 219–237.

[3] Cf. Paul Hindemith, *The Craft of Musical Composition I* (trans. by Arthur Mendel), New York, Associated Music Publishers, 1945, pp. 68–74.

The first movements of the following compositions were analyzed: *Clarinet Quintet,* Op. 30, by Paul Hindemith (1923), *String Quartet,* Number Four, by Béla Bartók (1927), *String Quartet,* Number Three, by Arnold Schoenberg (1928), and *String Quartet,* Number Six, by Hindemith (1943).[4]

The root of every structure that contained representatives of at least two pitch classes was determined.[5] The constituent interval that was the best according to Hindemith's Series 2 was found;[6] the root of this interval became the root of the structure. Where the best—and therefore only—interval was the tritone, that member of the tritone forming the smaller interval with the root of the next structure became the root; where both members were equidistant from that root, the member of the tritone lower in pitch became the root. Hindemith treats the augmented triad, the three-note chord in fourths, the diminished triad, and the diminished seventh chord differently from other structures; in this study these structures were not treated differently.

All structures were analyzed; immediate repetitions were deleted. No attempt was made to distinguish between essential and nonessential tones. Trills were assumed to be measured and were arbitrarily considered half the value of the smallest measured value sounding at the same time. Grace notes were analyzed before the beat, with values small enough to place them between the last measured note in any part and the note the grace notes embellish.

Root progressions were measured upward: movement up a perfect fifth and down a perfect fourth were grouped together as root progression of a perfect fifth. The category "No Movement" was withdrawn, since it was, in every case, about four times as large as the next largest category.

Preparation of the Data

The pitches were coded in a modification of the DARMS code.[7] The essence of pitch representation in DARMS is that each staff is treated alike; the pitch is deduced from the staff location, the clef, and the accidental. In this study the middle line was called 15, the second

---

[4] The Hindemith *Quartet* was analyzed through the first 54 measures, to the change of meter.

[5] "Structure" is used throughout rather than "chord," inasmuch as the latter usually implies representatives of at least three pitch classes.

[6] Cf. Hindemith, *The Craft,* p. 96.

[7] Cf. Stefan Bauer-Mengelberg and Melvin Ferentz, in the *ACLS Newsletter,* Special Supplement, June 1966, p. 38.

space 14, the third space 16, and so on. This was possible because of the relationship of the lowest notes of the instruments involved (violin, viola, cello, clarinet) to the clef in which these notes are normally written; had a composer written the cello part more than five ledger lines below the treble staff, a different numbering system would have had to have been used.

Since at one point it was necessary to keep the two violin parts separate from one another, both S and V were used for the treble clef; A was used for the alto clef, T for the tenor clef, B for the bass clef, and C (as in "clarinet") for the treble clef, B♭ transposition. The natural was indicated by a blank, the sharp by +, the double sharp by the 0–2–8 punch, the flat by − (11 punch), and the double flat by =. Silence was indicated by . (period) as the accidental and 99 as the staff location.

The punching was done by melodic line, one measure at a time; in order to be able to line up the pitches into vertical structures, it was necessary to space the pitch codes across the cards in such a way as to reflect their relative rhythmic values. Only as many subdivisions were used as were needed for all the lines in a single measure. A measure of $\frac{4}{4}$, the smallest value an eighth note and all larger values reducible to eight notes (that is, no quarter-note triplets), would require 8 subdivisions. On the other hand, a measure of $\frac{9}{4}$ in which all parts played a dotted whole note tied to a dotted half note would require but one subdivision. Most measures required 8 or 16 subdivisions, although $\frac{3}{2}$ bars with both eighth-note triplets and sixteenth notes required 72 subdivisions. A single beat of 7 against 6 required 42 subdivisions.

Each card could handle 24 pitch codes; additional cards were used for those measures calling for more than 24 subdivisions. Double- and triple-stopping doubled and tripled the number of lines and therefore the number of cards required for a measure. A change of clef in the middle of a measure was considered the entrance of a new line.

The card format was as follows:

Column 1:   collating sequence, necessary when more than one card is required for a single line in a measure
Columns 2–5: the measure number
5–6:   the number of rhythmic subdivisions in this measure
7:       the clef for this card
8:       the first accidental code
9–10:   the first staff location
11:      the second accidental

12–13: the second staff location

.

.

.

77: the twenty-fourth accidental
78–79: the twenty-fourth staff location
80: a letter indicating the piece: *B* for Bartók *Quartet,*
H for Hindemith *Quartet, S* for Schoenberg *Quar-*
tet, and *C* for Hindemith *Clarinet Quintet*

Root Extraction

All the pitch codes for one measure were read into core. If there
was only one line, and therefore no structures as defined above, the
measure was skipped. Otherwise, the pitch codes were rearranged into
vertical structures. The pitches for the first structure were calculated.
The structure was examined for unisons and octave duplications;
these were set at pitch zero. The pitches were then sorted into
ascending order and the zeros—representing both doublings and rests
—removed. If, as a result of this process, the structure was reduced to
a representative of a single pitch class, the structure was abandoned
and pitch calculation for the next structure in this measure was
undertaken. Otherwise, it was compared with the structure immediately preceding it. If it was the same, it was abandoned; otherwise, it
was stored for comparison with the next structure. The root counter
was advanced after this step.

The intervals constituting the structure were then calculated. If the
structure contained only the tritone, a zero root was stored, and the
two pitches were stored for comparison with the next root. If the best
interval was other than the tritone, the root of this interval was stored
as the root of the structure. The preceding root was checked: if it was
zero, it was replaced by the pitch forming the smaller interval with
the current root or with the lower pitch if the current root was a minor
third away from both pitches.

If more structures remained in the measure, pitch calculation for
the next structure was initiated; otherwise, the pitch codes for the next
measure were read in.

After all the roots were extracted and stored, the root progressions
were calculated. These were all reckoned upward: an upward root
progression and its inversion downward were grouped together. In
those cases where the successive roots were the same, resulting in no

motion, the repetitions were deleted. Motion between successive groups of two roots (1–2, 2–3, 3–4, etc.) was calculated, as was motion between three successive roots.

Statistical Manipulations

The statistical procedures used were frequency and probability, information (entropy and redundancy),[8] and probability of chance occurrence (chi-square and chi-square probability).[9] The frequency

Table XII-1. Frequency, probability, redundancy, and chi-square probability

	H2 *		H1 †		B ‡		S §	
	F	P	F	P	F	P	F	P
MIN 2	16	0.065	45	0.067	133	0.124	94	0.064
MAJ 2	25	.101	77	.115	80	.075	125	.085
MIN 3	31	.125	55	.082	82	.077	155	.085
MAJ 3	22	.089	57	.085	89	.083	135	.092
PFT 4	32	.129	101	.151	119	.111	138	.094
AUG 4	19	.077	40	.060	102	.095	147	.100
PFT 5	26	.105	76	.114	115	.107	140	.095
MIN 6	22	.089	70	.105	81	.076	132	.090
MAJ 6	24	.097	51	.076	91	.085	175	.119
MIN 7	14	.056	57	.085	79	.074	102	.069
MAJ 7	17	.069	40	.060	99	.093	128	.087
REDUN ‖		1.275		1.695		.645		.550
CHI-PROB #		0.128		0.132×10^{-7}		0.171×10^{-3}		$0.372 \times 10^{-}$

* H2 = Hindemith *Quartet;* † H1 = Hindemith *Quintet;* ‡ B = Bartók *Quartet;* § S = Schoenberg *Quartet;* ‖ REDUN = redundancy; # CHI-PROB = probability of chance occurrence.

[8] Cf. Claude E. Shannon and Warren Weaver, *The Mathematical Theory of Communication,* Urbana, University of Illinois Press, 1949, pp. v, 117. Entropy (H) is found by summing the products of the probability of each event or category and the logarithm of that probability: $-\Sigma P_i \log P_i$. Relative entropy (H_r) is the ratio of the entropy to the maximum possible information $\frac{H}{\log_n}$ where n is the number of categories. Redundancy is the difference between 1 and the relative entropy; in this study it is expressed as a percentage $R = 100(1 - H_r)$. For a recent study using both information theory and chi-square, cf. Lejaren Hiller and Ramon Fuller, "Structure and Information in Webern's *Symphonie,* Op. 21," *Journal of Music Theory* XI (1967) 60–115.

[9] Cf. Edward E. Lewis, *Methods of Statistical Analysis in Economics and Business,* Boston, Houghton Mifflin Company, 1963, pp. 307–329, especially pp. 318–322. The method for calculating the chi-square used in this study is $\sum \frac{(F_o - F_e)^2}{F_e}$, in which F_o are the observed frequencies and F_e the expected frequencies.

and probability of the eleven admissible root movements were calculated; the redundancy associated with the individual roots was calculated; and the probability of chance occurrence was calculated, using $n/11$ as the expected frequency in each case. These data are summarized in Table XII-1.

The same calculations were carried out with two successive root progressions considered as a unit. Transition probabilities for each row were also figured, with the redundancy and the chi-square probability. These calculations are summarized in Table XII-2, along with

Table XII-2. Percentage of redundancy for two and three root-progressions at a time

	IJ	I,J *	IJK	IJ,K *
H2	8.472	15.25	26.878	80
H1	5.269	9.32	17.302	53
B	5.105	9.14	16.132	43
S	1.662	2.77	8.484	25

* Average. For other abbreviations, cf. the note to Table XII-1.

the same calculations for three successive roots considered as a unit and for transition probabilities from the first two root progressions to the third. Table XII-3 shows the chi-square probabilities of each sample having been extracted from each other sample.

Table XII-3. Chi-square probabilities *

	H1	B	S
H2	0.228	0.015	0.521
H1		$.134 \times 10^{-9}$	$.144 \times 10^{-9}$
B	$.173 \times 10^{-22}$		$.510 \times 10^{-14}$
S	$.523 \times 10^{-28}$	$.181 \times 10^{-14}$	

* The observed frequencies are on the left; the expected frequencies are along the top. For the abbreviations, cf. the note to Table XII-1.

The amount of redundancy is quite different between the second Hindemith example, the Bartók example, and the Schoenberg example; there is, however, very little difference between the first Hindemith example and the Bartók example. One would suspect that, as the amount of data grew and the Hindemith examples were combined, these divergencies would be even more pronounced. The likelihood of chance occurrence of these frequencies can be ruled out except in the case of the second Hindemith example, which was also the smallest sample. Curiously, there is a greater than 1-in-100 chance of any one of the three having written the second Hindemith example, with the chances better than 50–50 that Bartók wrote it. Among the pre-1930 pieces, on the other hand, the chances are quite slim—fewer than 1 in 100,000,000—that one composer wrote another's piece.

All of the programs were run on the IBM 7040/1401 at the University of Miami Computing Center. The entire program was written in FORTRAN IV. Two routines developed by the Biometric Laboratory at the University of Miami were used: CHIPR, which calculates the probability of the chi-square, and NSORT, which sorts numbers into ascending sequence.[10] The total time for the main program was 8 minutes, 55 seconds, of which 6 minutes, 17 seconds represented execution. The chi-squares and chi-square probabilities shown in Table XII-3 were run separately, in the WATFOR compiler; the total time was 5.25 seconds, of which 1.484 seconds was execution. The program and the operating system of the computer together use approximately 29,000 of the 32,000 available core locations.

[10] Cf. Dean J. Clyde, Elliot M. Cramer, and Richard J. Sherin, *Multivariate Statistical Programs*, Coral Gables (Florida), University of Miami Biometric Laboratory, 1966, pp. 50, 54.

ETHNOMUSICOLOGY

CHAPTER XIII

Computer-Aided Analysis
of Javanese Music

by FREDRIC LIEBERMAN

This paper is a progress report on one facet of a continuing research project at the Institute of Ethnomusicology of the University of California at Los Angeles, under the direction of Dr. Mantle Hood.[1] It deals only with computing techniques and approaches; results and their interpretation will be published elsewhere.[2]

The main goal of the project is to clarify the concept of *paṭet* (mode) in Javanese *gamelan* music, and to learn how requirements of paṭet affect and guide group improvisation (an integral element of gamelan performance). The first task set for computer-aided analysis was to test on a large data base theoretical hypotheses previously proposed by Dr. Hood from examination of a relatively limited corpus.[3] Two phases of the job may be treated separately: (a) preparation of a computer-readable data base; and (b) processing. Before moving on to this discussion, however, a brief sketch of gamelan music will aid those unfamiliar with its terminology and terrain.

The Gamelan and Its Music [4]

Gamelan music is organized around a *cantus-firmus*-like theme here called "Fixed Melody" (abbreviated FM), performed by a family of

[1] All contributors to this project cannot be acknowledged here. Assisting Dr. Hood are Dr. Leon Knopoff, Hardja Susilo, Gertrude Robinson, and Max Harrell; research assistants for computer analysis include Robert Kauffman, Richard Meyers, Max Brandt, John Gardner, and the present writer. Access to computing equipment has been made possible through the cooperation of U.C.L.A.'s Computing Facility and Western Data Processing Center. Moreover, it should be understood that the author of this paper presents it not as a principal researcher but simply as the one of the group of workers to whom has fallen the task of preparing a public report.

[2] In a forthcoming book by Dr. Hood.

[3] Mantle Hood, *The Nuclear Theme as a Determinant of Paṭet in Javanese Music*, Groningen, Djakarta, Wolters, 1954.

[4] This brief introduction contains only enough information to clarify the material under analysis. For complete information, see Jaap Kunst, *Music in Java*, 2nd ed., The Hague, Nijhoff, 1949, and works of Mantle Hood cited earlier.

one-octave metallophones (*saron*); a set of gong kettles (*bonang panembung*) plays a simpler version of the melody. Interpunctuating gongs provide a colotomic structure, dividing the FM into regular phrases; *gong, kempul, kenong*, and *ketuk* are the main colotomic instruments. *Panerusan* instruments are those that improvise intricate elaborations on the FM; these include *gendèr* (multioctave metallophone), xylophone, flute, vocalists, and *rebab* (two-string spike fiddle). Finally, a pair of drums (*kendang*) provides agogic accentuation, and together with the rebab functions to coordinate the ensemble.

Two tuning systems are found: *sléndro* and *pélog*. Sléndro has five pitches arranged in large seconds and small thirds (1 2 3 5 6); pélog, with seven available pitches (of which five are used at one time), has smaller seconds and wider thirds.[5] In each tuning system are three patet; these are shown, together with typical cadential formulae, in Figure XIII-1.

Sléndro paṭet nem	6 5 3 2	
Sléndro paṭet sanga	2 1 6 5	
Sléndro paṭet manyura	3 2 1 6	
Pélog paṭet lima	5 3 2 1	or 5 4 2 1
Pélog paṭet nem	2 1 6 5	
Pélog paṭet barang	3 2 7 6	

Figure XIII-1. The paṭet

The traditional notation system makes use of a vertical staff, one line per pitch. Horizontal lines mark time units. Round notes indicate the FM, hook-shaped notes the bonang panembung part. Symbols on the left and right of the staff are colotomic structure and drum patterns, respectively. Recently a simplified cipher notation has been adopted. In Figure XIII-2 the same phrase is given in traditional, cipher, and Western notations.

Preparing the Data

The first data to be encoded were a collection of thirty-eight gendèr improvisations, part of a tape-recorded field collection, which were

[5] An incomplete definition, barely hinting at the nature of sléndro and pélog; further, see Mantle Hood, "Sléndro and Pélog Redefined," *Selected Reports, Institute of Ethnomusicology* I, 1 (1966), 28–48.

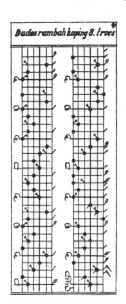

621 161232165353235 62132165312
2 1 6 1 2 1 6 5 2 5 2 1 2 6 3 2
T W T K T W T K

161268651216531211215682353221635
6 2 6 5 1 6 3 2 3 1 6 2 3 2 6 5
T W T K T W T G

Figure XIII-2. Traditional, cipher, and Western notations, where T = *Ketuk*, W = *Wela* (colotomic rest), K = *Kenong*, G = Gong. (Traditional gamelan notation from Jaap Kunst, *Music in Java,* The Hague, Nijhoff, 1949, used by permission of Martinus Nijhoff.)

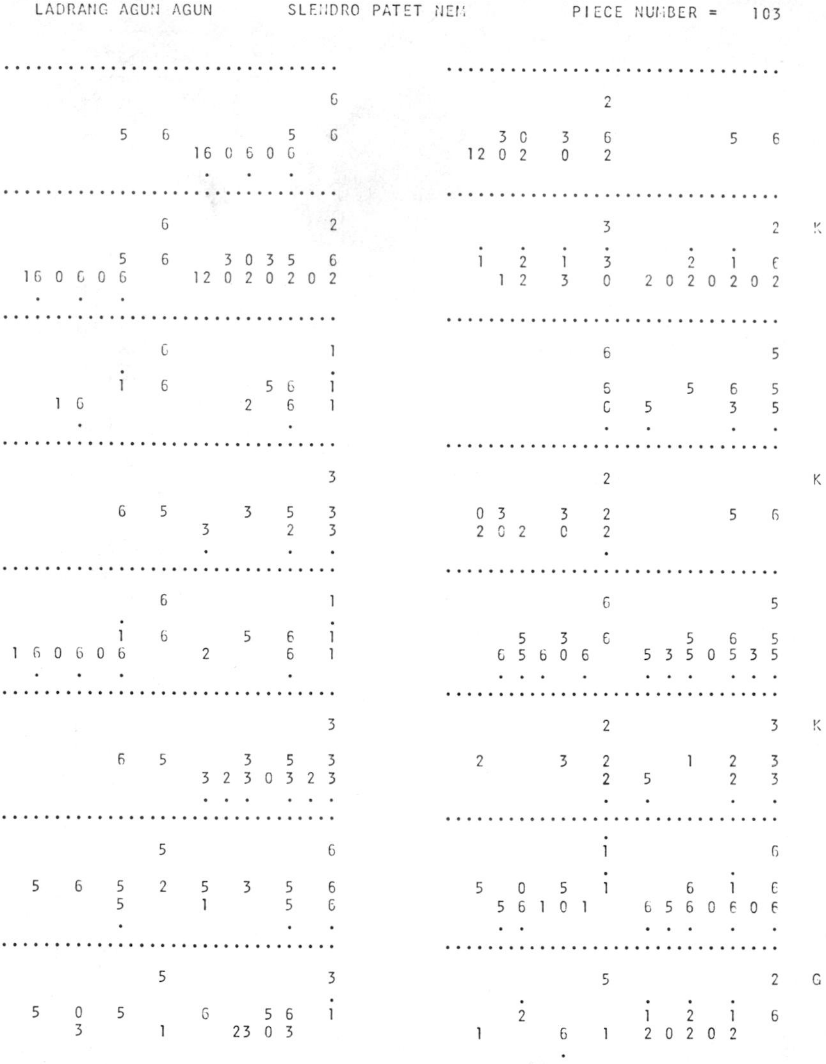

LADRANG AGUN AGUN   SLENDRO PATET NEM   PIECE NUMBER =   103

Figure XIII-3. Gendèr transcription

transcribed into cipher notation. The coding system devised may be termed "attributive," that is, each note is qualified by attributes (octave, duration, damping, and so on), and the resulting note groups joined into a string. This procedure soon proved troublesome. A single coding or punching error of duration-attribute would throw everything else out of phase. Code errors were difficult to detect because proofreading involved decoding and cross-checking with cipher notation.

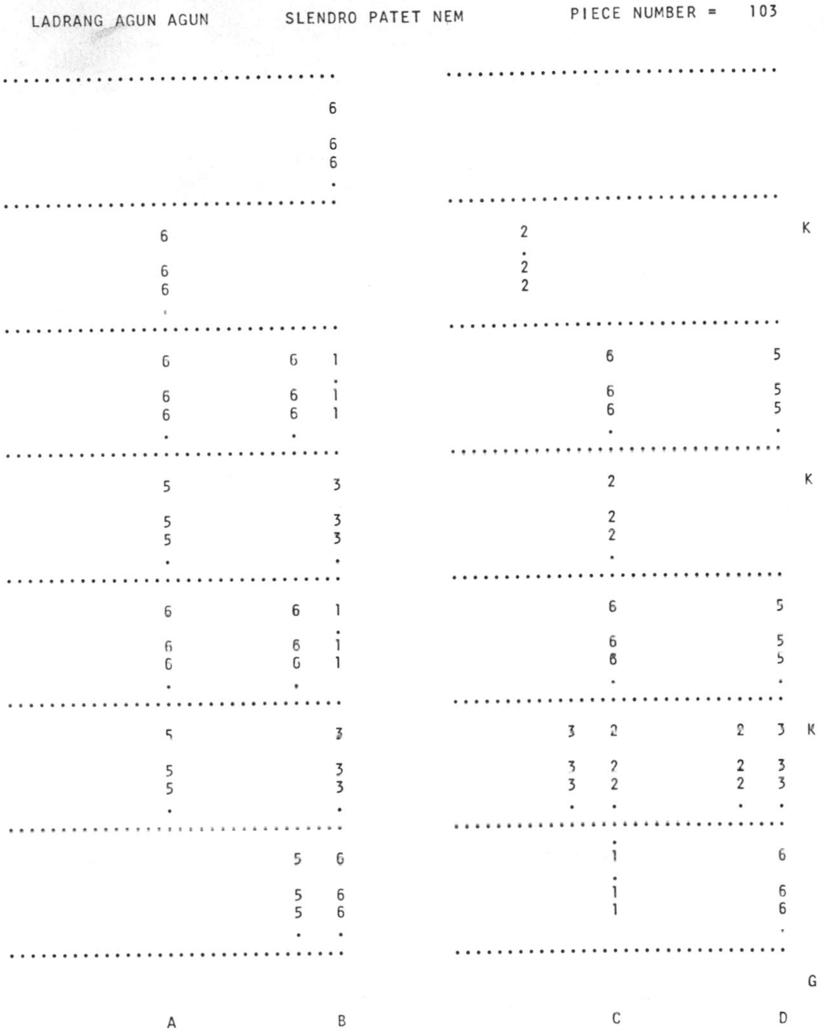

LADRANG AGUN AGUN   SLENDRO PATET NEM   PIECE NUMBER =   103

Figure XIII-4. Gendèr transcription, selected events only (see text)

To remedy the situation, a positional notation was proposed in which each card-field space represents a predetermined time unit. This leads to a card format essentially like cipher notation itself, making for simple proofreading and keypunching directly from the cipher notation, eliminating costly intermediate coding. The gendèr transcriptions have three musical lines: FM, right-hand, and left-hand pitches (see Figure XIII-3). In cipher notation a dot placed above or below a note indicates high or low octave, and this convention is retained in the keypunch format. Thus a group of six cards with aligned fields is necessary to reproduce cipher-notation format—three "note cards" and three "dot cards." In core storage the six fields are arranged as rows of a matrix ($6 \times n$, where n = piece length); therefore a given column of the matrix will contain all information about the selected time unit (in PL/1 the conceptual format is an array of character strings, but the principle remains identical).

Once this convenient coding system had been established, a second dataset was selected for keypunching, consisting of eighty-two representative pieces from a large Djogjakarta *kraton* (palace) music manuscript.[6] Keypunching was accomplished directly from traditional notation; each four-card group includes Fixed Melody, bonang panembung part, and colotomic structure. Finally, the two corrected datasets, each about 10,000 cards, were transferred to tape for ease in processing (no processing applications have yet been necessary which would justify the extra expense of disk storage).

Processing: Display

Listing the dataset tapes can normally be accomplished on peripheral equipment, with stock programs available at most computing centers. However we found it helpful to write a tape-to-print program that checks for illegal characters and rearranges the output into a more readable format (adding spaces between card groups, and so on). With one small modification this basic program becomes a useful analytical tool. A PRINT/NO PRINT branching network, inserted at the appropriate point, establishes a "variable event-display gate," allowing the researcher to concentrate on a particular musical event in its rhythmic and structural context by suppressing irrelevant notes. Figure XIII-3 is a normal page from a gendèr transcription; Figure XIII-4 shows the same segment of music with all notes suppressed except where FM, gendèr right and left coincide in pitch. The tendency of these octaves to fall on main structural points (quadratic subdivisions of the kenong phrase, marked A, B, C, D) is clearly apparent. Six event displays have been produced so far from the gendèr dataset, two from the FM dataset, mainly dealing with dissonance treatment. This technique, of course, generates prodigal amounts of output, and might be considered inefficient in terms of "machine time." However, in "people time"—results per man-hour—it

---

[6] Microfilm and Xerox copies of this multivolume collection are on deposit at the Ethnomusicology Archive, U.C.L.A.

is in fact highly efficient and productive, which is, after all, the more relevant measure.

Processing: Statistics

Computer statistics are facile to the point of glibness, and one must take care to avoid being seduced into "statisticulation." [7] Statistics have the advantage, however, of objectivity; and since ethnomusicologists frequently deal with musical cultures as external observers rather than as native practitioners, objective techniques are welcome safeguards against unconscious superimposition of alien values, which seldom apply.

The first statistical programming related to this project was an experiment in computer synthesis of Fixed Melodies, by Dr. Leon Knopoff, based on statistics from Mantle Hood's earlier manual analyses. [8] A set of nine syntactical rules were established; those governing pitch choice were programmed using a nearest-neighbor Markoff process, with transition probabilities derived from the analysis; other rules determined form and cadence pattern. The resulting tunes were not inconsistent with the literature, but neither were they wholly satisfactory imitations, leading to the inference that more refined analysis was necessary to define the style adequately.

The FM dataset was then processed to provide more detailed and extensive statistics. Frequency counts were obtained for all pitches (to construct weighted scales), for pitches at selected structural points (gong and kenong tones), and for two-, three-, and four-note patterns. In Figures XIII-5, XIII-6, and XIII-7 part A in each figure shows nearest-neighbor transition frequencies for sample Fixed Melodies; conjunct intervals are shaded (including unisons). The first line of part B summarizes the percentages of conjunct intervals (77, 83, 76 per cent), which deviate significantly from the expectation of conjunction in a random system (44 per cent). Further, examining the other figures, one discovers marked differences in melodic treatment of the various pitches, though relatively similar percentages occur across the three patet. Pitch 8 (high 1) occurs infrequently and must be examined separately. Pitches 1 and 6 behave consistently with less conjunction than 2, 3, or 5. This may be explained by thinking of 1

[7] This convenient term was aptly coined by Darrell Huff and Irving Geis, *How to Lie with Statistics*, New York, Norton, 1954.

[8] Leon Knopoff, "A Progress Report on an Experiment in Musical Synthesis," *Selected Reports, Institute of Ethnomusicology* I, 1 (1966), 49–60.

A.

	1	2	3	5	6	8
1	0	23	0	0	32	0
2	53	6	93	6	43	2
3	0	124	42	63	33	0
5	0	19	102		24	5
6	2	20	24	75	26	29
8	0	12	1	6	17	0

B.

	All	Conjunct only	Per cent conjunct
Total:	883	678	77
1	110	76	69
2	401	299	75
3	482	424	88
5	301	265	88
6	325	171	53
8	72	46	64

Figure XIII-5. Gending Lungkeh. Sléndro paṭet nem

and 6 as the outer boundaries of the normal melodic compass, hence more prone to skips (for example, a descending phrase 3 2 1 6̣ would be possible on instruments with a low 6; but the FM-carrying saron normally spans only the 1 to i octave, hence a skip up to 6 is forced). One may also note that these statistics do not violate the prominent

A.

	1	2	3	5	6	8
1	39	33	3	0	22	0
2	40	13	55	8	16	4
3	1	63	15	80	3	1
5	3	17	68	25	34	1
6	14	7	20	53	18	22
8	0	2	2	2	22	0

B.

	All	Conjunct only	Per cent conjunct
Total:	726	600	83
1	155	112	72
2	258	204	79
3	311	281	90
5	311	280	90
6	251	169	67
8	56	44	79

Figure XIII-6. Gending Gendrehkemasan. Sléndro paṭet sanga

	1	2	3	5	6	8
A. 1			23	0	5	0
2	55		64	3	29	1
3	27	73		45	15	3
5	0	8	42		46	5
6	9	9	31	52		16
8	0	0	2	1	22	

		All	Conjunct only	Per cent conjunct
B.	Total:	713	542	76
	1	182	118	65
	2	319	269	84
	3	347	246	71
	5	202	185	92
	6	262	164	63
	8	50	38	76

Figure XIII-7. Gending Mantra Kendo. Sléndro paṭet manyura

features of the paṭet cadential formulae—sanga and manyura reveal prominent 1-6 skips (2 1̄ 6̄ 5, 3 2 1̄ 6̄), nem stresses highly conjunct 5-3 (6 5̄ 3̄ 2)—and hence might reflect some kind of mutual influence or interaction between cadential formula and overall melodic motion. More positive statements would not be justified at this point. However, several interesting avenues of exploration have been opened, and additional effort spent analyzing these statistics would perhaps be fruitful, surely justifiable.

Processing: Pattern-search

The paṭet cadential formulae are not frequently sounded in a direct fashion, but rather are varied with complex and subtle techniques. To investigate the various cadence forms, a program was developed which, once provided with the archetypal four-note formula, could recognize, isolate, and label direct or retrograde patterns with embellishments or extensions of any length. The program's vocabulary includes sixteen positive identifications and four negative responses. Figure XIII-8 is a summary of all cadence patterns found in the FM dataset, paṭet sanga. Figure XIII-9 is a segment of output with the relevant cadence pitches circled. Most identifications are unequivocally correct, admitting of no other interpretation; when dealing with "ambiguous" situations (insufficiently defined by program logic) the

```
SLENDRO PATET SANGA
DIRECT
       8
DIRECT,EMBELLISHED
      62
DIRECT,PRE-EXTENSION
       3
DIRECT,POST-EXTENSION
       6
DIRECT,EMBELLISHED,PRE-EXTENSION
      18
DIRECT,EMBELLISHED,POST-EXTENSION
      23
DIRECT,EMBELLISHED,PRE AND POST-EXTENSION
       8
DIRECT,PRE AND POST-EXTENSION
       0
RETROGRADE
       0
RETROGRADE,EMBELLISHED
       4
RETROGRADE,PRE-EXTENSION
       0
RETROGRADE,POST-EXTENSION
       1
RETROGRADE,EMBELLISHED,PRE-EXTENSION
       0
RETROGRADE,EMBELLISHED,POST-EXTENSION
       4
RETROGRADE,EMBELLISHED,PRE AND POST-EXTENSION
       2
RETROGRADE,PRE AND POST-EXTENSION
       0
NOT COMPLETE OR NOT RECOGNIZABLE
      31
PRE-EXTENSION NOT COMPLETE
       0
NO GONG
       3
SONG LENGTH EXCEEDS ARRAY MAXIMUM
       0
```

Figure XIII-8. Summary of sanga cadence types

program's choices are always understandable but often the weaker of the available choices. Further development of program logic may be guided by these "wrong" responses. Programming is considerably more complex for even this kind of elementary pattern search than for the statistical and display techniques previously outlined. Nevertheless, this area of research promises to be extremely valuable as the pattern-recognition vocabulary grows larger.

Summary and Perspective

Since the inception of this project in 1964 a great deal has been learned from false starts, setbacks, and occasional successes; from these experiences the following general observations may be drawn. A research project utilizing computer-aided analysis is a complex system involving numerous interacting variables and must be treated as such if efficient production of results is desired. If at all possible, the principal researcher should have programming knowledge. If not, it appears more satisfactory to train music students in programming rather than to hire programmers untrained in music; students will generally maintain close contact with the project for longer periods of time, will be more interested in research problems and musical results, and will be able to capitalize on their new programming ability as a tool in their own research. It follows that processing methods producing useful results with simple techniques (such as display programs) are doubly efficient when used as on-the-job training for apprentice programmers. Much thought should be given the choice of a music representation code, whether to use one of the general-purpose codes now available, or to design a system to meet the special needs of the data at hand; care taken at this step can dramatically improve later programming efficacy.

This paper has dealt with the nature of the research problem, and methodologies of data preparation and processing. By means of short examples three processing types were distinguished: display, statistics, and pattern search—each capable of effective contributions toward the project's goal, learning more about patet. We will continue to construct statistical models of patet operation and check these by means

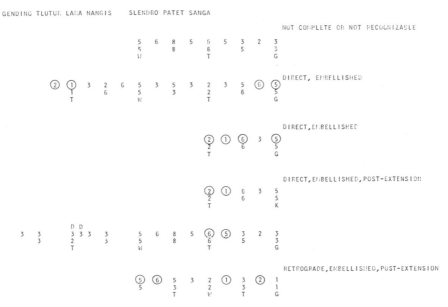

Figure XIII-9. Some sanga cadence patterns

of music synthesis programs. The most promising area for future development seems to be pattern recognition, and efforts will be concentrated in that direction. Though we have barely scratched the analytical surface, progress to date can be described as stimulating and most encouraging.

CHAPTER XIV

Computer-Oriented
Comparative Musicology

by BENJAMIN SUCHOFF

The published scientific studies resulting from Béla Bartók's researches into folklore contain frequency-of-occurrence statistics upon which certain conclusions are based in his description of characteristic musical and textual features.[1] The data were compiled by common although primitive means—as can be seen in the facsimile of Bartók's holograph (see Figure XIV-1); his "five-finger" calculations are, of course, the product of tedious, time-consuming hand-eye effort.

As I have shown elsewhere,[2] use of machine data processing provides the researcher with a powerful tool in such humanistic enterprise. The computer is useful not only in retrieval of information in amazingly quick time and with exceptional accuracy but also in permitting examination of Bartók's folk music material from viewpoints other than those he chose to survey. In fact, computer applications to this material have resulted in the disclosure of otherwise hidden variant relationships, classification discrepancies, and stylistic aspects.

The purposes of this essay are to present more specific details concerning procedures followed in the comparison of different musical materials and to publish the findings obtained from related computer programs—all as a means of suggesting possible guidelines for future investigation by interested researchers.

---

[1] See B. Bartók and A. B. Lord, *Serbo-Croatian Folk Songs*, New York, Columbia Univ. Press, 1951; and B. Bartók, *Rumanian Folk Music* (ed. Benjamin Suchoff), Vols. I–III, The Hague, Martinus Nijhoff, 1967. The music examples and illustrations appearing in this essay are used by permission of the Trustee of the Estate of Béla Bartók.

[2] B. Suchoff, "Computer Applications to Bartók's Serbo-Croatian Material," *Tempo* (London), No. 80, 1967.

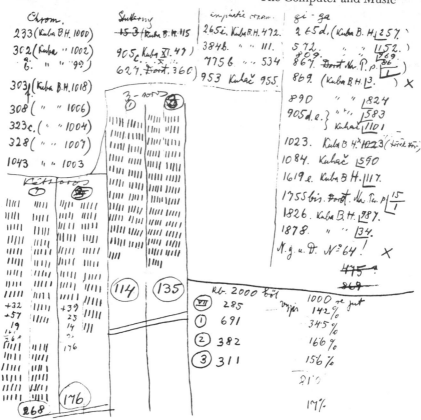

Figure XIV-1. Page of statistical jottings from Bartók's *Serbo-Croatian Folk Music* MS. The calculations have to do with section structure of the melodies and peculiarities of performance. Reproduced by permission, Estate of Béla Bartók.

PROCEDURES

The first problem is the determination of those parts of a given musical material which should be treated for data-processing purposes. In the case of the Bartók folk song collections used here—The Parry melodies [3] (see Figure XIV-2) and the Rumanian Colindas [4]— Bartók analyzed both materials for their content structure, that is, he determined the form of the individual melodies, tabulating them in

---

[3] The 75 women's songs contained in *Serbo-Croatian Folk Songs.*
[4] Winter-solstice songs, which include carols and Bethlehem songs, contained in Bartók's *Rumanian Folk Music,* Vol. IV (454 melodies, including variants) and Vol. V (27 Colindas, including variants).

Figure XIV-2. Sketch of melody No. 12C from Bartók's *Serbo-Croatian Folk Music* MS. See Figure XIV-3 for his skeleton form of the first melody section of this piece. Reproduced by permission, Estate of Béla Bartók.

terms of capital letter designation (A B A, A B B, and so on) to indicate like or different content of the melody sections. (A melody section generally is that portion corresponding to one line of underlying poetic text.) [5] As a case in point, Figure XIV-3 shows first the skeleton

[5] Text-line length, moreover, is determined on the basis of syllabic structure, ranging from three- or four-syllable lines to those with fourteen or more. (It

form, prepared by Bartók himself, of the first melody section appearing in Figure XIV-2 (the signed digits are editorial additions derived from the interval sequence extraction program described below.)

The different content structures are considered to be independent entities, even those which are contained in a single melody, for "contaminations" (melodies containing sections borrowed from foreign or urban sources) are not uncommon. These content structures, or "strings," are numbered consecutively in order of appearance in the collection: the Parry melodies from 1–156, the Colindas from 1–1,150. Their music notation is then transmuted by means of the Ford-Colum-

Serbo-Cr. F.S. No. 12C

Figure XIV-3. Skeleton and encoded forms of first melody section from Bartók's *Serbo-Croatian Folk Music* MS.

bia Representation into machine-readable graphics, which are pencilled onto special mimeographed forms, as in the encoded version of Figure XIV-3.

should be mentioned that in certain cases, because of inadvertency or other reason, omitted [Bartók] analyses had to be provided by the present writer.) Furthermore, melismata had to be skeletonized—reduced to principal tones—in accordance with underlying text-line syllabic structure (cf. Bartók's procedures in this regard in *Serbo-Croatian Folk Songs*, p. 90).

The Ford-Columbia Representation

This representation, developed by Stefan Bauer-Mengelberg,[6] was selected because of its versatility—particularly with regard to its future use in music printing [7]—and is only partially illustrated in our encoding (above). Pitches are indicated by a system of 50 space codes numbered from 10 leger lines below the staff to 10 above. Rhythmic values are indicated by such mnemonics as W for whole note, H for half note, Q for quarter note, and so forth. Note the use of space code abbreviations for notes which lie on the staff (that is, 0–9 in place of 20–29). Such abbreviation requires additional programming to later prefix the single digits with 2. A duration code need be given only once for successive notes of the same value. Here, too, additional programming will be required to restore omitted graphics. It is possible to omit space code redundancies, of course, especially with regard to tied notes. Indexing programs, unless programmed otherwise, treat tied notes as repeated ones. Although abbreviations and truncations are economical means, their excessive use may complicate reading of strings.

Punched card preparation

Keypunched cards as input medium are perhaps best for musicological purposes, since they also provide a handy reference file.[8] Referring again to our encoded version of Figure XIV-3, note the use of blank columns to separate graphic sets into "words" which are spaced in the same manner as they appear in actual music notation. Observe, too, that the bar line (/) is considered to be a word. Columns 1–14 are usually reserved for encoding clef, key, and meter.[9] The string itself occupies columns 15–65 (or 71),[10] and the remaining fifteen (or nine)

[6] I am indebted to Mr. Bauer-Mengelberg for permission to quote the representation shown in Figure XIV-3. As indicated below, the encoding of clef, key, and meter differs somewhat from his system.

[7] Messrs. Bauer-Mengelberg and M. Ferentz, under a grant from the Ford Foundation, are working on a project at Columbia University to develop a computer-controlled photocomposition process for music printing.

[8] Particularly if micro-aperture or Xerox Semi-Micro cards are used. For further details see H. B. Lincoln, "Musicology and the Computer: The Thematic Index" in *Computers in Humanistic Research* (ed. E. A. Bowles), Prentice-Hall, Englewood Cliffs, 1967, Chap. 18.

[9] The extended guide lines (columns 8, 15, 66, 68, 72) serve as signals for the special encoding procedures explained below.

[10] Observance of the col. 15–65 field limitation will permit data processing for indexing purposes at the Computer Center of State University of New York at

are used for serial numbers or similar data. In our folk song encoding, however, clef indication can be omitted, since Bartók transposed all melody sections to g^1 as *tonus finalis*. Replacement of key-signature code by accidental code throughout the string seems to facilitate reading as well as simplify programming for certain purposes. Our example, then, shows Bartók's classification designation [11] in columns 1–7, content structure in column 8 (a blank indicates A content structure), and meter (numerator only) in column 9. Change of time or additive meter is indicated in the following columns by integers separated by plus sign: 2 + 3, and so forth.

If only one card is needed to encode the melody section—usually the case in our materials—the record mark (0–2–8 multiple punch) is placed in column 66 to indicate end of data, otherwise 1, 2 . . . are used to indicate the card serial number of that specific set devoted to one string. The last card of the set must contain the record mark. Columns 67–71 are used for melody designation, 72–73 for researcher's initials, and 74–79 for string or serial number.[12]

After the encoded data are keypunched, the cards are listed for proofreading purposes (computer printout or IBM 407).

PROGRAMS

In most of his folk music studies Bartók groups the materials according to "grammatical" rather than "lexicographical" principles. The former, he states, is of higher importance, since it permits the researcher "to get a clear idea of the relationship of the melodies." [13] But, as Bartók himself admits, "one must have some previous familiarity with the material and a thorough knowledge of the rather complicated grouping system." [14] Without such familiarity and knowledge, of

---

Binghamton. A description of card preparation for this program, which was prepared in FORTRAN by Mrs. Cay Gill, can be obtained by writing to the Center. A similar indexing program, prepared in PL/I by Professor Jack Heller, Director of the New York University Institute for Computer Research in the Humanities, can be obtained from the ICRH (University Heights, N.Y.).

[11] Bartók's morphological procedures employ capital and lower-case letters, roman and arabic numerals to designate syllabic and rhythmic structures, caesura (end tone of a melody section), and other musical characteristics.

[12] Allowance is thus made for 999,999 cards under any one researcher's initials. Column 80, in the Harpur Incipit Interval Extraction Program, is used for special designation (see fn. 10).

[13] *Serbo-Croatian Folk Songs,* p. 15. The grammatical system, as developed by Bartók, is based (in order of importance) on the number of melody sections, syllabic structure, rhythmical character, and so forth.

[14] *Loc. cit.*

course, location of variants or of specific melodies is at best a long and arduous task. The solution to the foregoing problem is the construction of an index of melodies based on lexical principles, the most important one—according to Bartók—having to do with melodic structure in which "the contour line is entirely or partly similar." [15] H. B. Lincoln [16] has developed a computer-derived thematic index (see fn. 8) whose program, slightly modified, has been successfully applied to Bartók's folk music material. [17]

Incipit Interval Sequence Extraction Program

This is a FORTRAN program which computes the first seven intervals of an incipit, ignoring repeated notes, that has been encoded in the Ford-Columbia music representation. The computation involves extraction of the string interval sequences in terms of plus or minus digits. [18] The derived sequences are then sorted and compared. The last step is printed output in which the strings are ordered so that lesser precedes greater digit and plus precedes minus, and identical strings are juxtaposed in single-spaced vertical format. Figure XIV-4 shows actual computer output, printed as final copy (excepting headings and ruled lines) for typesetting purposes. [19]

In terms of frequency of occurrence the Colinda material string interval sequence +2 +2 −2 −2 is met nineteen times, followed closely by −2 −2 −2 (eighteen), −2 −2 (sixteen), and +3 −2 −2 (fourteen). The smaller Parry material, about one-eighth the number of Colinda strings, shows three occurrences of −2 −2 −2 −2 and −3 +3 −3; [20] other matches, involving only two strings, are either identical with or similar to the above-mentioned Colinda sequences. In fact, there are twenty-nine occurrences of matching strings between the two collections. It should be noted that either syllabic structure (dif-

---

[15] *Ibid.*, p. 17. His statement thus may be interpreted as contour lines containing similar sets or subsets.

[16] Professor of Music, State University of New York at Binghamton.

[17] See fn. 2.

[18] Intervallic quality (major/minor, augmented/diminished) is omitted from consideration in this indexing system, although it can be programmed for more refined comparative purposes.

[19] This sample page is one of thirty-six similar ones which comprises the Addenda to Bartók's *Rumanian Carols and Christmas Songs* (*Colinde*), Vol. IV, *Rumanian Folk Music* (see fns. 1, 4 above).

[20] This alternation of thirds occurs only in the Parry material as a kind of "closing formula" in the last section of a melody (see my essay in *Tempo*, No. 80, *op. cit.*, for further details).

Index No.	Class	Melody No.	String Interval Sequence	String No.
69	AIII	29	+2+2-2+2+3	224
70	BIII	100D.	+2+2-2+2-3+3	797
71	AII	12F.	+2+2-2-2	56
72	AII	12N.	+2+2-2-2	77
73	AII	18	+2+2-2-2	128
74	AIII	29	+2+2-2-2	222
75	AIII	30A.	+2+2-2-2	228
76	AIII	32	+2+2-2-2	236
77	BIII	62C.	+2+2-2-2	394
78	BIII	62D.	+2+2-2-2	395
79	BIII	62H.	+2+2-2-2	403
80	BIII	62J.	+2+2-2-2	407
81	BIII	62R.	+2+2-2-2	421
82	BIII	62V.	+2+2-2-2	429
83	BIII	62X.	+2+2-2-2	431
84	BIII	62DD.	+2+2-2-2	444
85		62FF.	+2+2-2-2	448
86	BIV	121A.	+2+2-2-2	970
87	BIV	121E.	+2+2-2-2	986
88	BIV	M3	+2+2-2-2	1086
89	BIV	M18	+2+2-2-2	1144
90	BIV	122A.	+2+2-2-2+2+2	1033
91	BIV	125	+2+2-2-2+2+2+2	1046
92	BIII	104A.	+2+2-2-2+2+2-2	844
93	BIII	104B.	+2+2-2-2+2+2-2	847
94	BIII	104D.	+2+2-2-2+2+2-2	853
95	BIII	104E.	+2+2-2-2+2+2-2	856
96	BIII	104F.	+2+2-2-2+2+2-2	859
97	BIII	104H.	+2+2-2-2+2+2-2	865
98	BIII	104J.	+2+2-2-2+2+2-2	871
99	BIII	104K.	+2+2-2-2+2+2-2	874
100	BIV	121R.	+2+2-2-2+2+2-2	1031
101	BIII	62V.	+2+2-2-2+2-3	430
102	BIII	73R.	+2+2-2-2+2-3+2	560
103	BIII	62C.	+2+2-2-2+2-4	393
104	BII	44B.	+2+2-2-2-2	273
105	BII	44C.	+2+2-2-2-2	275
106	C	130	+2+2-2-2-2	1067
107	BIV	115B.	+2+2-2-2-2+2	935
108	BIII	92A.	+2+2-2-2-2+3	735

Figure XIV-4. Actual computer output

ferent number of syllables in the underlying text line of a melody) or
—more frequently—the presence of one or more repeated notes account for the different lengths of the various sequences.

Figure XIV-5 indicates those types of interval sequences, involving

Colindas ☐ Parry ▨ Frottole ■ Cabezón ⠿

Figure XIV-5. Prevalent types of identical interval sequences in the
merged materials

ten or more matches, that occur in merged folk and art materials:
1,306 (combined) Colinda and Parry melody sections, together with
3,977 *Frottole* [21] incipits indexed by H. B. Lincoln, and 253 incipits
from the works of Antonio Cabezón (1510–1566) prepared by Earle
Hultberg.[22]

[21] A common type of early sixteenth century vocal music.
[22] Professor of Music, State University College at Potsdam, New York. I am
indebted to Prof. Hultberg for permission to quote from his Ford-Columbia representation of Cabezón's *Obras de Musica para Tecla, Arpa y Vihuela* (published
by Hernando Cabezón, Antonio's son, in Madrid in 1578).

There are fifty-eight other matches in the merged indices; none of them involves all four materials either. Interesting similarities turn up which seem to point toward folk-based or folk-styled characteristics of the art melodies: more than half (2,931) of the 5,536 interval sequences begin with plus or minus 2; indeed, conjunct motion by seconds is by far the most prevalent intervallic progression.

String Interval Sequence Extraction Program

The same index described in the preceding section has been programmed in PL/I and designated BARSIX (Bartók ARchives String Interval Xtraction).[23] Strings encoded in the Ford-Columbia representation are converted to plus or minus digits and stored in separate files. The "plus" file holds sequences whose first digit is plus, the "minus" file those whose first digit is minus. Each file is sorted, both are merged, and the lexicographical index is printed in the desired format. Features of the program include printing of coded strings and other keypunched data for reference and comparative purposes, and printing of the running total of occurrence of matches and the subtotal of specific number of strings in each match. The latter are expressed as digits (separated by a slash) and printed in the margin of the index.

Another program is available for printing the index in a different format from that illustrated in Figure XIV-4 (above). Below each interval sequence or set of matching sequences are printed the pertinent Ford-Columbia representation(s) and related data.

Substring Interval Sequence Extraction Program

Recalling Bartók's instruction that a variant relationship occurs when the contour line of a melody is also *partly* similar to that of another melody,[24] extraction of subsets from melody sections is therefore a desirable adjunct program for comparative analysis. BARSUBX (Bartók ARchives SUBstring Xtraction) employs the same format as BARSIX but with the exception that matches are linked to identicalness of a specific number of digit positions in the interval sequence.

---

[23] This and the following programs were developed by Professor Heller (see fn. 10).
[24] *Serbo-Croatian Folk Songs*, p. 17.

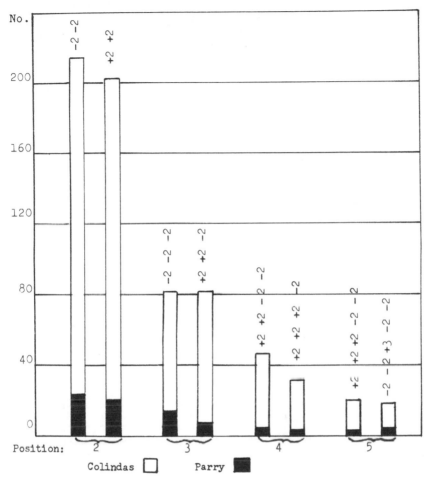

Figure XIV-6. Prevalent types of identical substring interval sequences in the merged Bartók materials

Figure XIV-6 shows the number of occurrences of the most frequent matching substring sequences, positions 2–5, in the merged Colinda and Parry melodies.[25]

Examination of the *Frottole* and Cabezón subsets [26] presents further

[25] Position 1 occurrences are shown in Table XIV-1. There are three types of identical substrings in Position 6, of which +2 +2 +2 −2 −2 −2 is prevalent (two occurences in each material).

[26] The punched cards of these collections were not available for substring programming; the following quotations therefore represent the manual extraction of data.

evidence of the kinship of these art music materials to the Bartók folk music collections. The prevalent type of *Frottole* substrings are the same as the Bartók ones (Figure XIV-6) in positions 2 and 3. The other positions involve a series of descending seconds. The Cabezón melodies are different in terms of subset frequencies: position $2 = -2 +2$; $3 = +3 -2 -2$; $4 = -2 +2 -2 +2$; $5 = -2 +2 +2 -2 +2$; $6 = -2 +2 +2 -2 +2 +2$ (or -2). It should be noted, however, that there are substring matches among all materials; indeed, a number of cases show a frequency of occurrence that seems to indicate more than just accidental matching.

Signed Digit Position Frequency of Occurrence

BARDFO (Bartók ARchives Digit Frequency Occurrence) lists quantity and percentages of the various types of plus and minus digits in each position. The Rumanian (Colindas) and Serbo-Croatian (Parry) melodies, as Table XIV-1 indicates, have a number of common characteristics.

Note that ascending intervals occur most often in position 1, descending intervals in positions 2, 3. The proportion of interval types as well as frequency of occurrence are also alike in both materials.

Table XIV-1. Signed digit position frequency of occurrence in the Colinda and Parry melodies (Parry statistics are in italics)

Signed digit	Per cent of occurrences in each position							Total no. of occurrences	Per cent of total
	1	2	3	4	5	6	7		
+2	24 *25*	24 *20*	20 *19*	14 *13*	9 *11*	6 *7*	2 *3*	1,479 *200*	27 *23*
−2	17 *13*	21 *18*	19 *16*	17 *18*	15 *15*	8 *11*	3 *8*	2,229 *369*	41 *43*
+3	33 *22*	17 *20*	20 *21*	18 *14*	6 *14*	4 *5*	2 *3*	541 *94*	10 *11*
−3	13 *12*	16 *17*	19 *20*	22 *15*	16 *14*	8 *15*	5 *7*	672 *120*	12 *14*
+4	35 *29*	18 *18*	18 *7*	14 *21*	8 *14*	7 *4*	1 *7*	173 *28*	3 *3*
−4	13 *19*	20 *6*	19 *25*	15 *38*	14 *6*	13 *6*	6	204 *16*	4 *2*
+5	60 *50*	16	9 *9*	8 *14*	5 *18*	1 *9*	1	93 *22*	2 *3*
−5	12	33 *33*	21 *33*	5	19	12	*33*	43 *3*	0.78 *0.35*
+6	57	29		14				7	0.12
−6	25		25		25		25	4	0.07
+7									
−7									
+8	50			50				2	0.03
−8									
Total all occurrences								5,447 *852*	

Table XIV-2. String interval distribution percentages in the Colinda and
Parry melodies (Parry statistics are in italics)

Interval	One type of digit	One and two types of digits				
		2	3	4	5	6
2	94 *86*	27.64 *24.39*	53.82 *60.97*	10.89 *6.50*	4.38 *4.06*	0.33
3	4 *11*		1.34 *3.25*	0.78	0.22	
4	2 *3*			0.56 *0.81*		

String Interval Distribution Program

BARSID1[or 2] (Bartók ARchives String Interval Distribution)
determines the number of strings in a given material that contain one
or two types of digits. Table XIV-2 indicates the percentages involved: note the similarity between the two Bartók collections. In
melodies comprised of one type of digit the Parry strings contain a
larger proportion of wider intervals (thirds, fourths). The Colinda
melodies, on the other hand, show more variegated intervallic structure. The particular value of BARSID is archeological, that is, it serves
as an indicator of primitiveness or acculturation.[27]

Table XIV-3. Percentage of string length
distribution in the Colinda and
Parry melodies

Length	Colindas	Parry
1	1.04	0.64
2	6.80	1.92
3	13.00	8.97
4	21.46	12.82
5	23.99	21.79
6	19.98	22.43
7	13.69	31.41

[27] In Vol. IV, *Rumanian Folk Music*, pp. 1–2, Bartók describes the Colindas as
a mixture of older and comparatively recent melodies. Moreover, a number of the
poetic texts are based on pagan epics that apparently date from pre-Christian
times. Bartók also mentions possible influence of Serbo-Croatian folk music on
that of the Rumanians; our programs seem to support his hypothesis (more con-
clusive evidence may be forthcoming upon completion of data processing of the
ca. 3,500 Bartók-tabulated Serbo-Croatian melodies now being prepared by the
present writer).

Distribution of String Lengths Program

BARDSL (Bartók ARchives Distribution String Lengths) specifies the number and percentages of string lengths (positions 1–7). Thus, as Table XIV-3 shows, an indication of characteristic syllabic structure of folk song material can be obtained.

IIIIIIIIIIIIIIIIIIIIIIIIIIIIIIIIIIIIII **Part Five**

MUSIC HISTORY AND

STYLE ANALYSIS

CHAPTER XV

Numerical Methods of Comparing Musical Styles

by FREDERICK CRANE and JUDITH FIEHLER

The availability to musicologists of fast, high-capacity computers has stimulated much effort in applying them as aids in analysis of musical structures and styles. It is natural that analysts should look to the computer for assistance, as music lends itself well to alphanumeric notation, and because so much of analysis (counting chords and the like) is mechanical and tedious.

Analysis can serve to define a style, as an end in itself, but commonly it is done in order to compare styles—to show in what ways they are similar and in what ways different. The computer promises to be as useful in comparison as in analysis; if anything, it promises more striking results in comparison applications. A musical style is so complex an organism that common-sense methods can hardly deal with it, except one element at a time. The computer's capacity and speed (and immunity to tedium) allow it to deal effectively with the intricately structured data. Computer methods are not qualitatively different from those that would be used to do the same job with paper and pencil, or desk calculator. For this reason, we will scarcely mention computers in describing some methods by which they can be used for stylistic comparison.

Numerical methods of comparison of the sort to be described here are well established in a number of other fields, although still new enough that particular techniques are not universally agreed on, and even that the validity of using the methods at all is questioned by some. In biology, numerical methods promise a greatly improved taxonomy of living organisms. In psychology, the results of testing are used to group related tests on one hand, and related personality types on the other. In ecology, homogeneous environments are listed with their biological populations, and either the species can be correlated according to the environments in which they appear, or environment types can be shown to be more or less closely related according to their species contents.

Three humanistic fields of study, archaeology, linguistics, and literary history, have made significant use of such numerical methods of comparison. Like musicology, archaeology studies products of human industry, and the archaeologist's purposes are close to those of the musicologist. Archaeology's interest in the techniques is for the establishment of artifact types through comparison of features of many examples, and for the establishment of affinities among sites and cultures through comparison of what is found in each of them. Archaeological use of methods essentially the same as those described below dates back at least to 1925, but only the availability of the computer promises to make these methods a tool of great power. Linguistics is particularly interested in the identification of language families on the basis of selected features of each language, and in reconstructing the evolutionary history of languages. Numerical methods have been used for these purposes since about 1908. Recently, a number of literary studies have used numerical techniques to good effect, particularly to settle questions of disputed authorship.

Other data units to which similar methods of comparison have been applied or for which they have been proposed include soils, complex molecules, human physical types, diseases, geological formations, coins, legislators (compared as to voting patterns) and library classifications.

That the relations of such units to each other are not unlike the interrelations of musical styles allows the whole apparatus of comparison techniques developed for use in other fields to be tested for its relevance to the particular problems of musical style. These techniques are mathematical (belonging to the category of multivariate statistics), and operate on any sort of data, indifferent to the phenomena they represent.

The objectives of such a science of musical styles will be similar to those of the familiar more subjective studies. At least until the degree of their effectiveness can be established, these numerical methods can have rather ambitious goals: (1) to distinguish fully between different personal styles—to show in what way any given work has more affinity for other works of the same composer than for works of other composers; (2) to distinguish substyles within personal styles, either as sharply differentiated styles or as a continuum of styles from one extreme to the other (these styles may be period styles, or distinct styles that the composer may have consciously adopted for different works in any temporal order); (3) to show the affinities of personal styles, or their relative closeness to each other, and to distinguish groups to which they belong, if these suprapersonal styles are suffiently discrete, and even to distinguish groups of groups.

The following elementary discussion of comparison techniques is organized according to the logical sequence of procedure: a discussion of types of raw data and their numerical representation is followed by an account of some methods of estimating affinities, and finally by some methods of establishing and displaying the mutual affinities within sets of works.

Stylistic Data and Their Numerical Representation

It seems self-evident that the more numerous and more varied the elements[1] on which stylistic comparisons are based, the more valid will be the results. The structure of even the simplest musical work is so complex, and yields meaningful data from so many viewpoints, that no simple formula can comprehend it. For some purposes, it may be desirable to base the computation of affinities on certain selected elements only, or to give extra weight to selected elements. But any subjective or a priori choice of elements should generally be avoided. For accurate results, the analysis of each work must yield as many discrete features as possible, and must be comprehensive in covering all possible aspects of the work.

Ideally, the characters to be processed should be truly elementary ones, logically self-sufficient, and not subject to subdivision. Where any other than such elementary "unit characters" are used, redundancy may result, with the effect that a single character may have more than its due weight in determining affinity. For an example, one might wish to consider as characters the highest note in a part, the lowest note in that part, and the range of the part. But the range is determined by the highest and lowest notes. Any one of the three could be omitted for zero redundancy. In practice, some redundancy will probably be unavoidable.

Data for comparison will normally be arranged in a matrix whose columns represent the works to be compared, and whose rows represent the characters on which the comparison is to be based. Either the works or the characters may be taken as the units for comparison.

[1] The terms elements, features, aspects, and characters will be used here interchangeably.

Comparison of characters will show which ones tend to be associated in different works. Taking the works as the units of comparison will result in grouping them according to their mutual affinities. The present paper is oriented toward comparison of works, which probably will be the commoner activity.

With regard to encoding for computations, three classes of characters may be distinguished: two-state, multistate, and continuous.

Two-state (or binary) characters may be such as are either present or absent in a composition (imitation, a tonal center, a figured bass), or such as are present in each of the works under study in one of two states (major or minor, tonal or real answer, exact or varied recapitulation). Normally, the value of a two-state feature will be encoded as either 1 or 0, 1 indicating presence and 0 absence. In the case of alternate states, the 1 will be arbitrarily assigned to one, the 0 to the other.

Multistate characters (meter, in a set of works that show several different meters) may be encoded as a set of two-state characters, only one of which would have the value of 1 for any given work.

Continuous characters are those that may have any value within a certain range. These may be of several types, including counts (number of measures in the work), fractions (the portion of chords that are tonic), and those features representable as a mean and a standard deviation (beats per chord might best be so represented). The ranges of values will vary greatly among different characters. In one set of pieces, the number of measures might vary between 20 and 70, while the fractions of tonic chords varied between .20 and .40. In the calculation of affinities, the larger figures would give very much more weight to the characters they represent. For this reason it is necessary to convert continuous character values to a uniform range. It is also particularly desirable to give each continuous character the same weight as each two-state character.

The conversion may take the form of compressing or expanding the scale of values linearly into the range 0–1, so that the lowest value L in the set for a certain character is made equal to 0, and the highest value H is made equal to 1, according to the formula

$$S = \frac{M - L}{H - L},$$

where M is the measured value, and S is the standardized value.

When calculating the coefficient of association, as will be seen below, only two-state characters can be used. If continuous characters must be considered, they can be converted to binary representation, but the results are at best not fully satisfactory. Binary encoding of continuous data inevitably leads to a combination of disadvantages: loss of information, distortion of the affinities of works in respect to the character involved, and undue weight given to each such character with respect to authentic two-state characters. Where two-state representation must be used exclusively, it seems desirable to seek to find more characters that are naturally so represented, rather than to convert continuous characters.

When gaps occur in the data because of a lack of complete or reliable sources, the missing characters for a work should be given a special label, such as *NC*, for "no comparison." The *NC* should also apply in the case of characters dependent on missing characters. If, for example, "imitation" is a presence-absence character, accompanied by such qualifying characters as "overlapping subjects," "rhythmically varied imitation," or "intervallically varied imitation," a work that lacked imitation would be encoded o under "imitation," and *NC* under all the characters that qualify the imitation. If these were encoded o, they would falsely show affinity in each character with works with imitation, but lacking these characters.

Measures of Affinity

Several methods can be used to convert the values of all the corresponding aspects of two works into a single measure of the affinity of the works for each other. Robert R. Sokal and Peter H. A. Sneath [2] divide the methods by which affinity can be calculated into three classes, according to whether they measure association, correlation, or distance.

Coefficients of association are calculated from data consisting of two-state features only. Sokal and Sneath [3] distinguish sixteen formulae by which the numbers of features in which the two works do or do not agree can be reduced to a single coefficient representing the degree to which the elements of the works are associated. For the present, we would suggest adoption of only the simplest formulae,

[2] Robert R. Sokal and Peter H. A. Sneath, *Principles of Numerical Taxonomy*, San Francisco, W. H. Freeman, 1963. The present paper is much in debt to the principles and techniques presented in this book, and the reader is referred to it for further information.

[3] *Ibid.*, pp. 129–130.

such as that for what Sokal and Sneath [4] call the "simple matching coefficient." If it can be shown that some other formula is more effective in associating works either according to the best definition of natural affinities, or according to their known origins, that formula should be substituted.

Where at least part of the characters have continuous values, the *mean character difference* [5] may be easily calculated. The mean character difference is conceptually the opposite of the simple matching coefficient, as it decreases rather than increases with increasing affinity. However, the mean character difference is more flexible, in that it can deal with differences between pairs of continuous values, rather than only with constant differences of one or zero. Where there are n characters in which works j and k are being compared, and the value of character i in work j is X_{ij},

$$d_{jk} = \frac{\sum_{i=1}^{n} \left| X_{ij} - X_{ik} \right|}{n}.$$

The mean character difference has the advantage of easy calculation, but a number of disadvantages in comparison to the coefficient of distance discussed below.

The *coefficient of correlation* may be used where some or all of the characters have continuous values. The type called the *product-moment correlation coefficient* will normally be preferred. Its value can be expected to vary between 0 (completely random relation of the values of corresponding characters in the two works) and 1 (agreement in all values). Negative correlations as great as −1 are theoretically possible, but in the present application they are not likely to be numerous or to have values far from 0.

The correlation coefficient has several drawbacks. It is far more difficult to conceptualize the computation than those of the coefficients of association and distance, and the calculations are much larger in number—probably no consideration when computers are used.

The third type of measure of affinity, the *coefficient of distance*, depends on conceiving the style of a work as represented by a point in multidimensional Euclidean space. Each character contributes a dimension, and the value for that character is, in effect, the distance

---

[4] *Ibid.*, p. 133.   [5] *Ibid.*, pp. 146–147.

from the Cartesian zero point on a unique directional axis. As the Euclidean distance increases with the number of characters whose values are computed, an average distance will normally be preferred.[6] This average distance compares to the mean character difference in just the same way that a standard deviation compares to a mean deviation. The relative advantages are similar in both cases.

The coefficient of distance and the mean character difference are unlike the other coefficients in that their value decreases with increasing affinity. In order to be able to use the same programs to process all the types of coefficient, the coefficients of distance and mean character differences must be converted to their reciprocals or complements, particularly by subtracting them from 1 or 10, depending on the range of the coefficients' values.

Calculation of any of the coefficients of affinity is affected by the presence of one or more NC's among the character values by which the two works are to be compared. Characters coded NC in either or both works must be totally eliminated from the computations. The validity of the affinity coefficient of any pair of works with many inapplicable characters is reduced. For this reason, NC's should be kept at a minimum, and works with many NC's should perhaps be eliminated from the study.

The result of the affinity computations will be a matrix like a mileage-between-cities table, whose columns and rows are headed by the identifications of each work. At the intersection of row i and column j will be entered the affinity between works i and j.

Methods of Clustering Styles

The concept of a work's style as a unique point in hyperspace is a very useful way of thinking not only of the relative distance of two works, but of the mutual relations among a set of works. If all the styles to be compared in a study are thought of as points scattered through hyperspace, objective answers can be sought to a number of questions about their distribution. Are they scattered at random, or do they form clouds or clusters, even slightly distinct from each other? Do the smallest clusters tend to form groups of clusters separate from each other? Are the clusters quite distinct from each other; in other words, are all points in each cluster closer to each other, or to their closest neighbors in the cluster, or to the cluster's center, than they are to comparable points outside the cluster?

[6] *Ibid.*, p. 147.

Much variety is possible in the procedures by which the clusters may be analyzed. The computer program must begin by linking the two works with the highest affinity. The succeeding steps will link other pairs, link single works to established clusters, and link clusters to each other. The order of joining, and often the membership of a cluster, will be the result of the criteria for membership. These may be: Which point outside the formative cluster is closest to any point in the cluster? Which point (or midpoint of a cluster) outside the cluster is closest to the midpoint of the cluster? Which point outside the cluster has the shortest average distance to all points in the cluster? Which point (or cluster) outside the cluster has the smallest maximum distance to any point in the cluster?

Each of the methods based on one of these criteria begins by joining the two closest points, and ends by combining all points into one cluster. But in between, the clusters established at each successive stage by different methods will not necessarily agree.[7] If any choice is to be made among clustering methods, it must be on a pragmatic basis: which method gives the most reliable clustering of a composer's works?

The results of the clustering procedure can be shown most fully in a reordered matrix of similarity coefficients, in which the order of columns and rows keeps together the works that have been linked at each stage of the clustering.[8] However, a *dendrogram*, like that in Figure XV-1, shows the structure of the clusters more graphically.

Sets of works, each set by a different composer or school, can be compared among each other by means like those with which single works are compared among each other. In comparing groups, each may be represented by its "center of gravity," or the point in space represented by the mean value of each of its features. In the case of comparisons based on two-state characters only, each character for the group can be represented by the fraction of works in which it has the value of 1.

Interpretation of the Results of Comparison

Ideally, a distinct cluster of styles will include works not only relatively similar to each other, but also of common origin, particu-

[7] Three basic clustering methods (single linkage, average linkage, complete linkage) are well illustrated in Robert R. Sokal, "Numerical Taxonomy," *Scientific American*, Vol. 215, No. 6 (December, 1966), p. 112.

[8] *Ibid.*, p. 113, and illustration, p. 110.

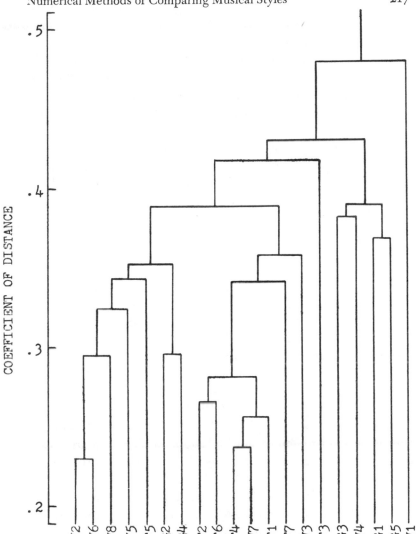

Figure XV-1. A dendrogram showing twenty chansons clustered according to style. Each horizontal line shows the coefficient of distance at which the two works or clusters below it join. A lower coefficient of distance indicates a greater affinity.

larly of a single composer. However, observed affinity and genetic proximity may not coincide in practice, and certainly are separate as concepts. Two works are genetically most similar if they were composed by the same composer, one right after the other. But perhaps another composer deliberately imitated one of the works, with the result that these two works are observably closer than are the works genetically closest to each other.

Different methods of calculating affinity and of grouping styles will undoubtedly have different results. Perhaps the genetic test will help choose among methods. The methods can best be tested on sets of works whose attributions are certain, and that are accurately dated.

Can compositions of different types be compared effectively with each other? The kind of comparison that takes into account any attribute found in a set of works, without discrimination, will normally be applied only within a set that is at least fairly coherent in origin, performance medium, and composition type, such as English madrigals, baroque secular solo cantatas, or classical symphonies. But it may be desired to apply numerical comparison to show the relations among different functional sets of the same composer, school, or period, or among different composers, schools, or periods within a single functional set. It may be desired to identify the composers of works of one type on the basis of known attributions of works of another type. Great care will be necessary to determine whether certain complexes of features will produce parallel groupings within functionally different sets of works.

Other Methods of Analyzing Stylistic Data

Cluster analysis is only one of several statistical techniques that might be used for processing stylistic data. Seriation analysis, factor analysis, and discriminant analysis all use a data matrix like that for cluster analysis, and all promise to have their own uses.

The applicability of seriation analysis to musical style is suggested by the assumption that a composer's style will change by degrees, without returning to a state that has been abandoned. If the assumption is correct, it should be possible to establish the order of a composer's works by listing them in such an order that the most similar works are side-by-side, and the least similar works are at opposite ends of the list. One end of the list should have the earliest works, and the other the latest, with at least approximate chronological order in between.

Factor analysis can be expected to show which aspects tend to vary together in the set of works under study. Our first studies show that many of the results are obvious; for example, note lengths vary with meters. But some less obvious relations also turn up, so that factor analysis promises some insights into what the composers considered related aspects of a work.

When the problem is to decide which of two or some other small number of composers wrote a disputed work, discriminant analysis should be the most useful technique. If, as a basis for comparison, there exist some other works known to be by each composer, discriminant analysis will furnish a probability that each composer produced the work in question.

An Application to Some Fifteenth-century Chansons

A first test of some of the techniques described above was made on a group of twenty chansons by three composers of the early fifteenth century. All the chansons attributed by the sources to Pierre Fontaine (7), Nicolas Grenon (5), and Jacques Vide (8) were chosen for comparison. The choice of composers as close together as possible in space and time promises the most exacting test of the methods' effectiveness; if their works can be distinguished effectively, those of composers more distant from each other should be still more easily separated.

Grenon's activities are documented between the years 1385 and 1449. He was in the Burgundian court chapel from 1412 to 1421, and otherwise was active especially in Cambrai and Bruges. Fontaine flourished from 1404 to 1447. He was in the Burgundian court chapel from 1404 to 1419 and 1428 to 1447. Vide was active from 1410 to 1433. He was at the Burgundian court from 1423 to 1433 as *valet de chambre* and *secrétaire*, but did not belong to the chapel. Thus, the three were contemporaries (Grenon older than the others), and in the Burgundian service (Grenon and Vide not simultaneously).

The eleven manuscripts in which the chansons are found are also quite close to each other, mostly copied between about 1430 and 1440, or between about 1420 and 1450 at the extremes. Seventeen of the twenty works are in the Ms. Oxford, Bodleian Library, Canonici misc. 213, all with composer attributions. There is no particular reason for questioning any of these attributions, or the three that are unique to other manuscripts. However, these manuscripts and others of the time sometimes attribute the same work to different composers, so there is a possibility that one or two of the twenty chansons are not by the composer named.

The following list of the chansons studied is in the order of the identifications assigned to each one for the project.

F1. *A son plaisir volentiers serviroye* (Fontaine)

F2. *De bien amer quant l'ay empris* (Fontaine)

F3. *J'ayme bien celui qui s'en va* (Fontaine)

F4. *Mon cuer pleure mes des yeulx me fault rire* (Fontaine)

F5. *Pastourelle en un vergier* (Fontaine)

F6. *Pour vous tenir en la grace amoureuse—Mon doulx amy, tenés vous tout temps gay* (Fontaine)

F7. *Sans faire de vous departie* (Fontaine)

G1. *Je ne requier de ma dame et m'amie* (Grenon)

G2. *Je suy defait se vous ne me refaites* (Grenon)

G3. *La plus belle et doulce figure* (Grenon)

G4. *La plus jolie et la plus belle* (Grenon)

G5. *Se je vous ay bien loyaulment amée* (Grenon)

V1. *Amans, doublés, or doublés vos amours* (Vide)

V2. *Espoir m'est venu conforter* (Vide)

V3. *Et c'est assez pour m'esjouir* (Vide)

V4. *Il m'est si grief, vostre depart* (Vide)

V5. *Las, j'ay perdu mon espincel* (Vide)

V6. *Puisque je n'ay plus de maystresse* (Vide)

V7. *Qui son cueur met a dame trop amour* (Vide)

V8. *Vit encore ce faux Dangier* (Vide)

The chansons were analyzed for a total of 145 aspects each. In 21 of these aspects, either 19 or 20 of the chansons were identical. These 21 aspects were not included in the computations, as contributing nothing to the calculation of affinities. Of the 124 aspects used, 23 are binary and 101 continuous. The attempt was made to cover nearly all aspects of the work except notation. The aspects chosen fall into the categories Voices and ranges (20), Scale (7), Diastematics (14), Rhythm and meter (23), Melody (5), Counterpoint (20), Modality (4), Form (13), and Text and its relations to music (18).

The computer program that processed the resulting data was designed to test a number of techniques, to see which yielded the best results. The nonbinary data were standardized by two slightly different methods, one of which brought them precisely, the other approximately, into the 0–1 range. The data standardized in each way were used to calculate a mean character difference, a coefficient of correlation, and a coefficient of average distance for each pair of chansons.

The resulting six affinity matrices were treated by three clustering methods—single linkage and two varieties of average linkage.

Both standardizations and all three affinity measures gave about the same results, giving each pair of works approximately, but not exactly, the same ranking on a scale from high to low affinity. Particularly, the mutual affinities among works F1, F2, F4, F6, and V7 are high according to all methods, so that they always cluster together. In general, the highest of all affinities are between works by the same composer, and the lowest ones are between works by different composers, but the contrary is true in a large part of the cases.

The results of all the clustering procedures are similar, although clustering by average linkage seems to be somewhat superior. In this procedure, linkage occurs when the average affinities of one work or cluster of works for another work or cluster are greater than for any other pair existing at the moment. The dendrogram (Figure XV-1) shows the results of the combination of 0–1 standardization of data, calculation of coefficients of average distance, and clustering by average linkage, weighted pair-group method—a combination that produced slightly better results than any other. Three distinct clusters are produced, with works V2-V6-V8-V5-F5-G2-G4, F2-F6-F4-V7-F1-F7-V3, and G3-V4-G1-G5. It can be seen easily that each of these clusters contains predominantly the works of one composer, respectively Vide, Fontaine, and Cronon. Six of the twenty works, however (F5-G2-G4, V7-V3, and V4), fall into the wrong groups, as far as authorship is concerned, and two works (F3 and V1) do not join any cluster.

The general agreement of the results of various combinations of techniques suggests that all the techniques are working effectively on the given data. The program was also run on some sets of partial data, with similar results in each case, suggesting that further refinements in the data gathered would not substantially change the results, as long as the attempt is made to include a wide variety of data.

The result of the project must be called disappointing, if it was hoped that all the works would be grouped according to their composers. Of course, this set of works was chosen to make a difficult test, and the outcome encourages the hope that, with composers a little farther apart, clusters will be more in accordance with origin. The small doubt about the reliability of the sources' composer attributions leaves open the possibility that more than twelve out of twenty of the works are clustered according to their composers. For an ideal test of the techniques, it is necessary that the composer of each work be known with certainty. A number of such tests will prove whether these numerical comparison methods can be useful in determining authorship.

Music Style Analysis
by Computer *

by A. JAMES GABURA

Music, Style, and Computers

Musical style analysis is useful variously to the artificial intelligence worker as a means of studying the composing process, to the composer as a part of his basic training, to the performer for interpreting scores, and to the musicologist for classifying scores, identifying composers, tracing stylistic influences, and reconstructing chronologies. Owing to its large capacity for data handling, the modern digital computer offers exciting new possibilities for style analysis. This article presents methods for musical parameter extraction and classification by computer, and describes experiments aimed at analyzing and identifying the keyboard styles of Haydn, Mozart, and Beethoven as exhibited in their pianoforte sonatas. The first section outlines the problem and some relevant work by other authors. The second section describes a music keypunch code and some techniques for storing music data. The third section describes methods for extracting certain numerical parameters from a musical score. The fourth section outlines a method for pattern classification by separating hyperplanes, and discusses the results of some experiments in distinguishing between similar styles on the basis of a limited number of parameters extracted from the musical score.

Style is a characteristic method of organizing musical materials, and can be associated broadly with a creative epoch, and more narrowly with an individual within an epoch. For example, the styles of Haydn, Mozart, and Beethoven are particular instances of eighteenth century musical style. In this paper, style will usually refer to individual style.

* Based on a thesis submitted for M.Sc. degree in computer science at the University of Toronto.

If statistics can be found which are related to style, we shall begin to have an objective measure of an otherwise elusive phenomenon. The evaluation of statistics depends on an ability to recognize and count events, and since traditional techniques for music analysis generally depend on the identification in the score of musical events defined by a complex set of rules, many of these techniques are capable of being automated, depending on whether the corresponding classes of musical events can be adequately defined. It is important to choose events relevant to the musical style in question; the analyst must draw on existing knowledge of music theory for guidance in choosing the pertinent musical parameters. Some trial and error may be necessary; one possible correction procedure would be to use the results of a particular analysis to synthesize an excerpt in the style under consideration and then examine the result. This can be done using a computer. In theory an analysis based on computer techniques could be carried out by hand, but in practice the amount of work involved would be prohibitive. Thus in a statistically oriented musical analysis, the computer is a key tool.

Without being overcomplicated, a statistical description of a style should embrace its important features. Given descriptions of more than one style, techniques are available for sorting out those features which distinguish one style from another—hence the feasibility of using a computer to identify the style, or the composer, of a given musical excerpt. If a certain statistic proves to be a style differentiator, we might claim to have found a measurement which is related to style, even though its musical interpretation may be somewhat obscure. However it is best to consider only statistics which can be interpreted musically.

Obviously it is impossible to perform all possible analyses of all the music that has ever been written; a number of restrictions have to be imposed before an actual experiment can be done. First it must be decided what styles are to be analyzed, and what composers will be chosen to represent those styles. Second, excerpts should be selected having as many common features as possible, to facilitate comparisons. Finally it should be decided what statistics are to be computed and how they will be related to style. Within this framework, it should be possible to find a statistical description of a particular style in terms of the musical features being examined. The problem can be restricted still further to an investigation of those features which distinguish one style from another, ignoring all common features. It is chiefly this restricted problem which is dealt with here.

Early musical applications of information theory sought to model the composing process by estimating the transition probabilities found in simple tunes. Analyses of transition probabilities have been successfully carried out for Western cowboy songs,[1] nursery songs,[2] Stephen Foster tunes,[3] and hymn tunes.[4] Synthesis based on transition probabilities can produce three kinds of results,[5] depending on the order of the analysis (in an Nth order analysis the transition probabilities for any note are conditional on the previous N-1 notes) as follows: (1) for too low an order of analysis, the results are not typical of the sample members; (2) for too high an order of analysis, the results duplicate the sample members; and (3) for an intermediate order of analysis, the results are typical of, but do not duplicate, the sample members.

A more extensive statistical analysis is reported by Fucks,[6] who computed statistical parameters related to the first-order skip distributions (frequency vs. pitch interval between successive notes) of sample melodies from 1600 to the present. One such parameter, the excess (excess $= \mu_4/\sigma^4 - 3$), is reported to show a positive correlation with historical time from the baroque to the contemporary nonserial era. Autocorrelation graphs for the sample melodies showed that the Bach melodies were less correlated than those of Beethoven, and that the Webern melodies were highly uncorrelated.

In a similar experiment, Bean[7] made first-order frequency counts of pitches in the exposition sections of four sonatas: by Mozart, Beethoven, Berg, and Hindemith. Results showed a different pattern of fluctuation of note frequency with measure number in the Hindemith

[1] H. Quastler, "Studies of Human Channel Capacity," in *Information Theory— Third London Symposium* (E. C. Cherry, ed.), Academic Press, New York, 1955, p. 361.

[2] R. C. Pinkerton, "Information Theory and Melody," *Scientific American*, 194 (1956), 77.

[3] H. F. Olson, and H. Belar, "Aid to Music Composition Employing a Random Probability System," *Journal of the Acoustical Society of America*, 33 (1961), 1163.

[4] F. P. Brooks, Jr., A. L. Hopkins, Jr., P. G. Newman, and W. V. Wright, "An Experiment in Musical Composition," *IRE Transactions on Electronic Computers*, EC-6 (1957), 175.

[5] These results were predicted and confirmed by F. P. Brooks, Jr., et al., *op. cit.*

[6] W. Fucks, "Musical Analysis by Mathematics; Random Sequences; Music and Accident," *Gravesaner Blätter*, 6, 23/24 (1962), 146, and "Mathematical Analysis of Formal Structure of Music," *IRE Transactions on Information Theory*, IT-8 (1962), 225.

[7] C. Bean, Jr., "Information Theory Applied to the Analysis of a Particular Formal Process in Tonal Music," Ph.D. dissertation, University of Illinois, 1961.

sonata than in the other three. Bean, counting each occurrence of a pitch as a single event, regardless of duration, and treating the individual notes as symbols, calculated the rate of information transmission and found it to be between 21 and 25 bits per second for Mozart, Beethoven, and Hindemith.

Extending the work of McHose,[8] who made first and second order statistical analyses of eighteenth century contrapuntal harmony, Baker[9] made a statistical study of the chords found in samples drawn from the Haydn, Mozart, and Beethoven string quartets. The samples chosen were all in major mode, in common meter, and nonmodulatory. A preanalysis was performed in which all triads were analyzed in relation to their tonal centers, thus eliminating the problem of key. Three main variables were considered: harmony, duration, and "strike" position within the measure. Harmony was considered to be the coincidence of three variables: root, inversion, and alteration status (altered or not altered). Transition probabilities up to fifth order were computed, and dependent relations between variables were investigated using chi-square tests of significance. One interesting observation was that Haydn tends to change his harmony more frequently than either of the other two composers. Both McHose and Baker also investigated the distribution of intervals between successive chord roots, considered by both to be of stylistic importance.

Music Keypunch Code

The use of a keypunch notation for music is one means of obtaining a data base for experiments in music style analysis. At present, keypunching is the simplest, cheapest, and most accurate means of coding music, although other methods are theoretically possible. One possibility is the use of an optical scanner which would accept a printed or handwritten musical score, but such a device is unfeasible at present. Data could be obtained through the use of an audio spectrum analyzer which would accept music as sound, but even were such an analyzer perfected, much of the original data would be lost. Still another possibility is the use of an electromechanical music keyboard which would transmit information directly to a computer or to an off-line storage device. This last is a reasonable solution, and would

[8] A. I. McHose, *The Contrapuntal Harmonic Technique of the 18th Century*, F. S. Crofts, New York, 1947, and *Basic Principles of the Technique of 18th and 19th Century Composition*, Appleton-Century-Crofts, New York, 1951.

[9] R. A. Baker, "A Statistical Analysis of the Harmonic Practice of the 18th and Early 19th Centuries," D.M.A. dissertation, University of Illinois, 1963.

provide rapid transcriptions, but is inherently inaccurate and would necessarily omit many of the details of the original score. Thus the keypunch code, using available equipment and manpower, is still the most accurate and inexpensive means of transcribing music into digits.

Aside from style analysis, a keypunch code for music has other uses. One of these is in a computer scheme for high-quality note setting using a photocomposition device, being developed at Columbia University.[10] A form of music code is also used by composers experimenting with a computer scheme for sound synthesis such as the one implemented in the BTL "MUSIC4" program.[11]

A keypunch notation should be simple and easily learned. It should closely follow traditional notation, for easy coding and verifying. The code should be complete, so that the data will be useful for a variety of analyses, and flexible, so that it can be adapted easily to different musical styles and notational conventions. In addition, the code should contain a certain degree of redundancy, so that some automatic checking can be provided. Clearly, a standard code for analysis, note setting, and sound generation would be highly desirable as long as keypunching remains the primary source of input for these activities. Several methods for keypunching have already been described;[12] however, these were not available at the time the present system was developed.

Described below is a code which, since 1963, has been used to transcribe a considerable body of piano music. A catalogue of the works which exist in this coded form is given in the Data Base at the end of this chapter. Various experiments on analysis of the music listed in the catalogue have been carried out.

The basic objective of the music code is to specify the pitch and duration of each note in the musical score. Other data, such as

[10] An abstract of the project is printed in Edmund Bowles (Compiler), "Computerized Research in the Humanities," ACLS *Newsletter*, Special Supplement, June (1966), 38.

[11] M. V. Mathews, and Joan E. Miller, "Music IV Programmer's Manual" (mimeographed), Murray Hill, N.J., *Bell Telephone Laboratories*, 1965.

[12] Murray Gould, and George W. Logemann, "An Alphanumeric Language for Music Analysis (ALMA)," New York University, Institute for Computer Research in the Humanities, 1966; Barry S. Brook, "The Simplified 'Plaine and Easie Code System' for Notating Music—A Proposal for International Adoption," *Proceedings of the Seventh International IAML Congress*, Dijon, 1965, in *Fontes Artis Musicae*, 12 (1965), 156; Michael Kassler, "A Representation of Current, Common Musical Notation—Manual for Key-Punchers," Project 295D, Princeton, N.J., Department of Music, Princeton University, June, 1963; Eric Regener, "A Linear Music Transcription for Computer Input," Princeton, N.J., Department of Music, Princeton University, March 23, 1964.

performance instructions, clef signs, stem directions, and so on, tend to be either unreliable or redundant and are not included, although they might be useful in other contexts. The music code is punched on standard 80-column IBM cards. Each voice is coded as a separate deck, one bar per card, and each card is uniquely identified and sequenced. To code the pitch of a note, three card columns are needed: one for the letter name, one for the accidental, and one for the octave. A two-digit integer codes the duration in terms of some minimum time unit. Thus five columns altogether are needed to specify the pitch and duration of one note. If the last 8 columns of each card are reserved for identification and sequencing, then space remains for 14 notes of 5 columns each. Thus bars of less than 15 notes can be coded one per card; bars containing more than 14 notes can be continued on the next card. The pitches and durations are coded separately: the pitches on the left side of the card, and the corresponding durations on the right. The key signature and title are

Figure XVI-1. Division of a composition into sections

included on additional cards which precede each voice, and the end of each section is marked by a special end card.

The various blocks of coding form a hierarchy as follows: (1) composer, (2) composition within composer, (3) section within composition, (4) voice within section, (5) bar within voice, and (6) note within bar. Each composition is divided into sections, or excerpts, such that each section has the same key signature throughout. The end of each section is marked with a double asterisk. The division into sections is shown schematically in Figure XVI-1.

The sections are coded one voice at a time, as shown schematically in Figure XVI-2. Each voice begins with an asterisk card, which also contains the key signature, the title, the composer, and other identification.

Two methods for storing music data in numerical form are suggested below.

In unpacked format, the most convenient structure for analysis, each note is represented by an integer which is replicated n consecutive times in n consecutive words of storage, where n represents the duration of the note in terms of the minimum time unit. The first of these replications bears a minus sign, indicating the strike position of the note. Semitones are numbered consecutively. Middle C, the 40th note of the piano keyboard, is represented by the number 40; rests are represented by zeros. Note that in this system the diatonic letter-name information contained in the original data is not retained.

An entire section is stored as an $m \times n$ matrix, where m is the number of voices in the section, and n is the number of time units. In this format, the rows represent "melodies" and the columns represent "harmonies." From this starting point, a more compact (but less useful) code can be generated if needed.

Some attention has been given to developing a special, packed format for storing music data efficiently. Such a format might be useful for analyzing an extended composition such as a symphony, or

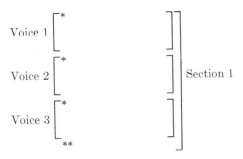

Figure XVI-2. Division of a section into voices

for more convenient handling of otherwise bulky data. A general outline of the packing scheme is given below.

The pitch and duration of each note are represented by a sequence of 12 bits: 5 for the duration, and the remaining 7 for the pitch, as illustrated in Figure XVI-3a. If the 5-bit field is insufficient for coding the duration, the following 12-bit field is used in addition, and the total duration is represented by the sum of the contents of the two fields. If these fields together are still insufficient, another 12 bits is used, and so on until the entire duration has been accounted for. The format for coding a note with a duration greater than 30 but less than 5,126 is shown in Figure XVI-3b.

Each voice is represented by a string of words, and these strings are joined together in sequence to form the code for the entire section. Each voice is preceded by a header word which points to the serial location of the header word of the next voice. The header word of the

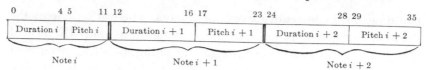

Figure XVI-3a. IBM-7094-machine-word format for packed notes

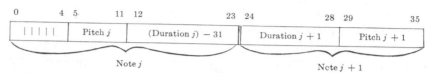

Figure XVI-3b. Format of a note with duration greater than 30 and less than 5,126

last voice points to the first unused word, which contains both a pointer of 77777_8 as an end of file indicator, and also the number of time units in the section. The entire sequence is preceded by a word which contains the number of words in the sequence. The resulting sequence is illustrated in Figure XVI-4 below:

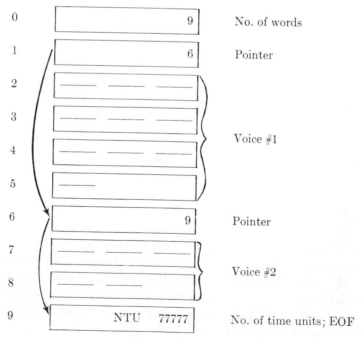

Figure XVI-4. Word sequence in the packed score

The overall saving of storage with respect to the unpacked format is at least an order of magnitude.

Musical Parameters

This section summarizes some experiments in identifying and classifying musical parameters. These parameters are determined from analyses of scale, melody, and harmony.

By *scale* is meant a set of pitches used by the composer as a basis for composition. The tonality of an excerpt is related to the scale used, which in turn can be determined by analyzing the pitch distribution.

For musical purposes, the frequency range from approximately 16 to 6,000 Hz. (vibrations per second) is divided into a series of logarithmically spaced, discrete pitches, of which there are 12 per octave. These are traditionally grouped into 12 pitch classes such that two pitches belong to the same pitch class if and only if they are an integral number of octaves apart. In the tuning scheme known as equal temperament, the pitches are related to frequencies in the following manner:

Octave ϵ $\{0, 1, 2, 3, 4, 5, 6, 7, 8\}$
Pitch class ϵ $\{0, 1, 2, 3, 4, 5, 6, 7, 8, 9, 10, 11\}$
F_b = base frequency = middle C frequency$/16$
Pitch (octave, pitch class) $= 2^{\text{octave + pitch class}/12}\ F_b$

For concert work, middle C is tuned to approximately 261 Hz. ($C_4 = 261.626$, $A_4 = 440$).

In the work described, the distributions were expressed as sets of normalized fractions x_i, such that $\Sigma x_i = 1$ over the sample space $i = 1$, $2, \ldots, n$, where $n = 88$ for pitch distributions, and 12 for pitch-class distributions. In this notation:

Mean $= \Sigma x_i i = q$
p^{th} moment $= \Sigma x_i\ (i - q)^p = \mu_p$
Standard deviation $= \mu_2^{1/2} = \sigma$
Curtosis $= \mu_4/\sigma^4 = \kappa$
Excess $= \epsilon = \kappa - 3$

Other measurements, related to pitch distributions, are suggested by information theory but were not computed here. Parameters such as rate of information transmission, entropy, and redundancy have been measured by other workers for similar data.[13]

---

[13] C. Bean, Jr., *op. cit.*; R. A. Baker, *op. cit.*

The distribution of pitches or of pitch classes provides elementary statistics which characterize certain general features of a musical score. Considering only pitch distributions of keyboard music, we might expect that the spread or standard deviation would increase with historical time, due to increasing keyboard ranges. However, pitch spread is not generally indicative of historical period, since a

Table XVI-1. Pitch-distribution parameters for excerpts in Part 1 of the Data Base

Excerpt *	Key	Mean	σ
1	A −	41.3	11.8
2	A −	49.7	8.4
3	A −	42.8	12.2
4	E♭+	41.7	12.3
5	E♭−	38.9	11.9
6	E♭+	42.1	12.1
7	E −	41.7	11.8
8	G −	45.1	10.6
9	E♭+	39.4	13.1
10	G −	42.5	13.6
11	G+	43.7	6.2
12	G+	44.0	11.0
13	G+	37.5	9.3
14	G+	43.7	14.8
15	G+	40.3	9.8
16	B♭−	46.6	12.9

* Excerpt numbers are defined in Data Base at end of this chapter.

given composer may use different spreads in different compositions, depending on the musical form and on the instrumentation. For excerpts in Part 1 of the Data Base (see Data Base at the end of this chapter), a pitch distribution was tabulated for each section, using an 88-note basis corresponding to the range of a modern piano. For each distribution, the corresponding mean, standard deviation, and second, third, and fourth moments were also tabulated. The parameters for the various sections are summarized in Table XVI-1. Note that the means of the pitch distributions do not seem to depend on key.

The pitch-class distributions were computed for the same excerpts,

ignoring octave duplications.[14] These distributions have been transposed into two standard keys for ease of comparison, C+ for excerpts
written in major keys, and A− for excerpts in minor keys, and are
presented in Table XVI-2, below. The excerpts have been rearranged
to group the major keys together. The first 10 excerpts are from
Brahms, and the last 6 are from Bartók.

Table XVI-2. Transposed pitch-class distributions for excerpts in Part 1
of the Data Base

Excerpt *		A	A♯	B	C	C♯	D	D♯	E	F	F♯	G	G♯
4	C+	.023	.163	.023	.080	.015	.068	.247	.017	.075	.014	.206	.071
6	C+	.087	.000	.082	.254	.000	.061	.008	.211	.073	.022	.202	.000
9	C+	.094	.004	.123	.165	.023	.099	.018	.173	.050	.063	.149	.030
1	A−	.234	.000	.112	.131	.022	.071	.033	.162	.074	.046	.065	.052
2	A−	.157	.021	.095	.083	.033	.161	.033	.161	.116	.029	.050	.062
3	A−	.216	.005	.108	.087	.049	.086	.043	.154	.052	.078	.050	.074
5	A−	.144	.051	.097	.108	.034	.125	.023	.199	.059	.042	.076	.044
7	A−	.121	.045	.124	.045	.058	.111	.032	.167	.104	.055	.032	.110
8	A−	.208	.008	.083	.128	.008	.108	.079	.121	.113	.068	.025	.051
10	A−	.194	.015	.088	.126	.015	.117	.076	.129	.082	.084	.025	.051
11	C+	.199	.000	.105	.141	.000	.073	.000	.189	.094	.000	.209	.000
12	C+	.247	.000	.000	.226	.032	.075	.000	.172	.022	.032	.194	.000
13	C⏐	.214	.000	.085	.231	.000	.035	.000	.168	.139	.000	.168	.012
14	C+	.218	.003	.000	.249	.032	.058	.000	.194	.038	.051	.158	.000
15	C+	.271	.000	.000	.213	.000	.058	.000	.250	.000	.000	.208	.000
16	A−	.212	.035	.025	.114	.161	.070	.044	.041	.177	.029	.025	.067

* Excerpt numbers are defined in Data Base at end of this chapter.

The pitch-class distributions were made by accumulating, over all
time units in the excerpt, the distinct pitch classes present for each
time unit, and normalizing as described. These distributions turned
out to be surprisingly useful, as shown below.

For each of the excerpts coded, it was possible to determine the key
simply on the basis of the pitch-class distribution of the excerpt. To
do this, the excerpt distribution is matched against a set of *key numbers,* which define the diatonic pitch classes contained in each of the
24 possible keys.[15] The key is determined using a maximum dot-

---

[14] In later pitch-class distribution calculations, octave duplications were normally included in the distributions.

[15] It could be argued that the members of the pitch-class collections which define the keys should themselves have weights, reflecting their relative importance

product criterion as follows: if $K = \{1, 2, \ldots, 24\}$ represents the set of key indexes, p represents the pitch-class distribution of the excerpt, and a_i, $i \in K$ are the key numbers, then the key is assigned by finding $i \in K$ such that $a_i \cdot p$ is a maximum.[16] After determining the key of each excerpt, the computer would transpose its pitch-class distribution into a standard key, either $C+$ or $A-$, for comparison with other excerpts.

It was shown above how the key of a tonal composition can be estimated on the basis of its pitch-class distribution. In an excerpt containing modulations, the key changes with time, and in order to follow the key changes, yet retain the same analytical approach, the overall pitch-class distribution over the whole excerpt has to be replaced with a series of *short-time* pitch-class distributions, employing a *time window* comparable in duration to the shortest modulatory passages.[17]

At a given point in the score, the pitches actually sounding contain the most pertinent information concerning the presence of a key change at that point. Thus a reasonable approach to the construction of a short-time pitch-class distribution at a given point is to give progressively less weight to the preceding pitches, and no weight to the following ones.[18] Although other sloping functions could have

---

as key indicators. However, such weights would necessarily be arbitrary, and experience has shown that their introduction has a tendency to confuse the key-determination procedure.

[16] An alternative method replaces the dot-product by an absolute deviation function. All distributions are first normalized so that their elements, which must be nonnegative, sum to unity. The absolute deviation between two normalized distributions x and y is defined as $0 \leq \Sigma |x_i - y_i| \leq 2$. A similarity index between x and y is defined as $0 \leq 1 - 1/2 \, \Sigma |x_i - y_i| \leq 1$. For key identification, x is replaced by the pitch-class distribution p, y is replaced by a key number a_i, and the key is assigned by finding $i \in K$ such that the similarity index between a_i, and p is a maximum. Results obtained using this method of comparison are very similar to those obtained using a dot-product. For the same excerpt, the two methods consistently yield the same predominant key, but occasionally assign a slightly different ordering to the competing keys.

[17] An alternative approach, used by Jackson and Bernzott of Roosevelt University, deduces key changes from a functional analysis of chord progressions. See R. Jackson and P. Bernzott, "Harmonic Analysis with a Computer—A Progress Report," *ICRH* (Institute for Computer Research in the Humanities), *Newsletter*, Vol. 1, 9 (1966) 3.

[18] Although a rectangular time window can produce a short-time pitch-class distribution more simply, a sloping weight function has two advantages for use in analyzing key changes: first, if the pitches at the leading edge of the time window

been used (for instance a linear ramp), an exponential weighting scheme was adopted in which the weights increase by a factor of 10 over the width of the time window, as illustrated in Figure XVI-5.

The short-time pitch-class distributions are evaluated at successive chord positions, since chords define convenient locations at which to estimate the local key (a chord is defined here as a collection of pitches, sounding together, and having a duration equal to the number of consecutive time units for which all the pitches remain un-

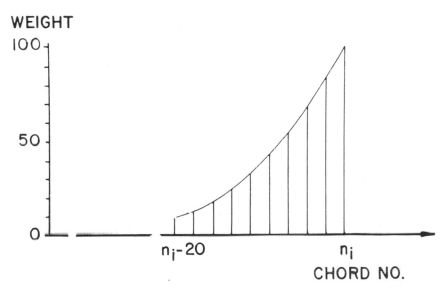

Figure XVI-5. Exponential weighting of pitch classes over a short time interval for the construction of a local pitch-class distribution (from A. James Gabura, "Computer Analysis of Musical Style," ACM Proceedings of the 20th National Conference, copyright © 1965, Association for Computing Machinery, Inc.; used by permission)

have the most weight, it seems reasonable to expect that whenever the time window reaches a key change in the score, that change will be registered immediately, whereas the region of uncertainty using a rectangular window would be of the order of the width of the window; second, in forming a mathematical definition of a subjective phenomenon such as the perception of key changes, it is desirable to make the model correspond to reality in some sense, in this case to build into it an approximation of the way one hears, acknowledging that the pitches actually sounding make the strongest impression on the listener, that with the passage of time he tends to forget what he has heard, and that he has no awareness (on first hearing) of pitches not yet sounded.

changed). Each of these short-time distributions is then used to determine a key, in the manner described earlier, which is then associated with its corresponding chord.[19]

Since it is the intention of the composer to produce key ambiguity during a modulatory passage (as opposed to a transition, which is characterized by an abrupt key change), an oscillation between the two keys present might be expected using the algorithm described. However, with an adequate time window,[20] the key changes were always indicated decisively and at the proper time, with only an occasional lag of a chord or two. A method of analyzing key ambiguity quantitatively has been implemented by printing for each chord, two or more of the highest-ranking keys, along with their associated ranking criteria. From this data, the relative abruptness of the various modulations can be deduced. The chord function in each of the various keys is computed and printed also, providing a more detailed

133	134	135	136	137	138	139	140	141	142	143	144	145	146	147
E♭+	E♭+	E♭+	E♭+	G♭+	G♭+	G♭+	F+	E♭+	E♭+	E♭+	E♭+	E♭+	E♭+	E♭+

148	149	150	151	152	153	154	155	156	157	158	159	160	161
G−	G−	F+	C+	C+	A−	A−	A−	A−	A−	A−	G♯−	G♯−	G♯−

Figure XVI-6. Computer analysis of key in Mozart's *Symphony No. 41*, K.551, Movement No. 1, Development Section, Bars 133–161 (Excerpt 6, Part 3 of Data Base appearing at end of this chapter). The key given is the predominant key at the end of the corresponding bar.

analysis of how the modulations were accomplished. An explanation of the methods used to determine chord function is provided further on in connection with the analysis of harmony. An example of a computer analysis of key is illustrated below in Figure XVI-6.

The methods described for detecting the occurrence of modulations in a musical score are effective for a wide range of styles, since they depend only on the local pitch-class distributions, rather than on a detailed analysis of chord function. Due to the nature of the approach,

[19] For chords near the beginning, the key estimates are unreliable since there are too few pitch classes represented in the short-time distributions due to the shortened time window. To correct this difficulty, an optional modification has been implemented in which the excerpt is considered to be reflected in the $t = 0$ origin. Because the short-time pitch-class distributions for chords for the beginning are by this device allowed to include pitches from future chords, their corresponding keys have a greater likelihood of being assigned correctly.

[20] In typical experiments a time window of 10 seconds was used; shorter time windows tended to result in spurious key fluctuations.

the sensitivity to key change can be made greater or less simply by decreasing or increasing the length of the time window used. Thus the model can be made to: (1) yield the hierarchical key structure of the excerpt, in which each successive level corresponds to a shorter time window, and (2) mirror the overall "sense of key" experienced by the listener at one or more of these levels.

By definition, it is meaningless to analyze an atonal composition using the concept of key. In the following paragraph a useful alternative concept is demonstrated for analyzing atonal excerpts.

Although the concept of key has no value in describing an atonal composition, it turns out that often it can be replaced by the idea of *axis*, which mathematically is nothing more than the most frequent pitch class. The method is to compute short-time pitch distributions as before, and to determine from each the most frequent pitch class.[21] An example of a computer analysis of axis is shown in Figure XVI-7.

46	47	48	49	50	51	52	53	54	55	56	57	58	59
F♯	F	C	A♯	G♯	D♯	F	G♯	E	E	C♯	C♯	C♯	C

60	61	62	63	64	65	66	67	68	69	70	71	72	73
D♯	D♯	D♯	A	A	B	F♯	F	A♯	A♯	G♯	G♯	B	C♯

Figure XVI-7. Computer analysis of axis in Stravinsky's *Movements for Piano and Orchestra*, Bars 46–73, Movement No. 2 (Excerpt 6, Part 3 of Data Base appearing at end of this chapter). The axis given is the predominant pitch class at the end of the corresponding bar.

It is instructive to analyze both tonal and atonal excerpts with respect to both key and axis. It was found that each method of analysis works best for its intended application: that is, tonal excerpts analyzed in terms of axis tend to show spurious axis fluctuations, and atonal excerpts analyzed in terms of key tend to exhibit spurious "key" changes. However, the patterns of key change and axis change seem to be more stable for tonal and atonal excerpts respectively. This conclusion is supported by the typical results shown in Table XVI-3 below. The values shown were obtained by analyzing a tonal and an atonal composition: once using the program for finding key changes,

[21] In practice this is accomplished with the same program described in the preceeding subsection, by setting each of the first 12 "key numbers" (representing the major keys) to zero except for the element representing the pitch class of the key note, and setting the second 12 "key numbers" (representing the minor keys) to all zeros.

and again with the program for finding axis changes. In each column the number in italics indicates the more stable mode of analysis for that excerpt.

These results demonstrate a computer-based analysis technique which can yield useful data for a wide range of atonal compositions which are otherwise unapproachable with traditional harmonic, or specialized atonal decomposition tools. The same approach could be

Table XVI-3. Comparison of the number of key and axis changes in both a tonal and an atonal excerpt. The excerpts are the same ones used to produce Figures XVI-6 and XVI-7.

Changes	Mozart tonal excerpt 2	Stravinsky atonal excerpt 6
Number of key changes	9	40
Number of axis changes	20	29

used also for the analysis of *modal* compositions, replacing the "key numbers" by similarly defined "mode numbers."

In a discussion of *melody* as a musical parameter, one recognizes first that historically the application of computers to music analysis began with statistical investigations of simple tunes, since these were easily coded and could be modeled by a simple time series with a finite number of states.[22] The experiments described here are essentially repeats with new data of experiments originally described by Fucks.[23] The present work supports his values for the excesses of melody skip distributions representative of the eighteenth century, and confirms the utility of the autocorrelation graph as a convenient means of determining the periodicity (or lack of same) in a given melodic excerpt.

For the excerpts represented in Part 1 of the Data Base appearing at the end of this chapter the melodies were identified during the coding process and designated as Voice 1 of the code. After converting to note number representation, the melodic skips were computed by subtracting each note number from the note number preceding it. Thus a repetition was designated by a skip of 0, a downward move-

[22] H. Quastler, *op. cit.*; R. C. Pinkerton, *op. cit.*; H. F. Olson and H. Belar, *op. cit.*; and F. P. Brooks, Jr., et al., *op. cit.*

[23] W. Fucks, "Musical Analysis by Mathematics," *op. cit.* and "Mathematical Analysis of Formal Structure of Music," *op. cit.*

ment of one semitone by a skip of −1, and so on. For the analysis of skips, the durations of the notes were not used.

A distribution of the skips occurring in each of the melody lines coded was tabulated by the computer, as in the example given in Figure XVI-8. Some of the distributions are shown graphically in Figure XVI-9, and the values obtained for the skip distribution parameters for each section of the data base are given in Table XVI-4.

BRAHMS INTERMEZZO OP 117 NO 1 IN E FLAT MAJOR MVT 1 20 BARS

DISTRIBUTION OF CONSECUTIVE INTERVALS
VOICE 1

N = 118

MEAN =	0.008
2ND MOMENT =	11.483
3RD MOMENT =	12.886
4TH MOMENT =	687.007
SCATTER =	3.389
CURTOSIS =	5.210
EXCESS =	2.210

-49	-48	-47	-46	-45	-44	-43	-42	-41	-40	-39	-38	-37	-36	-35	-34	-33	-32	31	-30

-29	-28	-27	-26	-25	-24	23	-22	-21	-20	-19	-18	-17	-16	-15	-14	-13	-12	-11	-10
																	.0085		

-9	-8	-7	-6	-5	-4	-3	-2	-1	0	1	2	3	4	5	6	7	8	9	10
	.0085	.0169		.0256	.0169	.0085	.3305	.1441	.0256	.0678	.1695	.0424	.0339	.0678		.0085	.0085	.0085	

11	12	13	14	15	16	17	18	19	20	21	22	23	24	25	26	27	28	29	30
		.0085																	

31	32	33	34	35	36	37	38	39	40	41	42	43	44	45	46	47	48	49	50

Figure XVI-8. Skip distribution for the melody line of Brahms' *Intermezzo,* Op. 117, No. 1, Movement 1 (Excerpt 1, Part 1 of Data Base appearing at end of this chapter)

The means of the distributions could be made exactly zero by considering the last note of the melody as proceeding circularly to the first. The high excess values reflect the steepness of the distributions relative to the normal distribution, and confirm the similarly high values obtained by Fucks for eighteenth century music, lending support to his suggestion that excess may be useful as a historical indicator.[24] Apparent exceptions include the Brahms, Op. 116, No. 5 (excess = −.56), in which the melody is composed chiefly of large skips and is relatively uncorrelated, and the second movement of the Brahms, Op. 116, No. 2 (excess = −1.25), in which upward and downward octave skips account for over 52 per cent of the total skip distribution. However in these two instances, the "melody" lines were chosen inappropriately during the coding process, and produced

[24] W. Fucks, "Musical Analysis by Mathematics," *op. cit.*

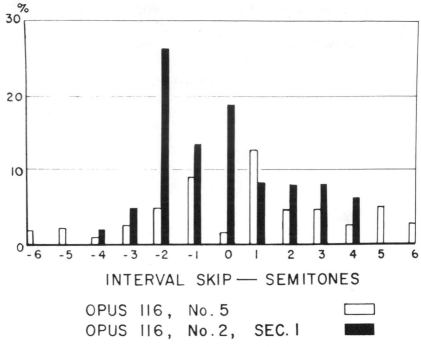

INTERVAL SKIP — SEMITONES

OPUS II6, No. 5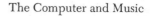
OPUS II6, No. 2, SEC. I

Figure XVI-9. Skip distributions for two Brahms melodies (from A. James Gabura, "Computer Analysis of Musical Style," ACM Proceedings of the 20th National Conference, copyright © 1965, Association for Computing Machinery, Inc.; used by permission)

anomalous results also when tested for periodicity, as explained below.

By plotting the autocorrelation function of a given melody, one can immediately determine the periodicity of the melody by inspecting the graph to a length corresponding only to the duration of the periodicity. Even if the melody is nonperiodic, some idea of its degree of predictability or randomness can be inferred from the initial portion of the autocorrelation function. If the function decays rapidly and remains near zero, the melody is uncorrelated or random (that is, contains many large skips); if it decays slowly, the melody is well behaved and predictable (that is, consists mainly of small skips). This latter interpretation of the autocorrelation graph is the one employed by Fucks, since his samples apparently consisted of too many separate melodies strung together to show a consistent periodicity.

To begin, the note scale is interpreted as a number scale, and the

Table XVI-4. Skip distribution parameters for melodies in Part 1 of the Data Base appearing at the end of this chapter

Excerpt	Number of notes in melody	Mean	σ	κ	ϵ
1	64	−.23	3.25	10.46	7.46
2	151	.03	8.78	1.75	−1.25
3	128	−.09	4.07	10.30	7.34
4	118	.01	3.39	5.21	2.21
5	65	−.19	9.04	2.98	−.02
6	131	.03	4.35	9.52	6.52
7	231	.00	7.72	2.45	−.56
8	166	.00	5.73	5.54	2.54
9	153	.00	3.72	5.09	2.09
10	161	.08	4.85	7.25	4.25
11	31	−.39	2.95	2.49	−.51
12	44	.05	3.26	2.52	−.48
13	31	−.39	2.95	2.49	−.51
14	70	.07	3.31	2.19	−.81
15	32	.38	5.14	14.20	11.20
16	61	.44	5.15	6.60	3.60

melody is considered to be a series of n notes x_i, represented by numbers on this scale. The correlation coefficients $r(n, k)$ between x_i and x_{i+k} over $i = 1, 2, \ldots, n - k$ are computed for each of $k - 1, 2, \ldots, 20$ and plotted against k. In this notation:

$$r(n, k) = \frac{\dfrac{\Sigma xy}{n - k} - \dfrac{\Sigma x}{n - k}\dfrac{\Sigma y}{n - k}}{\left\{\left[\dfrac{\Sigma x^2}{n - k} - \left(\dfrac{\Sigma x}{n - k}\right)^2\right]\left[\dfrac{\Sigma y^2}{n - k} - \left(\dfrac{\Sigma y}{n - k}\right)^2\right]\right\}^{1/2}}$$

where
$$x = x_i$$
$$y = x_{i+k}$$

For Brahms, the resulting correlograms were relatively smooth and well behaved (Figure XVI-10a), but for Bartók they had a more scattered appearance (Figure XVI-10b), due mainly to the short length of the samples used. The Brahms, Op. 116, No. 5, noted in the previous subsection as being relatively uncorrelated, has a correlogram which drops to zero at about $k - 10$, and stays there showing only small oscillations (Figure XVI-10c). The section previously noted for its high percentage of octave skips (Op. 116, No. 2, Mvt. 2) produces a correlogram which reflects strikingly the octave skips which appear on alternate beats in the score (Figure XVI-10d).

It is apparent from the above examples that the correlogram provides an easily interpreted summary of the periodicity and predictability of a melody excerpt. Such a correlogram can help characterize the excerpt: orderly or random, repetitive or nonrepetitive; and together with the skip distribution parameters, could be used as a basis for a crude classification procedure for melodies. An alternative classification procedure would involve the identification of melodic themes in the test sample, and the comparison of these, using a table look-up procedure, with a dictionary of themes mechanically extracted from a data base, or obtained from an independent library source.

In piano music of the style being considered, a great deal of stylistic information may lie in the ornamentation of melody. The ornaments, which include turns, mordents, trills, and so on, are superimposed on the melody line, and were originally used to prolong the force of the sustained notes, particularly in early piano and harpsichord music. The sound of a harpsichord dies away rapidly after the key has been struck, compared with the tone of a modern piano. Variations in the way ornaments are used by different composers do assist a trained listener in recognizing the composer's style. These variations include: (1) the actual form of the figuring, and (2) the voice in which it occurs.

For the present melodic analysis, ornamentation was not given special attention, although it was coded explicitly into the appropriate voice wherever it occurred. The analysis of melodic ornamentation might well be performed as a separate study.

A collection of tones sounding together is here referred to as a chord, having a duration represented in terms of an integral number of time units. A chord can be described in terms of its original pitches, or given as a bass note plus the intervals formed above it, or stated as a collection of pitch classes. The analysis of *harmony* is much influenced by the notation used; described below are several notations used as bases for classifying chords, and for summarizing the harmonic content of a given musical excerpt. It is proposed that harmonic content embraces style differentiators. Some approaches to the problem of extracting the root tone of a given harmony, which may be stated in either diatonic or chromatic notation, are outlined here.

In diatonic harmony, the root of a chord is the diatonic scale po-

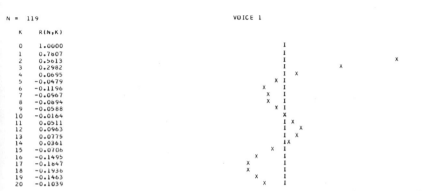

BRAHMS INTERMEZZO OP 117 NO 1 IN E FLAT MAJOR MVT 1 20 BARS

CORRELOGRAM

N = 119   VOICE 1

K	R(N,K)
0	1.0000
1	0.7807
2	0.5613
3	0.2982
4	0.0695
5	-0.0479
6	-0.1196
7	-0.0967
8	-0.0894
9	-0.0588
10	-0.0164
11	0.0511
12	0.0963
13	0.0775
14	0.0361
15	-0.0706
16	-0.1495
17	-0.1847
18	-0.1936
19	-0.1463
20	-0.1039

Figure XVI-10a. Correlogram for the melody line of Brahms' Op. 117, No. 1, Movement 1

BARTOK TEN EASY PIANO PIECES MVT 5   14 BARS

CORRELOGRAM

N = 33   VOICE 1

K	R(N,K)
0	1.0000
1	0.0806
2	-0.0978
3	-0.0951
4	-0.0723
5	0.2259
6	0.1647
7	0.2130
8	0.5044
9	-0.2581
10	-0.4411
11	-0.2416
12	0.0473
13	0.3800
14	-0.0189
15	-0.0840
16	0.1200
17	-0.5415
18	-0.4491
19	-0.0412
20	0.3966

Figure XVI-10b. Correlogram for the melody line of Bartók's *Ten Easy Piano Pieces,* V

BRAHMS INTERMEZZO OP 116 NO 5 IN E MINOR   77 BARS

CORRELOGRAM

N = 232   VOICE 1

    K   R(N,K)

    0   1.0000
    1   0.3592
    2   0.3272
    3   0.4950
    4   0.4342
    5   0.1720
    6   0.4118
    7   0.1283
    8   0.2522
    9   0.2250
   10   0.0488
   11   -0.0136
   12   0.2304
   13   -0.0949
   14   -0.0489
   15   0.0127
   16   0.0412
   17   -0.0445
   18   0.0998
   19   -0.0581
   20   0.0255

Figure XVI-10c. Correlogram for the melody line of Brahms' Op. 116, No. 5

BRAHMS INTERMEZZO OP 116 NO 2 IN A MINOR MVT 2   32 BARS

CORRELOGRAM

N = 152   VOICE 1

    K   R(N,K)

    0   1.0000
    1   0.1805
    2   -0.4301
    3   0.1864
    4   0.8202
    5   0.1868
    6   -0.4682
    7   0.1370
    8   0.7733
    9   0.1315
   10   -0.5242
   11   0.0737
   12   0.6949
   13   0.0597
   14   -0.5817
   15   0.0271
   16   0.6148
   17   -0.0452
   18   -0.6755
   19   -0.0583
   20   0.5101

Figure XVI-10d. Correlogram for the melody line of Brahms' Op. 116, No. 2, Movement 2

sition (I, II, III, IV, V, VI, or VII) upon which the chord is constructed. Above this root, in ascending thirds, are the pitches p_1, p_2, p_3, . . . which form the remaining chord tones. The resulting chord is said to be in root position: the ith inversion is formed by rearranging the constituent pitches so that p_i forms the lowest sounding tone. Thus it can be seen that in order to compute the inversion of a given chord, the root tone must first be identified.

Both Schillinger [25] and McHose [26] attach a stylistic significance to root movement, or interval between successive roots. In particular, Schillinger defines six possible root motions. In his terminology, Cycle 3 or C_3 occurs when the root moves down a third (or up a sixth); Cycle 5 or C_5 occurs when the root moves down a fifth (or up a fourth); and Cycle 7 or C_7 occurs when the root moves down a seventh (or up a second). The negative motions—C_{-3}, C_{-5}, and C_{-7} —are in the opposite direction. For example, C_{-3} occurs when the

Table XVI-5. Distribution of root movements
in typical eighteenth century composition

Root movement	Per cent	Schillinger terminology
Fifth	58	C_5, C_{-5}
Second	23	C_7, C_{-7}
Third	10	C_3, C_{-3}
Prime	9	C_0

root moves up a third (or down a sixth). Together, these exhaust all possible root motions. Schillinger termed these motions *cycles* since each one produces a unique, repetitive root pattern. He believed it a virtue in composition to use root cycles consistently and systematically, and thus evolved a theory of *cycle styles*. He concludes that C_5 is predominant in eighteenth and early nineteenth century music, as typified by Mozart and Beethoven. Similarly, he concluded that Bach shows evidence of C_7, and that C_3 appears both in Wagner and in fifteenth century Germanic compositions.

McHose, as a result of a later and presumably more extensive study of typical works of Bach, Handel, Graunn, and Telemann, estimated the occurrences of the various root motions as shown in Table XVI-5.

These root motions were further analyzed in terms of upward or downward motion as shown in Table XVI-6.

This data confirms Schillinger's conclusion that C_5 is the predominant root motion for eighteenth century music. It was therefore considered reasonable that a computer tabulation of root motion frequencies would be useful as a style-classification parameter.

To accumulate statistics on root cycles using the computer, it is

[25] J. Schillinger, *The Schillinger System of Musical Composition*, 2 vols., Carl Fischer, Inc., New York, 1941.
[26] A. I. McHose, *Basic Principles, op. cit.*

Table XVI-6. Distribution of root movements, subdivided
by direction of movement

Root movement	Relative frequency	Schillinger cycle
Fifth downward	Frequent	C_5
Second downward	Infrequent	C_{-7}
Third downward	Frequent	C_3
Fifth upward	Less frequent	C_{-5}
Second upward	Frequent	C_7
Third upward	Infrequent	C_{-3}

necessary to have an algorithm by which the computer can find the
root of any given chord. The method evolved here is based on diatonic
spelling, and is independent of accidentals. Thus for a particular
chord, the selection of the root depends upon the spelling used;
however it is known that in the epoch being considered for this type
of analysis, composers were generally quite careful in their delineation
of harmonies.

To begin, the seven diatonic letter names are placed in a cycle of
thirds, clockwise, as in Figure XVI-11.

From any starting point as a root, a chord can be constructed by
proceeding clockwise around the circumference. Conversely, the root
of a chord might be thought of as the note furthest counterclockwise
around that part of the circumference marked by the notes which
appear in the chord. Using this principle, the root of each of the four
triads shown in Figure XVI-12 can be identified as C, since each triad
is spelled with the same letters: CEG.

However, the principle stated turns out to be ambiguous in practice,
since it is not always clear which is the note "furthest counterclockwise" around the cycle of thirds. This point can be clarified with

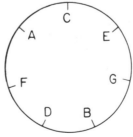

Figure XVI-11. Cycle of thirds, diatonic notation

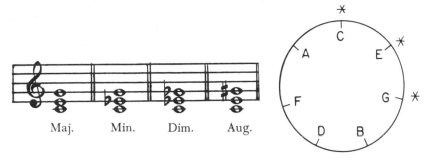

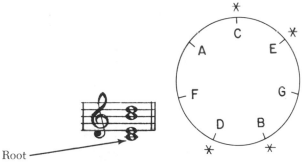

Figure XVI-12. Superposition of triads on the cycle of thirds (from A. James Gabura, "Computer Analysis of Musical Style," ACM Proceedings of the 20th National Conference, copyright © 1965, Association for Computing Machinery, Inc.; used by permission)

reference to the two examples shown in Figures XVI-13a and XVI-13b.

In Figure XVI-13a, one can find the largest unoccupied arc of the circumference, DC, and identify its clockwise extremity, C, as the root of the chord. However, an identical procedure fails for the example in Figure XVI-13b, since there is more than one unoccupied arc of maximum size, namely FC, CC, and GD. However, D is most likely the root, since it appears with a third above, viz. F. Hence, if the first

Figure XVI-13a. Letter name configuration, type 1 (from A. James Gabura, "Computer Analysis of Musical Style," ACM Proceedings of the 20th National Conference, copyright © 1965, Association for Computing Machinery, Inc.; used by permission)

procedure fails, one can find the largest occupied arc of the circumference and identify its counterclockwise extremity as the root of the chord. In the event that the letter names all appear simultaneously, the root is considered undefined.

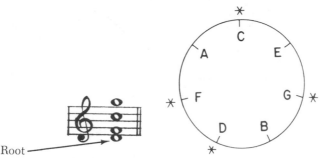

Figure XVI-13b. Letter name configuration, type 2 (from A. James Gabura, "Computer Analysis of Musical Style," ACM Proceedings of the 20th National Conference, copyright © 1965, Association for Computing Machinery, Inc.; used by permission)

The root extraction algorithm was coded for the computer, and the machine was used to compute distributions for each section in Part 1 of the Data Base (appearing at the end of this chapter) showing the percentage use of each of the six root cycles. Root cycles were computed at each time unit, and a summary was made of their distribution over each individual section. Table XVI-7a and Table XVI-7b below summarize the root-cycle distributions found in the various excerpts in the data base.

Comparing Tables XVI-7a and XVI-7b with Table XVI-6, it is apparent that there is some qualitative agreement with Brahms, but not with Bartók, as would be expected, considering that McHose's tables were based on eighteenth century harmonic practice. Table XVI-7a averages do not agree well with those in Table XVI-5; however, Table XVI-7b averages are in complete disagreement with those in Table XVI-5, suggesting that Bartók's pattern of root motions is quite different from the traditional pattern. The overall agreement with McHose is better than would be expected, considering the difficulties inherent in the particular computational method used for determining the root cycles.

There is a great deal of variability from excerpt to excerpt in the distribution of cycles within Tables XVI-7a and XVI-7b, which tends to mask the differences between the two tables. The variations might result in part from the fact that the sample excerpts were not specifically chosen for consistency, or from the possibility that these particular composers are themselves inconsistent in their use of root progressions. Also, certain difficulties with the analysis tend to result

Table XVI-7a. Root-cycle distributions in Brahms
as determined by the computer

Excerpt	C_{-7}	C_{-5}	C_{-3}	C_3	C_5	C_7
1	.255	.137	.118	.118	.216	.157
2	.312	.000	.026	.143	.234	.286
3	.192	.131	.061	.141	.313	.162
4	.165	.132	.176	.154	.242	.132
5	.088	.088	.363	.176	.209	.077
6	.120	.133	.253	.205	.193	.096
7	.238	.117	.176	.103	.154	.212
8	.049	.159	.134	.390	.085	.183
9	.204	.111	.156	.178	.147	.204
10	.080	.167	.120	.320	.167	.147
Average *	.170	.118	.158	.193	.196	.166

* Avg $C_3 + C_{-3}$ = .351; avg $C_5 + C_{-5}$ = .314; avg $C_7 +$
C_{-7} = .336.

in the computer-derived cycles being more evenly distributed than those of McHose.

One difficulty with the present technique results from the inability of the computer to distinguish nonessential tones (passing notes, suspensions, anticipations, and so on). When one of these occurs, a new chord is sometimes assumed to be present, and is given equal weight with those chords which form the underlying harmonic "skeleton." Thus the resulting root cycles are not the same ones obtained by ordinary hand analysis, although they are well defined and might be equally useful for the purpose of style classification. The difficulty is illustrated in the chorale excerpt shown below in Figure XVI-14. First

Table XVI-7b. Root-cycle distributions in Bartók as
determined by the computer

Excerpt	C_{-7}	C_{-5}	C_{-3}	C_3	C_5	C_7
11	.214	.071	.143	.286	.214	.071
12	.139	.139	.194	.167	.056	.306
13	.091	.000	.182	.455	.182	.091
14	.105	.000	.368	.421	.026	.079
15	.250	.071	.179	.286	.107	.107
16	.256	.105	.281	.175	.105	.088
Average *	.174	.064	.225	.298	.115	.124

* Avg $C_3 + C_{-3}$ = .523; avg $C_5 + C_{-5}$ = .179; avg $C_7 + C_{-7}$
= .298.

Figure XVI-14. Traditional analysis of the root cycles in a chorale excerpt compared with the computer analysis

is given the true "skeleton" analysis, then the analysis which would be produced by the computer. It is shown how a root cycle is decomposed by the computer into two different root cycles.

A second difficulty, also a result of near-sightedness on the part of the computer, arises in the vicinity of a broken chord bass. On certain beats the root is sometimes implied, rather than stated explicitly, and the real root is not detected on those beats, as shown in the example in Figure XVI-15.

Figure XVI-15. Illustration of implied root; beats on which the root is implied are indicated by asterisks

One way to avoid these difficulties might be to analyze chord roots only on strong beats, ignoring all harmony changes which occur on weak beats. However, for the purposes of style classification, it might be a disadvantage to restrict the analysis in this way, since less of the given data would be used. The advantage of using the computer in performing this task lies precisely in its ability to tirelessly execute the same root extraction procedure for each time element.[27] Preliminary results indicate a different pattern of root cycles in a Bach Chorale, particularly a predominance of C_7, as predicted by Schillinger. Thus the root cycle distribution test shows some promise as an indicator of style, and should be investigated in more detail.

The above diatonic method of finding the root of a chord can be used only if the spelling of the chord is known. However, if the only information available is the chromatic note number of each note in the chord, a new method for finding the root is needed. In contemporary music, chords are not, in general, carefully spelled, and the concept of root is often meaningless. Even when dealing with tonal composition, the problem of extracting roots is much more difficult when it is necessary to use a chromatic representation of chords, rather than a letter-name representation.

An algorithm is presented which will find roots for a certain class of chords, namely the major and minor triads and chords formed from them by adding additional thirds in an alternating major-minor sequence. This means that the triad may possess an added seventh, ninth, and so on, requiring only that the complete chord can be represented as a sequence of alternate major and minor thirds. Tones may be omitted from the sequence with no effect on the outcome of the root-finding algorithm. The algorithm is based on a 24-element tone wheel which has around its circumference an alternating sequence of major and minor thirds, as illustrated in Figure XVI-16.

Each of the 12 chromatic tones appears twice, once on the inner and once on the outer circumference. The pitches of a given chord are noted as pairs of positions on the circumference of the tone wheel, and the initial task is to delete one member of each pair. This is done by considering each pair in turn and deleting that member of the pair which is farthest from its closest neighbor. The deletion process is continued until one member of each pair has been deleted, or until no further deletions can be made (in which case no root is produced). If only one member of each pair remains, then the counterclockwise extremity of the largest arc formed by unoccupied circumference

---

[27] Since the approach described uses an analysis procedure which is simple to communicate, it seemed of questionable value to attempt to imitate a human analyst more precisely, as to do so would involve the difficult extraction of contextual information and the heuristic application of a wide range of ill-defined, ambiguous, and arbitrary rules.

positions is the root. By numbered steps, the procedure is as follows:
(1) mark all the different notes appearing in the chord; the notes will
appear in pairs, one in the inner and one on the outer circumference;
(2) with each note thus marked, associate an index which is equal to
the number of positions along the circumference to its nearest marked
neighbour; (3) consider each pair of notes, and delete the mark from

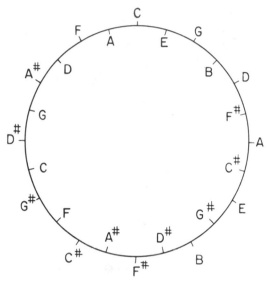

Figure XVI-16. Cycle of major and minor thirds, chromatic notation
(from A. James Gabura, "Computer Analysis of Musical Style," ACM Proceedings of the 20th National Conference, copyright © 1965, Association
for Computing Machinery, Inc.; used by permission)

the member of the pair which has the greatest index; (4) compute
new "proximity indexes" for all members of pairs yet intact, and repeat
step 3; if one member of each pair has been deleted, then proceed to
step 5, otherwise repeat steps 3 and 4 five or six times before conclud-
ing that no root exists by this definition; and (5) compute the lengths
of the arcs between all adjacent pairs of notes; the note at the
clockwise extremity of the widest arc is the root.

Having extracted the root, the chord inversion may be determined
by noting the position of the bass note (lowest sounding note) with
respect to the root on the circumference of the "tone wheel." That is, if
the bass note is the root, the chord is in root position; if the bass note
is the first position above the root in the sequence of clockwise

positions on the "tone wheel," the chord is in first inversion; and so on.

This method will not produce a correct root for the dominant seventh chord, which has a major third followed by two minor thirds, or for the diminished or augmented triads, which consist of two minor and two major thirds respectively. Therefore, the root and inversion determination for these chords was implemented by special tests.

There are many possible algorithms besides the one outlined above, for instance the one suggested by Hindemith.[28] His method is to find the lowest fifth, or failing that, the lowest fourth, and so on for other intervals in a predefined sequence, taking either the upper or lower tone of the interval, also prespecified, as the root. However, some disagreement with traditional analysis is inevitable whatever root extraction algorithm is used. It often happens that the root of a chord remains ambiguous until the chord resolves, that is, until its successor chord is known. Perhaps an improved algorithm might be found which can look ahead for clarifying details. However, it is much more practical, it has been found, simply to list all possible chords and their roots in a table. Then a simple look-up can be performed whenever a root is needed. This latter method has been successfully developed and implemented, and is described in greater detail below with reference to pitch structures.

The following is a description of experiments in which various chord notations are used in the process of classifying and identifying chord types used in music. For the purpose of making chord frequency counts, it was desired to use a technique which would retain the explicit structure of the chords, believed to contain the important style-bearing information, in contrast to a technique requiring a preanalysis of the score into traditional harmonic symbols, which would be restricted in application to a very small area of music which can be reduced to such limitations. By retaining the explicit structure, it was considered plausible that more of the stylistic information would be retained, since style is conveyed by the specific variations which occur within the traditional harmonic classification. The chords could not be retained in their original pitches, since a classification method was needed which would not depend on the particular key in which the excerpt was written. Thus chord types were constructed by retaining the chromatic intervals above the bass, omitting the bass itself.

[28] P. Hindemith, *The Craft of Musical Composition*, Vol. I (trans. by Arthur Mendel), N.Y., Associated Music Publishers, 1941, Chap. 3.

A table of harmonies was assembled by the computer in which each different combination of intervals was printed along with the percentage of the total time it was used in the excerpt. Each chord structure is tabulated as a group of integers arranged one above the other, where each integer denotes an interval, measured in semitones, above a common bass note. Thus a major triad in root position and close structure would be coded $\frac{7}{4}$.

From the table of harmonies a distribution of the intervals above the bass note was computed and printed, together with the mean and standard deviation of the distribution. The standard deviation as a measure of interval range might be useful as a historical style parameter, and should be smaller, for example, for harpsichord music than for piano music, due to the greater range of the latter instrument.

Distribution parameters for all samples in Part 1 of the Data Base appearing at the end of this chapter are given in Table XVI-8.

The frequency measurements were weighted in two ways: (1) by duration, and (2) by attack or "strike tone." Little difference was noted between the results corresponding to the two methods of weighting, and all subsequent measures were evaluated only by durational weighting.

The results of this particular experiment took the form of a large number of tables that proved hard to digest, and it was decided that in future experiments the computer should be instructed to arrange the output in such a way that would facilitate a direct comparison of the results corresponding to the different composers whose works were being analyzed.

The chief purpose of the experiment on chord comparisons was to provide information concerning the use of interval structure and harmony in the music of Haydn, Mozart, and Beethoven. The piano sonatas were chosen rather than the string quartets since the former were more readily accessible and the latter had already been analyzed statistically by Baker.[29] The experiment suggested itself as a logical extension of previous work. It was considered desirable that the results be easily interpreted, and that a test of machine implementations of various standard music-analysis techniques be demonstrated. In comparing composers with respect to frequencies of various chord types, it was expected that infrequent chord types might be particularly significant as differentiators of style. It was thus desired to compare the harmonies used by Haydn, Mozart, and Beethoven in

[29] R. A. Baker, *op. cit.*

order to discover which were used most frequently, and by which composer, and also to identify the differences between the three sets of harmonies which might provide insight into their stylistic individuality. For example, it would be expected that Beethoven would use intervals spanning a wider range than either Haydn or Mozart, since he wrote for a physically larger piano. In this experiment, type, root, inversion, key, bass note, and accent were all recognized as distinct

Table XVI-8. Interval distribution parameters for excerpts in Part 1 of the Data Base

Excerpt	Mean	σ
1	20.8	7.9
2	11.5	7.5
3	18.9	8.9
4	20.6	10.5
5	17.6	10.3
6	19.0	9.6
7	18.0	10.4
8	17.9	9.7
9	20.0	12.1
10	24.1	13.9
11	7.6	4.0
12	11.8	9.7
13	11.1	8.1
14	15.5	15.0
15	13.3	6.4
16	16.9	13.0

parameters of a chord, and chords differing in any one of these parameters were classified separately.

The selection of a scheme for coding harmonies was governed by a desire to retain as much information as possible concerning chord structure and function. An obvious approach is to divide the musical score into a series of vertical slices corresponding in width to the duration of the smallest time unit used, for example:

$$
\begin{array}{ccc}
-47 & 47 & -35 \\
-23 & 23 & -23 \\
-11 & 11 & -11
\end{array}
$$

Here each column represents the tones sounding during a single time unit. Each number corresponds to the serial number of a note on the piano keyboard. The minus sign indicates that the corresponding note is struck, and a number without a sign indicates that the tone is to be held over from a preceding attack. A difficulty arises in attempting a statistical analysis on the basis of the original pitches. Music of this style may be in any of 24 different keys, half of which are major, and half of which are minor. The note number representations of the 12 major scales are identical except for the addition of an integral constant, and the same is true for the minor scales. Hence to compare compositions written in different keys, it is necessary to obtain them in the same common key by transposition. But even single excerpts contain key changes, and so we must either restrict our input to nonmodulatory passages or devise some system by which the computer can recognize key changes automatically. Assuming that modulations can be so recognized, the above example could be recoded by the computer as shown below, in terms of semitones sounding above the lowest note. The key to which the chord belongs, and the position of the bass note with respect to the key note, are indicated below the numbers specifying the interval structure. (In these examples, columns are coded as single machine words.)

$$
\begin{array}{ccc}
-36 & 36 & -24 \\
-12 & 12 & -12 \\
1 & 1 & 1 \\
G+ & G+ & G+
\end{array}
$$

In the example, the first column specifies a chord consisting of two intervals, 12 and 36 semitones above the bass, which are both struck. The "1" indicates that the bass note is also the key note G, and the G+ indicates a G major context. The same example may be recoded more efficiently, in terms of storage space required, as shown below:

$$
\begin{array}{cc}
-36 & -24 \\
-12 & -12 \\
1 & 1 \\
G+ & G+ \\
2 & 1
\end{array}
$$

Here the integers in the bottom row specify the durations of the corresponding chords (columns), in terms of the smallest time unit used.[30]

―――――――

[30] For the purposes of constructing a time-series model of the compositional process, a symbol set composed of elements such as the above is likely to be awk-

The coding scheme used for the input data specifies each note of the musical score in terms of pitch and duration, and is described in detail under the heading Music Keypunch Code. In order to achieve some degree of consistency, the sonata excerpts chosen were all in common meter. A total of 72 excerpts were coded,[31] requiring approximately 15,500 bar-cards (Part 2 of Data Base appearing at the end of this chapter). Computer editing of the data as it was being keypunched proved to be of major importance during this phase of the project. The excerpts were limited in length so that each could be fitted into the available active storage area of the computer.

Algorithms were used to detect key changes within an excerpt, to extract roots and find inversions of chords from their chromatic representations, and to identify the chord types: major, minor, diminished, and dominant seventh. Details of these algorithms have been discussed earlier. They were coded to demonstrate that a machine could automatically perform some types of analysis traditionally done by hand, and to make the computer output more meaningful. However, since all the information about the chord is implicitly contained in its interval structure, the classification where possible into traditional harmonic symbols may have been an unnecessary complication. The analysis was carried out to first order only; higher order statistics would have to be obtained by additional programming. The excerpts were analyzed one at a time, in blocks by composer, and the resulting chord structures were tagged with their composer, and stored on magnetic tape. Finally, these structures were combined, sorted, and tabulated in a form facilitating a direct comparison of the harmonies used by the three composers studied.

Results of the comparison show that the octave (12) is by far the most common chord, and is used nearly twice as much by Haydn as by either Mozart or Beethoven. Three-note chords were less common than two-note structures, since there are more variations possible. The minor chord ($\frac{15}{3}$) for example, was used about one tenth as much as the major third (4), and more often by Beethoven than by Haydn or Mozart. In general, it was observed that Beethoven used more notes per chord than did either of the other two composers.

wardly large, and because of the high ratio of possible different symbols to the available quantity of data, it is clear that a synthesis based on such a process would degenerate at a very low order. For an experimental verification of the principle involved see F. P. Brooks, Jr., et al., *op. cit.*

[31] This phase of the project was completed by F. E. Braunlich and A. Mudgett in approximately six weeks.

One might expect that a limited number of different chord structures would appear in the works of each composer. That is, a graph of the number of different chords found plotted against the chord number analyzed might be expected to rise sharply at first, with a slope near unity, then eventually decrease in slope, and finally level off. In the present analysis, however, chord structure was complicated by chord function, so that a single interval structure might be found under several classifications, depending on the degree of the scale on which it was used, whether it occurred on a strong or weak beat, and so on. Thus the number of possibilities for different chords was greatly increased over the number that would be obtained only from differences in interval structure and discounting secondary classifications resulting from key and position within the measure. The amount of this increase was approximately 220 per cent in the experiment described. Due to the large number of separately distinguished chords, the graph of number of different chords versus chord number shows no sign of leveling off after the initial rapid increase, but appears to continue rising with constant slope in all three cases corresponding to the three composers (Figure XVI-17).

The curve for Beethoven is distinctly higher than those for Haydn and Mozart, and rises with a steeper slope. A relevant measurement is the number of *different* harmonies per harmony number, which is simply the slope of the line joining the origin to a point on the curve. This measurement decreases with increasing sample size; values are tabulated as follows for the total available samples: Haydn .22; Mozart .29; Beethoven .40. The limiting values of the slopes of the straighter portions of the curves (.15, .17, .26) indicate the same general trend, which reflects the fact that Beethoven's harmonic texture is thicker than Haydn's or Mozart's. Thus, in general, a greater harmonic variety is to be found in a sample of Beethoven, compared with samples of Haydn or Mozart of similar length.

Another observation of interest is the average number of time units per harmonic unit. This measurement confirms the observation, previously verified by Baker, that Haydn tends to change his harmonies more frequently than either Mozart or Beethoven. The two sets of results are presented below, for comparison:

                                 Baker
Haydn. . . . . .3.95 eighth notes per harmonic unit
Mozart. . . . . .4.25 eighth notes per harmonic unit
Beethoven. . . . . .4.21 eighth notes per harmonic unit

Gabura

Haydn . . . . 1.67 sixteenth notes per harmonic unit
Mozart . . . . 1.73 sixteenth notes per harmonic unit
Beethoven . . . . 1.73 sixteenth notes per harmonic unit

The discrepancy in the magnitude of the numbers is in part a result of the fact that in the present analysis, smaller harmonic units are acknowledged as being distinct. The important thing to observe is that the figures are smaller for Haydn than for Mozart or Beethoven.

In this experiment, as in the previous one, the quantity of output is almost overwhelming, due in this case to the large number of different chord types recognized. Hence a new method was developed, to be described next, which was specifically intended to reduce sharply the number of different chord classifications.

A technique was desired by which it would be possible to code the various common chord types, in such a way that the chord type and

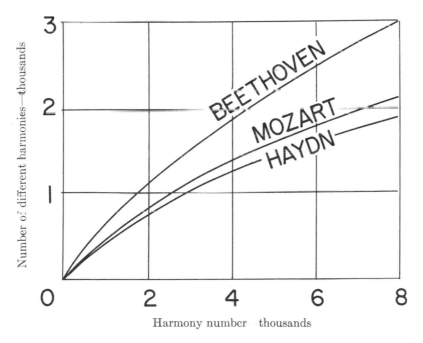

Figure XVI-17. Graph of number of different harmonies versus harmony number in the Piano Sonatas of Haydn, Mozart, and Beethoven (from A. James Gabura, "Computer Analysis of Musical Style," ACM Proceedings of the 20th National Conference, copyright © 1965, Association for Computing Machinery, Inc.; used by permission)

the inversion of a given chord could be quickly looked up in a table, thus avoiding the problem of finding a general algorithm for extracting the root of a given chord. The solution arrived at was to code each common chord type in a normalized form (root position) as a sequence of 12 ones and zeros (called a pitch structure) corresponding to the pitch classes the notes would occupy on the chromatic scale from C to B if the root of the chord were C. Since the chords are always coded in root position, the first element of the pitch structure is always "1." Using this table of chord types, the root and inversion of any chord can be easily determined,[32] provided its root position form is in the table. The list of chord types used in the present analysis is given in Table XVI-9.

A harmonic analysis of both tonal and atonal composition has been carried out using the table of chord types to determine both the roots and the inversions of chords occurring in the given musical scores.[33] The output format for the tonal harmonic analysis is illustrated below in Figure XVI-18.

Four of the highest ranking keys are shown with each chord; the first of these is the predominant one. At the end of the harmonic analysis, the ranks of the 24 keys have been determined by averaging over the entire excerpt, and were presented in order of decreasing rank.

The same chord-type table was used also for analyzing atonal compositions, but in this case the key-determination procedure was replaced by a simple determination of the predominant local pitch class, or axis, as explained above in the section headed Musical Parameters. The format for the atonal version of the harmonic analysis is shown below in Figure XVI-19.

At the end of the harmonic analysis, the 12 pitch classes, averaged over the entire excerpt, were presented in order of decreasing rank.

The use of a pitch-structure table for finding the root of a chord coded in chromatic notation is more efficient than the algorithm described previously, since it treats each chord type as a special case. A logical extension would be to compile a table of all pitch structures

---

[32] The pitch structure of the given chord is shifted cyclically until a "1" again appears in the first position. The number of times this operation must be performed to achieve a match with one of the pitch structures in the table gives the inversion of the chord, and the bit number of the root in the original pitch structure can be extracted at the same time.

[33] Many of the specifications for these programs were worked out in collaboration with P. Pedersen, a graduate student in the Faculty of Music.

Table XVI-9. Table of chord types, and their
corresponding pitch structures

Chord type	Mnemonic	Pitch structure
Rest	REST	000000000000
Unison	UNISON	100000000000
Dominant major 13th	D+13TH	100010000110
Dominant minor 13th	D−13TH	100010001010
Dominant minor 9th	D− 9TH	110010000010
Dominant major 9th	D+ 9TH	101010000010
French 6th	FR 6TH	100010100010
Diminished diminished 7th	00 7TH	100100100100
Augmented major 7th	X+ 7TH	100010001001
Diminished major 7th	0+ 7TH	100100100001
Diminished major 7th *	0+. 7TH	100000100001
Minor major 7th	−+ 7TH	100100010001
Minor major 7th *	−+. 7TH	100100000001
Major major 7th	++ 7TH	100010010001
Major major 7th *	++. 7TH	100010000001
Augmented minor 7th	X− 7TH	100010001010
Diminished minor 7th	0− 7TH	100100100010
Diminished minor 7th *	0−. 7TH	100000100010
Minor minor 7th	− − 7TH	100100010010
Minor minor 7th *	− −. 7TH	100100000010
Major minor 7th	+− 7TH	100010010010
Major minor 7th *	+−. 7TH	100010000010
Augmented triad	X TRI	100010001000
Diminished triad	0 TRI	100100100000
Minor triad	− TRI	100100010000
Minor triad *	−. TRI	100100000000
Major triad	+ TRI	100010010000
Major triad *	+. TRI	100010000000
Minor 2nd	− 2ND	110000000000
Major 2nd	+ 2ND	101000000000
Perfect 4th	P 4TH	100001000000
Diminished 5th	0 5TH	100000100000

Note: Asterisk indicates that an element is missing.

found in the given excerpt, regardless of whether they had been
previously entered manually into the table of chord types. To do this
requires a technique for normalizing pitch structures, or assigning a
root position arbitrarily, so that two pitch structures differing only by
an inversion could be identified as being the same. The procedure
used here is first to reverse the bit sequence in the pitch structure,
then cyclically to rotate the bits to form the smallest possible binary

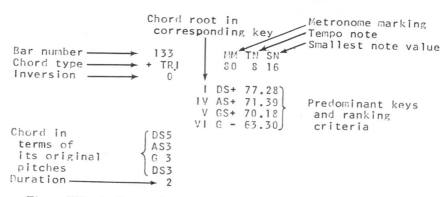

Figure XVI-18. Output format for tonal harmonic analysis

integer, and finally to reverse the bit sequence again. The result is a unique 12-bit binary number having a "1" in the first position.[34] Thus the pitch structure can be identified by a 4-digit octal number representation of either the normalized sequence of bits or the reverse normalized sequence.

Table XVI-10 and Table XVI-11 show the pitch structures, normalized according to the procedure described, contained in some typical excerpts from Mozart and Stravinsky. The tables show both the octal and binary representations of the pitch structures, and the chord types according to Table XVI-9 are shown where applicable.

Using the data obtained from all the individual excerpts in Part 2 of the Data Base appearing at the end of this chapter, averages were obtained for Haydn, Mozart, and Beethoven. A record was retained of the percentage of the total duration accounted for by each pitch structure, and also of the number of times it occurred. Only 75 unique pitch structures were found in the entire data base, including the null structure, which was used to represent a rest. With such a small set of elements, it would be not impractical to make frequency counts of pitch-structure sequences, without creating an unreasonably large set of classifications. The pitch structures for Haydn, Mozart, and Beethoven are shown in Tables XVI-12a, XVI-12b, and XVI-12c below. It is apparent that the most frequent structures are the common chord types listed in Table XVI-9.

[34] A similar representation has been adopted by H. S. Howe, Jr., who gives a FORTRAN program for computing the complete set of pitch structures in "Some Combinatorial Properties of Pitch Structures," *Perspectives of New Music,* Vol. 4, 1 (1965) 45.

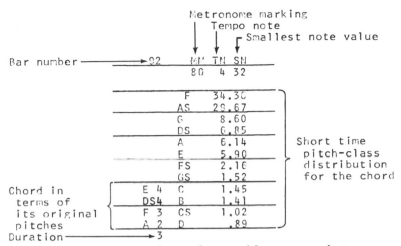

Figure XVI-19. Output format for atonal harmonic analysis

Table XVI-10. Pitch structures in Mozart, *Symphony No. 41*, K.551, Movement 1, Development Section, Bars 133–161

	Pitch structure 3 representations		Chord type	No. of occurrences	Per cent of total duration
1	0000	0000 000000000000	REST	1	2.586
2	0001	4000 100000000000	UNISON	18	8.190
3	0005	5000 101000000000	+ 2ND	1	0.431
4	0011	4400 100100000000	-.TRI	20	8.621
5	0015	5400 101100000000		2	0.862
6	0021	4200 100010000000	+.TRI	4	1.724
7	0025	5200 101010000000		1	0.431
8	0041	4100 100001000000	P 4TH	3	1.293
9	0051	4500 100101000000		6	2.586
10	0055	5500 101101000000		1	0.431
11	0061	4300 100011000000		3	1.293
12	0065	5300 101011000000		1	0.431
13	0101	4040 100000100000	0 5TH	3	1.293
14	0105	5040 101000100000	+-.7TH	3	1.293
15	0111	4440 100100100000	0 TRI	21	9.052
16	0211	4420 100100010000	- TRI	30	14.655
17	0221	4220 100010010000	+ TRI	27	12.931
18	0245	5120 101001010000		1	0.431
19	0251	4520 100101010000		1	0.431
20	0311	4460 100100110000		12	5.172
21	0431	4610 100110001000	X+ 7TH	2	0.862
22	0443	6110 110001001000	++ 7TH	5	2.155
23	0445	5110 101001001000	0- 7TH	2	0.862
24	0451	4510 100101001000	-- 7TH	1	0.431
25	0511	4450 100100101000	+- 7TH	30	12.931
26	0513	6450 110100101000		6	2.586
27	0531	4650 100110101000		1	0.431
28	0551	4550 100101101000		2	0.862
29	1111	4444 100100100100	00 7TH	6	3.448
30	1145	5144 101001100100		1	0.431
31	1225	5224 101010010100		2	0.862

Computer Identification of Style

Some experiments are described here which make use of a linear pattern recognition technique for distinguishing between the musical styles of Haydn, Mozart, and Beethoven.

In most pattern-recognition schemes, a set of measurements is made on each pattern, and these sets are subsequently classified into groups or patterns by a processor. A critical question is the selection of appropriate measurements which adequately describe the patterns. For the purpose of classifying musical excerpts, for example, any of the numerical parameters given in the section on Musical Parameters above, as well as many others, could potentially serve to characterize the style of the excerpts. Assuming that an adequate set of measurements has been selected, the problem becomes one of classifying sets of measurements. One method for performing this classification was originally called the error correction procedure by Rosenblatt, a system he invented for training his simple three-layer series-coupled Perceptron.[35]

The training procedure used in the experiments to be described was adopted directly from a formulation of Rosenblatt's error correction procedure presented by Greenberg and Konheim.[36] First, a measurement vector is determined for each musical excerpt, where each vector contains n values corresponding to a set of n numerical parameters, plus an $n + 1^{th}$ element which is given the value "1." The composers are then treated in pairs. For composer A, there are p measurement vectors x_i, $i = 1, 2, \ldots, p$, one for each excerpt, and similarly for composer B there are q measurement vectors y_i, $i = 1, 2, \ldots, q$. An $n + 1$-dimensional vector w, called the weight vector, is computed by an iterative *training* procedure to be described. The object of the training procedure is to find a weight vector w such that for an arbitrary $\theta > 0$:

$$w \cdot x_i > \theta, i = 1, 2, \ldots, p, \text{ and}$$
$$w \cdot y_i < -\theta, i = 1, 2, \ldots, q.$$

[35] F. Rosenblatt, *Principles of Neurodynamics*, Buffalo, N.Y., Cornell Aeronautical Laboratory, 1961.

[36] A number of less sophisticated classification techniques were tried and abandoned in favor of the one described, which is sometimes referred to as the method of separating hyperplanes. See H. J. Greenberg and A. G. Konheim, "Linear and Nonlinear Methods in Pattern Classification," *IBM Journal*, Vol. 8, 3 (1964) 299.

Table XVI-11. Pitch structures in Stravinsky, *Movements for Piano and Orchestra*, Bars 46–73 (Movement 2, complete)

	Pitch structure 3 representations	Chord type	No. of occur- rences	Per cent of total duration
1	0000 0000 000000000000	REST	4	4.478
2	0001 4000 100000000000	UNISON	6	7.276
3	0003 6000 110000000000	– 2ND	6	6.530
4	0005 5000 101000000000	+ 2ND	4	3.731
5	0007 7000 111000000000		4	3.358
6	0013 6400 110100000000		1	0.373
7	0015 5400 101100000000		3	1.306
8	0017 7400 111100000000		1	1.119
9	0021 4200 100010000000	+.TRI	2	1.306
10	0023 6200 110010000000	–+.7TH	2	1.679
11	0025 5200 101010000000		1	0.560
12	0033 6600 110110000000		1	2.239
13	0041 4100 100001000000	P 4TH	9	10.075
14	0043 6100 110001000000	++.7TH	1	0.746
15	0045 5100 101001000000	––.7TH	4	4.104
16	0047 7100 111001000000		2	0.933
17	0053 6500 110101000000		1	0.746
18	0061 4300 100011000000		4	3.172
19	0063 6300 110011000000		1	0.746
20	0065 5300 101011000000		1	0.746
21	0071 4700 100111000000		1	0.187
22	0101 4040 100000100000	0 5TH	1	0.560
23	0103 6040 110000100000		2	0.373
24	0105 5040 101000100000	+–.7TH	1	0.560
25	0115 5440 101100100000	0– 9TH	1	0.746
26	0117 7440 111100100000		2	2.239
27	0121 4240 100010100000	0–.7TH	1	0.933
28	0125 5240 101010100000	0+ 9TH	2	5.224
29	0141 4140 100001100000	0+.7TH	6	3.545
30	0143 6140 110001100000		1	0.746
31	0145 5140 101001100000		1	0.746
32	0161 4340 100011100000		1	1.493
33	0205 5020 101000010000		7	4.478
34	0207 7020 111000010000		4	3.731
35	0211 4420 100100010000	– TRI	1	0.560
36	0215 5420 101100010000		1	1.493
37	0223 6220 110010010000	0+ 7TH	1	1.119
38	0243 6120 110001010000		2	0.560
39	0245 5120 101001010000		2	2.052
40	0251 4520 100101010000		1	1.493
41	0253 6520 110101010000		1	2.985
42	0315 5460 101100110000		1	0.746
43	0321 4260 100010110000		1	1.493
44	0345 5160 101001110000		1	0.187
45	0443 6110 110001001000	++ 7TH	1	0.187
46	0453 6510 110101001000		2	1.679
47	0513 6450 110100101000		1	0.187
48	0523 6250 110010101000		1	0.560
49	0543 6150 110001101000		1	1.493
50	0615 5430 101100011000		1	0.746
51	0617 7430 111100011000		1	0.373
52	0625 5230 101010011000		1	0.933
53	0723 6270 110010111000		1	0.373

Table XVI-12a. Pitch structures used in the Haydn Piano Sonatas

Pitch structure	No. of occur-rences	Per cent of total duration	Pitch structure	No. of occur-rences	Per cent of total duration
0000	189	3.878	0205	140	0.798
0001	3490	24.608	0211	485	2.993
0003	215	1.066	0213	8	0.032
0005	696	4.059	0215	14	0.061
0007	2	0.008	0221	1099	9.494
0011	2093	14.542	0223	3	0.020
0013	39	0.205	0225	14	0.057
0015	34	0.176	0243	2	0.012
0021	2122	15.653	0245	21	0.148
0023	10	0.053	0251	18	0.082
0025	82	0.457	0261	7	0.028
0031	23	0.193	0305	1	0.004
0041	1498	9.358	0311	6	0.024
0043	91	0.514	0321	5	0.020
0045	174	1.375	0421	33	0.193
0051	201	1.313	0423	6	0.024
0053	1	0.008	0425	2	0.016
0055	7	0.032	0431	1	0.004
0061	76	0.432	0443	26	0.148
0101	364	2.264	0445	5	0.020
0103	40	0.263	0451	29	0.123
0105	184	1.218	0511	195	1.284
0111	229	1.877	0513	4	0.016
0115	3	0.020	0551	9	0.037
0121	46	0.283	0711	6	0.024
0125	2	0.020	1111	49	0.321
0141	4	0.028	1125	11	0.049
0151	2	0.037			

If such a vector w exists, it can be shown that the training procedure below will eventually terminate. In this case the measurement vectors are said to be linearly separable. In general, the linear separability of the measurement vectors cannot be assumed; however, there is no practical method for deciding whether the vectors are separable other than by applying the algorithm for determining the weight vector w.

The algorithm for determining the weight vector is as follows. After initially setting $w := 0$, the following four conditions are tested for the result of the dot-product $w \cdot z$, where z is replaced in turn by each of the measurement vectors x_i, $i = 1, 2, \ldots, p$, and y_i, $i = 1, 2, \ldots, q$.

$$\text{If } w \cdot z > \theta \text{ and } z \, \epsilon \, \{x_i\}, w := w$$
$$\text{If } w \cdot z \leq \theta \text{ and } z \, \epsilon \, \{x_i\}, w := w + z$$
$$\text{If } w \cdot z < -\theta \text{ and } z \, \epsilon \, \{y_i\}, w := w$$
$$\text{If } w \cdot z \geq -\theta \text{ and } z \, \epsilon \, \{y_i\}, w := w - z$$

Table XVI-12b. Pitch structures used in the Mozart Piano Sonatas

Pitch structure	No. of occur- rences	Per cent of total duration	Pitch structure	No. of occur- rences	Per cent of total duration
0000	273	4.139	0213	11	0.080
0001	3223	23.622	0215	14	0.062
0003	234	1.314	0221	1184	12.451
0005	676	4.032	0223	5	0.022
0007	4	0.035	0225	11	0.075
0011	1778	12.785	0231	4	0.026
0013	35	0.240	0245	14	0.106
0015	28	0.200	0251	17	0.089
0021	1833	13.578	0261	4	0.022
0023	31	0.267	0305	3	0.013
0025	74	0.423	0311	10	0.142
0031	18	0.133	0321	6	0.044
0041	1377	8.239	0421	32	0.245
0043	107	0.730	0423	2	0.008
0045	152	1.163	0443	5	0.049
0051	209	1.893	0445	7	0.053
0061	58	0.347	0451	10	0.080
0071	2	0.008	0455	4	0.017
0101	332	1.920	0507	1	0.004
0103	47	0.316	0511	97	1.069
0105	220	2.027	0513	5	0.053
0107	4	0.017	0551	4	0.017
0111	225	2.241	0655	1	0.004
0113	8	0.146	0711	1	0.008
0121	45	0.360	1111	15	0.427
0125	1	0.035	1113	2	0.017
0131	1	0.004	1125	4	0.017
0141	16	0.102	1133	1	0.008
0147	1	0.004	1145	2	0.008
0205	129	0.967	1325	1	0.004
0211	432	3.458			

If the entire set of measurement vectors is tested, and no change in w is required, the training procedure terminates; otherwise, the process is repeated, again replacing z by each of the measurement vectors in turn. Each such pass through the set of measurement vectors is termed an *iteration*.

Note that after a finite number of iterations, the weight vector w can be expressed as a linear combination of the measurement vectors, where measurement vectors corresponding to composer A have non-negative *coefficients*, and vectors corresponding to composer B have nonpositive ones. These coefficients should be accumulated during the training procedure, since they can indicate which *patterns* (excerpts) are relatively more significant for the purpose of separating the classes.

Having computed a weight vector w, the measurement vector z of a

Table XVI-12c. Pitch structures used in the Beethoven Piano Sonatas

Pitch structure	No. of occurrences	Per cent of total duration	Pitch structure	No. of occurrences	Per cent of total duration
0000	144	3.316	0211	407	6.105
0001	2118	19.896	0213	13	0.139
0003	147	0.957	0215	11	0.183
0005	516	3.461	0221	983	14.720
0007	5	0.094	0223	5	0.094
0011	1233	9.745	0225	45	0.434
0013	32	0.361	0231	6	0.038
0015	21	0.150	0245	59	0.634
0021	1244	10.184	0251	28	0.283
0023	9	0.083	0261	19	0.283
0025	50	0.417	0305	22	0.328
0031	9	0.105	0311	29	0.261
0041	1059	7.274	0321	5	0.061
0043	42	0.439	0345	2	0.011
0045	108	0.929	0421	13	0.116
0051	208	2.476	0423	2	0.011
0053	3	0.044	0425	6	0.055
0055	7	0.044	0431	5	0.039
0061	25	0.167	0443	36	0.384
0065	2	0.016	0445	31	0.295
0071	1	0.011	0451	68	0.717
0101	257	1.786	0453	2	0.044
0103	20	0.205	0455	3	0.100
0105	197	2.059	0505	1	0.005
0107	1	0.005	0511	313	4.363
0111	208	2.103	0513	9	0.283
0113	34	0.417	0551	7	0.094
0115	6	0.061	0651	1	0.005
0121	45	0.383	0711	4	0.038
0125	6	0.033	1111	48	0.974
0131	6	0.089	1113	8	0.211
0141	11	0.083	1115	4	0.116
0151	11	0.172	1125	2	0.027
0205	105	0.940	1315	2	0.011

new excerpt of unknown classification is identified by forming the product $\mathbf{w} \cdot \mathbf{z}$ and noting whether the result is greater or less than zero. If $\mathbf{w} \cdot \mathbf{z} > 0$, the decision will be made that the new excerpt belongs to composer A. Note that this is equivalent to asking whether $\mathbf{v} \cdot \mathbf{z}'$ is greater or less than c, where

$$\mathbf{v} = (w_1, w_2, \ldots, w_n),$$
$$\mathbf{z}' = (z_1, z_2, \ldots, z_n), \text{ and}$$
$$c = -w_{n+1}.$$

If there are m classifications, $m(m-1)/2$ vectors $\mathbf{v}_{ij}$ can be constructed, such that $\mathbf{v}_{ij}$ distinguishes between class i and class j. If we choose $\mathbf{v}_{ij}$ such that

$$\mathbf{v}_{ij} \cdot \mathbf{b} < c_{ij} < \mathbf{v}_{ij} \cdot \mathbf{a} \ (\mathbf{a} \ \epsilon \ \text{class} \ i \ \text{and} \ \mathbf{b} \ \epsilon \ \text{class} \ j),$$

then the class of an unknown measurement vector $\mathbf{z}'$ may be identified by noting that if $\mathbf{z}'$ is a l.c. of the training vectors in class j, then

$$\mathbf{v}_{ij} \cdot \mathbf{z}' - c_{ij} < 0 \ \text{where} \ 1 < i < j, \text{and}$$
$$\mathbf{v}_{jk} \cdot \mathbf{z}' - c_{jk} > 0 \ \text{where} \ j < k < m.$$

Therefore, if the measurement vectors for the excerpts of three composers can be shown to be linearly separable in pairs, the three corresponding weight vectors may be used to identify the style of a new excerpt written by one of the composers.

In the experiments here described, the relative durations of pitch structures (chords normalized with respect to transposition, inversion, and octave displacement), were used as a basis for differentiating between musical excerpts composed by Haydn, Mozart, and Beethoven. To begin, the percentage of the total duration occupied by each pitch structure was determined for each excerpt of Part 2 of the Data Base, as shown in Table XVI-10 for an individual excerpt. For all excerpts combined, a total of 75 different pitch structures was found, and these were given in Table XVI-12. A measurement vector is therefore defined for each excerpt, and contains the percentage duration of each of the 75 pitch structures in that excerpt. Since the musical excerpts were all drawn from the general category of eighteenth-century pianoforte sonatas, it seems reasonable to assume that the quantity being classified is closely related to the composer's individual style.

Some difficulty was experienced in applying the iterative training procedure to the measurement vectors corresponding to excerpts from the Haydn/Mozart composer pair, in that the weight vector did not, at first, converge. Since the convergence of the classification algorithm is an all-or-nothing affair, and since it was not known in advance whether or not the measurement vectors were in fact linearly separable, a method was needed for guiding the classification algorithm so that needless computation could be avoided, and so that intermediate successes could be achieved.

An essential feature of the training procedure is that the conditions for convergence are not affected by the order in which the measurement vectors are presented. Taking note of this, a subset of the measurement vectors is selected for which the training procedure *will* converge, and additional excerpts are added one at a time.[37] If the training procedure does not converge after K iterations with a new measurement vector, that vector is momentarily set aside and another substituted. The process terminates when all of the measurement vectors have been used to form a separating weight vector; otherwise, at least a linearly separable *subset* of the measurement vectors will have been determined.

In the event that all the measurement vectors are linearly separable, it is natural to ask what is the smallest subset of the original measurements actually needed to produce a separation of the excerpts into classes. As suggested by Greenberg and Konheim, it seems reasonable that the weights assigned to the various measurements by the weight vector would give some indication of the relative importance of those measurements. An obvious method of reducing the number of measurements required would be to delete repeatedly the measurement corresponding to the smallest weight, reconverging the weight vector if necessary. The process would terminate when the weight vector would no longer converge in a reasonable length of time. However, it has been found that in practice this method does not yield a sufficiently compact subset of the original set of measurements. Apparently, critical measurements tend to be discarded at an early stage, and the elimination process terminates prematurely.

Several other methods for reducing the number of measurements needed were tested experimentally. The particular method which was found to give the smallest subset of the original measurements proved to be identical to the method described in the above paragraph, with the exception that the weight vector **w** is cleared to zero each time the measurement set is reduced. Although this means retraining each time from scratch, a more reliable estimate of the least important of the remaining measurements is thereby obtained.

Assuming that a weight vector **w** can be found which will correctly classify all the given measurement vectors, it would be desirable to determine the error rate for classifying *new* excerpts. This can be done using the weight vector **w** to classify a number of new measurement vectors of known classification. However, since musical excerpts are expensive to code in large numbers, a random choice of

[37] In order to ensure that an excerpt which is difficult to classify will not be included in the beginning stages of the process, the initial subset of the measurement vectors is selected by taking those with the smallest coefficients resulting from a test run of, say, 2,000 iterations.

approximately 10 per cent of the sample excerpts was used to provide an independent test, and the remaining 90 per cent were used for training. The experiment was repeated several times with different random choices for the independent test excerpts, and the results were averaged to produce an estimate of the predictive power of the classification scheme.

From the above discussion it is evident that there are an infinite number of weight vectors which will classify a given linearly separable set of measurement vectors, and that these can be ranked according to their ability to correctly classify new patterns. However, the question of finding the "best" weight vector in this clearly defined sense is still a difficult unsolved problem.

As indicated in Part 2 of the Data Base appearing at the end of this chapter, there are 78 excerpts, 29 of which are Haydn, 30 are Mozart, and 19 are Beethoven. Approximately equal numbers of bars from each composer are represented. The first experiment was to determine the three weight vectors corresponding to the three composer pairs. The convergence of the weight vector for classifying excerpts of the first composer pair, Haydn/Mozart, came only after much computing, but, as it turned out, the other two weight vectors converged readily. Using a value of $\theta = 10$,[38] the computer running times for determining the weight vectors were 20.0 min. for Haydn/Mozart, 1.6 min. for Haydn/Beethoven, and 0.6 min. for Mozart/Beethoven. These times confirm the previously known fact that Haydn's work is quite similar to Mozart's. The training process proceeded at a rate of approximately 1,000 iterations per minute, with the given numbers of excerpts, and the maximum (75) number of measurements.

An estimate was made of the error rate on independent test data using randomly chosen test excerpts, according to the procedure outlined in the preceding subsection. The resulting error rates were 51.8 per cent, 29.5 per cent, and 24.2 per cent, for the Haydn/Mozart, Haydn/Beethoven, and Mozart/Beethoven composer pairs respectively. These percentages are supported by the experimental values given in Table XVI-13.

Note that in Table XVI-13, when the number of iterations required

[38] A very large value of θ was found to result in an excessive use of computer time. R. O. Duda and H. Fossum, in "Pattern Classification by Iteratively Determined Linear and Piecewise Linear Discriminant Functions," *IEEE Transactions on Electronic Computers*, Vol. EC-15 (1966), 220, estimate that θ should be near $|x|^2$, where x is a typical pattern value, but that the exact value is not critical.

Table XVI-13. Classification error rates on independent test data

Haydn/Mozart 53 training excerpts 6 test excerpts		Haydn/Beethoven 43 training excerpts 5 test excerpts		Mozart/Beethoven 44 training excerpts 5 test excerpts	
No. of iterations	No. correct	No. of iterations	No. correct	No. of iterations	No. correct
21,221	6	927	4	765	5
22,133	4	1,673	4	549	4
19,876	3	878	4	926	4
14,645	2	1,629	4	712	4
9,832	2	1,452	4	772	4
6,867	1	883	3	240	2
17,548	4	796	3	622	3
22,081	4	1,781	3	640	3
15,700	4	1,374	3	774	5
22,930	5	1,642	3	713	3
12,244	1	2,024	5	704	5
11,634	2	1,749	2	907	4
17,212	3	1,441	3	530	4
16,757	3	1,742	3	743	3
12,236	2	1,765	4	706	5
7,936	3	1,089	3	533	4
16,627	2	1,370	3	561	4
11,024	2	1,909	4	447	2
17,827	2	2,030	5	417	4

to generate the weight vector is small, the number of test samples correctly identified also tends to be small.

The qualitative characteristics of experiments of this kind are aptly summed up by Duda and Fossum: "When . . . the training patterns were linearly separable, convergence was achieved. When the training patterns were not linearly separable, the error rate for the training data dropped rapidly at first and eventually fluctuated about some limiting value. The error rate for testing data stabilized at a higher limiting value considerably sooner, the difference between the performance on training and testing data decreasing as the number of training patterns was increased." [39]

Using the method described in the preceding paragraphs, it was possible to reduce substantially the number of pitch-structure measurements required for classifying the music excerpts by composer. For

[39] R. O. Duda and H. Fossum, *op. cit.*

instance, it was found that to produce a separation of the Haydn/Bee-thoven excerpts, duration values for only 16 pitch structures were required. Similarly, the number of pitch-structure measurements required to separate the Mozart/Beethoven excerpts was reduced to 18. However, the Haydn/Mozart excerpts provided a problem at first, since the weight vectors required were initially produced at the rate of only one every 20 minutes. However, it was noticed that for both the Haydn/Beethoven and the Mozart/Beethoven pairs, the pitch structures finally remaining had been among the highest ranking 50 per cent of those in the corresponding weight vectors determined using all the measurements. This fact suggested a short-cut procedure by which the 40 per cent of the pitch structures in the originally determined weight vector having the lowest weights could be eliminated immediately. Thus it was possible to run the measurement-elimination program for the Haydn/Mozart composer pair, which eventually terminated with only 22 measurements remaining. The reduced pitch-structure sets which are sufficient to distinguish the music excerpts by composer are given below in Table XVI-14.

In conclusion it is most encouraging to note that convergence was achieved in each of the three cases, and that the convergence could be maintained using only a relatively small fraction of the available number of measurements. The relatively poor error rates on independent data can be attributed to the relatively small number of samples available for excerpts having so much variability, and are typical for this kind of experiment in which iteratively determined weight vectors are used for classifying patterns not contained in the training set. However, the 52 per cent error rate given for the Haydn/Mozart composer pair on independent test data reflects a real difficulty in distinguishing between the styles of this particular pair of composers. The main reason for this difficulty stems from the fact that the two composers in question were contemporaries, and borrowed freely from each other's work. Additional uncertainty may have been introduced by the fact that some of the excerpts have been arranged for piano by secondary composers. The lower error rates for the other two composer pairs suggest that the weight vectors computed are of some limited value for the machine recognition of the composer of a test excerpt.

It has been demonstrated how various nontrivial parameters of a music score (chord type, root, inversion, key, modulation, and so on) can be extracted by a computer from basic pitch and duration data. It

Table XVI-14. Reduced pitch-structure sets sufficient to classify the Sonata excerpts of Haydn, Mozart, and Beethoven

Haydn/Mozart		Haydn/Beethoven		Mozart/Beethoven	
Pitch structure	Sign of weight	Pitch structure	Sign of weight	Pitch structure	Sign of weight
0113	−	0061	+	0511	−
0023	−	1111	+	1111	+
0141	−	0451	−	0043	+
0443	+	0045	+	0225	−
0423	+	1125	+	0443	−
0261	+	0103	−	0031	−
0231	−	0141	−	0311	+
0101	+	0423	−	0111	+
0225	+	0151	−	0451	−
0151	+	0205	+	0305	−
0125	+	0101	+	0151	−
0421	−	0305	−	0251	+
0031	+	0421	+	0231	+
0251	−	0113	−	0023	+
0107	−	0511	−	0211	−
0455	−	0261	−	0061	+
1113	−			0005	−
0115	+			0425	−
0013	+				
0055	+				
1133	−				
1145	−				

has also been shown how measurements of one of the simpler of these, pitch structures, can be used as a basis for differentiating between two or more musical styles. The basic techniques for discriminating between similar styles using a computer might be refined in two ways. First, techniques might be developed for coding additional parameters such as rhythm and form, a wider range of musical features could be used to represent the excerpts, and some of the existing parameters, such as pitch structures, might be extended to higher order to represent, for example, chord progressions. Second, the classification or processor algorithm might be improved, possibly by employing some of the more promising methods based on statistical decision theory. Were a high order of success eventually achieved in the direction of style recognition by computer, we would expect, through a detailed knowledge of the methods and weights employed by the machine, to

have gained insight into some of the essential distinguishing features
of individual musical styles.

DATA BASE

Part 1

Excerpt	Composer and composition
1, 2, 3	Brahms, *Intermezzo* in A minor, Op. 116, No. 2, Movements 1, 2, 3.
4, 5, 6	Brahms, *Intermezzo* in E flat major, Op. 117, No. 1, Movements 1, 2, 3.
7	Brahms, *Intermezzo* in E minor, Op. 116, No. 5.
8, 9, 10	Brahms, *Capriccio* in G minor, Op. 116, No. 3, Movements 1, 2, 3.
11, 12, 13, 14, 15	Bartók, *Ten Easy Piano Pieces*, V.
16	Bartók, *Ten Easy Piano Pieces*, VII.

Part 2

Excerpt	Haydn Sonatas
1	Sonata in D major (Peters), No. 7, Mvt. 1
2	Op 31, No. 4, Mvt. 1
3	Sonatina No. 6, Mvt. 2, from Six Sonatinas for Piano (Schott & Co.)
4	Op 31, No. 2, Mvt. 2
5, 6, 7	Sonata in C major (Peters), No. 24, Mvt. 2
8, 9	Sonata in E major (Schirmer), No. 17, Mvt. 1, 3
10, 11	Sonata in E flat major (Peters), No. 26, Mvt. 1
12, 13, 14	Sonata in B flat major (Peters), No. 27, Mvt. 2
15	Sonata in C major (Peters), No. 43, Mvt. 1
16	Sonata in B minor (Peters), No. 39, Mvt. 3
17	Sonata in D major (Peters), No. 28, Mvt. 2
18, 19, 20, 21, 22, 23	Sonata in G major (Schirmer), No. 11, Mvt. 1, 3
24, 25, 26	Sonata in E major (Peters), No. 30, Mvt. 3
27, 28	Sonata in E flat major (Peters), No. 35, Mvt. 1
29	Sonata in F major (Schirmer), No. 20, Mvt. 3

Excerpt	Mozart Sonatas
30, 31, 32	Sonata in A major (K. 300i), 3rd Movement
33, 34	Sonata in C major (K. 284b), 1st Movement
35, 36, 37, 38, 39	#1 in C, Movements 1, 3, 4
40, 41, 42	#2 in A, Movements 1, 3, 4
43	#3 in D, Movement 1
44, 45	#4 in B flat, Movements 1, 3
46	#5 in F, Movement 1
47, 48	#6 in C, Movements 1, 3
	(From a set arranged by an unknown composer from K. 439b, trios for 2 basset horns and bassoon)
49, 50	Sonata in B flat major (K. Anh. 136), 1st Mvt.
51, 52, 53	Sonata in D major (K. 284c), 1st & 2nd Movements

54	Sonata in C major (K. 545), 3rd Movement
55	Sonata in G major (K. 189ʰ), 2nd Movement
56, 57	Sonata in C major (K. 300ʰ), 1st Movement
58, 59	Sonata in E flat major (K. 189ᵍ), 1st & 3rd Mvts.
	(Koechel numbers from the 6th Edition [1964])

Excerpt	*Beethoven Sonatas*
60	Op. 13, Mvt. 2
61	Op. 22, Mvt. 1
62	Op. 10, No. 2, Mvt. 3
63, 64, 65	Op. 10, No. 3, Mvt. 1
66, 67	Op. 14, No. 1, Mvt. 1
68, 69, 70, 71	Op. 27, No. 1, 1st, 6th, and 8th sections
	(Andante, Allegro vivace, and Presto)
72, 73, 74	Op. 26, Mvt. 3
75	Op. 57, Mvt. 2
76	Op. 14, No. 2, Mvt. 2
77, 78	Op. 49, No. 1, Mvt. 1

Part 3

Excerpt	*Composer and composition*
1, 2, 3, 4, 5	Stravinsky, I., *Movements for Piano and Orchestra* (1958–1959; London, Boosey & Hawkes c 1960), Miniature score (20 pp.) 10 min., Mvt. I, II, III, IV, and V (complete)
6	Mozart, W. A., *Symphony No. 41* (K. 551), Movement 1 Development Section, Bars 133–161.
7	Bach, J. S., Chorale No. 176

CHAPTER XVII

Toward a Comprehensive
French Chanson Catalog

by BARTON HUDSON

A few years ago, during an attempt to locate sources for the chansons of several fifteenth-century composers, it was impressed upon me how difficult an undertaking this can be. One must rely chiefly either upon published inventories of individual sources or upon the laborious process of personal examination of many manuscripts and early prints. (Editions of music and chance references also provide some help.) In the former case one is confronted by widely varying degrees of completeness and accuracy, ranging from a simple listing of titles and composers to detailed listings of concordances, musical incipits, and textual sources. After constructing as complete an enumeration of sources of a group of pieces as possible through this method, one then turns to the sources lacking published inventories. Assuming the availability of manuscripts and prints, on microfilm or otherwise, this is not too terribly difficult, so long as composer or text, or both, are given, though one does need elaborate files with cross indices, which are time-consuming to construct and to use.

But suppose that only a textual incipit is given. The presence of the text of a known piece is no reliable indication of a concordance with that piece. It may be a different setting of the same text, or even of a different text that begins in the same way. Or it may be a reworking of an original piece through addition or substitution of voices. On the other hand, a piece may occur in the disguise of a contrafactum, with a translation of text, or with no text at all. In the final analysis, the only reliable way to discover all concordances for a given piece is through comparison of musical incipits of each voice of the piece under study with each piece in every source that contains works of the repertory. Discovery of all concordances for even a relatively small repertory of one hundred pieces can be a formidable untertaking.

Is there no easier way to approach the problem? Perhaps not, but there is a means whereby the task can be accomplished with a high degree of completeness once and for all. Suppose that incipits of each voice of every chanson in every source were indexed in a very large file provided with a system for locating any melodic contour. Then it would be a relatively simple matter to look up each of the one hundred pieces and find complete information. But if all existing chansons were already in a file, would it not be possible to compare each with all the others and tabulate chosen items of information concerning each separate piece and make the results available? Only if a highly efficient means of making all the comparisons, tabulations, and cross indices could be found. The computer is the obvious answer. And it is my hope, by this means, to produce such a catalog for the entire literature of polyphonic French chansons from its beginning in the thirteenth century up to about 1520.

What must such a catalog contain? As presently envisioned it will include the following divisions:

A. A complete listing of all manuscript and printed sources (some three hundred of them) containing pieces from this repertory. After each should appear a list of the relevant pieces contained in it, identified by numbers keyed to the listing described under B below.

B. An alphabetized list of all the separate pieces is needed, numbered in sequence, with cross entries for those pieces with different texts in one or more voices and for contrafacta.

(1) Musical incipits given in some easily deciphered form are required. Ideally, this would be actual music notation on staff lines, provided computer hardware is available in time. Otherwise an acceptable equivalent using only symbols available on the computer printer must be used. Several systems are already in existence.

(2) Under each piece should appear a list of the sources, with a folio or page number, in which the piece occurs, identified by sigla keyed to the list of sources described under A above.

(3) For each source there should appear such other information as composer ascription and text incipit (or lack of either), any verbal canons, indication of missing voices if the source is defective, and an indication of the amount of text given in each voice (whether full text, textual incipit, or no text).

C. A melodic index, described below, is needed, whereby any desired melodic contour may be easily located.

D. A composer index should be included, with all necessary variants of each name cross-indexed, facilitating the location of any work ascribed to a given composer.

To further clarify, we may show some examples of what the entries in each section would look like. It should be understood that no claim is made for completeness or accuracy, though the examples are not fabricated. They have been constructed manually for purposes of illustration only.

A typical entry in the listing of sources would look as follows:

F112   Florence, Biblioteca Nazionale Centrale, Magl. XIX. 112.
            (Nos. 141, 657, 876, 2026, 2085, 2270, 2310, 2407, 2415,
            2419, 2633, 2687, 3380, 3818, 3853, 4017, 4493)

Four examples, including three related pieces, may show the format envisioned and some uses for the catalog (see Examples XVII-1, XVII-2, XVII-3, XVII-4).

Example XVII-1.
185. *Bergerette savoyenne*

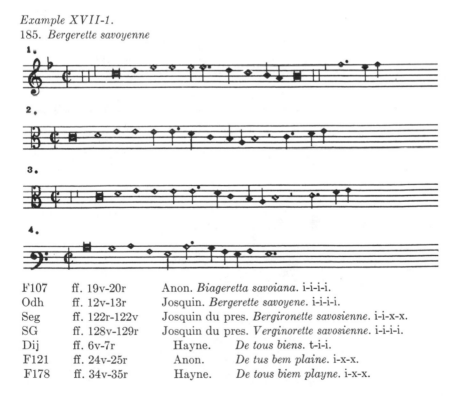

F107	ff. 19v-20r	Anon. *Biageretta savoiana.* i-i-i-i.
Odh	ff. 12v-13r	Josquin. *Bergerette savoyene.* i-i-i-i.
Seg	ff. 122r-122v	Josquin du pres. *Bergironette savosienne.* i-i-x-x.
SG	ff. 128v-129r	Josquin du pres. *Verginorette savosienne.* i-i-i-i.
Dij	ff. 6v-7r	Hayne. *De tous biens.* t-i-i.
F121	ff. 24v-25r	Anon. *De tus bem plaine.* i-x-x.
F178	ff. 34v-35r	Hayne. *De tous biem playne.* i-x-x.

Example XVII-2.
619. *De tous biens plaine*

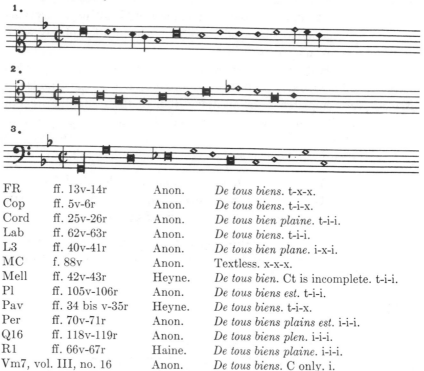

FR	ff. 13v–14r	Anon.	*De tous biens. t-x-x.*
Cop	ff. 5v–6r	Anon.	*De tous biens. t-i-x.*
Cord	ff. 25v–26r	Anon.	*De tous bien plaine. t-i-i.*
Lab	ff. 62v–63r	Anon.	*De tous biens. t-i-i.*
L3	ff. 40v–41r	Anon.	*De tous bien plane. i-x-i.*
MC	f. 88v	Anon.	Textless. x-x-x.
Mell	ff. 42v–43r	Heyne.	*De tous bien.* Ct is incomplete. *t-i-i.*
Pl	ff. 105v–106r	Anon.	*De tous biens est. t-i-i.*
Pav	ff. 34 bis v–35r	Heyne.	*De tous biens. t-i-x.*
Per	ff. 70v–71r	Anon.	*De tous biens plains est. i-i-i.*
Q16	ff. 118v–119r	Anon.	*De tous biens plen. i-i-i.*
R1	ff. 66v–67r	Haine.	*De tous biens plaine. i-i-i.*
Vm7, vol. III, no. 16		Anon.	*De tous biens.* C only. *i.*

Example XVII-3.
620. *De tous biens plaine*

| Glar | pp. 452–453 | Jodocus Pratensis. *De tous bien playne.* Ct canon: Fuga ad minimam. x-x-x. |
| Odh | ff. 102v–103r | Index: Josquin. *De tous biens playne.* Ct canon: Petrus et Joannes current In puncto. i-i-i. |

Example XVII-4.
621. Textless.

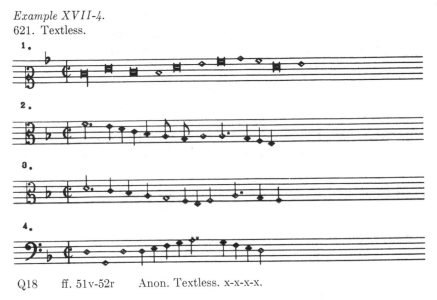

Q18   ff. 51v-52r   Anon. Textless. x-x-x-x.

Provided all the necessary data are given the computer, it should be possible to provide a similar listing of sources for every existing piece. And in many cases there should be found concordances not heretofore known.

We turn now to the melodic index. Some means must be found to locate any melodic contour one may want to identify. A system like that of Barlow and Morganstern [1] immediately comes to mind. Here melodies are represented in letters transposed to the Key of C. There are several objections, however. For one thing, in music of the early sixteenth century and before, it is at best anachronistic to speak of music in a particular key. Thus transposition to another "key" is likely to lead to difficulty. In addition, chromatic alterations and repeated notes are carefully accounted for, and, as we shall see, this can pose serious problems for this particular repertory. Conceivably a system involving the letter names of the notes of a melody could be used. But this would make no allowance for possible transpositions. A method such as that proposed by Nanie Bridgman [2] seems much more useful. Here the first note of a voice part is represented by zero. After this the

[1] Harold Barlow and Sam Morganstern, *A Dictionary of Musical Themes*, New York, Crown, 1948; *A Dictionary of Vocal Themes*, New York, Crown, 1950.

[2] "L'Etablissement d'un catalogue par incipit musicaux," *Musica Disciplina*, IV (1950), pp. 65–68. See further in N. Bridgman, "Nouvelle visite aux incipit musicaux," *Acta Musicologica*, XXXIII (1961), pp. 193–196.

intervals are represented by 2 for seconds, 3 for thirds, and so on. A plus sign denotes an ascending interval, minus a descending one. No distinction is made between major, minor, augmented, and diminished intervals, as this becomes involved with the appearance or nonappearance of accidentals, and no consistency in this respect can be expected during the period. Nor are repeated notes taken into account, since a longer note in one source is often matched by two or more shorter ones in another. Mme. Bridgman quotes the following example (see Example XVII-5)[3] pointed out in a much earlier article by O. Koller.[4]

Example XVII-5.
Trent 89, f. 420, and Paris, Bibl. Nat., ms. fr. 15123, f. 156.

Florence, Bibl. Naz., Magl. XIX. 59, f. 61.

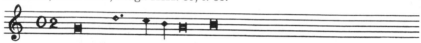

Such instances are common. Through ignoring accidentals and repeated notes, the difficulty due to many minor nonessential variants is avoided. Thus the superius of *Bergerette savoyenne* would be represented as shown in example XVII-6 (I prefer to regard the initial zero as understood).

Example XVII-6.

+2 +2   -2 -2 -2 -2 +2 +5 -2 +2

Each incipit consists of the first ten *pitch changes* (not the first ten notes), so that their numerical representation consists of ten numerals. If, then, each incipit is represented by a number sequence in an ordered listing keyed to the alphabetic listing, it would be possible to locate the beginning of any voice of any piece. This can be useful, for instance, in discovering borrowed material, the identity of melodies

---

[3] "L'Etablissement," p. 67.

[4] "Die beste Methode, Volks- und volksmässige Lieder nach ihrer melodischen Beschaffenheit lexikalisch zu ordnen," *Sammelbände der Internationalen Musikgesellschaft,* IV (1902–1903), p. 4.

with different texts, and the sources of unidentified *cantus firmi*. A similar procedure, for instance, enabled me to identify the *cantus firmus* of a Kyrie and Gloria in a manuscript at Annaberg[5] as the *Bergerette savoyenne* superius, and thereby discover that they belong to Brumel's Mass based upon it.

The melodic index will be arranged like the following example, which is a complete finding index for the four examples cited in Figures XVII-1–4.

+2	+2	−2	−2	−2	−2	+2	+2	+2	+2	185(2, 3)
+2	+2	−2	−2	−2	−2	+2	+5	−2	+2	185(1)
+2	+2	−3	+3	+2	+2	−5	+5	−3	+3	620(3)
−2	+2	−3	−2	+4	−2	−2	−2	+2	−2	185(4)
2	2	2	2	2	2	2	2	2	−2	621(2)
−2	−2	−2	−2	−2	−2	+2	+3	−2	−2	621(3)
−2	−2	−2	+4	−2	+2	+2	+2	−2	−2	619(1), 620(1)
+3	−2	−2	+3	+2	+2	+2	−2	−3	+2	619(2), 620(2), 621(1)
−5	+5	+2	+2	+2	+2	−2	−2	−2	−2	621(4)
+8	−4	+2	+3	−2	−3	−2	+2	+4	−5	619(3)

Note that the superius of the textless piece of Bologna Q18 is correctly identified as the tenor of *De tous biens plaine*.[6]

It may be objected that this system ignores a very important element: rhythm. This is true. And when it is not taken into account, there will be times when the same number sequence can represent two very different melodies, which will then be made to look like an identity. Nevertheless, a system which took rhythm into account would be cumbersome to use, and the number of misleading instances will be small. Moreover, the accompanying voices provide a check.

Certain problems arise which require special programming provisions to assure a match between incipits of two sources of a piece which contain minor variants. It is not our purpose to describe in detail the program to be used, but it may be of some value to call attention to some of the procedures which must be incorporated into it.

To begin with, the musical incipits are encoded in linear representa-

---

[5] Annaberg (Erzgeb.), Kirchenbibliothek, Ms. 1284 (*olim* Mus. Ms. 2), pp. 60–71.

[6] It must be admitted that the piece actually occurs with the words *De tous bien plen*. This harmless falsification was perpetrated here only to point up the possibilities for finding other instances of borrowing which are less easily discovered.

tion using the Digital Alternate Representation of Music Symbols (DARMS—also known as the Ford-Columbia Representation), developed by President Stefan Bauer-Mengelberg of the Mannes School of Music. Since a detailed description of this system presumably will soon be available, there is no need to go into it here. Let us merely remark that it is sufficiently powerful to describe the musical notation *as it appears* so that the score could be reproduced from it if desired.[7]

Once the incipits are introduced and certain abbreviations are expanded to complete form, the computer derives from them sequences of numbers representing melodic motion, which we shall call *pitch positions*. These are not the same as intervals, as shown in Example XVII-7.

Example XVII-7.
Pierre de la Rue, *Pour ung jamais*, bassus.

```
Intervals:        +2  -3    +2  -2   -2  +5  +2  -2   -2  +2
Pitch positions: +1  -2    +1  -1   -1  +4  +1  -1   -1  +1
```

Each of the pitch positions represents the interval from the beginning pitch, 2 for a second, 3 for a third, and so on. The plus sign indicates that the pitch is higher than the beginning pitch; minus, a lower pitch.

This has important practical applications in discovering matches when there are minor melodic variants. Suppose, for instance, that one source has a leap while another has the interval filled in with scalewise motion, as in Example XVII-8.

Example XVII-8.
A.   B.

```
        +3              +1      +1      +1     (= +3)
```

When the computer compares the interval at A with the first at B it will not find a match. It can then be instructed to compare it with the

<hr />

[7] Editor's note: The Bauer-Mengelberg system is described briefly in Chapter XIV.

next note; again no match is found. But when the next note at B is
considered, it will be recognized that it forms the same interval with
the starting pitch as at A. If the two melodic incipits agree in other
respects, the computer may tentatively assume that the two are the
same melody with only a minor variant.

This procedure will be particularly useful in cases like that shown
in Example XVII-9, which occur frequently in music of the period
around 1500.

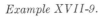

Example XVII-9.

A.

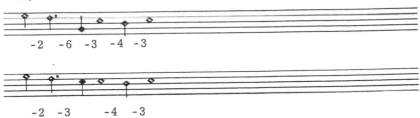

The computer will easily recognize that the first three notes and the
last of each melodic fragment are identical, while in A one additional
pitch has been inserted.

This method would circumvent another type of variant which occurs occasionally, shown in Example XVII-10.

Example XVII-10.

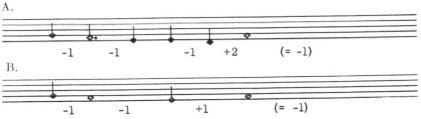

This procedure will also make matches despite scribal errors in the
sources and the inevitable encoding mistakes, provided, of course, that
they are not too serious. On the other hand, it is quite probable that
fortuitous matches will be found where none actually exist. This
should not be serious, however, as there are always the other voices to
use as checks. If the upper voices of two pieces are made to match
only through this kind of manipulation, it may be assumed that the
two are the same, with only minor variants, only if the lower voices of
each match.

A second problem concerns the choice of pieces to be encoded. Obviously those with French texts. But if part of the problem is to identify as many pieces with texts other than an original French one, other incipits must be included as well. For instance, Caron's *Tanto l'afano* is actually the same as *Le desporvue infortuné*. The *Cent mille escus* ascribed to both Busnois and Caron also appears as *Cento mille escute*. Most of the motets of Walter Frye turn out to be contrafacta of his own chansons. *Myn hertis lust* also occurs as *Grant temps* and *Beata es; So ys emprentid* as *Pour une suis desconfortée, Soyez aprantiz,* and *Sancta Maria succurre.*[8] Clearly much material must be taken into account which is only suspected to be related to the chanson repertory. However, if pieces are included which are not shown to be disguised chansons, false impressions will be created, and irrelevant and incomplete information will creep in. The solution is to tag the data for each piece with a text in a language other than French. If no match with a French piece occurs, a tagged piece can then be deleted. This still leaves textless pieces. The procedure will be to include them without the tag unless they are obviously of another repertory.

At one point it was seriously considered whether ligatures should be encoded as such, or whether representation as single notes would be sufficient. The latter course has been followed. While ligatures may indeed be of interest to the scholar, their appearance in the sources is far from consistent, and their inclusion would lead to an unacceptably cumbersome catalog in most cases. On the other hand, chansons of the thirteenth century, for example those of Adam de la Halle, are written in pre-Franconian notation. Here the ligatures are so important that they cannot be omitted.

The best method of dissemination of information contained in a catalog such as that described here is still an open question. I have assumed that it should be published in traditional book form, so that it can be perused at leisure. The cost of publication need not be prohibitive. If a high quality computerized music printer is achieved, and practical devices of this nature are currently under development, then the computer output should be ready for offset printing, requiring only minor touch-up. The expense of typesetting would be eliminated.

There is another possibility, however, which should not be overlooked, at least in the future. This is the storage of the completed

[8] Sylvia W. Kenney, *Walter Frye and the Contenance Angloise,* New Haven and London, Yale University Press, 1964, p. 64.

catalog on tape at a central location so that anyone needing information could have access to it. Presumably university computer centers
will be interconnected by telephone lines within a few years, enabling
a scholar to request information of computer A at his local installation.
Computer A will then contact computer B at the information center,
perhaps hundreds of miles away. The requested material is quickly
found and relayed to computer A, which immediately prints it out for
the scholar's use. Whether browsing by telephone, via computer, will
replace browsing in a book in an office or library remains to be seen.
Very much more elaborate information retrieval systems are seriously
anticipated within a few decades, systems which would render libraries as we know them obsolete.[9]

The comprehensive index and concordance described here is a vast
project which will require considerable time for completion. It is,
however, quite unlikely that it will be more time-consuming than an
exhaustive inventory of two or three large manuscripts. And if done
successfully, only occasional corrections or refinements should be
required in the future. Moreover, the experience derived from it and
other similar ones currently in progress should serve as models and
springboards for similar, or even more extensive, treatment of other
repertories. Complete bibliographical control of source materials is
now a possibility. The scholar can be relieved of much of the tedious
work that is merely preparatory to his main problem.

[9] J. C. R. Licklider, *Libraries of the Future,* Cambridge, Mass., M.I.T. Press,
1965.

CHAPTER XVIII

Transcription of Tablature
to Standard Notation

by W. EARLE HULTBERG

Research conducted over a span of several years indicates that as yet only a relatively small portion of Spanish Renaissance musical literature has been brought to light. Despite the many contributions of highly qualified scholars, significant gaps still exist in the knowledge of this repertoire. In its original form, much of the material is written in sixteenth century notation; a considerable amount, particularly that for keyboard, lute, or vihuela, appears in various kinds of tablatures.

Among Spanish composers of this period, Antonio de Cabezón is one of the most prominent. The collected works, published in 1578, were set in tablature by his son, Hernando de Cabezón, and many of Cabezón's compositions are available today in editions suitable for performance or study. The long-range goal of the present project is to make available for these purposes much more of the repertoire of the Spanish Renaissance.

A microfilm of Cabezón's collected works as published by his son was obtained at the Escorial Library near Madrid, Spain. Most of the works are original compositions of Antonio de Cabezón; several, however, are glossed settings by Cabezón of works by other writers such as Hernando de Cabezón, Josquin, and Verdelot.[1]

Cabezón works were selected for the project because they offer ample opportunity to solve various problems of transcription typical of tablature from this period. Two to six voices are used; hexachord orientations are indicated at the beginning of most pieces. Time

[1] *Obras de Musica para Tecla, Arpa y Vihuela,* de Antonio de Cabeçón, Musico de la Camara y Capilla del Rey Don Philippe nuestro Señor. Recopiladas y puestas en Cifra por Hernando de Cabeçón, su hijo.

signatures are usually either $\frac{2}{2}$ or $\frac{3}{2}$; note values range from whole to sixteenths. Whenever the composer deems them necessary, rhythmic values which apply ordinarily to the most active voice are assigned above the appropriate pitch designations.

The research project [2] has attempted to develop processes designed to transcribe to standard notation, through utilization of the capabilities of computer programming, tablatures of the type used by Cabezón and other writers contemporaneous with him. It is hoped that similar processes will be developed which will aid in the transcription of other tablatures.

The focus, intent, and purposes of the project are first, to develop appropriate programs designed to transfer tablature to the Ford-Columbia music representation, and second to encode in Ford-Columbia representation by this process a large, representative body of material. The availability of this data offers several further possibilities, as noted.

(a) A printout eventually can be made of the music in transcription to standard notation using the PHOTON process developed by the Ford-Columbia project.

(b) Because the Ford-Columbia representation is in essence the complete musical score, analysis of the music from any of several standpoints becomes possible through the use of additional programs. For such purposes languages such as FORTRAN IV or SNOBOL IV have been found extremely helpful. Important comparisons can be made on a large scale between the theory and practices of any given period or styles.

(c) Accurate, detailed indexing and comparisons of large numbers of incipits, glosses and other embellishments, and cadence formulae come within the realm of possibility. As part of the present project, a complete thematic index in Ford-Columbia representation of Cabezón's works has been included.

A third purpose of the project is to establish bases for the development of additional computer programs which will in turn provide means to transcribe other types of keyboard, lute, and vihuela tablature to standard notation via intermediate languages.

---

[2] Supported by a Grant-in-Aid from the Research Foundation of the State University of New York, the project has been developed at the State University College at Potsdam, New York, with the assistance and cooperation of the Computer Science Department, Alan Stillman, Director, and John Short, Programmer.

Thematic Index

A complete thematic index of Cabezón's works has been prepared in Ford-Columbia music representation. Pitch and duration codes have been given for the first ten to twelve notes of each composition; in each case the voice which seemed most appropriate has been selected for encoding. Sharps, flats, and natural signs have been included wherever they appear in the original.

The index, an important reference source for the repertoire of the Spanish sixteenth century, is part of the collection of computer-readable thematic indices currently being established.

Computer Programs

The computer programs developed as the principal part of this project have as their primary objective the transference of a key-punched form of Cabezón's tablature to standard notation. Necessary and pertinent procedures include the following.

(1) A linear, key-punched representation of the tablature in a simple, intermediate input code is required. Basic data (title, clefs, signatures, number of voices) are stated at the beginning of each composition. Rhythmic indications (W, H, Q, E, S) and signs for sharp ($\sharp$), flat (-), and natural (°) are initially encoded as they appear in Ford-Columbia representation. Pitch designations, ties, and measure bars are indicated in a manner similar to that in which they appear in the tablature. In order to provide the necessary information for each note, four spaces are reserved on the encoding form to show: Number, Range, Accidental, and Value. Thus, for example, F with the value of a quarter note appears as: 1 Q; a tied quarter note appears as: , Q. Figure XVIII-1 shows bass and treble clef pitches as they are designated by Cabezón, the intermediate input code, and Ford-Columbia representation. Additional clefs are used when necessary.

(2) Computer programs to transfer the intermediate input code described above to Ford-Columbia representation are necessary. The programs (a) transfer each note and rest to the appropriate form in Ford-Columbia representation (pitch and duration codes are included); (b) align all vertical simultaneities; (c) coalesce measure bars; (d) indicate ties; (e) add all necessary stems, showing direction designated for various voices and staff position.

Figures XVIII-2, XVIII-3, XVIII-4, and XVIII-5, based on a short homophonic piece selected from Cabezón's works, demonstrate the process outlined above.

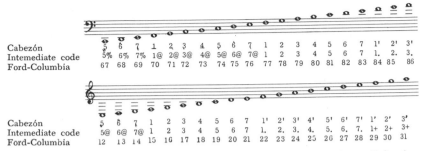

Figure XVIII-1. Bass and treble clef pitches as designated by Cabezón, by intermediate input code, and by Ford-Columbia representation.

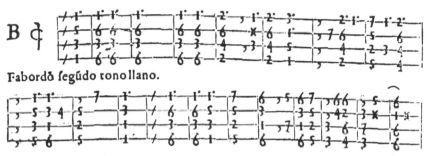

Figure XVIII-2. Tablature in original form

```
CABEZON,FABORDON SEGUNDO TONO LLANO 14                                      CAB   001
101,/102,/103,/104,/                                                        CAB   002
231G,77!F !K1-    M2:2                                                      CAB   003
101 R   H1. H/      1. H1.  H/     1.  W/     1. H1.  H/     2.  H,   Q1.#Q/     2. H3.  HCAB  010
/    ,   H2.  Q1.   Q/      7   Q1.  Q2.  H/     ,   Q1.  Q1.  H/     ,   H7   H/     1.  W/   CAB   011
R   H1.  H/     1. H1.  H/     7   W/     6   H,   Q5   Q/     6   H7   H/     ,   Q6   Q6   HCAB  012
/    ,   H5 #H/     6   W//                                                  CAB   013
102 R   H5   H/     6   H6   H/     6   W/     6   H6   H/     6   W/     6   H1.  H/     ,   QCAB  014
7   Q6   H/     5   H6   H/     ,   Q5   Q3   C4   Q/     5   W/     3   W/     R   H6   H/   CAB   015
6   H5   H/     5   W/     3   W/     3   H5   H/     ,   Q4   Q2   H/     3   W/     1 #W//   CAB   016
103 R   H3   H/     3   H3   H/     3   W/     3   H3   H/     4   H,   Q3   Q/     4   H5   HCAB  017
/    ,   H4   H/     2   Q3   C4   H/     ,   C3   Q1   H/     2   W/     1   W/     R   H3   HCAB  018
/    3   H3   H/     2   W/     1   H,   Q7a  C/     1   H2   H/     3   H6a H/     7a   W/   CAB   019
6a  W//                                                                      CAB   020
104 R   H1   H/     6a  H6a H/     6a  W/     6a  H6a H/     2   W/     2   H1   H/     ,   HCAB  021
2   H/     5a  H4a H/     ,   Q5a  Q6a H/     5a   W/     1a   W/     R   H6a H/     6a  H1  HCAB  022
/    5a  W/     6a   W/     6a  H5a H/     3a  H4a H/     3a   W/     6%   W//               CAB   023
```

Figure XVIII-3. Intermediate input code

```
CABEZON,FABORDON SEGUNDO TONO LLANO 14                                      CAB   001
231G,77!F !K1-    M2:2  RH,RH,RH,RH 22HU,19HD,79HU,77HD / 22HU,20HD,79HU,75CAB  002
HD 22HU,20HD,79HU,75HD / 22W,20W,79W,75W / 22HU,20HD,79HU,75HD 22HU,20HDCAB  003
,79HU,75HD / 23HUJ,20W,80HUJ,78W 23CU,80CU 22#QU,79QU / 23HU,20HD,80HU,7CAB  004
8HD 24HUJ,22HDJ,81HUJ,77HDJ / 24HU,22QD,81HU,77HD 21QD 23QU,20HD,80HU,78CAB  005
HD 22QU / 21QU,19HD,78QU,74HD 22QU,79QU 23HUJ,20HDJ,80HUJ,73HDJ / 23QU,2CAB  006
0QD,80QU,73QD,23QU,19QD,79QU,74CD 22HUJ,17QD,77HU,75HD 18QD / 22HU,19W,7CAB  007
8W,74W 21HU / 22W,17W,77W,70W / RH,RH,RH,RH 22HU,20HD,79HU,75HD / 22HU,2CAB  008
0HD,79HU,75HD 22HU,19HD,79HU,77HD / 21W,19W,78W,74W / 20HUJ,17W,77HUJ,75CAB  009
W 20QU,77QU 19QU,76QU / 20HU,17HD,77HU,75HD 21HUJ,19HDJ,78HU,74HD / 21QUCAB  010
,19QD,79HU,72HD 20QU,18QD 20HUJ,16HD,75HU,73HD / 20HU,17W,76W,72W 19#HU CAB  011
/ 20W,15#W,75W,68W //                                                       CAB   012
```

Figure XVIII-4. Ford-Columbia representation

Figure XVIII-5. Score in standard notation

The process offers several advantages. First, because of its simplicity, the intermediate input code provides a way for a person of limited musical training to encode the tablature quickly and accurately; and second, the initial encoder makes only basic decisions; most other decisions are made by the program. Ad hoc decisions are made by the researcher. Third, because of the several steps involved, the process provides an automatic double-check of data validity; and fourth, with modification, similar procedures can be applied to transcription problems involving other tablatures.

This project and the proposed development of future programs demonstrate the valuable contributions the computer can make to the needs and demands of contemporary musicological research.

CHAPTER XIX

A Test for Melodic Borrowings among Notre Dame *Organa Dupla*

by THEODORE KARP

The fact that numerous melodic interrelationships, both large and small, exist among Notre Dame *organa dupla* has been noted by many scholars. The large correspondences are undoubtedly deliberate borrowings. The small ones are probably no more than melodic formulae, building blocks that together furnish an index of melodic style. An intimate knowledge of both sorts of borrowings would help us achieve a more precise understanding of Notre Dame melodic style. It would also enable us to distinguish points of similarity and disparity between this and other styles of the twelfth and early thirteenth centuries. Lastly, such knowledge might shed considerable light on both harmonic and rhythmic problems. A complete command of this material can be achieved through the use of the computer. Indeed, this author has processed the entire repertoire toward this end.

In order to compile information on *unsuspected* borrowings as well as on those partly identified by human means, a mechanical set of tests was employed. In this set, the digits 2, 3, 4 represent ascending intervals of a second, third, and fourth, while the digit 5 represents all ascending intervals of a fifth or more. The digits 6–9 indicate the descending counterparts of the aforementioned, while the digit 1 indicates a tonal repetition. The digit o signifies the end of a note graph, whether ligature, conjunctura, or nota simplex. From the numbers 1–999 I first deleted all those that, when translated into musical equivalents, represented musical impossibilities. Then the decades representing musical rarities were each consolidated into two-place numbers, while those representing extremely common patterns were expanded into either four or five places. In the end, the full series, representing all possible combinations of musical motion, comprised

371 numbers. For the purposes contemplated, a more precise interval code and test series actually would have presented serious musical disadvantages. In addition, great increases in both programming complexity and running costs would have resulted.

The *dupla* were encoded according to the principles just outlined, the first card of each series indicating source, title, and approximate length. Proceeding interval by interval, the machine searched the first piece for the presence of the first test configuration, and then, by means of a do-loop, moved through the succeeding tests of the series. The entire repertoire was processed in this fashion, one work at a time. In all, more than 100,000 citations were located for the 371 configurations.

When a test pattern was unearthed, the computer was directed to perform several operations. The title of the piece, source, and exact location of the configuration were noted, together with the 10 preceding and the 10 following digits. Merely as a by-product, this information was made available through a printout which furnishes a summary of the melodic content of each piece. Since a search for a cadential pattern involves a note-by-note comparison proceeding backwards from the final tone, the 10 digits preceding the configuration were reversed in order. For reasons of handling speed, the reversed series as well as the normal series following the configuration were then each consolidated into one 10-place number—the maximum number of places possible—and all pertinent information was put onto a pair of tape records that varied only slightly in order and content. At the end of the testing procedure the tape was put through a three-way sorting process. First the duplicate pairs were separated so that one might concentrate either on the melodic context preceding the configuration or on that following. Then each resultant series was sorted according to the configuration being tested. Lastly, within each configuration, the citations were arranged in numerical order. By means of still a third program, the sorted material was made available in a format spaced to facilitate rapid scansion.

Because the test configurations employed are themselves too small to possess intrinsic musical value, the process described yields chaff as well as wheat. Fortunately, the two can be separated with little expenditure of time. Immediately above and below each citation there appear, in spaced alignment, those passages that resemble it most closely, either in terms of the context that precedes the test configuration or in terms of the context that follows. If, in scanning consecutive entries, one finds differences in the first two columns of sorted figures, the likelihood of significant musical resemblance is almost nil. The danger of overlooking even this slight possibility is further reduced in that all significant resemblances are cited more than once. The presence of weak resemblances may be revealed only in the strongest of their citations. As the columns of identical figures increase so does the likelihood of significant musical resemblance. Indeed, the fashion in which certain formulae are capable of varied extension is illustrated with a high degree of graphic clarity. If one finds complete agreement not only between the 10 columns of sorted digits and the 2–5 columns of the test configuration, but also between successive digits of the unsorted columns, then one may conclude the likelihood of extensive, deliberate borrowing. This may be verified quickly by checking the pieces involved with the aid of the precise citations that accompany.

If one is studying a given piece, it is possible to ascertain quickly whether or not there exist passages of content similar to *any* specific passage that may be of interest. All patterns are arranged in numerical order, and one can proceed directly to the citations for the relevant motion pattern. On the other hand, it is also possible to work in the opposite sense, by scanning the figures to find out where significant resemblances occur and then returning to the music to observe the way in which these borrowings are treated. In either case certain cautions must be observed. It is possible for a pattern to occur in varied interval forms. The presence of such variations will not be indicated by the program. Foreknowledge of the possibility is required, and a search among different related patterns must be instituted. Similarly, a significant resemblance may occur in slightly different notational patterns. Again this will be revealed only by consulting appropriate notational variants. Modifications of the program—deleting, for example, the notational o and adding rhythmic data—may be appropriate to the investigation of melodic borrowing in many other repertoires.

Part Six

MUSIC INFORMATION RETRIEVAL

CHAPTER XX

MIR—A Simple

Programming Language for

Musical Information Retrieval *

by MICHAEL KASSLER

There follows a description, in the form of a programmers' manual, of a special-purpose programming language called MIR—the acronym of the phrase "musical information retrieval." [1]

The MIR language was developed in early 1964 as part of a pilot project concerned with experiencing how digital computers could assist musicologists in answering internal-evidential questions about a certain corpus of music—in this project, the Masses of Josquin des Prez To this end, the full score of each Mass (and of a few related pieces) was entered into computer-acceptable form by manual keypunching according to a system of conventions that preserves all internal-evidential information,[2] and an IBM-7094 computer program

---

* This article describes work done at the Department of Music, Princeton University, on a project advised by Professors Arthur Mendel and Lewis Lockwood and supported in part by the National Science Foundation through an institutional grant to Princeton University. The article forms part of the author's Ph.D. dissertation (Princeton University, 1967).

[1] An unspecialized description of MIR is given with some general remarks on musical information retrieval in my article, "Toward Musical Information Retrieval," in *Perspectives of New Music*, Vol. 4, no. 2 (Spring-Summer, 1966), 59–67.

[2] An incomplete list of these conventions is given in Alexander M. Jones and Hubert S. Howe, Jr., *I.M.L.: An Intermediary Musical Language*, (mimeographed), Princeton, Princeton University Department of Music, 1964. In principle, all of these conventions could be followed by automatic machinery—most likely, by an optical character-recognition machine that recognizes and discriminates amongst the "primitive symbols" of current common musical notation (some aspects of such a machine are sketched in my article, "An Essay toward Specification of a Music-reading Machine [in preparation],) and by a suitably programmed digital computer. (The Josquin Masses were keypunched from the critical *Vereniging voor Nederlandse Muziekgeschiedenis* edition in which the music is noted in the current common musical notation.)

was written to convert the punched-card data, one movement at a time, to magnetic-tape data representative not only of the original written music but of some sounded-musical properties computable therefrom such as pitch and attack-time.[3] The MIR language was fashioned so that any effectively computable music-theoretical propositional function—i.e., any predicate whose truth-value is computable from the notes, rests, clefs, and other "primitive symbols" of musical notation that in some order constitute one or another particular composition—could be represented as a MIR program. And the "software" system to carry out automatically any MIR program—i.e., finite ordered set of MIR instructions—was designed for the IBM-7094 computer so that any magnetic tape produced by the aforementioned conversion program could serve as input data to any MIR program.[4]

That the pilot project might achieve its principal purpose as soon as possible, certain limitations of the "dialect" of the current common musical notation in which the critical edition of the Josquin Masses is noted were accepted as limitations of the entire project and therefore became limitations of MIR. These limitations include not only trivial thresholds—e.g., the allowance of triply dotted but not quadruply dotted notes,[5] and the allowance of groupettes (e.g., duplets, triplets) but not nested groupettes—but also the salient restriction that all scores treated in the project exist in a lynear partition, i.e., in a partition in which each part is a lyne.[6]

For the same reason, MIR was restrained from being as flexible as it might have been. The writing of MIR as a "macro-language" of FAP,

---

[3] Indeed, a linkage from the conversion program to a version of the MUSIC IV program (described in M. V. Mathews and Joan E. Miller, *Music IV Programmer's Manual* [mimeographed], Murray Hill, N.J., Bell Telephone Laboratories; and in Godfrey Winham, *The Reference Manual of Music 4B* [mimeographed], Princeton, Princeton University Department of Music (n.d.), in detail and in M. V. Mathews, "The Digital Computer as a Musical Instrument," *Science*, Vol. 142 [1963], 553–557, without detail) has been programmed by Tobias Robison. This linkage allows automatic generation of a sounded-musical realization of a composition from the punched cards which represent only its written-musical properties. Although this realization is neutral with respect to timbre, loudness, and absolute tempo, and does not reproduce text, it has proved useful in "proof-hearing" the contents of the punched cards.

[4] This "software" system has been written in BE FAP, the Bell Telephone Laboratories' version of FAP, by Tobias Robison with some help from Hubert S. Howe, Jr., and me.

[5] Throughout this article, the word "note" is used as a generic name for whole-notes, half-notes, quarter-notes, etc., and also for whole-rests, half-rests, quarter-rests, etc.

[6] Roughly speaking, a part is a *lyne* if it is performable on an instrument that, at any one time, can produce at most one pitch.

the FORTRAN Assembly Program, although providing the power to intercalate FAP instructions at any place in a MIR program, rules out some machine-independence; the setting of MIR's music-theoretical primitives at a level far more primitive than is realized customarily in music-theoretical investigations requires the user who would manipulate (for example) Neapolitan sixths to construct such a concept from the MIR primitives; [7] the readily conceivable extensions to permit as part of a MIR program modification of the input data tape or "composition" of an output data tape have bever been implemented.[8]

MIR is, to the best of our knowledge, the only actualized special-purpose programming language for the expression and evaluation of music-theoretical propositional functions. But to intimate that it soon may be wiser to supersede MIR by a system in which considerably more advantage is taken of those aspects of musical data processing that can be delegated to machinery than to improve MIR fragmentarily is merely to reflect recent advances in computer technology.[9]

MIR supplements FAP essentially in two ways. MIR reserves a virtual area of core storage: this consists of 36-bit *computer words* named by *symbolic addresses* suggestive of the types of musical data the computer words will store. And MIR includes *instructions* which provide for the interrogation and alteration of data stored in computer words.

It is convenient though heterodox to view MIR instructions as direct commands to a special machine that performs specific operations on musical data.[10] The most striking aspect of this hypothesized machine is that its central memory can hold, at any one instant, data represen-

[7] Of course, once such a concept is constructed in the form of a MIR subroutine, it may be recalled for use by its name alone, i.e., without reconstruction.

[8] The capability to "compose" an output data tape in the same format as the input data tape is essential to the implementation of a "derivational" musical analysis: for each stage in a derivational analysis consists of production of a musical composition whose notes are computed from previously produced compositions by application of specific rules of analysis. Since several important traditional systems of musical analysis can be reviewed as systems of derivational musical analysis, this capability would be significant.

[9] The notion of delegation is taken from R. A. Fairthorne, *Towards Information Retrieval*, London, Butterworths, 1961. For a view of the possible effects of this new technology—particularly the development of time-shared systems and new graphical input-output devices—on libraries, see J. C. R. Licklider, *Libraries of the Future*, Cambridge, Mass., The M.I.T. Press, 1965.

[10] The proper view is that MIR instructions are data that the FORTRAN Assembly Program assembles into the machine language of some IBM 700-series computer in accordance with the "macro-definitions" that belong to the "software" system mentioned above.

tative of at most one note. This note (or rest) is called the *current note* for that instant. Whenever a note of the composition being processed is made the current note (by MIR instructions described later), a whole set of data pertinent to that note and to the musical interval between that note and the immediately previous current note is stored automatically in the computer words reserved by MIR. The contents of these computer words immediately after a note has been made current are described next in tabular form: the left-hand column gives the symbolic address of each computer word; the right-hand column has a description of its contents.[11]

Name of computer word	Contents
LYNENØ	The number of the lyne on which the current note is located. (By convention, the topmost lyne in each system of staves in a lynear partition is numbered one, the next lower lyne is numbered two, and so on.)
MEASNØ	The number of the measure in which the current note is located. (By convention, the leftmost measure in each movement is numbered one.[12] The "dialect" of the current common musical notation employed requires that the ith measure in each part of a lynear partition coincide with the ith measure of each other part of that partition, for each positive integer i not greater than the number of measures in the movement.)
NØTENØ	The number of the current note on its lyne within its measure. (Counting is from left to right, starts with one at the beginning of each new measure, and includes rests as notes.)

[11] The following conventions are used: "Ø" designates the letter; "O" designates the Arabic numeral; sequences of (just) Arabic numerals denote according to the decimal system and are stored in computer words in the usual binary representation, right-justified with leading zeroes; sequences of six characters which are capital Roman letters, the character "b" (representing a space), or a few other signs (including Arabic numerals—but at least one of the six characters must not be an Arabic numeral), represent data stored in computer words according to the standard binary-coded data representation which allows six bits for each character.

[12] It is possible to have the measure counter reset to one other than at the beginning of a new movement if the keypunched musical data is marked by the proper keypunched comment at the appropriate place.

Name of computer word—*Continued*   Contents

CURN

This word contains the *note index* of the current note—a unique identifier of the place of the current note in the composition being processed. CURN is provided for use with the TØCURN instruction described below; the exact bit structure need not be known for that application and is not detailed here.

REGCL

14 if the current note is a rest. Otherwise, the register-class of the pitch represented by the current note, taking instrument transposition into account. Following Young,[13] Middle C through the next higher B (which may be noted as C♭) are assigned to register-class 4; notes in the next higher octave are assigned to register-class 5; etc.

NØTECL

14 if the current note is a rest. Otherwise, the note-class of the current note (i.e., the pitch-class of the pitch represented by the current note), taking instrument transposition into account. All C's, B♯'s, and D♭♭'s are assigned to note class 0; all C♯'s are assigned to note-class 1; . . . ; all B's are assigned to note-class 11.

SEMITØ

0 if the current note is a rest. Otherwise, taking instrument transposition into account, the number of semi-tones that the current note is "above" any note whose register-class and note-class both are 0 (e.g., SEMITØ would contain 78 if the note just made current is in register-class 6 and note-class 6).

DNC

bbbbbb if the current note is a rest. Otherwise, taking instrument transposition into account, the *diatonic note-class* of the current note, i.e., Abbbbb, Bbbbbb, Cbbbbb, Dbbbbb, Ebbbbb, Fbbbbb, or Gbbbbb, according as the current note is an A or an A♯ or an A✕ or an A♭ or an A♭♭ or an A♮, a B or a B♯ or . . . , etc.

TIEIND

1 if the current note is tied to the immediately preceding note on the same lyne; otherwise 0.

BARLIN

0 if the current note is not followed directly (i.e., without any intermediate note or rest) by a barline; 1 if the cur-

---

[13] Robert W. Young, "Terminology for Logarithmic Frequency Units," *Journal of the Acoustical Society of America*, Vol. 11, no. 1, 1939, 134 ff.

	rent note is followed directly by a single barline that does not end a staff; 2 if the current note is followed directly by a single barline that does end a staff; 3 if the current note is followed directly by a double barline.
PRECAC	0 if the current note is not preceded immediately by an accidental; otherwise, according to the following table:

Contents of PRECAC	Immediately preceding accidental
1	Sharp
2	Flat
3	Double-sharp
4	Natural
5	"Naturalized" sharp [14]
6	"Naturalized" flat
7	Double-flat

STAFPØ	55 if the current note is a rest. Otherwise, the number of the staff-position of the current note, as depicted in the following diagram:

---

[14] I.e., a sharp preceded immediately by a natural.

Name of computer word—*Continued*   Contents

DURAT   According to the following table:

Contents of DURAT	Current note
1	Long
2	Breve
3	Semibreve, whole
4	Minim, half
5	Crotchet, quarter
6	Quaver, eighth
7	Semiquaver, sixteenth
8	Demisemiquaver, 32nd
9	Hemidemisemiquaver, 64th
10	128th
15	Grace-note

DURINT
DURNUM
DURDEN   By the *note-durational value* of a note is meant the rational number of whole-note units that is the ideal duration of the note, except that, by convention, the note-durational value of a grace-note is 0. If a note is dotted or an element of a groupette, this is taken into account in computing the note's note-durational value; however, affection by a fermata is not taken into account. The note-durational value of a note may be represented uniquely as a "mixed number" consisting of an integer plus a proper fraction in lowest terms so conventionalized that if its numerator is 0 then its denominator is 1. The note-durational value of the current note is so represented and stored: integer, numerator, and denominator, in DURINT, DURNUM, and DURDEN, respectively.

DØTIND   0, 1, 2, or 3, according as the current note is undotted, single-dotted, double-dotted, or triple-dotted. (Reference here is made to note-durational dots, not staccato dots.)

GRPNØ   0 if the current note is not an element of a groupette. Otherwise, the groupette-number of the groupette containing the current note. (For example, 3 if the current note is in a triplet.)

DYNMRK   0 if the current note is affected directly by no dynamic mark; otherwise, according to the following table:

Name of computer word—*Continued*   Contents

Contents of DYNMRK	Dynamic mark directly affecting current note
1	*pppp*
2	*ppp*
3	*pp*
4	*p*
5	*mp*
6	*mf*
7	*f*
8	*ff*
9	*fff*
10	*ffff*
11	Beginning of crescendo
12	End of crescendo
13	Beginning of decrescendo
14	End of decrescendo

DYNVAL — The contents of DYNVAL will represent the "dynamic-mark value" pertaining to the current note, even if the current note is not affected directly by any dynamic mark. Until it is necessary to employ the concept of dynamic-mark value, the contents of DYNVAL will automatically be set to 0, as the programming necessary to produce other contents of DYNVAL has not yet been accomplished.

SPECSN
SPECSN+1 — These two computer words, adjacent in computer memory, both contain 0 if no special signs affect the current note. If the current note is affected by a fermata, SPECSN contains 12 and SPECSN+1 contains 0. Other special signs will be accommodated as they are needed for research.

SUGGAC — 0 if the current note is not affected by an editorial or parenthetic "suggested" accidental. Otherwise, 1, 2, or 3, according as the suggested accidental affecting the current note is a sharp, a flat, or a natural.

BRACK — 0 if the current note is not affected by any ligature-denoting brackets. Otherwise, 1, 2, or 3, according as the current note is affected by the beginning, the

Name of computer word—*Continued*   Contents

middle,[15] or the end, of a bracket—i.e., as the current note is at the beginning, in the middle, or at the end, of a bracket.

PHRMRK

o if the current note is not affected by any phrase-mark (i.e., tie or slur). Otherwise, 1, 2, 3, or 4, according as the current note is affected by the beginning, the middle (see note 15), the end, or the "simultaneous" beginning and end, of some phrase-mark(s).

TEXT

bbbbbb if no text accompanies the current note. Otherwise, that text, six letters maximum, left-justified with trailing spaces, stored in computer memory according to the standard binary-coded data representation.

MESINT
MESNUM
MESDEN

SYSINT
SYSNUM
SYSDEN

By the *measure attack-time* of a note is meant the rational number of whole-note units that separate the beginning of the measure containing that note from the time at which the note ideally should be attacked. Similarly, by the *system attack-time* of a note is meant the rational number of whole-note units that separate the beginning of the system of staves that contains the note from the time at which the note ideally should be attacked. Both the measure attack-time and the system attack-time of a note may be represented uniquely as "mixed numbers," each consisting of an integer plus a proper fraction in lowest terms so conventionalized that if its numerator is o then its denominator is 1. The measure attack-time of the current note is so represented and stored: integer, numerator, and denominator, in MESINT, MESNUM, and MESDEN, respectively. The system attack-time of the current note is so represented and stored: integer, numerator, and denominator, in SYSINT, SYSNUM, and SYSDEN, respectively.[16]

---

[15] By "middle," any noninitial and nonterminal portion is meant.

[16] For example, both the measure attack-time and the system attack-time of the first four notes in the Violin 1 part of the first movement of Beethoven's *Fifth Symphony* are, in order, o o/1, o 1/8, o 1/4, and o 3/8. The next note in that part has measure attack-time o o/1 and system attack-time o 1/2, presuming that the first system of staves exends at least through the second measure. Observe that, of two adjacent notes on the same lyne in the same system (the notes may

Name of computer word—*Continued*   Contents

INSTRU
INSTRU+1

The name of the musical instrument or voice scheduled to perform the current note is stored in the adjacent computer words INSTRU and INSTRU+1, left-justified with trailing spaces. (If the name of the instrument or voice is longer than 12 letters, only the first 12 letters of the name are stored.)

CLEF

According to the following table:

Contents of CLEF	Clef affecting current note
1	Treble clef with "8" above
2	Treble clef with "8" below
3	Bass clef ⎫ F-clefs
4	Baritone clef ⎭
5	Tenor clef ⎫
6	Alto clef ⎪
7	Mezzo-soprano clef ⎬ C-clefs
8	Soprano clef ⎭
9	G-clef located on first staff line ("French violin" clef)
10	Treble clef

KEYSIG
KEYSIG+1
KEYSIG+2
KEYSIG+3
KEYSIG+4
KEYSIG+5

The keypuncher of the music is given, in the I.M.L. system of conventions,[17] the option of representing a key-signature either by naming the major key which the key-signature is a key-signature of, or by listing each element of the key-signature. If the former option were taken, each of KEYSIG through KEYSIG+6 would con-

---

have a barline between them but there is no intermediate note), the difference of the system attack-time of the left note from the system attack-time of the right note is the note-durational value of the left note, except if the left note is a whole-rest or a breve-rest and is the only note on its lyne in its measure (in which case its note-durational value is the value of the time-signature affecting that measure). Observe too that, on any lyne, the sum of the note-durational values of each note in a measure equals the value of the time-signature affecting this measure. For more detail, see Chapter 5 of my article, "A System for the Automatic Reduction of Musical Scores," in Papers Presented at the Seminar in Mathematical Linguistics, Vol. 6, 1960 (on deposit at Widener Library, Harvard University, Cambridge, Mass.).

[17] Jones and Howe, *op. cit.*

Name of computer word—*Continued*   Contents

KEYSIG+6 KEYREP	tain o and KEYREP would contain a binary-coded data representation of the key "of" the current note, e.g., FSHARP. If the latter option were taken, KEYREP would contain bbbbbb and each computer word from KEYSIG to KEYSIG+6 would correspond to one key-signature sharp or flat (key-signature naturals are discounted), as follows: for each natural number n less than 7, KEYSIG+n contains o if the $(n+1)$th (from left to right) key-signature element (i.e., sharp or flat) does not exist, or otherwise KEYSIG+n contains an eight-bit "byte" right-justified with leading zeroes—the "byte" consisting of a two-bit prefix, that is 1 or 2 according as the $(n+1)$th key-signature element is a sharp or a flat, catenated to a six-bit suffix that is the binary representation of the number of the staff-position on which the $(n+1)$th key-signature element is. (The numbers of staff-positions have been given above in describing the contents of the computer word addressed by STAFPØ.)
TSNUM TSDEN	The time-signature affecting the current note is stored in TSNUM and TSDEN as follows. If the time-signature comprises a numerator and a denominator (e.g., $\frac{3}{16}$), then the numerator is stored in TSNUM and the denominator is stored in TSDEN: storage of both is in the binary-coded data representation, left-justified with trailing spaces. (Hence, pursuing this example, TSDEN would contain the number denoted by "010660606060" in the octal system, because octal "01," octal "06," and octal "60," are the binary-coded data representations for the alphanumeric symbols "1," "6," and "b," respectively.) If the time-signature comprises a sequence of one or more Arabic numerals (e.g., 3), then that sequence is stored in TSNUM in the binary-coded data representation, left-justified with trailing spaces, and TSDEN contains bbbbbb. If the time-signature is C, O, ₵, or Φ, then TSDEN contains bbbbbb and TSNUM contains Cbbbbb, Øbbbbb, C/bbbb, or Ø/bbbb, respectively. (Representation of other time-signatures or mensuration signs could be handled similarly if needed.)

Name of computer word—*Continued*   Contents

TSVNUM
TSVDEN

The "value" of the time-signature affecting the current note is considered to be a rational number of whole-note units and is stored as a fraction in lowest terms: numerator in TSVNUM and denominator in TSVDEN. (For example, corresponding to the time-signature $\frac{12}{8}$: TSVNUM would contain 3 and TSVDEN would contain 2.)

INSTRN

The musical transposition of the instrument or voice scheduled to perform the current note is stored in INSTRN as a signed number [18] of semitones: the sign is negative if the instrument or voice "sounds lower than written"; otherwise, the sign is positive. Thus, if the current note were scheduled to be performed by a B-flat clarinet, INSTRN would contain −2.

INSDIR
INSREG
INSNØT

The musical transposition of the instrument or voice scheduled to perform the current note is stored in INSDIR, INSREG, and INSNØT, as follows. If the instrument or voice "sounds lower than written" then INSDIR contains 1; otherwise, INSDIR contains 0. The amount of the transposition, in terms of register-classes and note classes, is stored "properly" in INSREG and INSNØT, respectively: "properly" signifying that the contents of INSNØT is not greater than eleven. Thus, if the current note were scheduled to be performed by a B-flat clarinet, INSDIR, INSREG, and INSNØT, would contain 1, 0, and 2, respectively.

NUMLYN

The total number of lynes in the system of staves containing the current note.

---

[18] An unsigned number and a positively signed number are stored in computer words as identical sequences of binary digits if the magnitudes of the two numbers are the same. A negatively signed number is stored in a computer word in the same way that the number's absolute value would be stored, except that the left-most bit of the computer word containing a negatively signed number is set to one. The MIR arithmetic instructions introduced below all are algebraic in the sense that the usual rules for computing with signed numbers apply: the MIR programmer using just these and no other arithmetic instructions can be indifferent to the way that negative numbers are stored.

Name of computer word—*Continued*   Contents

DATE	I.M.L.[19] allows the keypuncher to include a certain amount of external-evidential information about the composition being processed, and this information is retained for use in MIR programs. If the year of composition or the year of publication or some other date associated with the composition being processed has been entered suitably onto the punched cards, this number will be stored in DATE; otherwise, DATE will contain 0.
PØSER PØSER+1 PØSER+2 PØSER+3 PØSER+4	The first thirty letters of the name of the composer of the current note are stored in these consecutive computer words, six letters per word with trailing spaces. If the keypuncher has not keypunched appropriately a composer's name, then each of PØSER through PØSER+4 will contain bbbbbb.
AUTHØR through AUTHØR+4	Similarly, the name of the writer of the text that accompanies the current note is stored here.
LISHER through LISHER+3	Similarly, the name of the publisher of (the composition containing) the current note is stored here.
EDITØR through EDITØR+4	Similarly, the name of the editor of (the composition containing) the current note is stored here.
RANGER through RANGER+4	Similarly, the name of the arranger of (the composition containing) the current note is stored here.
PLACE through PLACE+3	Similarly, the name of some place associated with (the composition containing) the current note—e.g., the place of publication, is stored here.
TITLE through TITLE+5	Similarly, the title of (the composition containing) the current note is stored here. It is required that every composition being processed have a title: hence, when a note is made current, TITLE will not contain bbbbbb.

[19] Jones and Howe, *op. cit.*

SUBTIT through SUBTIT+3	Similarly, the subtitle of (the section or movement containing) the current note is stored here. When a note is made current, SUBTIT may contain bbbbbb, as it is not required that a subtitle affect every note of the composition being processed. However, the presence of different subtitles for different parts of the composition allows effective use of the TØSECT instruction described below.
TEMPØ through TEMPØ+2	Similarly, a tempo indication (e.g., ADAGIØ) affecting the current note is stored here.
PUNXER through PUNXER+4	Similarly, the name of the person who keypunched the portion of the musical composition containing the current note is stored here.
INTVL	The musical interval between the current note and the immediately previous current note is stored in INTVL as a signed number of semitones: the sign is negative if the current note is "lower in pitch than" the immediately previous current note: otherwise the sign is positive.[20] Exceptions to the above: if the current note is a rest, or if the immediately previous current note is a rest, or if there is no immediately previous current note (as at the start of a MIR program), then INTVL contains bbbbbb.
INTDIR INTREG INTNØT	The interval between the current note and the immediately previous current note is stored in INTDIR, INTREG, and INTNØT, as follows. If the current note is "lower in pitch than" the immediately previous current note, then INTDIR contains 1; otherwise, INTDIR contains 0. The amount of the interval, in terms of register-classes and note-classes, is stored in INTREG and INTNØT, respectively. For the computation of

[20] More precisely—letting w and x denote the register-class and note-class, respectively, of the current note, and letting y and z denote the register-class and note-class, respectively, of the immediately previous current note—the sign is negative if and only if ($12w+x$) is less than ($12y+z$).

Name of computer word—*Continued*   Contents

INTDIR, INTREG, and INTNØT, only, the "pitch" of a rest is considered to be: register-class 0, note-class 0. E.g., if the immediately previous current note were Middle C and the current note were an eighth-rest then INTDIR, INTREG, and INTNØT, would contain 1, 4, and 0, respectively. If there is no immediately previous current note, then INTDIR contains 2, INTREG contains the register-class of the current note, and INTNØT contains the note-class of the current note.

DINTVL
GENUS
DIØCT

If the current note is a rest, or if the immediately previous current note is a rest, or if there is no immediately previous current note, then DINTVL contains 0 and GENUS contains 0 and DIØCT contains 0. Otherwise, the "diatonic interval" between the current note and the immediately previous current note is represented in DINTVL, GENUS, and DIØCT, as follows:

Contents of DINTVL	Interval
1	Unison, octave, double octave, etc.
2	Second, ninth, etc.
3	Third, tenth, etc.
4	Fourth, eleventh, etc.
5	Fifth, twelfth, etc.
6	Sixth, thirteenth, etc.
7	Seventh, etc.

Contents of GENUS	Interval
1	Doubly diminished
2	(Singly) diminished
3	Minor
4	Perfect
5	Major
6	(Singly) augmented
7	Doubly augmented
8	Some other interval

Name of computer word—*Continued*   Contents

Contents of DIØCT	Interval
0	Smaller than an octave [21]
1	An octave or larger but smaller than
⋮	two octaves
n	n octaves or larger but smaller than $(n+1)$ octaves

DINDIR   Let z denote the current note and y the immediately previous current note. If z or y is a rest, or if there is no immediately previous current note, then DINDIR contains 2. Otherwise, roughly, DINDIR contains 1 if z is "diatonically lower" than y and 0 otherwise. More precisely: if the diatonic interval between z and y is greater than a fourth (of any genus)—this is meant "absolutely": a tenth is greater than a fourth—then DINDIR contains 1 or 0 according as z is or is not "lower in pitch than" y. Also, if the diatonic interval between z and y is a unison (of any genus) then DINDIR contains 1 or 0 according as z is or is not "lower in pitch" than y. In all other situations, DINDIR contains 1 or 0 according as the diatonic note-class of z is or is not one of the three letters preceding (any instance of) the diatonic note-class of y in the following sequence of letters: [22] A B C D E F G A B C.

WA1
WA2
WA3
WA4
WA5
WA6
WA7
WA8
WA9
     Twenty consecutive computer words are reserved for the MIR programmer to use as "work areas." Each of WA1 through WA20 is set to 0 before the first instruction of any MIR program is executed. Additional "work areas" may be introduced in any MIR program by use of the FAP BSS pseudo-operation.

[21] The term "octave" here refers not to pitch but to notation. The diatonic interval from Middle C to the B-double-sharp thirteen semitones away is a doubly augmented seventh and hence an interval smaller than an octave (in this sense of this term).

[22] It should be apparent—e.g., from the preceding footnote—that there are cases in which, when a note is made current, the contents of DINDIR and INTDIR will not be identical.

Name of computer word—*Continued*   Contents

WA10

WA11

WA12

WA13

WA14

WA15

WA16

WA17

WA18

WA19

WA20

MIR instructions consist of three fields: a *location* field, an *operation* field, and a *variable* field. Each MIR instruction is to be keypunched, following the standard FAP format, on a separate 80-column Hollerith punch card.[23] The content of the operation field of each MIR instruction and the types of variable field that legitimately can follow each such operation field are described next. The location field of a MIR instruction may be entirely blank or may contain a MIR symbolic address—i.e., any catenation of up to six capital roman letters or Arabic numerals that does not consist entirely of Arabic numerals—other than a symbolic address that names a computer word described above. An instruction whose location field is not blank will be said to be *located at* the symbolic address contained in the instruction's location field. The existence of the location field permits departure, in the way described below, from the normal mode of operation wherein the instruction executed after executing instruction i is the instruction next after i in the presented program.

---

[23] The following acceptable but not immutable format specification allows use of a "program card" on standard IBM keypunch machines: location field comprising columns 1–6, column 7 blank, operation field comprising columns 8–13, columns 14 and 15 blank, variable field comprising columns 16–72, optional numeric sequencing (of the punched cards) comprising columns 73–80. Keypunching of each field of a MIR instruction then should begin at the leftmost column allocated for that field; if not all allocated columns are filled, trailing blanks are permissible. If desired, comments—ignored when a MIR program is executed—may be punched in columns allocated for the variable field of a MIR instruction provided that at least one blank column separates the beginning of the comment from the end of the regular variable-field data.

MIR instructions that make a note current and bring data representative of it into the computer words described above

Operation field: TØSECT (mnemonic for "To section")

Variable field: Within parentheses, the name of a subtitle of the composition being processed.

Effect: If the subtitle so named has been defined properly in the keypunched representation of the composition being processed then the first note on the first lyne in the first measure of the section named by this subtitle becomes the current note. Otherwise, computation terminates and an appropriate error message is provided on the printout from the computer. (For example, the instruction: TØSECT (ET IN TERRA) presumably would cause an error message to appear if the composition being processed were Beethoven's *Fifth Symphony*.)

Operation field: TØMEAS (mnemonic for "To measure")

Variable field (direct-address type): A sequence, of one through five Arabic numerals, possibly preceded immediately by + or by −.

Effect: Let n be the number denoted by the sequence of numerals according to the decimal system. Suppose that, before this instruction is executed, the current note is in measure numbered m. (If there is no current note before this instruction is executed, m is presumed to be o.) Then execution of this instruction causes the new current note to be, if such exists, the first note on the first lyne in measure numbered $m+n$, $m-n$, or n, according as the sequence of numerals is preceded (in the variable field) by +, by −, or by no sign. If no such note exists in the composition being processed (e.g., if the instruction: TØMEAS 99999 is given when the composition being processed belongs to Bartók's *Mikrokosmos* set), then computation terminates and an appropriate error message is provided.

Operation field: TØMEAS

Variable field (indirect-address type): Within parentheses—the left parenthesis preceded immediately by +, by −, or by C—a MIR symbolic address defined in the MIR program.[24]

Effect: Let n be the unsigned number stored in the computer word whose symbolic address is given in the variable field. Suppose

[24] A MIR symbolic address is *defined in* a MIR program if it constitutes the location field of a MIR or FAP instruction (or pseudo-instruction) in the program, or if it is the symbolic address of one of the computer words described above. In any MIR program, a symbolic address cannot be used to name more than one computer word.

that, before this instruction is executed, the current note is in measure numbered m. (If there is no current note before this instruction is executed, m is presumed to be 0.) Then, execution of this instruction causes the new current note to be, if such exists, the first note on the first lyne in measure numbered $m+n$, $m-n$, or n, according as the left parenthesis is preceded in the variable field by $+$, by $-$, or by C. If no such note exists in the composition being processed (e.g., if the instruction: TØMEAS C(WA13) is given when WA13 contains 999999 and the composition being processed belongs to Bartók's *Mikrokosmos* set), then computation terminates and an appropriate error message is provided. (The letter "C" may be thought of as an abbreviation of the phrase "the contents of.")

Operation field: TØLYNE (mnemonic for "To lyne")
Variable field (direct-address type): A sequence, of one through five Arabic numerals, possibly preceded immediately by $+$ or by $-$.

Effect: Let n be the number denoted by the sequence of numerals according to the decimal system. Suppose that, before this instruction is executed, the current note is on lyne numbered p in measure numbered m. Then, execution of this instruction causes the new current note to be, if such exists, the first note in measure numbered m on the lyne numbered $p+n$, $p-n$, or n, according as the sequence of numerals is preceded in the variable field by $+$, by $-$, or by no sign. If no such lyne exists in measure numbered m, or if there is no current note before this instruction is executed, then computation terminates and an appropriate error message is provided.

Operation field: TØLYNE
Variable field (indirect-address type): Within parentheses—the left parenthesis preceded immediately by $+$, by $-$, or by C—a MIR symbolic address defined in the MIR program.

Effect: Let n be the unsigned number stored in the computer word whose symbolic address is given in the variable field. Suppose that, before this instruction is executed, the current note is on lyne numbered p in measure numbered m. Then, execution of this instruction causes the new current note to be, if such exists, the first note in measure numbered m on the lyne numbered $p+n$, $p-n$, or n, according as the left parenthesis is preceded in the variable field by $+$, by $-$, or by C. If no such lyne exists in measure numbered m, or if there is no current note before this instruction is executed, then computation terminates and an appropriate error message is provided.

Operation field: TØNØTE (mnemonic for "To note")

Variable field (direct-address type): A sequence, of one through five Arabic
numerals, possibly preceded immediately by + or by −.

Effect: Let n be the number denoted by the sequence of numerals according to the decimal system. Suppose that, before this instruction is executed, the current note is note numbered q on lyne
numbered p in measure numbered m. If the sequence of numerals is preceded in the variable field by no sign then execution of
this instruction causes the new current note to be, if such exists,
the note numbered n on lyne numbered p in measure numbered
m. If the sequence of numerals is preceded in the variable field
by + or by − then execution of this instruction causes the new
current note to be, if such exists, the nth note on lyne numbered
p after or before, according as the sign is + or −, the note numbered q on lyne numbered p in measure numbered m. (Observe
that the new current note need not be in measure numbered m
if the sequence of numerals is preceded in the variable field by
+ or−: only for sufficiently small n will the new current note be
the note numbered $q+n$ or $q−n$ on lyne numbered p in measure
numbered m. However, if the sequence of numerals is preceded
in the variable field by no sign then the new current note, if it
exists, will be in measure numbered m.) If no such new current
note exists, or if there is no current note before this instruction
is executed, then computation terminates and an appropriate
error message is provided.

Operation field: TØNØTE

Variable field (indirect-address type): Within parentheses—the left parenthesis preceded immediately by +, by −, or by C—a MIR symbolic address defined in the MIR program.

Effect: Let n be the unsigned number stored in the computer word
whose symbolic address is given in the variable field. Suppose
that, before this instruction is executed, the current note is note
numbered q on lyne numbered p in measure numbered m. If the
left parenthesis is preceded in the variable field by C then execution of this instruction causes the new current note to be, if
such exists, the note numbered n on lyne numbered p in measure
numbered m. If the left parenthesis is preceded in the variable
field by + or by − then execution of this instruction causes the
new current note to be, if such exists, the nth note on lyne numbered p after or before, according as the sign is + or −, the note
numbered q on lyne numbered p in measure numbered m. (Observe that the new current note need not be in measure num-

bered m if the left parenthesis is preceded in the variable field by + or by −, but will be in measure numbered m (if the new current note exists) if the left parenthesis is preceded in the variable field by C.) If no such new current note exists, or if there is no current note before this instruction is executed, then computation terminates and an appropriate error message is provided.

Operation field: TØCURN (mnemonic for "To current note")
Variable field: A MIR symbolic address defined in the MIR program.
Effect: If the computer word whose symbolic address is given in the variable field contains the note index of some note in the composition being processed then execution of this instruction causes that note to be the new current note. Otherwise, computation terminates and an appropriate error message is provided. (For example, if execution of the instruction: MØVE   CURN,WA6 is followed when executing a MIR program by execution of the instruction: TØCURN   WA6 and if the execution of all intermediate instructions has not caused alteration of the contents of WA6, then execution of: TØCURN   WA6 causes the new current note to be that note which was the current note when: MØVE   CURN,WA6 was executed.[25] It will be seen that the inclusion of CURN and TØCURN in the MIR system makes convenient the determination of the musical interval between any two notes in the composition being processed.)

Operation field: NØTEU (mnemonic for "Note up")
Variable field: A symbolic address at which some MIR (or FAP) instruction is located in the program.
Effect: Suppose that, before this instruction is executed, the current note is on lyne numbered p and has system attack-time x in some system s of staves. Then, if $p > 1$, execution of this instruction causes the new current note to be that note, on lyne numbered $p-1$ in system s, whose system attack-time y has the following property: y is the greatest of all system s, lyne numbered $p-1$ system attack-times that are less than or equal to x. (I.e., if $p > 1$, the new current note "attacks simultaneously with" or "holds through the attack of" the current note before this instruction is executed.[26]) If $p = 1$ then execution of this instruction does not

[25] In general, transferring data from a computer word does not alter the contents of that word, but transferring data to a computer word is destructive of the previous contents of that word.
[26] None of this terminology is meant to suggest that any of the various notes mentioned cannot be a rest.

alter the current note (or the contents of any computer word) and the instruction to be executed after this instruction is the one located at the symbolic address given in the variable field. (If $p>1$ the instruction to be executed after this instruction is—as is normally the case—the one next in sequence.)

Operation field: NØTED (mnemonic for "Note down")
Variable field: A symbolic address at which some MIR (or FAP) instruction is located in the program.
Effect: Suppose that, before this instruction is executed, the current note is on lyne numbered p and has system attack-time x in some system s of staves. Let t be the total number of lynes in s. Then, if $p<t$, execution of this instruction causes the new current note to be that note, on lyne numbered $p+1$ in system s, whose system attack-time y has the following property: y is the greatest of all system s, lyne numbered $p+1$ system attack-times that are less than or equal to x. If $p = t$ then execution of this instruction does not alter the current note (or the contents of any computer word) and the instruction to be executed after this instruction (only if $p = t$) is the one located at the symbolic address given in the variable field.

Operation field: SNØTEU (mnemonic for "Simultaneous note up")
Variable field: A symbolic address at which some MIR (or FAP) instruction is located in the program.
Effect: Suppose that, before this instruction is executed, the current note is on lyne numbered p and has system attack-time x in some system s of staves. Then, execution of this instruction causes the new current note to be, if such exists, that note n, in system s at system attack-time x, such that n is on the greatest-numbered of all lynes in s having a lyne number less than p and having a note whose system attack-time is x. (I.e., n, if it exists, is the element, of a "chord" of simultaneously attacked notes, next "higher" to the note that is the current note before his instruction is executed—where "higher" is short for "having lesser lyne number"; but see note 26 above.) But if no such note n exists—e.g., if $p = 1$—then execution of this instruction does not alter the current note (or the contents of any computer word) and the instruction to be executed after this instruction (in this case only) is the instruction located at the symbolic address given in the variable field.

Operation field: SNØTED (mnemonic for "Simultaneous note down")
Variable field: A symbolic address at which some MIR (or FAP) instruction is located in the program.

Effect: Suppose that, before this instruction is executed, the current note is on lyne numbered p and has system attack-time x in some system s of staves. Then, execution of this instruction causes the new current note to be, if such exists, that note n, in system s at system attack-time x, such that n is on the least-numbered of all lynes in s having a lyne number greater than p and having a note whose system attack-time is x. But if no such note exists— e.g., if p is equal to the total number of lynes in s—then execution of this instruction does not alter the current note (or the contents of any computer word) and the instruction to be executed after this instruction (in this case only) is the instruction located at the symbolic address given in the variable field.

MIR arithmetic instructions [27]

Operation field: ADD3 (mnemonic for "Three-address add")

Variable field: A symbolic address defined in the program, immediately followed by a comma, which is immediately followed by a symbolic address defined in the program, which is immediately followed by a comma, which is immediately followed by a symbolic address defined in the program.

Effect: The algebraic sum of the contents of the computer words whose symbolic addresses are the first two given in the variable field is stored in the computer word whose symbolic address is the third given in the variable field. (E.g., if the contents of WA1, WA2, and WA12, just before execution of the instruction: ADD3 WA1,WA2,WA12 are, respectively, 3, -2, and 167, then the contents of WA1, WA2, and WA12, just after execution of this instruction are, respectively, 3, -2, and 1.)

Operation field: SUB3 (mnemonic for "Three-address subtract")

Variable field: A symbolic address defined in the program, immediately followed by a comma, which is immediately followed by a symbolic address defined in the program, which is immediately followed by a comma, which is immediately followed by a symbolic address defined in the program.

Effect: The algebraic difference of the contents of the computer word whose symbolic address is given second in the variable field from the contents of the computer word whose symbolic address is given first there is, stored in the computer word whose symbolic address is given third there.

[27] These instructions perform the arithmetic operations of addition, subtraction, and multiplication, on signed integers only (including zero). To perform these operations on other mathematical entities, or to perform the operation of division on signed integers, FAP subroutines can be written.

Operation field: MPY3 (mnemonic for "Three-address multiply")

Variable field: A symbolic address defined in the program, immediately followed by a comma, which is immediately followed by a symbolic address defined in the program, which is immediately followed by a comma, which is immediately followed by a symbolic address defined in the program.

Effect: The algebraic product of the contents of the computer words whose symbolic addresses are the first two given in the variable field is stored in the computer word whose symbolic address is given third there.

Observe that none of these arithmetic instructions alters the current note.

MIR logical instructions

Operation field: TRA (mnemonic for "Transfer") [28]

Variable field: A symbolic address at which some MIR (or FAP) instruction is located in the program.

Effect: An "unconditional" transfer: in every case, the instruction to be executed immediately after this instruction is executed is the instruction located at the symbolic address given in the variable field.

The following four MIR logical instructions, which effect "conditional" transfers, are described together because of their similarity each to each other.

Operation fields: TRGTH (mnemonic for "Transfer if greater than")
                  TRGEQ (mnemonic for "Transfer if greater than or equal to")
                  TRLTH (mnemonic for "Transfer if less than")
                  TRLEQ (mnemonic for "Transfer if less than or equal to")

Variable field (for each instruction): A symbolic address defined in the program, immediately followed by a comma, which is immediately followed by a symbolic address defined in the program, which is immediately followed by a comma, which is immediately followed by a symbolic address at which some MIR (or FAP) instruction is located in the program.

Effects: Let b and c be, respectively, the unsigned numbers stored in the computer words whose symbolic addresses are the first and second symbolic addresses given in the variable field. The instruction located at the symbolic address given third in the variable field is to be executed immediately after executing this

[28] This is a FAP instruction.

instruction if $b>c$ and the operation field contains TRGTH, or if $b \geq c$ and the operation field contains TRGEQ, or if $b<c$ and the operation field contain TRLTH, or if $b \leq c$ and the operation field contains TRLEQ. In all other cases, the instruction executed immediately after executing this instruction is the one next in sequence.

Operation field: CØMPAR (mnemonic for "Compare")

Variable field: A symbolic address defined in the program, immediately followed by a comma, which is immediately followed by a symbolic address defined in the program, which is immediately followed by a comma, which is immediately followed by a symbolic address at which some MIR (or FAP) instruction is located in the program; all this may or may not be followed immediately by a comma and the letter F.

Effect: The contents of the computer words whose symbolic addresses are the first two symbolic addresses given in the variable field are compared. If they are equal and the symbolic address given third in the variable field is not followed there by ",F" or if they are unequal and that symbolic address is followed there by ",F" then the instruction executed immediately after executing this instruction is the instruction located at the symbolic address given third in the variable field. In all other cases, the instruction executed next is the one next in sequence.

Operation field: CØMPTR (mnemonic for "Compare and transfer")

Variable field: A symbolic address defined in the program, immediately followed by a comma, which is immediately followed by a symbolic address defined in the program, which is immediately followed by a comma, which is immediately followed by a symbolic address at which some MIR (or FAP) instruction is located in the program, which is immediately followed by a comma, which is immediately followed by a symbolic address at which some MIR (or FAP) instruction is located in the program.

Effect: The contents of the computer words whose symbolic addresses are the first two symbolic addresses given in the variable field are compared. If they are equal then the instruction executed immediately after executing this instruction is the instruction located at the symbolic address given third in the variable field. If they are unequal then the instruction executed immediately after executing this instruction is the instruction located at the symbolic address given fourth in the variable field.

Operation field: MØVE (mnemonic for "Move")

Variable field: A symbolic address defined in the program, immediately followed by a comma, which is immediately followed by a symbolic address defined in the program.

Effect: The contents of the computer word whose symbolic address is given first in the variable field are stored in the computer word whose symbolic address is given second in the variable field. (So, immediately after executing this instruction, both computer words have equal contents.) [29]

Operation field: LØØKUP (mnemonic for "Look up")

Variable field: A symbolic address defined in the program, immediately followed by a comma, which is immediately followed by a symbolic address defined in the program, which is immediately followed by a comma, which is immediately followed by a sequence of one, two, or three, Arabic numerals not all of which are o, which is immediately followed by a comma, which is immediately followed by a symbolic address at which some MIR (or FAP) instruction is located in the program.

Effect: Let n be the number denoted by the sequence of numerals according to the decimal system. Execution of this instruction causes (in effect) the contents of the computer word whose symbolic address is given first in the variable field to be compared with the contents of the computer word w whose symbolic address is given second in the variable field and with the contents of each of the $n-1$ computer words that follow w consecutively in computer memory. If the computer word whose symbolic address is given first in the variable field has contents equal to that of any of the n computer words with which it is compared, then the instruction executed next is the one located at the symbolic address given last in the variable field. Otherwise, the instruction executed next is the one next in sequence.

Observe that none of these logical instructions alters the current note.

MIR output instructions

Operation field: CALL (mnemonic for "Call") [30]

Variable field: EXIT

Effect: This instruction should be the last instruction executed in any MIR program. It accomplishes necessary terminal bookkeeping.

---

[29] If it is desired merely to store zero in a computer word, the FAP instruction STZ is recommended; if it is desired merely to store a nonzero number (to whose magnitude the programmer is indifferent) in a computer word, the FAP instruction STL is recommended. A symbolic address of the particular computer word constitutes the variable field of each of these two instructions.

[30] CALL is a FAP instruction; EXIT is a FAP subroutine.

To have data that have been processed in a MIR program printed out, it is possible to write for this purpose a special subroutine in FAP or to utilize (by calling an already prepared FAP subroutine) a standard FORTRAN "write output tape" procedure. In addition, one may use an output routine recently incorporated into the MIR system: the operation field consists of MPRINT; the variable field consists of a sequence, enclosed by parentheses, of comma-separated mnemonics for each type of data to be printed out. For example, execution of the instruction: MPRINT (MEAS,LYNE,NØTE) would cause a printout of the measure number, the lyne number, and the note number (in that order) of the note that is the current note when the instruction is executed. Labelling the columns of data (e.g., with "MEAS NO" if appropriate), determining the number of spaces between columns on the printout, and several other features, can be controlled by the programmer. The MPRINT routine is, at least in part, dependent upon the peripheral equipment to be used, and is not described further here.

Two MIR programs—exclusive of input and output procedures—are presented next.[31] The first program locates the highest and lowest (in terms of pitch) notes in lyne numbered two of the composition being processed (Figure XX-1). The second program counts the number of times that a rising second is followed by a rising third, in both lyne numbered one and lyne numbered two of the composition being processed (Figure XX-2). A third illustration of a MIR program, together with a flow chart descriptive of it, has appeared in my article, "Toward Musical Information Retrieval," referred to in footnote 1.

The results of the first program are stored as follows: the measure number, note number, register-class, note-class, and semitone number (i.e., above a note in register-class 0 and note-class 0) of the extremal notes are stored in WA10 through WA14, respectively, for the highest note, and in WA15 through WA19, respectively, for the lowest note. The results of the second program are stored as follows: the number of times a lyne-1 rising second is followed by a lyne-1 rising third is stored in WA10; the number of times a lyne-2 rising second is followed by a lyne-2 rising third is stored in WA11; and in WA12 is stored the sum of the final WA10 and WA11 totals.

[31] In Figures XX-1 and XX-2 the letter O is distinguishable from the Arabic numeral 0 without the use of the slashed O.

```
                TOMEAS   1
                TOLYNE   2
ONWARD          COMPAR   REGCL, =14,REST TO LOCATION REST IF C.N. A REST
                MOVE     MEASNO,WA10
                MOVE     NOTENO,WA11
                MOVE     REGCL,WA12
                MOVE     NOTECL,WA13
                MOVE     SEMITO,WA14
NEWLO           MOVE     MEASNO,WA15
                MOVE     NOTENO,WA16
                MOVE     REGCL,WA17
                MOVE     NOTECL,WA18
                MOVE     SEMITO,WA19
RETURN          COMPAR   BARLIN, =3,STOP    STOP IF AT DOUBLE BARLINE
                TONOTE   +1                 TO NEXT NOTE
                COMPAR   REGCL, =14,RETURN TO RETURN IF C.N.  A REST
                TRGTH    SEMITO,WA14,NEWHI TO NEWHI IF ON NEW HIGH
                TRLTH    SEMITO,WA19,NEWLO TO NEWLO IF ON NEW LOW
                TRA      RETURN              GO TO RETURN
NEWHI           MOVE     MEASNO,WA10
                MOVE     NOTENO,WA11
                MOVE     REGCL,WA12
                MOVE     NOTECL,WA13
                MOVE     SEMITO,WA14
                TRA      RETURN
STOP            CALL     EXIT
REST            COMPAR   BARLIN, =3,STOP
                TONOTE   +1
                TRA      ONWARD
```

Figure XX-1. Program 1

Both programs make use of a convenient feature of FAP. If *s* is a sequence of Arabic numerals that denotes, according to the decimal system, a number *n* less than 2^{36}, then the so-called *decimal literal* consisting of an equal sign followed directly by the numerals of *s* in order may be used in variable fields of instructions in place of a

```
                TOMEAS   1
                TOLYNE   1
CHK42D          COMPAR   BARLIN, =3,STOP  STOP IF AT DOUBLE BARLINE
                TONOTE   +1
RETRY           COMPAR   DINTVL, =2,CHK42D,F
                COMPAR   DINDIR, =0,CHK42D,F   ON A SECOND
                COMPAR   BARLIN, =3,STOP       ON A RISING SECOND
                TONOTE   +1
                COMPAR   DINTVL, =3,RETRY,F
                COMPAR   DINDIR, =0,RETRY,F    ON A THIRD
                COMPAR   LYNENO, =2,LYNE2      ON A RISING THIRD
                ADD3     WA10, =1,WA10     INCREMENT WA10
                TRA      CHK42D
LYNE2           ADD3     WA11, =1,WA11     INCREMENT WA11
                TRA      CHK42D
STOP            COMPAR   LYNENO, =2,ADD
                TOLYNE   2
                TRA      CHK42D
ADD             ADD3     WA10,WA11,WA12
                CALL     EXIT
```

Figure XX-2. Program 2

symbolic address of a computer word containing a representation of n. (The Arabic numeral sequence may be preceded by a minus sign if a negative integer is to be represented by a decimal literal.) For example, execution of the instruction: ADD3 $=6,=-59$,WA1 would cause the contents of WA1 to become -53. Also available for use by the MIR programmer is the "Hollerith literal" capability of FAP: this would be especially useful in searching the text of vocal music for the occurrence of a particular syllable.[32]

---

[32] After this article was completed, my attention was directed to an article by Tobias Robison, entitled "IML—MIR: A Data-processing System for the Analysis of Music," recently published in Harald Heckmann (ed.), *Elektronische Datenverarbeitung in der Musikwissenschaft*, Regensburg, Gustav Bosse Verlag, 1967. The reader of both the present article and the Robison article will find a few terminological discrepancies and will find some other than nominal differences where the MIR system described by Robison is a development from the MIR system decribed here. For the record, I would note that Robison's statement that the IML representation for keypunchers "was originally designed by" me is untrue: IML was designed by Alexander M. Jones. Arthur Mendel's recent article, "Some Preliminary Attempts at Computer-assisted Style Analysis in Music (*Computers and the Humanities*, Vol. 4, no. 1, September 1969, pp. 41–52), describes some initial musicological results obtained at Princeton University with MIR programs applied to Josquin's *Missa L'homme armé super voces musicales*, and some nonmusicological problems encountered in implementing the MIR system there.

CHAPTER XXI

An Automated Music Library Catalog for Scores and Phonorecords

by JOHN W. TANNO, ALFRED G. LYNN, and ROBERT E. ROBERSON

Our purpose in this article is to give the reader some understanding of how an automated score and phonorecord catalog can benefit the university community. We shall describe the general attributes of the system, the process involved in implementing it, and the benefits over the traditional catalog in cost and service which accrue from it. We will not go into the history of the system or how one catalogs using the system. Our aim is to create an interest in a system that has increased service at a reduction of cost at the State University of New York at Binghamton.

There are three viewpoints represented in the development of this system, and each of us will discuss it as it relates to his viewpoint.

MUSIC LIBRARIAN

Before the music librarian can begin to automate a score and phonorecord catalog, he has to define the attributes of the catalog:

(1) The kind of catalog that is desired;
(2) What special ways he wants to be able to draw on the various attributes of scores and phonorecords;
(3) The way in which the information of the entry is to be used; and
(4) The entry and how each entry will be orderd in the catalog.

In the vernacular of the computer world, the input and the output must be defined. The systems analyst can then devise the necessary programming and formats for producing the desired output from the input, while the manager of the data-processing center determines the feasibility of developing such a catalog in view of his total commitment to the university. The music librarian need not know how this is done, but the system will be more effective if the librarian and analyst work closely together with a sympathetic knowledge of each other's requirements.

In a conventional card catalog, two types of entries are made: (1) the main entry which contains the call number, the composer (author), standard (conventional) title, actual (distinctive) title, publisher, collation, and additional descriptive information as required, and (2) all other entries which are formed by adding a header (such as subject, title, editor, and so on) to the main entry. All entries are filed alphabetically in the catalog, first by header (composer if main entry), then by composer, title, call number, and so forth.

To generate the two basic types of entries, the automated system makes use of two files: (1) a code file which is an authority file, and (2) a document file. The code file may be thought of as an alphabetical list of headers by category. A two-digit code represents the category and a six-digit code represents each header. A category is an attribute of a score or phonorecord that a user of the catalog might utilize in looking for an entry. The code file is divided into the ten categories shown below:

01	Composer	07	Performer
03	Instrument	08	Librettist
04	Subject	09	Editor
05	Translator	10	Compiler
06	Transcriber	11	Arranger

An entry to the code file is made by filling out the code file transmittal shown in Figure XXI-1.

Each line in the transmittal represents a card. Eight cards are available for each entry to the code file. This allows space to include biographical or explanatory information as needed. The complete information would only be printed in the catalog once; only card o will be used as the header for an entry after the first occurrence.

Once a name, subject, or instrument is assigned a code, it need never be written again. This insures that the name and date, subject, or instrument will be standardized, since they will be called for only by code from the single listing in the code file. By the same virtue, all

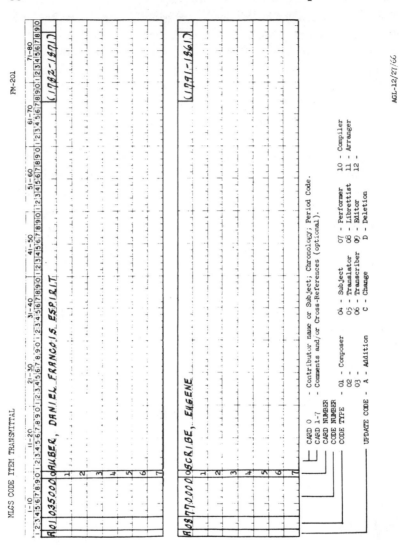

Figure XXI-1. Code file transmittal

corrections or changes to that name may be executed by a single change in the code file.

The document file is generated from the transmittal shown in Figure XXI-2.

This transmittal serves both for main entries and cross references. Each entry to the document file is assigned a control number. Each of the ten cards (lines) that make up the entry is also numbered, so that any part of the entry may be defined throughout the processing. Two areas may be defined in the transmittal: (1) the code area, cards 0 to 3, and (2) the text area, cards 4 to 9. The code area allows for forty-six different six-digit codes from the code file to be entered, namely:

1	Composer code	3	Transcriber codes
4	Librettist codes	3	Translator codes
4	Editor codes	9	Performer codes
3	Compiler codes	3	Arranger codes
6	Subject codes	10	Instrument codes

A six-digit code in the appropriate code area on the document file transmittal will enable an entry to be generated in the catalog. The header called for by code will be taken from the code file and placed above the text area taken from the document file. In this manner, a total of forty-six entries could be generated using the same text with different headers.

Because both standard (conventional) and actual (distinctive) titles are used in cataloging music, a way of handling both titles had to be developed. Three possibilities in title configuration exist:

Case A: Both a standard and actual title are used.

Case B: The standard title is identical to the actual title.

Case S: Only a standard title is used.

To enable the computer to discriminate among these cases, a box (labelled *T* on card 3 of the document file form) has to be filled in with the appropriate case designator. In case *A*, the standard title is used only to sort entries under the composer's name, while the actual title is the one used for the title entry. The title entry is formed, then, by using the title in card 5 as a header over the text area. As a further refinement in case *A*, a cross reference (from the actual title to the standard title) will be automatically generated for the composer catalog. This will enable a user who would not know the conventional

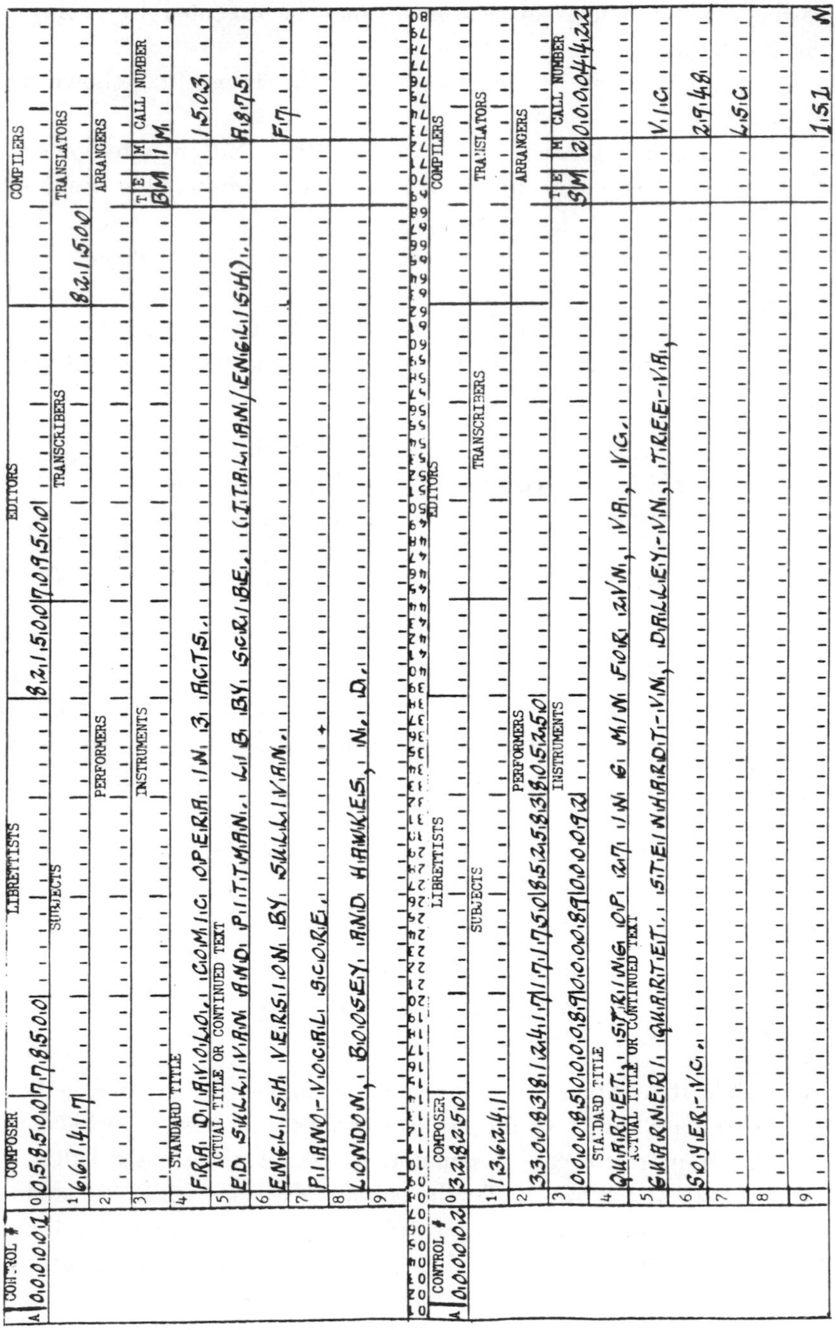

| CONTROL # | COMPOSER | LIBRETTISTS | EDITORS | COMPILERS |
| | SUBJECTS | PERFORMERS | INSTRUMENTS | TRANSCRIBERS | TRANSLATORS | ARRANGERS | T E | M | CALL NUMBER |

A 0000001 0 0585000778500 | 821500077850 0 | 821500077850 0 | 821500 0

1. 660.14.19
2.
3. STANDARD TITLE — FRA DIAVOLO, COMIC OPERA IN 3 ACTS.
   ACTUAL TITLE OR CONTINUED TEXT
4. E.D. SULLIVAN AND P.ITTMAN, W.B BY SCRIBE, (ITALIAN/ENGLISH).
5. ENGLISH VERSION BY SULLIVAN.
6. PIANO-VOCAL SCORE.
7. LONDON, BOOSEY AND HAWKES, N.D.
   BM / M / 1 M — 15.03, R.815, F.9

A 0000002 0 3282850

1. 1.3624.11
2. 33.00838.1.2411.191.17.1175085258318052500
3. 0100085100008910000092 — INSTRUMENTS
   STANDARD TITLE
4. QUARTET, STRING, OP. 127 IN 6 MIN FOR 12VN, VA, VC.
   ACTUAL TITLE OR CONTINUED TEXT
5. GUARNERI QUARTETT, STEINHARDT-VN, DALLEY-VN, TREE-VA,
6. SONER-VC.
   BM / M / 2000044222 — V.1C, 29.48, 4.5C, 1.51

Figure XXI-2. Document file transmittal

title to find the entry through the distinctive title. In case S, no title entry is generated. In case B, the title found in card 4 is used to also generate a title entry. This avoids entering the identical title twice. In this manner all unique titles will be used as headers to generate a title listing.

The input, then, consists of a code file and a document file. From both files the information necessary to form a catalog entry is generated.

For output, it was decided to generate twelve separate catalogs, rather than a dictionary catalog:

Composer	Instrumentation	Arranger
Title	Librettist	Transcriber
Subject	Editor	Translator
Performer	Compiler	Shelf list

This will permit the user to find easily any particular type of entry, and will make it easy to ascertain how the catalog is being used. Since it is possible to generate any type of catalog one would want, if this arrangement is not effective, it will be changed.

The formats for entries made in each of these catalogs may be seen from the sample catalog (Figure XXI-3) at the end of this article. All entries have basically the same format as the composer entry, with the addition of the appropriate header. The shelf-list entry is identical to the composer entry, but it is sorted by call number.

The instrumentation catalog is unique, in that it lists not only solo works for a particular instrument, but also all chamber music that includes any particular instrument, arranged by groups (duo, trio, quartet, and so on) under that instrument. For example, a quartet for flute, oboe, violin, and piano would be alphabetically listed under the following headers in the instrumentation catalog:

FLUTE—OB, PF, VN
OBOE—FL, PF, VN
PIANO—FL, OB, VN
VIOLIN—FL, OB, PF

This same procedure is followed for up to nine different instruments, with a further distinction being made for works that are concertos, sonatas, or suites.

To date there have been 5,000 entries made in the document file and 3,000 entries in the code file. Eight entries in the catalog are generated from the average document entry, resulting in a series of twelve catalogs containing 40,000 entries. The catalog is to be printed semi-annually with supplements as required. The cost of cataloging an item in this system has been $2.45, as compared to $5.50 by traditional cataloging methods.

Other advantages offered to the music librarian by such a system are manifold. Once the catalog data is in machine-readable form, a great flexibility is suddenly available. Specialized programming enables the librarian to request specialized catalogs. For example, a catalog of all cantatas on file, written between 1700 and 1750, could be written, or a list of all chamber works including a part for violin edited by Galamian could be made, or a list of works by Beethoven for which a record and a score are on file could be generated. There is no end to the ways one might generate catalogs, be it a merged dictionary catalog, a card catalog, or a separate listing. When the time arises that on-line inquiries can be made, then the user will be able to make his own specialized requests. In looking ahead, the same system could be enlarged to catalog books on music as well, which would pave the way for general information retrieval in the field of music.

The system enables the authority file (code file) actually to generate the entries, guaranteeing that each name or subject be correctly listed. All changes in the authority file would be reflected in all entries at the next print time. There is no limit to the number of added entries that could be made, and the labor necessary to add them consists of looking up the code for each one.

Cataloging by computer enables the librarian to analyze the process by computer. Accurate logs can be kept on the amount of material cataloged, making cost analysis over any period of time possible. Specialized machine checks on the data processed can assure uniformity and correctness of all entries to the two files. Update programs reject data incorrectly entered and make routine verifications of codes entered on the transmittal file forms.

In short, a greater efficiency in the cataloging process along with a greater diversity of service results from this system.

Now that the input and output have been defined, the systems analyst will show how the former begets the latter.

SYSTEMS ANALYST

The Music Library Catalog System design is based upon two presumptions which, trivial as they may seem, are critical to the applicability of automated library cataloging in a small-machine environment. Firstly, each document in the library will have associated with it some set of entries distributed throughout the printed catalog. In the main, these entries are identical, showing, in the case of music library documents, the same composer, title, and publishing information. The differences among these entries are primarily in the heading information by which the individual entries are filed. These headings associate with the document some attribute common to many other documents in the library, such as a particular subject, artist, or instrumentation.

Secondly, given a computer with capabilities of random associative access to high-volume storage, it is possible to sort much larger volumes of data than would otherwise be the case. In computer sorting, the only significant data is that being used as sort-control necessary only to sort the control data itself, plus providing a short information—any other data in the file is just so much wasted space during sorting. When random-access storage is available, it becomes reference code by which the complete source record may be recovered after sorting. In the present system this technique affords a virtual increase in storage capacity of 8-to-1 over a conventional sort, with a corresponding improvement of processing time. An additional dividend of this method is that corresponding sort data need not be constrained to fixed fields in the sorted records, since this data may be reorganized as it is selected for sorting.

Machine Configuration

From the outset it was planned to design the MLCS system for the smallest practical machine configuration, since it was recognized that in view of the perennial conversion problem confronting large, established libraries, the greatest appeal of an automated cataloging system would be to the smaller and newer libraries whose access to large-scale computing equipment might be severely limited. Compromise of this goal with the practical considerations of local needs led to a design configuration of a two-tape, two-disk, card/print system with medium core storage capacity. The Harpur computer is an IBM System/360-40 with 256K core storage (although this large core capacity is not exploited) and two 2311 disk drives having nominal capacity as used of 6.75 million characters each. The design goals satisfied by this configuration are 10,000 documents in the library and up to 10,000 attribute codes on file, although it is expected that additional capacity will become available before these limits are approached. Index generation rates approximate 40,000 entries per hour, corresponding to about 8 hours of catalog printing time per hour of generation. With the exception of standard sorting programs supplied by the system manufacturer, the entire system is programmed in basic COBOL, and is executed under IBM's standard Disk Operating System.

The capacity of the system is directly related to available disk storage, and is virtually independent of all other machine parameters except, of course, machine time. At current rates generally available to academic users, and assuming 8 entries (average) per library document, cost of computer time for cataloging 10,000 documents would be approximately $1,200, using the machine configuration described.

The Code File

Each line of the Code Transmittal Form (Figure XXI-1) represents one punched card, and ultimately a line of print. Eight such lines (560 text characters) comprise one code file record. The first of these lines expresses a distinctive attribute common to multiple documents in the library, that is, a particular subject, composer, instrument, performer, and so on. Subsequent lines provide for notation of such biographical, bibliographical, or other supplementary information as may be appropriate. The complete code record is printed only once in the catalog, immediately preceding the first appearance of the corresponding attribute. Thereafter, only the first line of the code record appears as the heading line of subsequent catalog entries, until all documents referencing the attribute have been listed.

Major attribute categories, such as composers, librettists, subjects, and so on are assigned arbitrary two-digit numbers, and each category appears in final form as a distinct subcatalog, rather than disseminated alphabetically throughout an integrated file as in the conventional library card catalog. Within each category unique attributes are assigned six-digit code numbers such that the codes correspond to the desired ordering of the alphabetic text which they represent. Thereafter these codes proxy for the alphabetic data throughout catalog generation until they are decoded for listing. The complete code, therefore, is comprised of a two-digit category prefix and a six-digit code number. However, the complete code, supplemented by a card number to facilitate file maintenance, is carried only in the code master file. Elsewhere in the system, the card number is not applicable, and the prefix is implied by the position of the six-digit code number within the record, resulting in a 30 per cent saving of space required for coding. It is evident that the prefix may be reinstated at any time on the basis of code position, and that arrangement of any set of code numbers in ascending numeric order implies a corresponding arrangement of the equivalent text in ascending alphabetic order.

The use of six numeric digits for each code provides a potential capacity of one million different entries in each code category. In practice, only a fraction of this capacity is employed, with the codes distributed throughout the available number set in such a way as to minimize the probability that additional code entires will be forced out of proper alphabetic sequence by lack of available code numbers. To this end, a supplementary program performs reorganization of each category into correct alphabetic sequence, with automatic reassignment of code numbers for optimum distribution, and appropriate update of code invocations elsewhere in the document file.

In this program, the first lines of all entries within each category are ordered in "natural" sequence, ignoring spaces between words and all punctuation except left parentheses. The first three digits of each code are then reassigned through reference to tables of frequency of occurrence of surnames as derived by the University of Oregon (1935). Sets of entries having identical partial codes are then distributed evenly within the remaining interval of 1,000 integers, thus completing the six-digit code. This process allows adequate space within the code set for interim manual assignment of additional codes. Reorganization may be performed immediately prior to each catalog run in order to rectify any possible errors in manual selection of codes.

The code file is maintained as a serial file, ordered in ascending category, code, and card sequence. Because the code master file is arranged, by definition, in the same order as the final catalog, the file may be processed in its serial format during catalog generation, with the reservation that no single catalog entry may invoke more than one code. In the Harpur system this restriction is transgressed by the requirement for a cross-indexed instrumentation catalog, wherein each catalog entry may require decoding of up to 10 separate instrument codes. Thus the file must be processed in a randomly accessible format. However, serial processing offers moderate advantages of time and equipment in systems where the one-code restriction can be tolerated.

The present machine system is storage-bound with respect to the equipment available for sorting and random-access files, and this factor has had a significant effect upon program design. It was initially suggested that major storage economies could be realized through utilization of alphanumeric coding, whereby three characters could serve in place of the present six-digit coding scheme. However, it soon became evident that the validity-checking capability afforded by a limited ten-digit coding set offered advantages of reliability which far outweighed considerations of storage capacity.

The Document File

The Document Transmittal Form (Figure XXI-2) contains three types of basic data, in addition to the control information used for file maintenance. The upper part of the form is partitioned into fixed fields for entry of code invocations, each of which ultimately creates an entry in the final catalog. The lower part of the transmittal is used for entry of free-form textual data descriptive of the individual document, which data appears essentially unaltered as the text of each catalog entry generated by the codes above. Within the area are three fields reserved for standard title, actual title (if any), and call number. The first of these is used to control the order of catalog entries within composer, while the other two generate one entry each in the title and shelf list catalogs, respectively. The third basic data type (to the left of the first call-number segment) is used for internal notation of the type and format of the document record, the error status of the record, and the medium upon which the subject document is recorded.

Early definitions of the document record transcription scheme provided for essentially free-form text entry, primarily in default of realization that format consistencies and transcription rules were applicable to the data at hand. However, it soon became painfully obvious that mechanical editing of free-form text could not reliably recover the context of the material, and that a moderate amount of format consistency could afford significant margins of reliability through programmed auditing of each input transmittal. Subsequently, coding rules and the transmittal form itself were gradually modified and improved to the point that it is presently possible to identify 30 types of significant errors in the input data without imposing any objectionable degree of "computeritis" upon library personnel.

The importance of programmed auditing of data cannot be overemphasized. The input path from cataloger to keypuncher to unit-record processing to the file-update program is fraught with hazard, as evidenced by the fact that upon first audit of approximately 1,500 original document records nearly 30 per cent were discovered to contain errors which would have significantly degraded the usefulness of the final catalog, while the rate of data rejection by the file maintenance program is still commonly as high as 10 per cent.

Catalog Generation

The music library catalog as defined here consists of a large number of catalog entries, each containing data derived from a document record, a code record, or some combination of the two. With the document and code files at hand in randomly accessible format, the remaining task is to develop appropriate control records for recovery, integration, formating, and arrangement of the desired combinations of basic data. This function is performed by an index generation program, which creates a simplified representation of each entry to appear in the final catalog. These index records contain reference numbers for code- and document-record recovery, control codes defining the format of the catalog entry, and sort-control data for determining the relative position of the entry within the catalog listing.

In order that the cataloging system may remain responsive to variations of input-output format and to future requirements for specialized catalogs, the index generator is written as a general-purpose interpretive program which depends upon an external table-of-control commands for its processing logic. In response to the parameters supplied by these commands, the program transfers selected data from master document records to index records. Such data may be left- or right-justified to any selected boundary in the index record, and may optionally be packed, with deletion of spaces and punctuation. The number of characters transferred may be defined by either input or output field limits, and fixed data or padding fields may be inserted directly from the control deck. In addition, the program may make logical decisions about the issuance and format of the index record, based upon variable data in the document record. Control commands may be continuously chained where extensive control data is required for generation of a complex index record, but in practice, ten or fewer commands on a single control card usually suffice.

Each command string generates one type of index record whenever the current document record satisfies the criteria for generation. The present catalog requires approximately 70 command strings for generation of the complete catalog. Each document record is tested against the entire set of command statements, and each results in generation of an average of 7.8 index records. The index records are 120 characters in length, comprised of 20 characters of fixed identification data and up to 100 characters of sort information which is used to arrange the raw index file in final catalog sequence.

The command set may be altered by the librarian to suit his immediate needs, without requiring the attention of the system programmer. Thus the librarian is afforded independent control of the content and organization of the catalog, and through the use of multiple control decks he may create any number of distinctive catalogs using the same base data.

Catalog Production

The raw index file produced by the index generation program is sorted on the 100-character field of control information, after which it represents a much-abbreviated form of the final catalog. The order of significance of sort data from most to least significant is, in general: attribute category, attribute, composer, standard title, recording medium, and call number, although various other arrangements are employed for special-purpose catalogs such as shelf lists.

The sorted index file is passed to a print-file-generation program which contains a formating subroutine for each type of catalog listing, selected by identification data in the index record itself. This program recovers any required code and document records from the random-access files, combines selected data from these records in a predetermined format, and issues a print-image record of the catalog listing to a magnetic tape file for subsequent printing as time permits. This file may of course be saved for later reproduction of all or part of the catalog, and allows production of the hard-copy catalog to be segmented at the convenience of computer operations personnel, avoiding commitment to long print runs on the order of 10 to 15 hours.

MANAGER—DATA PROCESSING CENTER

Music Holding—System Justification

The willingness of a computer center in an academic setting to undertake as a project to devise a music-holdings system may be for the same reasons which dictate industrial efforts: low cost, better efficiency, speed, and accuracy; or the project may be accepted for more subtle reasons: to gain knowledge while trying to accomplish a specific project, to determine if the approach is sound through the use of actual data, and, in some cases, to determine whether a different approach is required because of the failure of the project.

The Music Library Catalog System presented a real challenge to this center. It gave the center an opportunity to work on the development of a particular kind of cataloging system, one which is unique and for which we anticipate further refinements. The music data base was identifiable, limited, but expanding, and, since much effort was being exerted along the same lines at other institutions, the future possibilities for information retrieval were wide. If successful, we were confident that more information at greater speed, reduced cost, and higher accuracy would be available. This conclusion was based on the fact that once initial data was input to the system, changes would be required only of the cataloger, mistakes because of having to redo what was already accurate data would be eliminated, and errors in constant repetitious data (such as composer's name) would be avoided since any composition would use the same entry from a source file. Furthermore, looking forward to inquiry systems in many areas of activity, the Music Library Catalog System offered a data base which would prove readily accessible to any such inquiry. In other words, we could foresee the possibility, with what was being developed, of a typewriter terminal being used to inquire as to the nature of our music holdings.

One of the prime considerations was how to deal with the information related to the holdings, such as author (composer), title, editor, instruments, performers, and so on. It was agreed finally that as much information as possible would be coded. This conclusion was reached because the size of the existant holdings was limited, the on-line files on the computer could be better handled with numerical data of limited size, and we were looking for limited discrepancies, many of which could occur because of spelling errors if coding were not used. Although it is possible that in time we may elect to use actual names in this system, for the present we are confident that accuracy is enhanced through coding, speed is not lost (after a process of learning occurs for the personnel doing the work on the transmittals), and the processing of data in the Computer Center is expedited.

Cost considerations are ever present. We now know our machine cost will be less than we anticipated; our programming cost higher. To

obtain our first catalogs, which will include approximately 5,000 holdings, the costs break down as follows:

Keypunching	$ 2,000
Programming	4,000
Machine time	6,400
	$12,400
Transmittal labor by Music Department	12,250
Total cost	$24,650

Obviously, the programming cost is a one-time cost for accomplish-
ing our present objective and will not be repeated. Most of the
machine cost is for testing and development and will not be repeated.
Therefore, our cost for the catalogs for the next 5,000 holdings, which
will be integrated with our present 5,000 holdings for a combined
catalog of 10,000, will be:

Keypunching	$ 1,800
Machine time	1,200
	$ 3,000
Transmittal labor by Music Department	8,000
Total cost	$11,000

(It should be noted that, since the first time around, considerable
change in the transmittal form and a period of learning by the people
involved have allowed for less redoing and more expeditious processing, which reduces our costs in these areas.)

These costs must be compared to a totally manual system. The
Music Department estimates the cost to assimilate the data and type
the multitude of catalog cards in the same variations as the computer
system would cost $55,000 for 10,000 holdings, exclusive of the learn-
ing and programming cost, and operational cost for the computer
system for 10,000 items would be $22,000, or $33,000 less than a totally
manual system. From this point alone it is obvious what merit exists in
computerization of this data. However, we wish to emphasize that in
the long run what appeals even more to us than the present catalogs
and data are the myriad of information possibilities inherent in the
data base being developed.

The following pages (Figure XXI-3) illustrate the various types of
entries that could be generated from the information shown on the
document transmittal form (Figure XXI-2).

```
                 *  MUSIC LIBRARY CATALOG BY LIBRETTIST  *
*********************************************************************************
SCRIBE, EUGENE (1791-1861)
*********************************************************************************
SCRIBE, EUGENE (1791-1861)
 AUBER, DANIEL FRANCOIS ESPIRIT (1782-1871)                         M
  FRA DIAVOLO. COMIC OPERA IN 3 ACTS.                               1503
   ED SULLIVAN AND PITTMAN. LIB BY SCRIBE. (ITALIAN/ENGLISH).       A875
   ENGLISH VERSION BY SULLIVAN.                                     F7
   PIANO-VOCAL SCORE.
   LONDON, BOOSEY AND HAWKES, N. D.



......000001.............................................................

                  *  MUSIC LIBRARY CATALOG BY EDITOR    *
*********************************************************************************
PITTMAN, JOSIAH (1816-1886)
*********************************************************************************
PITTMAN, JOSIAH (1816-1886)
 AUBER, DANIEL FRANCOIS ESPIRIT (1782-1871)                         M
  FRA DIAVOLO. COMIC OPERA IN 3 ACTS.                               1503
   ED SULLIVAN AND PITTMAN. LIB BY SCRIBE. (ITALIAN/ENGLISH).       A875
   ENGLISH VERSION BY SULLIVAN.                                     F7
   PIANO-VOCAL SCORE.
   LONDON, BOOSEY AND HAWKES, N. D.



......000001.............................................................
*********************************************************************************
SULLIVAN, ARTHUR SEYMOUR (SIR) (1842-1900)
*********************************************************************************
SULLIVAN, ARTHUR SEYMOUR (SIR) (1842-1900)
 AUBER, DANIEL FRANCOIS ESPIRIT (1782-1871)                         M
  FRA DIAVOLO. COMIC OPERA IN 3 ACTS.                               1503
   ED SULLIVAN AND PITTMAN. LIB BY SCRIBE. (ITALIAN/ENGLISH).       A875
   ENGLISH VERSION BY SULLIVAN.                                     F7
   PIANO-VOCAL SCORE.
   LONDON, BOOSEY AND HAWKES, N. D.



......000001.............................................................

                 *  MUSIC LIBRARY CATALOG BY TRANSLATOR  *
*********************************************************************************
SULLIVAN, ARTHUR SEYMOUR (SIR) (1842-1900)
*********************************************************************************
SULLIVAN, ARTHUR SEYMOUR (SIR) (1842-1900)
 AUBER, DANIEL FRANCOIS ESPIRIT (1782-1871)                         M
  FRA DIAVOLO. COMIC OPERA IN 3 ACTS.                               1503
   ED SULLIVAN AND PITTMAN. LIB BY SCRIBE. (ITALIAN/ENGLISH).       A875
   ENGLISH VERSION BY SULLIVAN.                                     F7
   PIANO-VOCAL SCORE.
   LONDON, BOOSEY AND HAWKES, N. D.



......000001.............................................................
```

Figure XXI-3. Sample entries from music library catalog (continued on page 344)

```
                     *  MUSIC LIBRARY CATALOG BY INSTRUMENTS  *

********************************************************************************
VIOLA - VN, VN, VC.
********************************************************************************
VIOLA - VN, VN, VC.
  GRIEG, EDVARD HAGERUP (1843-1907)                                   0000442
    QUARTET, STRING OP 27 IN G MIN FOR 2VN, VA, VC.
      GUARNERI QUARTET. STEINHARDT-VN, DALLEY-VN, TREE-VA,            VIC
      SOYER-VC.                                                      LSC
                                                                     2948

                                                                     1S1    N
......000002..................................................................
********************************************************************************
VIOLIN - VA, VN, VC.
********************************************************************************
VIOLIN - VA, VN, VC.
  GRIEG, EDVARD HAGERUP (1843-1907)                                   0000442
    QUARTET, STRING OP 27 IN G MIN FOR 2VN, VA, VC.
      GUARNERI QUARTET. STEINHARDT-VN, DALLEY-VN, TREE-VA,            VIC
      SOYER-VC.                                                      LSC
                                                                     2948

                                                                     1S1    N
......000002..................................................................
********************************************************************************
VIOLONCELLO - VA, VN, VN.
********************************************************************************
VIOLONCELLO - VA, VN, VN.
  GRIEG, EDVARD HAGERUP (1843-1907)                                   0000442
    QUARTET, STRING OP 27 IN G MIN FOR 2VN, VA, VC.
      GUARNERI QUARTET. STEINHARDT-VN, DALLEY-VN, TREE-VA,            VIC
      SOYER-VC.                                                      LSC
                                                                     2948

                                                                     1S1    N
......000002..................................................................

                     *  MUSIC LIBRARY CATALOG BY SHELF LIST   *

..............................................................................
AUBER, DANIEL FRANCOIS ESPIRIT (1782-1871)                           M
  FRA DIAVOLO. COMIC OPERA IN 3 ACTS.                                1503
    ED SULLIVAN AND PITTMAN. LIB BY SCRIBE. (ITALIAN/ENGLISH).       A875
    ENGLISH VERSION BY SULLIVAN.                                     F7
    PIANO-VOCAL SCORE.
    LONDON, BOOSEY AND HAWKES, N. D.

......000001..................................................................
GRIEG, EDVARD HAGERUP (1843-1907)                                    0000442
  QUARTET, STRING OP 27 IN G MIN FOR 2VN, VA, VC.
    GUARNERI QUARTET. STEINHARDT-VN, DALLEY-VN, TREE-VA,             VIC
    SOYER-VC.                                                       LSC
                                                                    2948

                                                                    1S1    N
......000002..................................................................
```

Figure XXI-3 (continued)

```
            *   MUSIC LIBRARY CATALOG BY COMPOSER     *

***********************************************************************
 AUBER, DANIEL FRANCOIS ESPIRIT (1782-1871)
***********************************************************************
 AUBER, DANIEL FRANCOIS ESPIRIT (1782-1871)                        M
   FRA DIAVOLO. COMIC OPERA IN 3 ACTS.                             1503
   ED SULLIVAN AND PITTMAN. LIB BY SCRIBE. (ITALIAN/ENGLISH).      A875
   ENGLISH VERSION BY SULLIVAN.                                    F7
   PIANO-VOCAL SCORE.
   LONDON, BOOSEY AND HAWKES, N. D.
 ......000001.....................................................
***********************************************************************
 GRIEG, EDVARD HAGERUP (1843-1907)
***********************************************************************
 GRIEG, EDVARD HAGERUP (1843-1907)                                00004422
   QUARTET, STRING OP 27 IN G MIN FOR 2VN, VA, VC.
   GUARNERI QUARTET. STEINHARDT-VN, DALLEY-VN, TREE-VA,            VIC
   SOYER-VC.                                                       LSC
                                                                  2948

                                                                  1S1    N
 ......000002.....................................................
            *   MUSIC LIBRARY CATALOG BY SUBJECT     *

***********************************************************************
 CHAMBER MUSIC - QUARTET - STRING
***********************************************************************
 CHAMBER MUSIC - QUARTET - STRING
   GRIEG, EDVARD HAGERUP (1843-1907)                              0000442
   QUARTET, STRING OP 27 IN G MIN FOR 2VN, VA, VC.
   GUARNERI QUARTET. STEINHARDT-VN, DALLEY-VN, TREE-VA,           VIC
   SOYER-VC.                                                      LSC
                                                                  2948

                                                                  1S1    N
 ......000002..................................................
***********************************************************************
 OPERA - COMIC OPERA (INCLUDE OPÉRA BUFFA, OPERA COMIQUE).
***********************************************************************
 OPERA - COMIC OPERA (INCLUDE OPERA BUFFA, OPERA COMIQUE).
   AUBER, DANIEL FRANCOIS ESPIRIT (1782-1871)                      M
   FRA DIAVOLO. COMIC OPERA IN 3 ACTS.                            1503
   ED SULLIVAN AND PITTMAN. LIB BY SCRIBE. (ITALIAN/ENGLISH).     A875
   ENGLISH VERSION BY SULLIVAN.                                   F7
   PIANO-VOCAL SCORE.
   LONDON, BOOSEY AND HAWKES, N. D.
 ......000001.....................................................
            *   MUSIC LIBRARY CATALOG BY TITLE     *

 .................................................................
 FRA DIAVOLO. COMIC OPERA IN 3 ACTS.
   AUBER, DANIEL FRANCOIS ESPIRIT (1782-1871)                      M
   FRA DIAVOLO. COMIC OPERA IN 3 ACTS.                            1503
   ED SULLIVAN AND PITTMAN. LIB BY SCRIBE. (ITALIAN/ENGLISH).     A875
   ENGLISH VERSION BY SULLIVAN.                                   F7
   PIANO-VOCAL SCORE.
   LONDON, BOOSEY AND HAWKES, N. D.
 ......000001.....................................................
```

Figure XXI-3 (continued)

```
                    *  MUSIC LIBRARY CATALOG BY PERFORMER   *

*********************************************************************************
DALLEY, JOHN
*********************************************************************************
DALLEY, JOHN
   GRIEG, EDVARD HAGERUP (1843-1907)                              0000442
     QUARTET, STRING OP 27 IN G MIN FOR 2VN, VA, VC.
       GUARNERI QUARTET. STEINHARDT-VN, DALLEY-VN, TREE-VA,          VIC
       SOYER-VC.                                                     LSC
                                                                    2948

                                                                    1S1    N
......000002...................................................................
*********************************************************************************
GUARNERI QUARTET
*********************************************************************************
GUARNERI QUARTET
   GRIEG, EDVARD HAGERUP (1843-1907)                              0000442
     QUARTET, STRING OP 27 IN G MIN FOR 2VN, VA, VC.
       GUARNERI QUARTET. STEINHARDT-VN, DALLEY-VN, TREE-VA,          VIC
       SOYER-VC.                                                     LSC
                                                                    2948

                                                                    1S1    N
......000002...................................................................
*********************************************************************************
SOYER, DAVID
*********************************************************************************
SOYER, DAVID
   GRIEG, EDVARD HAGERUP (1843-1907)                              0000442
     QUARTET, STRING OP 27 IN G MIN FOR 2VN, VA, VC.
       GUARNERI QUARTET. STEINHARDT-VN, DALLEY-VN, TREE-VA,          VIC
       SOYER-VC.                                                     LSC
                                                                    2948

                                                                    1S1    N
......000002...................................................................
*********************************************************************************
STEINHARDT, ARNOLD
*********************************************************************************
STEINHARDT, ARNOLD
   GRIEG, EDVARD HAGERUP (1843-1907)                              0000442
     QUARTET, STRING OP 27 IN G MIN FOR 2VN, VA, VC.
       GUARNERI QUARTET. STEINHARDT-VN, DALLEY-VN, TREE-VA,          VIC
       SOYER-VC.                                                     LSC
                                                                    2948

                                                                    1S1    N
......000002...................................................................
*********************************************************************************
TREE, MICHAEL
*********************************************************************************
TREE, MICHAEL
   GRIEG, EDVARD HAGERUP (1843-1907)                              0000442
     QUARTET, STRING OP 27 IN G MIN FOR 2VN, VA, VC.
       GUARNERI QUARTET. STEINHARDT-VN, DALLEY-VN, TREE-VA,          VIC
       SOYER-VC.                                                     LSC
                                                                    2948

                                                                    1S1    N
......000002...................................................................
```

Figure XXI-3 (continued)

INDEX